THE LEAGUE OF NATIONS AND THE PROTECTION OF THE ENVIRONMENT

In the history of how the law has dealt with environmental issues over the last century or so, the 1920s and 1930s and the key role of the League of Nations in particular remain underexplored by scholars. By delving into the League's archives, Omer Aloni uncovers the story of how the interwar world expressed similar concerns to those of our own time in relation to nature, environmental challenges, and human development, and reveals a missing link in understanding the roots of our ecological crisis. Charting the environmental regime of the League, he sheds new light on its role as a center of surprising environmental dilemmas, initiatives, and solutions. Through a number of fascinating case studies, the hidden interests, perceptions, motivations, hopes, agendas, and concerns of the League are revealed for the first time. Combining legal thought, historical archival research, and environmental studies, a fascinating period in legal-environmental history is brought to life.

OMER ALONI is Research and Postdoctoral Fellow in the Faculty of Social Sciences, University of Bar-Ilan, Ramat-Gan, Israel. He received his PhD from Tel-Aviv University (Faculty of Law). He holds research affiliations with the University of Potsdam, the Rachel Carson Center for Environment and Society (LMU Munich), and the Max Planck Institute for Legal History and Legal Theory. He was awarded the Tallinn Prize by the European Society for Environmental History for the best research in 2018 and 2019.

CAMBRIDGE STUDIES IN INTERNATIONAL AND COMPARATIVE LAW: 159

Established in 1946, this series produces high quality, reflective and innovative scholarship in the field of public international law. It publishes works on international law that are of a theoretical, historical, cross-disciplinary or doctrinal nature. The series also welcomes books providing insights from private international law, comparative law and transnational studies which inform international legal thought and practice more generally.

The series seeks to publish views from diverse legal traditions and perspectives, and of any geographical origin. In this respect it invites studies offering regional perspectives on core *problématiques* of international law, and in the same vein, it appreciates contrasts and debates between diverging approaches. Accordingly, books offering new or less orthodox perspectives are very much welcome. Works of a generalist character are greatly valued and the series is also open to studies on specific areas, institutions or problems. Translations of the most outstanding works published in other languages are also considered.

After seventy years, Cambridge Studies in International and Comparative Law sets the standard for international legal scholarship and will continue to define the discipline as it evolves in the years to come.

A list of books in the series can be found at the end of this volume.

THE LEAGUE OF NATIONS AND THE PROTECTION OF THE ENVIRONMENT

OMER ALONI
Bar-Ilan University

CAMBRIDGE
UNIVERSITY PRESS

CAMBRIDGE
UNIVERSITY PRESS

University Printing House, Cambridge CB2 8BS, United Kingdom

One Liberty Plaza, 20th Floor, New York, NY 10006, USA

477 Williamstown Road, Port Melbourne, VIC 3207, Australia

314–321, 3rd Floor, Plot 3, Splendor Forum, Jasola District Centre,
New Delhi – 110025, India

79 Anson Road, #06–04/06, Singapore 079906

Cambridge University Press is part of the University of Cambridge.

It furthers the University's mission by disseminating knowledge in the pursuit of education, learning, and research at the highest international levels of excellence.

www.cambridge.org
Information on this title: www.cambridge.org/9781108838191
DOI: 10.1017/9781108937399

First published 2021

A catalogue record for this publication is available from the British Library.

Library of Congress Cataloging-in-Publication Data
Names: Aloni, Omer, 1982 – author.
Title: The League of Nations and the protection of the environment / Omer Aloni, Bar-Ilan University, Israel.
Description: Cambridge, United Kingdom; New York, NY: Cambridge University Press, 2021. | Series: Cambridge studies in international and comparative law; 159 | Based on author's thesis (doctoral – University at Tel-Aviv, 2019), issued under title: Back to the League of Nations: evaluation of the environmental regime: 1919–1939. | Includes bibliographical references and index.
Identifiers: LCCN 2020056951 (print) | LCCN 2020056952 (ebook) | ISBN 9781108838191 (hardback) | ISBN 9781108937399 (ebook)
Subjects: LCSH: Environmental law – History – 20th century. | League of Nations.
Classification: LCC K3585 .A46 2021 (print) | LCC K3585 (ebook) | DDC 344.04/609042–dc23
LC record available at https://lccn.loc.gov/2020056951
LC ebook record available at https://lccn.loc.gov/2020056952

ISBN 978-1-108-83819-1 Hardback

CONTENTS

ACKNOWLEDGMENTS

Above all, I owe my supervisor, David Schorr, a huge debt of gratitude for believing in this research project from the beginning. His enriching and precise guidance inspired me ever since I have started to think of the League of Nations.

In writing this study, I also owe a great deal to a long list of academic institutes and research centers in Israel and abroad for their generous and confident support in my developing project: the Tel-Aviv University Buchmann Faculty of Law, the Zvi Meitar Center for Advanced Legal Studies, the Taubenschlag Institute of Criminal Law, the Cegla Center for Interdisciplinary Research of the Law, the Professor Nathan and Judith Feinberg Fund for Advancing International Law Research, the Rachel Carson Center for Society and Environment of Munich's Ludwig-Maximilians-Universität, and the Max Planck Institute for Legal History and Legal Theory. I gratefully acknowledge the continuing and loyal support of the David Berg Foundation Institute for Law and History that enabled me to conduct a true legal history study from scratch.

I also thank the International Minerva Fellowship and the Max Planck Society for supporting my collaboration with a variety of research institutions and scholarly communities in recent years.

My archival research at the League of Nations Archives in Geneva would not be possible and fruitful without the most generous assistance of the professional team, led by Jacques Oberson.

I would like to thank Cambridge Studies in International and Comparative Law Series' editors, Larissa van den Herik and Jean d'Aspremont, for their belief in this project. I am also grateful to the editorial team at Cambridge University Press for their inspiring and careful work, and to Tom Randall, Laura Blake, Helen Kitto, Gayathri Tamilselvan, and Roger Bennett in particular.

Samantha Rothbart has done an excellent job as my English editor, for which I am grateful.

I thank Martin Beammann, Patricia Clavin, Ron Harris, Moshe Hirsch, Liat Kozma, Pnina Lahav, Christof Mauch, Susan Pedersen, Peter H. Sand, Shani Schnitzer, Natasha Wheatley, and Anna-Katharina Wöbse for their helpful advice. All errors, however, remain mine.

Introduction

Prologue

In recent years, historical study of the League of Nations has flourished, spawning new perspectives and calling into question long-held beliefs regarding this unique institution. Many of these studies explore questions regarding the centrality and importance of the League in the first half of the twentieth century. Additional studies have examined the League's influence on the international arena even beyond 1945, and the establishment of the League's successor, the United Nations. It seems that only today, after several decades of harsh historiography that governed the post-1945 era, has a more positive view of the League emerged.

The present study joins this renaissance, extending this field of research by including historical-legal and environmental aspects within the renewed exploration of the League of Nations. Remarkably, the role of the League in the history and evolution of international environmental law remains almost entirely unexplored. This project uncovers the ways in which the League, as one of the first institutions of its kind, constituted and regulated relations between nature, environment, and humankind. My revisionist retrospective will not limit its scope to the linear historical borders of 1919 and 1939, but also strives to identify the League's influence and place in, and its impact on, environmental regulation after the League was formally dissolved in 1946. As the environmental story of the 1920s and 1930s unfolds, I will not focus on dilemmas of environmental, conservationist, preservationist, and industrial-economic interests alone; rather, I include political, legal, and institutional motivations, both obvious and hidden, that took place in this complex environmental regime. As such, I will also draw attention to environmental issues that involved third-world exploitation in general, and the historical-environmental impact of these questions on colonialism and imperialism (and vice versa) in particular.

Given the abundance of different studies engaged in the eclectic tasks of the League, which takes into account researchers' legal studies in this area, we have not yet seen an attempt to systematically map or to thoroughly investigate the contribution of the League in terms of international law, environment, and nature.

By telling the story of interwar environmental perspectives, I wish to navigate and explain different trends in the history of global environmental law and in studies on the League. Using these questions to track possible links between history, law, and environment, I shall explore those opportunities in environmental law and international relations in which the League was so deeply involved. This reclaiming of the past enables us to deepen the conventional analysis beyond what we would describe as "historiographic amnesia," which is typically characteristic of research about the League, as exemplified by Scott's *Rise and Fall of the League of Nations*.[1] As such, the story of the League as a whole, with its different (and sometimes inconsistent) chapters and challenges – which up until now have been missing from both the history of international law and environmental history serves as fresh territory for new, unique exploration.[2]

Unlike the Soviet archives, which were kept locked behind the Iron Curtain and were thus unavailable to Western scholars until the early 1990s, the accessible archives of the League in Geneva have remained all but forgotten for half a century. As such, a traditionally hazy historical view of the League has inhibited thorough study in fields ranging from political science to international law. New readings and new findings about the League and its effect on the evolution of international environmental law call into question long-held conceptions of the League and the

[1] Among the few important works within the historiographic framework of the "decline and fall of the League" are: Elmer Bendiner, A Time for Angels: The Tragicomic History of the League of Nations (1975); or George Scott, the Rise and Fall of the League of Nations (1973). For another realistic analysis in this regard *see* F. S. Northedge, The League of Nations: Its Life and Times, 1920–1946 (1986).

[2] The memory of the League in the history of modern times underwent a changing historiographic evolution during the twentieth century, and into the dawn of the twenty-first century. These changing trends in the research have been affected, first, by certain new historical discoveries that focus on a variety of activities of the international forum. Second, they have also been affected by various historical and geopolitical circumstances of the twentieth century, such as the collapse of the Soviet Empire and the end of the Cold War. And third, some of the revisionist scholars argue that this image has changed as a result of the way in which the League's successor, the United Nations, was created and how it evolved in the second half of the twentieth century.

history of environmental law. Using this new historiography allows me to reveal the apparent indifference of the common environmental historiography to the role and involvement of the League in shaping the global legal-environmental regime – a regime whose development in the interwar world I will examine. In the following chapters, which cover almost every part of the Earth – from the depth of the oceans to wooded landscapes – I will prove the existence of a mutually influential relationship between the League and the developing environmental agendas and movements of its time, as well as the movement towards an international conception of environmental law.

The twentieth century was one of international cooperation on a variety of environmental issues. Governments worldwide, from Europe to Latin America and beyond, signed nearly 400[3] environmental treaties and agreements throughout the period, half of which were initiated as a response to different reflections on the modern question of nature and wildlife conservation. Indeed, many of these conventions and transnational agreements are "no more" than simple bilateral fishing agreements, which emerged as a result of neighboring states' common concerns – including concerns about certain geographical regions in which countries might experience species loss. The rest of these international legal agreements were more complex and they usually engaged several different countries, some of whom often did not even share a geographical border. This century, even without the League's presence, marks a period of commitment to nature protection in general, and to species and animal protection in particular.

The study of the Anthropocene tells us that environmental changes and crises as a result of humankind's activities occurred even prior to the first decades of the twentieth century.[4] However, the turn of that century is perhaps the first time that the impact of human behaviors threatened many of the planet's major bio-systems. Compared with earlier (sometimes, very early) implications of human societies on surrounding nature, this period introduced several *parallel* threats that humankind posed to the environment. It seems that the interwar period revealed a clear recognition and understanding of the overall negative impact of humans on surrounding nature, exemplified by instances of disappearing ocean species, shrinking forests, oil pollution and its related contamination of

[3] Marc Cioc, The Game of Conservation: International Treaties to Protect the World's Migratory Animals 2 (2009).

[4] Erle C. Ellis, Anthropocene: A Very Short Introduction (2018).

seawater and birds, and the environmental-sanitary dangers emerging from rural peripheries around the world. Prior to the League's environmental regime, there had never been such a collective, organized, and continuing (even if only for a relatively short period) general policy in terms of international law and international governance.

Just as environmental concerns guide some policymakers today, the League discussed numerous areas that it believed would have significant consequences for the basic conditions of all life in the future. Throughout the 1920s and 1930s, it discussed questions that are familiar to us today, including: How does one define an environmental risk or challenge? What action should the international community take? How should international law mobilize in response to environmental challenges? The League, sometimes together with other bodies, understood that the future of nature (and human society) as *they* knew it depended on *their* actions. Moreover, at least some of the current huge environmental challenges in terms of *our* twenty-first century, such as oil spills and pollution of the sea, ruthless whaling, spreading diseases and pandemics (not to mentioned the devastating outcomes of COVID-19), and accelerating forest loss (see the news from Brazil's Amazon rainforest in 2020) were – as the following interwar stories will show – there, or here on the still-suffering planet, also during the 1920s and 1930s.

Similarly to how we currently face global environmental dilemmas, the League's regime tackled various realms and fields: science, politics, economics, social tensions, history, and law too, of course. Nature protection considerations often competed with the economic interests of developing societies who were hungry for natural resources. Responsibility for future generations guided the League, alongside economic and industrial incentives and the race to the bottom in exploiting the planet's treasures. Many of the key interwar issues are the same as the ones that the international community (and, unfortunately, also the environment) is facing today, in the midst of the ecological crisis, such as pollution, overexploitation, food, raw materials, mass extinction, technological improvements, scientific exploration, water, diplomacy, ecosystem management, and more.

Indeed, the broad scope of history encompasses several periods that have never been considered to have anything – or very little – to do with environmentalism or nature protection. Recently, however, as the scholarship of environmental history has continued to expand, scholars have changed our perceptions of these periods. Some have argued that the Third Reich and the Nazi Movement were not just extremely violent or devastating phenomena, but that they also had a coherent or systematic approach towards nature.[5] Likewise, reinterpretation of the Venetian Empire has suggested that one understand it as a power that had an (early) environmental conception of trees and timber as a basis for its political, military, and engineering success.[6] Through my explorations of the interwar period over the last few years, I truly believe that it is an appropriate time to add this period, and that of the League in particular, to the developing chain of legal and environmental historiography.

Research Fields and General Structure: Bridging Two Separate Historiographies

This research presents a historical analysis of various policies, discussions, decisions, and acts related to the environment that were made by different organs, officials, and departments of the League or in their involvement; it also addresses the intersection of environment, humans, and law. My findings will reveal a bridge between two particular fields of research that up to this point have been treated as distinct and separate: the historiography of the League, and the development of international environmental law.

In order to better situate the context of this study, the following section will provide a general overview of the central building blocks in the relevant bodies of literature.

On the Emerging Historiography of the League of Nations

During the last two decades, and especially in recent years, scholars from different schools and disciplines have become increasingly interested in the League as an area of study. Fresh research has shed new light on the reality of the period between the two wars of the twentieth century, prompting a vigorous investigation of the history and significance of the institution that was tasked with maintaining world peace and order during that volatile time.

5 How Green Were the Nazis? Nature, Environment, and Nation in the Third Reich (Franz-Josef Brüggermeier, Marc Cioc & Thomas Zeller eds., 2005).

6 *See, e.g.*, Christof Mauch, The Growth of Trees: A Historical Perspective on Sustainability (2014).

New discoveries of the last few years have enabled a "reapproaching" to the intangible "spirit of Geneva."[7] A careful inquiry into the environmental perspectives that guided the diplomats and officials of the League, as well of those of the different bodies that negotiated with the League during the 1920s and 1930s, is therefore part and parcel of the broader renaissance of the League. A great variety of works have begun to emerge, offering new perspectives regarding the perceived bright new future for humankind in the post-1918 world; some of these perspectives impacted the evolution of international environmental law, leaving a thumbprint that can still be seen today.

These changing perspectives of the League's historical role are based on historical methodologies and archival research, which bring new readings to the history and analysis of the League's various activities, tendencies, and initiatives. The engagement of legal scholars – particularly legal historians – in studies of the League, has only of late been undertaken.[8] This engagement of legal historians stands to provide new angles that allow for deeper insights into the League's research community. Legal history can offer a better understanding of the relevance of different tasks performed by the League and its organs, and could fill in certain gaps in the body of historical knowledge.

The common historic perception of interwar Geneva is that of a failed and weakened capital of early internationalism – naïve and unrealistic. It has also repeatedly been blamed for failing to prevent World War II. As a result, historians and other scholars have almost completely avoided studying activities other than peacekeeping and collective security, two of the League's main responsibilities. As mentioned above, this historiography has been undergoing fundamental change of late.[9]

Dozens of studies conducted recently have argued that the League did much more than simply attempt to create a system of collective

[7] As described by Susan Pedersen, who is considered to be the "founding mother" of the revision of the League. Susan Pedersen, *Back to the League of Nations*, 112 AM. HIST. REV. 1091 (2007), 1113.

[8] Michael Fakhri, *The 1937 International Sugar Agreement: Neo-Colonial Cuba and Economic Aspects of the League of Nations*, 24 LEIDEN J. INT'L L. 899 (2011).

[9] For instance, a relatively large number of scholars are specifically interested in the interwar campaign the League led against the trafficking of women and children. *See, e.g.*, the studies of LIAT KOZMA, GLOBAL WOMEN, COLONIAL PORTS: PROSTITUTION IN THE INTERWAR MIDDLE EAST (2017); Paul Knepper, *The Investigation into the Traffic in Women by the League of Nations: Sociological Jurisprudence as an International Social Project*, 34 L. & HIST. REV. 45 (2016); Magaly Rodríguez García, *The League of Nations and the Moral Recruitment of Women*, 57 INT'L REV. SOC. HIST. 97 (2012).

security.[10] Issues such as refugees,[11] economic stability and recovery,[12] minority protection,[13] public health,[14] and the complexity of the mandate system,[15] for instance, stand today at the center of scholarship on the history of the League. Numerous works have shown that the League was identified and defined as much more than just an "International Security System"[16] – even by contemporary players of the interwar period, including its leading figures and jurists.[17] Another idea that seems to have lost its validity is the claim that the League (and the organs that operated its institutional structure) allegedly opposed the adoption of any agenda that could be interpreted as interfering in the sovereignty of nation states.

[10] Usha Natarajan, for instance, pointed to the link between the legacy of the League's mandate system (which was one of its central enterprises) and different approaches regarding the reconstruction of the Iraqi state at the beginning of the 2000s and in the aftermath of the overthrow of Saddam Hussein's regime: Usha Natarajan, *Creating and Recreating Iraq: Legacies of the Mandate System in Contemporary Understanding of Third World Sovereignty*, 24 Leiden J. Int'l L. 799 (2011). Gerald Halman's study echoes the gap or differences between the failed state concept of the early 1990s, and the League's understanding of this concept: Gerald B. Halman, *Saving Failed States*, 89 Foreign Pol'y 3 (1992–93). In that context, *see* also the work of Ralph Wilde: *From Danzig to East-Timor and Beyond: The Role of International Territorial Administration*, 95 Am. J. Int'l L. 583 (2001).

[11] Keith D. Watenpaugh, *The League of Nations' Rescue of Armenian Genocide Survivors and the Making of Modern Humanitarianism: 1920–1927*, 115 Am. Hist. Rev. 1315 (2010).

[12] Patricia Clavin, Securing the World Economy: The Reinvention of the League of Nations: 1920–1946 (2013).

[13] Christian Raitz von Frentz, A Lesson Forgotten: Minority Protection under the League of Nations – The Case of the German Minority in Poland: 1920–1934 (1999); Mark Mazower, *Minorities and the League of Nations in Interwar Europe*, 126 Daedalus 47 (1997); Carole Fink, Defending the Rights of Others: The Great Powers, the Jews and International Minority Protection 1878–1938 (2004).

[14] Iris Borowy, Coming in Terms with World Health: The League of Nations Health Organisations: 1921–1946 (2009).

[15] Natasha Wheatley, *Mandatory Interpretation: Legal Hermeneutics and the New International Order in Arab and Jewish Petitions to the League of Nations*, 227 Past & Present 205 (2015).

[16] On the change in the common perception of the League's task of securing the post–World War I world *see, e.g.*, Mark Mazower, No Enchanted Palace: The End of Empire and the Ideological Origins of the United Nations (2009), and Governing the World: the History of Idea, 1815 to the Present (2013); Susan Pedersen, The Guardians: The League of Nations and the Crisis of Empire (2015).

[17] Existing research on these legal-professional issues and the interplay within the League as an institution has looked into the question of how lawyers and legal thinking contributed to the shape of the League system. *See*, for example, Stephen Wertheim, *The League of Nations: A Retreat from International Law*? 7 J. Global Hist. 210 (2012).

However, in spite of this recent boost in interest in the League, especially in those issues that were or are considered to be part of the League's broad "humanitarian agenda,"[18] very little attention has been given to this period in the history of diplomatic and legal international environmentalism. Apart from minimalist references here and there, such as those that describe the interwar period as nothing more than a few groping attempts, the common perception is that environmental issues were never on the League's agenda, and that they only gained traction with the UN: "The UN system, weak as it is in terms of sovereign authority, *changed this.* A broad agenda established by mostly liberal powers that won World War II. It included concern for . . . a world-wide view of nature."[19]

The Common Historiography of the Evolution of International Environmental Law Has So Far Disregarded the League

In a similar pattern, the conventional historiography of the evolution of international and transnational environmental law also tends to skip over the interwar period almost completely. Indeed, although several scholars who have studied the development of this international-legal regime have lately identified "evidence of increasing domain structure"[20] in the last third of the nineteenth century, and especially during the *fin de siècle*, the period of the League remains, almost entirely, a legal-environmental-historiographic "black hole." Except for the historic investigation into the role of certain NGOs at that time, environmental historians almost exclusively begin their studies with the establishment of the United Nations. Therefore, the common environmental-history narrative places much of

[18] The League of Nations' Work on Social Issues: Visions, Endeavours and Experiments (Magaly Rodríguez García, Davide Rodogno & Liat Kozma eds., 2016).

[19] John W. Meyer, David J. Frank, Ann Hironaka, Evan Schofer & Nancy B. Tuma, *The Structuring of a World Environmental Regime, 1870–1990*, 51 Int'l Org. 623, 631–32 (1997) (emphasis added). For further reading on the institutional aspects of the role of the UN in shaping the international legal environmental regime – such as in the establishment of the Food and Agriculture Organization (FAO), or the World Health Organization (WHO), *see* Lynton K. Caldwell , International Environmental Policy (1990), and John McCormick, Reclaiming Paradise (1989).

Yet, one should note that new studies of the League deal in particular with the history of creating the technical organizations or internal professional agencies of the League (which are also known as "performative bodies") in the 1920s, and their legal-institutional aspects (*see, e.g.*, Kayo Yasuda, *From the League of Nations Health Organization to the WHO 1943–1946: The Succession and Development of International Functional Cooperation*, 2 Annals Japanese Pol. Sci. 194 [2010]).

[20] Meyer et al., *supra* note 19, at 624.

its emphasis on the post–World War II period, as most investigations tend to mark the starting point of international environmental history with the UN Environment Programme (UNEP), founded at the UN Conference on the Human Environment in Stockholm, in June 1972.[21] By introducing evidence that environmental thinking did in fact take place within the discussion, negotiations, and routine practice of internationalism and diplomacy in the interwar period (linking the issues of nature protection, endangered species, pollution, sanitation, natural resources and raw materials, superpowers, colonialism and imperialism), we might more effectively refine the "the prevailing narrative"[22] of the history of international environmental law.

This scholarly gap becomes even more apparent when one takes into account how overwhelmingly substantial the field of environmental history has become in recent years. As I will describe in each chapter, rich scholarship has been written on almost each and every realm in the history of nature, environment, and humankind – from the history of earthquakes, to volcanic eruptions, droughts, deforestation, climate change, nuclear and renewable energy, sanitation, and more. Where different studies *have* focused on environmental issues, periods, or institutions, no comprehensive study in the interdisciplinary field of environmental history has yet been conducted on the League.

Following the previously mentioned trend of "historiographic amnesia" regarding the League's presence in general, there is likewise a general indifference to the League's environmental role. Studies on the League and on the history of international legal environmentalism are both silent on this issues. The commonly accepted descriptions tend to emphasize that concerted global action in an environmental context did not occur, and perhaps could not have occurred, before 1945 – and more likely not before 1972 – the year in which the UN initiated its formal organized environmental program in terms of international law.[23]

[21] *See*, for instance, Wolfram Kaiser and Jan-Henrik Meyer, who focus on the UN as the true starting point of modern environmental protection: Wolfram Kaiser & Jan-Henrik Meyer, *International Organizations and Environmental Protection in the Global Twentieth Century, in* INTERNATIONAL ORGANIZATIONS AND ENVIRONMENTAL PROTECTION: CONSERVATION AND GLOBALIZATION IN THE TWENTIETH CENTURY 1 (Wolfram Kaiser & Jan-Henrik Meyer eds., 2017) [hereinafter INTERNATIONAL ORGANIZATIONS AND ENVIRONMENTAL PROTECTION].

[22] *See* Watenpaugh, *supra* note 11, at 1322.

[23] *See* Wolfram Kaiser & Jan-Henrik Meyer, *Introduction: International Organizations and Environmental Protection in the Global Twentieth Century, in* INTERNATIONAL ORGANIZATIONS AND ENVIRONMENTAL PROTECTION, *supra* note 21, at 2–3. Even

Regardless of what has been written, environmental changes had occurred as environmental problems long before the establishment of the UN. Moreover, the international arena, using legal discourse and introducing legal mechanisms, was aware of these challenges. As my research reveals, the League tried to solve a series of environmental crises such as the sea pollution caused by oil discharge from ships, which threatened the coastline of different countries (Chapter 1); dwindling fish stocks in general, and the growing threat of the extinction of the whale due to rapidly developing whaling techniques (Chapter 2); diseases that emerged from rural peripheries in Eastern Europe and East Asia, and which thrived and spread due to poor hygiene and public health conditions in the countryside (Chapter 3); and difficulties in the timber trade given the economic and commercial outcomes of the Great Depression and the dumping policy of the Soviet Union, which intertwined with a growing concern about deforestation that was presented as a phenomenon that dramatically changing the natural landscape (Chapter 4). All these environmental challenges urgently required solutions.

According to the common environmental history perspective, it was only in the second half of the twentieth century – and certainly not during the interwar period and the reign of the League – that measures of this kind could have been taken into consideration. Scholars have argued that two dramatic changes in world society that occurred in the second half of the twentieth century can serve as variables that explain the rise of contemporary environmental regimentation. The first change involved the expansion of rationalized scientific analyses of nature, while the other change was organizational and involved the rise of an international associational framework, principally the UN system,[24] which provided arenas that

minimalist descriptions given by scholars who study the origins and development of international environmental law, if they do refer to or mention the role of the League during the shaping of this international legal regime, do not lean on the League in and of itself, but ascribe much of the contribution of advancing international legal-environmental initiatives not to the League, but to other international developments. Instead of focusing on the League, these scholars choose to attribute such environmental measures to the growing involvement of scientists and other researchers, along with early environmental NGOs, as these factors screened and influenced the events and processes carried out in the institution. They argue that, despite the absence of a central international power, it is evident that environmental policy rallied behind a culture of "rationalism and science" (Meyer et al., *supra* note 19, at 625). However, could it be that the League had a role in that development?

24 *See, e.g.*, Meyer et al., *supra* note 19, at 629. For a broader and detailed description of the environmental history of the twentieth century, and of the awareness of changes between nature and humankind, as well as the shift between the nineteenth and twentieth centuries, *see*

encouraged mobilization around broad global interests and transcending nation-state agendas (and, in many cases, restrictions or reluctance). The expansion of rationalized scientific analyses of nature and the rise of the UN provided an expanding international framework, in which both a global-environmental discourse and legal-environmental transactions arose. The research literature emphasizes[25] the importance of the appearance of an international regime's framework on the historical timeline: "Together, these two forces provide an expanded world-level frame within which interaction and discourse about environmental issues could expand . . . ."[26]

To be certain, a rich legal history on the history of environmental law in modern times does already exist. Works such as those of Peder Anker,[27] for instance, aim to trace environmental policies that tend to mirror international law and international discourse, decades before the establishment of the UN. However, even when Anker, one of the pioneers of the historiography of environmental law, refers to the period under investigation, he attributes minor importance, if any at all, to the role and place of the League. Instead, his work analyzes the role of the British Empire, which adopted innovative environmental policies – most particularly what he describes as its experimental "ecological imperial legacy" outside Europe.

Layout of the Chapters

Remarkably, the role of the League in the history and evolution of environmental law remains almost entirely unexplored. I explore different aspects of the League's deep involvement in trying to solve global environmental problems in the 1920s and 1930s. Archival research in the Palais des Nations reveals some surprising – and relevant – discussions and ideas of the unique role played by transnational organizations, NGOs, civil society groups, and non-state actors in vigorous campaigns and intensive international efforts for the protection of nature or the

J. R. McNeill, Something New under the Sun: An Environmental History of the Twentieth Century World (2000).

25 *See, e.g.*, Erving Goffman, Frame Analysis (1974); David E. Snow, E. Burke Rochford Jr., Steven K. Worden & Robert D. Benford, *Frame Alignment Processes, Micromobilization, and Movement Participation*, 51 Am. Soc. Rev. 464 (1986).

26 Meyer et al., *supra* note 19, at 629.

27 Peder Anker, Imperial Ecology: Environmental Order in the British Empire: 1895–1945 (2001).

environment, and for the preservation of a variety of natural resources in the period under examination.

As the interwar environmental regime unfolds, my revisionist retrospective does not limit itself to the linear historical borders of 1919 and 1939, but also identifies the influence and position the League held, and its effect, on environmental regulation after 1945 – and sometimes considerably later.[28] I also identify the motivations and the political patterns, both obvious and hidden, which were present during this environmental regime.

This study is divided into four main chapters, each of which deals with a different real-time environmental, economic, political, and legal test case handled by the League. I will discuss these chapters and the challenges they cover in the fifth chapter.

The first chapter traces the intensive joint effort to reach an agreement on the International Convention Relating to the Pollution of the Sea by Oil. As I elaborate, several organs and officials of the League were involved in the complex legal consultations and coordination surrounding the promotion of an international convention that aimed to fight and put a stop to oil discharge from ships – pollution that threatened shores and communities in various countries. The special convention of the League aimed to improve an earlier transnational convention that was agreed on in 1926. However, as I will show, the League's campaign was more intense and dealt with the conflict of interests between the shipping industry and those parties that wished to protect the sea and nature from oil pollution. This legal-environmental effort was carried out by and under the auspices of the League, and it stands as a case study of the

[28] It should be noted that this project deals with a broader definition of *International Law*. I will generally discuss "law," "transnational law," or "global law." In this way, the dissertation will also examine the implications of the League policies and negotiations of the different legal systems that Geneva was interacting with, as a part of a global (or transnational) legal discourse in the interwar period. For an example of the overlap between environmentalism, transnational law, global law, and/or international law, which tends to blur our strict definitions, *see*, *e.g.*, Astrid Mignon Kirchhof & Jan-Henrik Meyer, Global *Protest against Nuclear Power. Transfer and Transnational Exchange in the 1970s and 1980s*, 39 HIST. SOC. RES. 165 (2014); Michael L. Hughes, *Civil Disobedience in Transnational Perspective: American and West German Anti-Nuclear-Power Protesters, 1975–1982*, 39 HIST. SOC. RES. 236 (2014). Naturally, this research does not intend to unpack the complexity of the sometimes "duel" conflict relations between these two broad terms. For a more direct, precise, and focused discussion on this theoretical field of international law studies, *see*, *e.g.*, Joseph S. Nye & Robert O. Keohane, *Transnational Relations and World Politics: An Introduction*, 25 INT'L ORG. 329 (1971).

evolution of environmental perspectives and voices who chose to turn to international law for help.

Although the antipollution campaign ultimately failed in terms of the interwar period, it is nevertheless important given the many relevant threads it weaves together: the joint effort of several states and agencies; the deep involvement of NGOs from various states, who advocated for the protection of migrating birds that were dying in their thousands as a result of poisoned sea water); supportive public opinion with relatively wide media coverage; international and transnational questions of law and inquiries relating to international relations; and the battle between the environmentalist agenda and competing industrial interests (along with their political lobby and pressures). Moreover, as I will show in the conclusion portion, the interwar effort was not in vain as it contributed to the postwar convention of 1954.

The second chapter covers the intensive diplomacy related to whaling, one of the central international campaigns that was led by the League. As technological developments in the field of whaling (by Norwegian, British, Japanese, and other fleets) rapidly increased, scientists and others became increasingly concerned that whales were about to become extinct, a claim that gained more and more attention. Given capabilities as a new, professional body of international law, the League became *the* center for a fierce battle between whaling powers (who were reluctant to accept any external intervention in "their" profitable industries, and the legal limitations this would undoubtedly entail for their fleets) and scientific associations and "neutral" voices (who urged the League to prevent a version of the tragedy of the commons on the high seas).

This chapter compares the different negotiations and proposals for the first international whaling conventions that were prepared by the League (and signed in 1931 and 1937), in order to regulate and control the boom in whaling expeditions. These had begun to travel farther and farther in the oceans, bringing the species to the brink of historical disaster.

I have placed the treatment of whaling in this chapter, as it follows on from the consideration of maritime pollution (covered in the first chapter). As both of these case studies relate or are entangled in the webs of waves, water, seas, and international law, it seems as they should follow each other, as they depict a certain sense of water security. Based on these first two chapters together, one can interpret the ways in which the League and other interwar participants saw the sea, at least to a certain extent, as a legal world.

The third chapter explores the League's "rural hygiene" campaign. During its work on different reflections of sanitary problems that put local, national, and global public health at risk, the League invested substantial scientific, comparative, and professional effort while it was considering different possible policies with which these dangers and challenges could be faced. These suggested policies, articulated in terms of international law, focused mainly on the eradication of a variety of environmental-sanitary risks and spreading diseases, which the League believed to be plaguing the countryside in Eastern Europe and across the "Far East" (as it was called by the participants). Among the international community's concerns were the need to protect water resources from human and nonhuman pollution, to treat refuse, to fight spreading diseases particularly in rural areas, to limit fly breeding, to control rats and pests, and more. Citing these concerns as threats to local, national, and international communities, the League conceptualized agricultural peripheries as a rural frontier from which humanity could better protect itself, using various means of sanitary engineering, special medical services, and political awareness.

This chapter tracks two main events that took up much of the League's attention. First, it assembled the European Conference on Rural Hygiene (1931) and, later, parallel to its main agenda and realms of inquiry and cooperation, the Intergovernmental Conference of Far Eastern Countries on Rural Hygiene, which was held at Bandoeng, Java in August 1937.

The fourth chapter uncovers the problem of timber production and trade following the Great Depression, and the increasing concerns of spreading deforestation in various areas around the world.

The Kingdom of the Forests gained particular attention during the interwar period: international bodies (including the League) were interested in controlling and coordinating the production and supply of different raw materials (such as coal, cotton, oil, gum, wheat, and sugar) to the international market, both in regular times and during times of crisis. Immediately after the World War I, the League became interested in timber in particular. At the end of the 1920s, about forty million cubic meters of sawn timber – the most popular product at this time – were exported worldwide per year.[29] This figure was cut almost in half when the Great Depression of 1929 started to affect international commerce and timber production. Accusations against

[29] Walter Grottian, Die Umsatzmengen im Weltholzhandel 1925–1938, 144 (1942).

a dumping policy of the Soviet Union, which stood as a central part of the Five-Year-Plan, have been heard. This alleged policy applied pressure of its own and put other national timber industries at risk. The League wished to support these industries and encouraged the development of an international regime of mutual cooperation and coordination between exporting and importing countries.

While independent international organizations, such as the International Institute of Agriculture in Rome, or the Comité International du Bois,[30] have focused on timber, different voices started in the late 1930s to advocate for the protection of trees and forests. These parties (mostly led by the French delegation to Geneva) encouraged the League to fight against deforestation – a phenomenon that was spreading as an environmental result of industrial-economic development – in Scandinavia, the Soviet Union, Europe, and North America. At that point, the interwar story of timber reflected a sort of harmony between the League and Western nations' commercial interests. With their profits severely reduced, some of these nations turned to international law and cooperation to protect their national industries and to stabilize dropping prices. The League, driven by its own agenda, wished to see the control of supply of the timber market and restricted production in order to prop up prices and thereby ensure the survival of the industry. With the merging of these threads, environmental considerations were woven into the plot, coloring the dilemma with urgent calls to restrict timber production and forest harvest in order to stop deforestation from expanding. These dimensions added another layer to the economic incentives and industrial interests surrounding the timber issue.

The fifth chapter will provide a broader comparative view of the League's environmental concerns. The main aim of the additional discussion in this chapter is to weave these different initiatives (which are described separately in each chapter) into a coherent and broad regime, one that has a common ground, continuity, and certain dynamics. As each chapter explains the role played by central theories, ideas, conflicting interests, environmental challenges, and scientific or professional concerns, this chapter will put them together and explain some of the differences and common patterns. Moreover, this analysis also revises the League's different endeavors from contemporary environmental perspectives, and assesses their relevance to current dilemmas where nature protection conflicts with human needs. Likewise, I will also deal in this

[30] The International Timber Committee.

part with some more general questions, such as the perennial problem of Eurocentrism.

Each of the following chapters explores a different dimension of the League's history of environmental policy. They focus, chronologically and thematically, on the environmental impacts of pollution of the sea by oil, the growing whaling industry and endangered whales, rural hygiene and sanitation problems in different regional peripheries, and timber production and fears of spreading deforestation. However, this study is not a comprehensive history that covers every aspect of the League's engagement with issues that had – to some extent – to do with nature or ecosystems. There may well be other concerns that the League handled that also involved environmental perspectives.[31] Rather, I present a broad, sweeping legal-historical overview of several of the most critical environmental challenges that the interwar world faced, in order to understand the notions and reasons behind the League's environmental leadership and to explain both its shortcomings and achievements.

The concluding part reviews several of the key patterns in the League's environmental regime as it unfolded. I will also use this opportunity to discuss some of the broader implications of this study for international environmental policymaking.

Next to the techno-environmental and legal questions covered in each chapter, the environmental story reveals the complex institutional framework of the League. Although this research does not intend to cover or analyze the complex institutional structure of the League, it will describe and deal with its meanings in relation to the case studies and the way they evolved during the period. It should be noted however, as this study covers the League as a complex organization, that the main organs of the League were the Assembly, the Council, and the Secretariat. One can find them, and their changing roles, in each chapter. The Assembly, which met once a year, consisted of representatives of all the member states and decided on the organization's policy. The Council, whose main mission was to settle international disputes, included four permanent members (British, France, Italy, and Japan) and four (later nine) others elected by the Assembly every three years. The Secretariat, the heart of the League in many aspects, carried out the day-to-day work of the League, under the

[31] Given the possible ways to conduct archive-based research in legal history, and although I have done my best not to omit the important policy areas and to capture all the major realms in which the League dealt with environmental perspectives as central part of its considerations, there might still be some hidden issues that involved these perspectives but which have not been covered in this study.

direction of the Secretary-General, prepared the agenda, and published reports of the meetings. The League's institutional framework also included autonomous bodies,[32] and a list of committees and commissions received mandates from the League.[33] Main parts of this research will analyze and interpret the work of these special bodies, sometimes working almost independently, under the auspices of the League. As the first chapter will show, for instance, the issue of oil pollution was discussed under the supervision of the League's Communications and Transit Organisation. The Organisation was one of the auxiliary bodies established by the Covenant of the League, and it had the authority to focus on and study various questions of a more or less technical character, or so it seemed.[34]

Moreover, the Organisation discussed the oil pollution problem in collaboration with the Economic Committee. The Committee was part of a series of several other functional fixed committees (next to the Financial, Fiscal, and Statistical Committees), all of which were part of the Economic and Financial Organisation, which was another auxiliary body of the League.[35] As central parts of my study show, the Economic Committee would make up most of what would become the League's environmental regime.

It should also be noted that although the chapters refer from time to time to the League as a whole, the institutional structure on the ground was obviously more complex. The League was not, either in the environmental questions or in any other issue, a single, unified entity, seeming to possess knowledge and will of its own. Therefore, in relevant places, the chapters will differentiate the views of the League's various organs (or individuals or groups within those organs).

[32] Such as the Permanent Court of International Justice (PCIJ), which its establishment was provided for the in the Covenant of the League; or the International Labour Organisation (ILO/BIT), that was established in 1919 at the Paris Peace Conference as an international organization working in cooperation with the League.

[33] Such as the Permanent Mandate Commission or Opium Advisory Committee (Advisory Committee on Traffic in Opium and Other Dangerous Drugs).

[34] For a review on the role of the Organisation for Communications and Transit as a mediator in the global process, *see*, among others, Frank Schipper, Vincent Lagendijk & Irene Anastasiadou, *New Connections for an Old Continent: Rail, Road and Electricity in the League of Nations Organisation for Communications and Transit*, *in* MATERIALIZING EUROPE: TRANSNATIONAL INFRASTRUCTURES AND THE PROJECT OF EUROPE 113 (Alexander Badenoch & Andreas Fickers eds., 2010). For a description of the institutional framework of the League, *see, e.g.*, NORTHEDGE, *supra* note 1.

[35] The Economic and Financial Organisation was created at a special institutional conference the League held in Brussels in September–October 1920.

The League's Environmental Regime As a Story of Legal History and Continuity

As I elaborate in each of the chapters, I have placed the League's endeavors in each specific legal, environmental, economic, and political challenge on its "own" relevant historical developing timeline. None of these issues – pollution of the sea by oil, the whaling dilemma, the rural hygiene campaign, or timber industry crisis and fear of deforestation – is isolated or without context. The League, too, was part of a developing process of emerging environmental awareness. As the historical background of each chapter highlights, in many of the case studies that formed the cornerstones of the interwar environmental regime (and prior to 1919 or before the League started to handle these missions), there were already relevant and influential national or transnational legal arrangements that tried to solve or address these problems.

The League was not alone in developing environmental awareness during the interwar[36] period. Power relations were often apparent in the discussions on environmental issues. The balance of power (or lack thereof) was frequently highlighted in the League's engagement with environmental issues. This was not unique to the League's regime. The early environmental treaties, signed outside the League, that dealt with wildlife in Africa in 1900[37] and 1933,[38] for instance, were a stitch on the warp and woof of colonialism; and the North American bird treaties[39] of the early twentieth century were largely an outcome of the actions of US scientists and activists (conservationists and ornithologists) – though not really Canadian or Mexican ones. Some issues of the interwar environmental regime reveal or reflect power relations, colonial hegemony, and the strong will of new states to take part in the game of international law per se.

There are individual histories that focus on interwar environmental challenges (as my study illustrates); but a systematic overview of the surveys that have aimed to cover the interwar period as part of a broad depiction of all of environmental history (such as the panoramic

[36] The environmental history of the League as a postwar period, correlates with a developing field within the intensifying spectrum of environmental history. This field or subfield focuses on the effects that conflicts in war and combat had upon nature and ecosystems. *See, e.g.*, Natural Enemy, Natural Ally: Toward an Environmental History of War (Richard P. Tucker & Edmund Russell, eds., 2004).

[37] The 1900 Convention for the Preservation of Wild Animals, Birds, and Fish in Africa.

[38] The 1933 Convention Relative to the Preservation of Fauna and Flora in the Natural State.

[39] The 1916 Migratory Bird Treaty.

overviews of John McNeill[40] or Ian Whyte[41]) shows that the interwar period is considered to be almost worthless in the greater scheme of modern environmental history. Even in his groundbreaking book, comprising no fewer than 421 pages, McNeill dedicated just one sentence (!) to the role of the League in the environmental history of the twentieth century: "By 1935 the clear decline in Blue Whales led to regulations overseen by the League of Nations. These had scant effect."[42]

McNeill says nothing further: either on the intensive involvement of the League in the convoluted campaign for international whaling law (which continued almost throughout the interwar period), or on the League as a whole and as an institution that promoted the environmental regime.

Certainly this introductory section cannot cover every book that seeks to provide an overview of all environmental history; however, there are a few notable examples that continue to overlook the interwar period (though they include other earlier periods, as I have mentioned), such as Whyte's A DICTIONARY OF ENVIRONMENTAL HISTORY, published in 2013.[43] Like others, Whyte ignores the role and the position of the League. However, in his detailed interdisciplinary environmental dictionary (in Whyte's own words), which covers several hundred different terms of environmental history over 500 pages, there is not a single term relating to the League. In contrast, institutions such as the Council for the Preservation of Rural England receive two different mentions;[44] the Royal Society for the Protection of Birds gets three separate references in his survey.[45] Terms relating to international environmental law do appear, but they refer to the term Globalization (on page 218).

40 McNEILL, *supra* note 24.

41 IAN D. WHYTE, A DICTIONARY OF ENVIRONMENTAL HISTORY (2013).

42 McNEILL, *supra* note 24, at 242. To reinforce my argument regarding the "hidden chapter" of the League in the history of international environmental law, one can also point to a clear reality: in the legal-historical overviews of international environmentalism, such as the work of Meyer et al. on the evolution of the global regime, no more than a single paragraph is dedicated to the role (successes and failures alike) of the League (See Meyer et al., *supra* note 19, at 631). This single paragraph, in a comprehensive description beginning in the year 1870 and ending in the early 1990s, is a poignant illustration of the common description and understanding of the genealogy of international environmental law and the role of the League in its evolution.

43 WHYTE, *supra* note 41.

44 On pages 122 and 202.

45 On pages 175, 347 and 424. However, it does not mention the role of the society in the interwar campaign against the pollution of the sea by oil, an initiative that drove the League to lead an international discussion on the first environmental convention of its kind (*see* the discussion in Chapter 1).

The same is true of another work that aims to explore a comprehensive environmental vision of human history. Like Jared Diamond's GUNS, GERMS, AND STEEL,[46] Clive Ponting's study[47] tells of the relationship between the environment and human history. Ponting examines a variety of historic world civilizations, from Sumeria to ancient Egypt, and from Easter Island to the Roman Empire. He argues that human societies have repeatedly built communities and structures that have grown and prospered by exploiting the Earth's resources, only to expand to the point where those resources can no longer sustain the societies' needs, populations or aims. One of his primary arguments is that the reason for these empires' collapse lies in the environmental history crises.

Was there an international environmental crisis during the interwar period? Ponting mentions the League only in two very brief remarks. First, he discusses the case of Nauru (on page 194), and mentions that the island was first a German territory (colony), then a League of Nations mandate, and then a United Nations mandate.[48] Second, he refers to the League in his discussion of the issue of food in the twentieth century (on page 246).[49]

I should be more accurate. There is quite a rich historiography that explores supranational dimensions of environmentalism – including their explicit legal policies – in periods that preceded the first half of the twentieth

[46] JARED DIAMOND, GUNS, GERMS AND STEEL: THE FATES OF HUMAN SOCIETIES (1997).

[47] CLIVE PONTING, A NEW GREEN HISTORY OF THE WORLD: THE ENVIRONMENT AND THE COLLAPSE OF GREAT CIVILISATIONS (revised edition, 2007; original ver. 1991).

[48] For another study that tracks the role of the Nauru in a shift in international environmental law later on in environmental history *see* Antony Anghie, *"The Heart of My Home": Colonialism, Environmental Damage, and the Nauru Case*, 34 HARV. INT'L L.J. 445 (1993).

[49] But the interwar period is being mentioned for comparative perspective. Ponting argues that the period was worse in terms of Western conditions (especially in the United States and in Britain). Following the Great Depression, the international community became threatened by the increasing problem of famine, as people "starved to death on the streets of New York and in Britain" (Ponting, *supra* note 47, at 246).

This can also explain the League's initiatives to present global standards of nutrition: the League collected worldwide information and officially estimated that a third of the population was too poor to buy the minimum diet that the League believed to be essential to maintain health.

Moreover, the only relevant reference, as I see it, in Ponting's study, appears in Chapter 8: "The Rape of the World." Here, under the subtitle "Whaling," he discusses the whaling industry's interest in devising a scheme to control catches "so that whaling could continue at a sustainable . . . level." Without mentioning the ongoing and intensive endeavors of the League in an explicit manner, Ponting mentions that "[s]ome attempts were made in the 1930s but they failed . . . ." (*Id.* at 166).

century. However, while these studies have moved beyond local, national-domestic questions of environmental history and have identified a transnational shift in environmental history, they have largely focused on imperial or colonial networks, dimensions, and frameworks. In that sense, one can easily find works that uncovered pre-1946 or pre-1972 transnational environmental law, such as Richard Grove's work. In his study, Grove was one of the first historians who found the origins of environmentalism in the unexplored realm of Western (British, French, and Dutch) colonial policies in East Asia, the Caribbean, and other regions. In this retrospective, Grove pointed out the significance of the colonial impact on the global environment beyond the European metropolis that controlled Western empires overseas. He further looked at the ways in which – for the first time in transnational contexts – conservationist notions were reflected in these empires' policies abroad, and how they handled the limitations of local and global natural resources.[50]

Likewise, Rachelle Adam[51] introduced the complexity of species extinction in different regions in Africa, and showed how the British intensive effort to protect these endangered species should be understood as part of early environmental law. Marc Cioc,[52] or Mario Prost and Yoriko Otomo,[53] also looked at international environmentalism that used legal terms and mechanisms beyond the nation-state model in imperial or colonial frameworks. Yet the historiography remains silent on international environmental law that is *not* part of imperial or colonial studies.[54]

Though there are a few scholars who have recognized or identified the preliminary formation of the early international environmental regime at

[50] Richard H. Grove, Green Imperialism: Colonial Expansion, Tropical Island Edens and the Origins of Environmentalism, 1600–1860 (1996).

[51] Rachelle Adam, Elephant Treaties: The Colonial Legacy of the Biodiversity Crisis (2014).

[52] Cioc, *supra* note 3. *See*, in particular, the ways in which Cioc describes the role of colonial legacy in the evolution of international whaling law, and regarding the protection of migratory birds.

[53] Mario Prost & Yoriko Otomo, *British Influences on International Environmental Law: The Case of Wildlife Conservation*, *in* British Influences on International Law: 1915–2015, 192 (Robert McCorquodale & Jean-Pierre Gauci eds., 2015).

[54] Moreover, compared to the general discourse that characterized early transnational imperial environmentalism, and the period of the League that followed, it would be rather hard to find the same "neo-colonial romanticisation" (Prost & Otomo, *supra* note 53, at 210) in its discussions on environmental challenges. In most cases, as I will describe, the League, in general, did not turn to exotic or mysterious features in its representation of the fauna and landscape of the non-Western world.

the turn of the twentieth century, they have tended too often to narrow the focus of their research. Some have chosen to focus on other frameworks, largely bypassing the League's legal-environmental activities during its reign – both those that were successful and those that failed. David Frank[55] and David Pepper,[56] for instance, have examined efforts in the first two decades of the twentieth century to place environmental concerns within the international legal discourse. Although both have claimed that these efforts provided "weak frameworks" in the operative international dimension, my work will study the League as a framework in the context of historical analysis of the evolution of international environmentalism, which promoted international legal activity and discourse. One can find therein different policies[57] that aim to protect wildlife[58] and the campaign for the prevention of whaling.[59] However, for instance, right after Prost and Otomo discuss different conservation treaties and international conferences that took part in the protection of wildlife in Africa and in setting rules for hunting management in the 1910s, they move on to describe the "post-war period," which marked "a further sea change for international conservation" as a whole.[60]

The "war" they refer to is, obviously, World War II, leaving the interwar period (the global arena after 1918) overlooked.

This tendency to overlook the League becomes even more apparent in scholarship that aims to disrupt common perceptions or concepts of environmental historiography, and to uncover the origins of international environmental law. Prost and Otomo describe the 1950 International

55 David J. Frank, *Science, Nature and the Globalization of the Environment: 1870–1990*, 76 Soc. Forces 409 (1997)

56 David Pepper, The Roots of Modern Environmentalism (1984).

57 Meyer and his associates, for instance, referred to the increasing ecosystem perspective in the late 1910s. However, they attributed it primarily to advances and scientific activity (in the local–national context), but not to an international–institutional policy, or to any legal interface. *See* Meyer et al., *supra* note 19, at 630.

58 *See*, for instance, the international conference of 1900, which was assembled for the protection and conservation of wild animals in Africa; as well as the convention which followed it – ironically, this convention simultaneously called for the rescue of the African Animal Kingdom and for the protection of hippos and giraffes, as well as for the eradication of dangerous species such as lions, baboons and pythons. *See* Sherman S. Hayden, The International Protection of Wild Life: An Examination of Treaties and Other Agreements for the Preservation of Birds and Mammals (1942).

59 For a broad analysis of the history of international efforts to make whaling sustainable in the twentieth century, *see* Kurkpatrick Dorsey, Whales and Nations: Environmental Diplomacy on the High Seas (2013).

60 Prost & Otomo, *supra* note 53, at 205.

Convention for the Protection of Birds alongside "the first treaty to tackle marine pollution"[61] – the International Convention for the Prevention of Pollution of the Sea by Oil (which was adopted on May 12, 1954, and amended in 1962 and 1969). However, even their revisionist work fails to mention that the same legal-environmental campaign took place not long before the development they analyze: during the 1930s, to be precise. This parallel chain of concerns about nature, industry, and the coastal landscape that led to the sketching of a similar legal solution under the auspices of the League is completely omitted from this description of environmental legal history. As my first chapter describes, the League led an international coalition (that faced bitter resistance from the shipping industry and its political lobby) that showed a growing concern for dying birds that were washing up on the shores by their thousands.[62]

While one can see a significant change in the course of the League historiography in general since the 1990s, there still has yet to be an equivalent development in the historiography of legal environmentalism. My study challenges this gap in the common historiography of environmentalism, while shattering or revising some of its arguments and premises.[63]

[61] *Id.* at 206.

[62] Indeed, as I will elaborate in the first chapter, the nascent environmental challenges the League faced as early as the 1920s seem to have failed to reach binding international conventions – if we are to discuss the final results. However, the very fact that comprehensive studies, which acknowledge by definition the role of the gradual historical evolution of international environmentalism, skip the interwar period as a whole seems to justify my claim. In one of their notes, for instance, Prost and Otomo mention that the 1950 International Convention for the Protection of Birds was "the result of *a series of conferences*, following on from a 1902 Convention for the Protection of Birds." And yet, they are satisfied with minimizing – in my opinion – the contribution of the efforts that had been invested in the battle over the interwar work-in-progress convention, which was according their (too) general observation "limited in its effectiveness" (Prost & Otomo, *supra* note 53, at 206, note 54 (emphasis added)).

[63] The need, or at least the possibility, to revise or reassess descriptions of the activities and history of the League as seen through the lenses of the history of international environmental law becomes even more pronounced, as I claim, when considering the primary and secondary literature on which scholars in the field have based their research. When Meyer and his colleagues state that all efforts to encourage the League to operate in environmental issues "failed in any respect," they refer to Hayden's assessment, made in 1942. Hayden, however, dealt with international environmental law in the 1940s, from the very specific perspective of the protection of wild animals. He also asserted that "the question [of protecting] whales was treated alone by the League" (HAYDEN, *supra* note 58, at 148).

Another "minimalist" estimation of the joint effort to promote environmental issues and concerns by the League appears in Ronald Mitchell's research. Yet, even in this kind

Indeed, in contrast to the limited historiographic perspectives I have briefly presented, several recent works have expanded the scope and reach of research on the League into environment-related subjects.[64] Though they examine certain environmental issues within the framework and history of the League,[65] they still lack, in my mind, a broader overview that brings to light a systematic and comprehensive analysis of the League's environmental legal activities. My analysis therefore weaves these activities into a regime that can be revised, studied, and compared in legal manners, interpretations, and methodologies.

As noted above, it seems that only recently has the historical view of the League become illuminated with new perspectives, contrasting to the former view that characterized it for almost half of the last century. Is it not then time, following the example of the changing historical research, to shatter old-fashioned images of the League also with regard to the interface between studies on the League and the history of international environmental law?

of study, the focus is given to scientific perspectives on a specific field (pollution of the sea by oil). *See* Ronald Mitchell, *International Oil Pollution of the Oceans*, *in* INSTITUTIONS FOR THE EARTH: SOURCES OF EFFECTIVE INTERNATIONAL ENVIRONMENTAL PROTECTION 183 (P. H. Hass, R. O. Keohane & M. A. Levy eds., 1993).

64 Sunil Amrith and Patricia Clavin's recent study, for example, which was published only in 2013, examines the infrastructure and the involvement of internal bodies of the League, and the networks that were established by the League from 1930 to 1945 to fight hunger and nutrition in rural areas, particularly in East Asia. The League, however, was also trying to initiate a similar move in 1939 to promote these conditions in rural areas of Europe. This economic-history research focuses on the realms of nutrition, health, and rural development, and one can see the environmental perspectives engaged therein. In addition, the study also seeks to examine the history of relations between the institutions that participated in this system. These kinds of missions, and others, set the framework for what later developed into the UN Food and Agriculture Organization (FAO), the World Health Organization (WHO), and the International Bank for Reconstruction and Development (IBRD). *See* Sunil Amrith & Patricia Clavin, *Feeding the World: Connecting Europe and Asia, 1930–1945*, 218 (suppl. 8) PAST AND PRESENT 29 (2013).

65 The work of Anna-Katharina Wöbse, for example, deals with the effort invested during the campaign for international environmental consent regarding a common ecological concern, as reflected in the (failed) Pollution of the Sea by Oil Convention. However, Wöbse does not look or go any further but the discussions and proceedings of that one complex convention. Wöbse, the first scholar who tried to find environmental international legal history in the interwar period, ends her revelation with yet another description of the common pattern of the rise and fall of the League, and expresses her findings with an awareness of the clichés about the history and the role of the League: "The failure to impose a comprehensive pollution control regime may seem to confirm the clichés about the League's shortcomings . . . ." *See* Anna-Katharina Wöbse, *Oil on Troubled Water? Environmental Diplomacy in the League of Nations*, 32 DIPLOMATIC HIST. 519, 519 (2008).

Before Concluding the Introduction

A few additional general remarks before I move on to the League's environmental regime. The following chapters will maintain a linear path of the historical timeline as far as possible; however, I will also try to avoid a mere chronological description and nothing more. My analysis is not entirely a "strict," laboratory-style analysis. History cannot, and should not, be explained in terms of separate and isolated factors alone. An approach that either tries to follow the historical evolution through a chronologic chain of events, or one that focuses only on one specific role or agency, might miss part of the almost chaotic, and very human, course of history. Economic reasons and commercial interests alone cannot give us a full picture – if there is any – of the campaigns for international environmental regime. Nor can an isolated examination of the environmentalist and conservationist agendas of that time reveal the entire story. The mixed variety of the (sometimes conflicting) parties involved had a direct effect on how the interwar questions of pollution, whaling, rural hygiene and sanitation, and timber unfolded.

Moreover, this is not the first study to claim that international interest in conservation existed before the 1970s, 1980s, and 1990s. Likewise, this is also not to suggest that this interest in conservation has always been translated or articulated into an agreement. In most cases, it was not. However, the urgent calls that pushed the League and the international community to act have not yet been studied thoroughly or as a part of a coherent, continuing, regime.[66]

Having provided this general introduction to the League's environmental regime, it should also be noted that it is hard to accurately compare the

[66] For example, the Convention on the International Trade in Endangered Species of Wild Flora and Fauna (1973) (better known as CITES), which scholars and environmental activists consider to be one of the most prominent stages of international environmental law in the post–World War II era, oversaw the import and export of listed (at risk of extinction) species. The legal mechanism used in CITES was based on a system of licensing authorization that operated very much like the method that was introduced in the interwar environmental conventions that I will discuss (*see* my discussion in Section 2.3.5 of Chapter 2, in which I elaborate on the first international whaling convention of 1931). Some scholars (such as Prost and Otomo, and other scholars who have focused on colonial environmental legacies) have claimed, however, that these legal mechanisms were shaped by the British Imperial legacy and experience overseas (Prost & Otomo, *supra* note 53, at 207–08). However, my study will show that the traditional scholarship in environmental history – which attributes most (if not all) of the landmarks of early international environmental law to the role of empires (and in particular the British Empire – *see* GROVE, *supra* note 50) – tends to skip other bodies and states of that period.

scope and volume of environmental initiatives that preceded 1946 with those that followed the year that the UN was established. Surely these two chapters of environmentalism differ considerably in their definitions, theoretical framework, and aims. Both the environmental achievements and ecological failures of the second half of the century easily overshadow those of the first half as a whole, and of the interwar period in particular. The second half of the century, for instance, stands out as a much more institutionalized period in terms of environmental cooperation and international coordination. The Food and Agriculture Organization (FAO), for example, joined the United Nations Educational, Scientific and Cultural Organization (UNESCO), the World Meteorological Organization (WMO), and the International Maritime Organization (IMO). Likewise, the 1946 International Convention for the Regulation of Whaling overcame both its earlier versions of 1931 and 1937, and compared to later international cooperation against the pollution of the sea by oil, the "early" (and precedential) convention of the League on that issue can be seen as almost amateur.

But that does not seem to be the right question. The evolution of international environmental law in the twentieth century, and also beyond it, definitely has visible roots in the 1920s and 1930s. Even if one were to claim that most of these activities were a colossal failure on the ground, the layered developing geology of international (environmental) law[67] owes at least some of its explanations to the interwar period, whether it is considered a success or not. Likewise, the main goal of this study is not to evaluate *how* were these environmental issues on the ground, and what was their impact in "real" or measured terms. I rather focused and was interested in the ways in which different perspectives on these concerns were reflected by terms and discourse of international law. Indeed, there is no doubt that the early 1950s marked a new chapter in the history of global environmentalism. The 1950 International Convention for the Protection of Birds (on the matter of the cause of sea pollution), for instance, was agreed on by various European nations. But should not environmental history judge this final and formal stage of 1950 *alongside* the interwar series of discussions and drafts of legal convention that had tried to establish a worldwide agreement for the protection of migratory birds?[68]

[67] J. H. H. Weiler, *the Geology of International Law – Governance, Democracy and Legitimacy*, 64 ZEITSCHRIFT FÜR AUSLÄNDISCHES ÖFFENTLICHES RECHT UND VÖLKERRECHT 547 (2004).

[68] Most of the environmental history that focuses on international protection for migratory birds tends to study the twists and turns of transnational conventions that mostly related

As I will argue, at least some of the natural or obvious characteristics of the ways in which international law as a whole, and international environmental law in particular, has been shaped over time, were already evident during the interwar period. The issues that follow in each chapter were part of an ongoing process that also included legal mechanisms as central tools with which these environmental challenges could be confronted.

This brings me to the notions of conservation and preservation in common environmental studies discourse. Biodiversity, wildlife protection, and sustainability are some of the most recognized terms of ecology today, but it seems that at the beginning of the previous century, words such as "conservation" reigned supreme.[69] As I will demonstrate in each chapter, at times, international and subnational actors simultaneously relied on reflections or interpretations of both of these theoretical terms in real-time test cases; sometimes, they articulated their demands using only one or the other.

This is not the place to launch into a discussion of the history of these two key notions in environmental history, but since my study aims to deal with the interplay between them as they were reflected in early international law, I shall present a brief overview of their definitions and differences.

The study tackles the question of whether or not the League's use of international law, governance, and diplomacy in the following test cases practiced conservationist approaches or preservationist ones. Environmental historians who have studied different chapters in the evolution of international environmentalism tend to suggest several interpretations of the theoretical and substantial tendencies that were used or implemented within legal discourse, agreements, conventions, and treaties of the relevant period being studied. This work will distinguish between Environmentalism (and those who share its perspectives as Environmentalists), or protection of the

to North America. However, following the 1902 Convention for the Protection of Birds (which, most scholars argue, was limited in its effectiveness), the interwar period did introduce a growing interest in attempts to reach an international convention on behalf of the League. In fact, as I elaborate and discuss in Chapter 1, the Convention Against the Pollution of the Sea by Oil was ignited by early efforts and fierce discussions regarding the post–World War I condition of certain shores, which were covered by thousands of dead birds that had been poisoned by the oily waters of the sea in the aftermath of the naval war transportation.

69 For a discussion on the history of conservation (in American context), *see*, *e.g.*, JUDSON KIND, THE CONSERVATION FIGHT: FROM THEODORE ROOSEVELT TO THE TENNESSEE VALLEY AUTHORITY (2009).

environment (as we understand it in its modern sense, as a political, social, and cultural phenomenon that has been defined as such since the late 1960s); and Environmental (and those who share its perspectives as Environmentals), which collects into itself any measures and actions that engage with the connection between nature and human environment.[70]

Likewise, I will also distinguish, where relevant, between conservation and preservation, and the ways these terms were used – and modified – by different interwar players. Conservation usually refers to the sustainable use and management of natural resources including wildlife, water, air, and earth deposits. The conservation of renewable resources ensures that they are not consumed or exploited faster than they can be replaced. The conservation of nonrenewable resources like fossil fuels involves ensuring that sufficient quantities are maintained for future generations to utilize. Conservation of natural resources usually focuses on the needs and interests of human beings, for example the biological, economic, cultural, and recreational value such resources have.[71]

Preservation, in contrast, attempts to maintain in their present condition areas of the Earth that are so far untouched by humans – regardless of their significance to human society, economy, and consumption. Preservationist agendas usually adopt a far less human-centered approach to environmental protection (than in conservationist approaches), placing a value on nature that does not relate to the needs and interests of human society and individuals. This conception of nature argues that ecosystems and individual species should be preserved whatever the cost, regardless of their usefulness to humans, and even if their continued existence would prove harmful to humankind. This follows from the belief that every living thing has a right to exist and should be preserved.

Between these (raw) definitions, the international whaling conventions of 1931, 1937, and 1946,[72] for instance, can be read, understood, and interpreted in several different, ways. On the one hand, the interwar conventions demonstrate or articulate the concept of conservationist

[70] For a preliminary sketch of the difference between these two "types" of environmentalism, *see* Danielle Tesch & Willet Kempton, *Who Is an Environmentalist? The Polysemy of Environmental Actions*, 8 J. Ecological Anthropology 67 (2004).

[71] Therefore conservationists accept that development is necessary for a better future, but only when the changes take place in ways that are not wasteful.

[72] As I elaborate in Chapter 2, although the 1946 Convention was introduced after the League was dissolved, it seems that it should still be considered as a legal product of the interwar period.

environmental policies: they promote the wise use of exploitable natural resources, and sustainability. "These treaties," as Marc Cioc puts it, "offered no protection to individual species until they had already become 'commercially extinct' (that is, too rare to hunt profitably)."[73] But on the other hand, as I will show further in Chapter 2, these conventions used a "preservationist" discourse, such as setting sanctions against the overexploitation of certain whale species, establishing geographical sanctuaries in certain marine areas, and forbidding whaling in certain seasons (these were articulated in legal terms as well).

Did the League express preservationist perspectives in its actions and discussions that involved environmental reflections? Should the League rather be considered a conservationist institution? How can we distinguish conservation from preservation in this matter? Perhaps the League is better treated as forum that expressed preservationist and conservationist views and concerns simultaneously, or interchangeably.

However, referring to environmental perceptions in the interwar period does not mean I am claiming that the different players involved in the battle on nature and natural resources used our own language. Although this is not the place to engage with some of these broad issues, I shall rather seize this opportunity to discuss briefly possible claims concerning certain weaknesses of the main methodology used in this research and the possible difficulties it might involve. As other scholarly debates have shown, the turn to history in international law has also demonstrated a certain complexity of methods, and mostly interpretation, used in international legal history. To state the obvious, we must be cautious, for instance, of anachronism.[74] Although I will use (and more than once) later concepts such as "NGOs," "regime," or even "environment," as I describe and analyze the League's activities in relation to nature, I am aware, of course, of the potential problems of this common mode of writing legal history. As the debate between Phillip Alston and Jenny S. Martinez on the possible risks of anachronism in international legal history in particular has already shown, one should not take out of context terms that were used in a certain period, or "force" one's current interpretation on contemporary terms that were used in the past.

[73] Cioc, *supra* note 3, at 8.

[74] For a debate on the possible risks of anachronism in the history of international law in particular, *see* the controversy between Phillip Alston and Jenny S. Martinez over the interpretation of human rights terms in different time periods: Phillip Alston, *Does the Past Matter? On the Origins of Human Rights: An Analysis of Competing Histories of the Origins of International Human Rights Law*, 126 Harv. L. Rev. 2043 (2013).

In other words, the ways in which I strive to "bring alive," if I am to borrow from Alston's analysis,[75] the environmental chapter of the League, primarily through archival research that provides a real feel for the ways in which the League developed its policies with regard to nature, cannot, and should not, overlook or dismiss the duty of being careful and mindful of the gap between different historical periods, the terms in use, and their interpretations. Legal scholars in particular sometimes tend to rely on the "search-engine mentality,"[76] which insists on interpreting certain terms without being sufficiently cautious about their historical context. Therefore, whenever I discovered an interwar use of discourse on nature, exploitation of natural resources, or nature protection I did my best to be aware of both the similarities and the differences between that period's contemporary context *and* our current environmental and legal discourse.

One more cautious remark. Although the main focus of the study is on the League, this is not to claim or to assume that it was the only body that considered environmental views. The League certainly was not the only organization that paid attention to or fought for environmental causes. As I will show, the League was part of an international network of independent or external bodies and agencies – national, regional, professional, transnational, industrial, political, and international – that took part in the continuing debates over timber production, pollution of the sea by oil, spreading diseases in the global periphery, and whaling. In each campaign or environmental challenge, I will sketch the role of other organizations that collaborated with or challenged the League (or those that "used" the League to promote their own environmental agendas). In each environmental issue, the League served as the center (or, at least, as one of the centers) of discussions and as the focus of the decision-making process, successful or unsuccessful as these decisions (ultimately) were.

The League's environmental experience (including, most certainly, its failures along the way) allowed it to develop its institutional relevance as well as "its" international law per se – the League was not simply a vehicle for the environmental agenda. A majority of the interwar environmental initiatives actually began as subnational initiatives or national endeavors, and were only later elevated into the international sphere. Historically, this meant that in most cases, domestic[77] legal attempts came first,

[75] *Id.* at 2047.
[76] *Id.* at 2049.
[77] Or colonial, depending on the relevant geopolitical context.

followed by transnational or international campaigns. The League was obviously not the first forum that fulfilled transnational opportunities and aspirations in terms of international law. However, it was the first *institutionalized* forum of international law and diplomacy, with an agreed founding document (the Covenant of the League of Nations, from April 28, 1919).

Indeed, in certain environmental issues, some other states paved the way. Germany, for instance, stood behind the initiative of the African treaties at the turn of the twentieth century,[78] while the Americans (and not the Canadian or the British) advanced the bird treaties of the early twentieth century.[79] Some scholars have argued that this was also the case with the whaling problem, in which Norway[80] played a leading role.

In an intriguing way, the League followed at least some of these early initiatives – it did not start everything from scratch. As I show, the League's endeavors in each environmental challenge followed up at least one (if not several) development(s) that preceded it. However, despite this general notion of continuity, the League marked a transition from local or national efforts to guarantee sufficient stocks (of birds for game, for instance, or of whales for the growing whaling industry) for current and future generations, to a much larger perspective – one that took into account all of humanity (or, at least, substantial parts of it). By analyzing the international regulations (be they against the pollution of the sea by oil, or the whaling conventions) or modes of international governance (in supporting, for instance, thoughts of controlling timber trade and securing prices after the Great Depression and Soviet dumping policy) that the League promoted, I will explain the ways in which the League created this shift in (international) environmental law.

An overview of interwar environmentalism reveals the common belief that the focus should be placed on regulating (rather than

[78] Especially the Convention for the Preservation of Wild Animals, Birds, and Fish in Africa, or the 1900 London Convention (signed in London, May 19, 1900); although it was absent from the following – the Convention Relative to the Preservation of Fauna and Flora in their Natural State, or the 1933 London Convention (signed in London on Nov. 8, 1933). *See* Bernhard Gissibl, The Nature of German Imperialism: Conservation and the Politics of Wildlife in Colonial East Africa (2016).

[79] Convention for the Protection of Migratory Birds Signed between the United States and Great Britain, or the 1916 Convention, which was signed in Washington, DC on Aug. 16, 1916; and the Convention between the United States of America and the United States of Mexico for the Protection of Migratory Birds and Game Mammals (or the 1936 Convention), signed in Mexico City on Feb. 7, 1936.

[80] *See* Cioc, *supra* note 3.

eradicating) activities like hunting, exploitation, and trade. Most conservationist agreements of the first half of the twentieth century were rooted in the perception that trade in endangered species[81] was "here to stay," and that a pragmatic approach aimed at controlling the problem's excesses was likely to be more effective than an "abolitionist approach."[82]

Indeed, this study does not to argue that "what was will be again" (Ecclesiastes 1:9). The justifications of environmentalism and the theoretical structure have certainly evolved since the 1920s and 1930s. Conservationist approaches, which dominated the field of pro-nature perspectives in modern times and shaped a large number of the environmental initiatives that were discussed by the League, were replaced with newer preservationist perspectives. The broad field of environmentalism changed fundamentally during the twentieth century. A significant change relates to the role of scientific concerns, which in many cases prompted environmental discussions during the studied period. The focus on protecting individual dominant species[83] shifted during the post–World War II period to the study of whole ecosystems instead. In other words, scientific scholarship, which contributed to and shaped international environmental law solutions at the time, moved from trying to defend one endangered species to a broader and more comprehensive view of nature as an ecosystem.

Going back to the interwar period, I chose the title of this study because it truly expresses the intensive and comprehensive involvement of the League in a list of complex, fierce, and problematic political, legal, economic, and social dilemmas that were entangled with fundamental environmental considerations. I will examine the role of the League from the perspectives of environmental policy, international law, and legal history. The following chapters address different interrelated questions, such as: To what extent did the League, its internal institutions, and other transnational organizations active during that time relate to environmental issues? How significant were environmental considerations in relation to other considerations and interests, such as economic development and the interests of the

[81] Most of which were considered to be raw materials. See my discussion in Chapters 2 and 4.

[82] Prost & Otomo, *supra* note 53, at 208.

[83] Such as whales. *See* my discussion in Chapter 2.

Great Powers, as can be viewed in the League's policy? In what ways were environmental concepts or approaches embodied and reflected in the League's policies, and how did they compete or conflict with other interests and incentives? To what extent did the League influence global environmental-legal arrangements of that time, and how did it affect the development of legal and diplomatic spheres after 1945?

1

Fighting Pollution Made by Humankind

The League of Nations and the Endeavors of the Convention against the Pollution of the Sea by Oil

1.1 Introduction

Four years after the guns had finally fallen silent, another alarming threat emerged from the sea. Communities in cities, towns, and resorts along the shore watched with growing fear how World War I endured, at least with regard to its dark environmental aftermath. A thick layer of oil covered the shores of many different countries, disturbing everyday life and badly affecting tourism, fisheries, and other commercial activities.

Great Britain and Germany were the first to notice this oil pollution near the shore. It was no surprise that two of the most industrialized European nations were also the first to be severely affected by the consequences of their technological and economic development. Soon after, several other states such as France, the Netherlands, and the United States reported on the same problem. The strange thick layer of filth that began to blanket different shores first appeared in countries that had been through the Industrial Revolution.

The oil was doing much worse than just damaging the view. People, especially nature lovers, started to notice a parallel disturbing phenomenon: thousands of dying seabirds started to cover the shores along shipping routes, poisoned by oil that polluted the water.

Although the League of Nations was coping with so many other – and to a certain extent more acute – consequences of World War I, some groups and states found that the 1930s were the right time to approach the League's high-ranking officials. These bodies wished for the League, along with the entire international community, to lead a campaign for an international convention that would control – and finally reduce – levels of oil pollution in the sea.

The first chapter will explore different discussions and legal acts of the League of Nations as it dealt with the growing problem of pollution of the seas and oceans by oil in the period under investigation. In the following sections, I will examine how different environmental perspectives, ideas, and solutions were defined and articulated while the League was challenged both by environmental pollution of the oceans, and by competing interest groups pushing the League to support their various agendas.

This chapter has three central parts (in addition to the introduction). First, in order to situate the interwar story of oil pollution as a part of a developing environmental-legal plot, the chapter starts with a short historical review of the issue of oil pollution of the sea. The first section will describe the evolving problem – and awareness – of seas becoming polluted by oil discharge. It will show that the interwar period was not the first time human communities were concerned about the implications of pollution of the sea on their interests. Relying on a linear-historical perspective, the role of the League will be examined and evaluated as part of a continuing transnational problem, such as the example of the Preliminary Conference on Oil Pollution of Navigable Waters,[1] which was triggered by a similar cause but chose to deal with the environmental challenge outside of the auspices of the League.

The second (and central) section of the chapter explores the ways in which the League became involved in the evolving challenge of solving the pollution crisis. I will start with the first calls that advocated for saving the birds from death. The focus on the role of NGOs will support my claim that this planned international environmental-legal advocacy deviated from domestic constraints and barriers.

In this section, I will further track the activity of a special committee of experts the League had assembled (through its Communications and Transit Organisation) in order to study the issue of oil pollution. I will explore the committee's intensive discussions on new means of international regulation that aimed to fight oil pollution of the sea as a consequence of oil discharge from ships, on the proponents and opponents of the legal campaign, and on the outcome of the League's efforts: the special convention against the pollution of the sea by oil, which was introduced in 1935.

Following this historical narrative, I will wrap up with some brief conclusions. Having looked at the legal and practical outcomes of the special campaign of the League, I will also provide an overview of the post-League era. Here, my main claim is that, in order to evaluate the League's historical role as an agent of environmentalist considerations,

[1] Mostly referred to as the Washington Conference of 1926.

we should also compare its antipollution efforts with later developments – and obstacles – in terms of international environmental law and pollution of the seas and oceans. In that sense, the timeline that the League was part of did not break once the League dissolved. Unfortunately, pollution of the sea continued to be a troubling environmental – and legal – problem in the second half of the twentieth century: as an international or regional, as well a local-national, problem. Although the League ceased to exist, some of the tensions and the suggested solutions it discussed in the 1930s were still on the table.

In this chapter, which is also the first tangible opportunity to revisit the League's complex environmental regime, I will examine the convention's intensive and ambitious efforts against the pollution of the sea by oil. This international effort engaged different bodies, some of which were affiliated with the League, and some of which were independent but still in the League's orbit. As I will show, this early environmental campaign turned to firm and explicit legal mechanisms in order to achieve its goals. By doing so, the campaign captured the attention and resourcefulness of some of the leading forces and persons of interwar diplomacy.

As I will elaborate, several officials and organs of the League were involved in the long and complex process of legal consultation and coordination that went into preparing an international convention. While the environmental problem was escalating, the League focused on the dangers and costs of oil pollution, given that it viewed the sea as an international common. Moreover, most of the discussions and consultations, which lasted several years, took place under the direct auspices of the League, and leaned on a new type of institutionalized international law that was, literally, under construction. This was not merely a "technical" fact, but also one that had historical, environmental, and legal significance.

Despite the bustling antipollution activity and fierce legal-environmental battle between conservationist groups from all around the world and pro-industrial bodies, both environmental history and legal studies have tended so far to skip this interwar story of birds, oil, and shipping.

The League of Nations was not the first body to deal with the outcomes of pollution. In the age of sailing, there was naturally no problem of pollution along coasts or harbors.[2] However, as sailing gave way to coal

[2] There was an incipient problem that resulted from the careless deposit of refuse. Thus, early preindustrial pollution legislation existed as early as 1814 in Great Britain to prohibit emptying rubbish or filth into any navigable, river, harbor, or haven. *See* 54 Geo. 3, c. 159. § 11 (1814).

and coal in turn gave way to oil after World War I, modern societies had to learn to cope with the side effects of the commercial and industrial development of shipping.

However, studies that have focused on polluted marine environments from the period that preceded the second half of the twentieth century are rather scarce. Moreover, most of the legal or environmental history that has studied the effects of oil pollution and legal remedies or reactions at the turn of the twentieth century has focused primarily on domestic and national legal campaigns – mainly in British and American contexts – but has not been very interested in transnational and international endeavors.[3] Joseph A. Pratt, for instance, focused only on the environmental legal campaign of the 1924 American Oil Pollution Act,[4] and analyzed the legal entanglements in that period.

Furthermore, although there are a few examples of legal history that have explored different legal measures that aimed to fight oil pollution and which moved beyond domestic and local test cases, they nevertheless skipped the interwar period. Joseph Sweeney, for instance, studied local legal campaigns as early as 1908 (in Britain and the United States), as well as transnational frameworks (such as the convention achieved at the 1926 Washington Preliminary Conference on Oil Pollution of Navigable Waters). However, even this kind of "multidimensional" broad description almost completely overlooks the role of the League. In his survey, which stretches over more than fifty pages, the League is mentioned only once and very briefly, to say the least: "During the interwar years, action to implement an international regime to control oil pollution was requested by the League of Nations; but nothing was accomplished."[5]

The international dimension of oil pollution only began to be revealed in environmental and legal literature after the late 1960s or 1970s, where studies exploring later or current periods used similar research questions to the ones that I use in this study.[6] Earlier attempts

[3] One well-known exception is the abundant discussion on the many interpretations of the Trail Smelter arbitration between the United States and Canada. *See*, among others, Alfred P. Rubin, *Pollution by Analogy: The Trail Smelter Arbitration*, 50 Or. L. Rev. 259 (1971).

[4] Joseph A. Pratt, Black Waters: Responses to America's First Oil Pollution Crisis (2008).

[5] Joseph C. Sweeney, *Oil Pollution of the Oceans*, 37 Fordham L. Rev. 155, 189 (1968).

[6] *See*, among others, Daniel Owen, *The Marine Implementation of the EC Birds and Habitats Directives: The Cases of Shipping and Oil Exploration Compared*, *in* Challenging Coasts Book Subtitle: Transdisciplinary Excursions into Integrated Coastal Zone Development 159 (Leontine E. Visser ed., 2004).

to regulate oil pollution by law other than domestic law, as argued in works such as those of Sweeney or Tafsir Johansson and Patrick Donner,[7] mostly classified oil pollution damage as maritime tort, while "other systems of law" were not and still are not very successful in their attempt to codify this procedure by means of international law.[8]

However, research that focused on the damage caused to birds by oil pollution seems to be more substantial. Besides current works that move between environmental and legal perspectives,[9] studies have described environmental history that warned of the dramatic impact of oil pollution on animals – and birds in particular. Early twentieth-century NGOs (such as the British Royal Society for the Protection of Birds, and the Royal Society for the Prevention of Cruelty to Animals) warned in the interwar period that all it took was a small amount of oil to cause lethal consequences to both birds and their eggs.[10]

Scholarship that analyzed international protection of birds was carried out in the early twentieth century and interwar period. Sherman Hayden, for instance, reviewed legal agreements that aimed to protect birds (and other animals) by means of international law.[11] G. A. Brouwer also studied the roots of institutional frameworks working to protect birds as part of international biodiversity.[12] It should be mentioned, however, that although these kinds of studies were interested in transnational patterns, the study of legal arrangements intended to protect bird life in various regions was not as widespread as the study of other legal arrangements (mostly in imperial contexts) that strove to preserve wildlife species such as lions, tigers, and elephants.[13]

[7] Tafsir Johansson & Patrick Donner, The Shipping Industry, Ocean Governance and Environmental Law in the Paradigm Shift: In Search of a Pragmatic Balance for the Arctic (2015).

[8] Sweeney, *supra* note 5, at 169.

[9] *See, e.g.*, G. Troisi, S. Barton & S. Bexton, *Impacts of Oil Spills on Seabirds: Unsustainable Impacts of Non-Renewable Energy*, 41 Int'l J. Hydrogen Energy 16549 (2016).

[10] A Dictionary of Birds 407 (Bruce Campbell & Elizabeth Lack eds., 1985).

[11] Sherman Strong Hayden, The International Protection of Wild Life: An Examination of Treaties and Other Agreements for the Preservation of Birds and Mammals (1942).

[12] G. A. Brouwer, The Organisation of Nature Protection in Various Countries (1938).

[13] *See*, among others, Rachelle Adam, Elephant Treaties: the Colonial Legacy of the Biodiversity Crisis (2014).

As I will elaborate, some scholars who have studied the issue of oil pollution in legal terms, such as Ekaterina Anyanova[14] and Edgar Gold,[15] entirely skipped the first half of the century and treated the problem as a clear post–World War II issue of international law.

Indeed, even before starting the story of this chapter in early environmental law, I am tempted to open with a (bitter) spoiler: this case study of the entanglements concerning the League's antipollution initiative is, ultimately, a history of failure. Most of the hopes and goals of the original plans were not fulfilled, at least not during that time.

However, numerous elements were reflected in the many convolutions of the antipollution convention: environmental notions and perspectives; the central role of professional experts and scientific expertise in the discourse of international law as a source of legitimacy; the economic interests that challenged environmental and scientific interests; the involvement of different NGOs, non-state actors, and other bodies in the game of international law; the interactions between traditional powers and traditional diplomacy vis-à-vis new emerging states eager to have a say in how international law was to be constructed – and formulated – by the League as an unfamiliar forum; the relatively wide media coverage; and the new routine and mechanisms of crafting and shaping international law.

In this chapter, I will argue that we should refer to the antipollution convention not only as a case study in environmental history, but also as an opportunity to deepen our understanding of the routine and work methods of different departments and organs of the League as an institution. The League developed internationalism and shaped international law as a whole, and not only with its environmental regime. In many ways, the players, organizations, and other interested parties that played a role in the battle of the convention were not only concerned for the sake of the polluted seas, or for dying poisoned seabirds. They were also advocating for what they saw as justified ways in which the League and other nations should shape (or not) international law per se.

Likewise, as with several other environmental issues the League was handling, different parties had interpreted the pollution crisis as an environmental issue, as well as one that projected dilemmas and basic

[14] Ekaterina Anyanova, *Oil Pollution and International Marine Environmental Law, in* Sustainable Development – Authoritative and Leading Edge Content for Environmental Management 29 (Sime Curkovic ed., 2012).

[15] Edgar Gold, Handbook on Marine Pollution (1998).

definitions of international law such as sovereignty, territorial waters, and relations between superstate organizations and nation states.

1.2 Historical Background of Polluted Seas and Human Concerns

Before the League took a hold of the oil pollution discussion, there were also earlier attempts to solve the problem: first by domestic means (in Britain and the United States), and then also beyond local and national barriers. The following section will briefly introduce the landmark developments of oil pollution along the evolving historical timeline: first, it was a national problem (Section 1.2.1); then, when local measures were not successful, the issue of oil pollution became a transnational regional concern (Section 1.2.2); and finally, it became an international issue that was given to the League to solve.

The sections that follow will mainly provide a linear-chronological overview. However, it should also be noted that, in certain places, I have chosen to describe the evolution of the discussion through a different lens: when the national-domestic character of the antipollution campaign transformed, becoming regional and then international in its dimensions. This kind of description also exemplifies the shift from local to international, and justifies the central role of the League as it treated the concern for pollution of the sea as an international matter that demanded collective action.

1.2.1 Polluted Seas As a Domestic Problem: Concerns of Oil Pollution in Britain and the United States

World War I marked not only the end of the long nineteenth century and a turning point in modern history, but also a time that introduced major changes in modern technology in general, and in means of transportation in particular. True, oil-fueled ships had been sailing back and forth prior to the bitter autumn of 1914, but combat needs and considerations[16] together with the efficiency of oil engines led to a fairly rapid change in that feature of naval (and then commercial) transportation. In fact,

[16] Compared to coal-fueled battleships, oil-fueled battleships were much safer to navigate in dangerous water, as they produced less smoke and were thus less visible and therefore less easily detected by the enemy. Moreover, the fact that oil-fueled ships were faster and quicker to navigate within the turbulent waters of World War I made the choice much easier.

already during the battles of World War I, Britain entrusted its navy with oil-fueled ships instead of the traditional nineteenth-century steam- or coal-fueled ships.[17]

Once the war was over, the naval fleets decided not to revert to the technology of their former ships; moreover, they encouraged the mercantile fleet to follow suit, not only in Britain, but in most of the leading maritime nations of that time. As the interwar period began, the naval and maritime world that unfolded was very different from the one that preceded it.[18] Before World War I, less than 3 percent of ships in operation used oil-fueled engines; in 1922, shortly after the establishment of the League, this figure was nearly a quarter.[19]

One of the outcomes of this technological shift in marine transportation was the phenomenon of polluted waters due to oil refuse. Experts were the first to identify the link between the technological developments in shipping and the negative effect on nature and animals.[20] At first, in the aftermath of World War I, ornithologists had assumed that sunken submarines and naval wrecks that had been lost during the battles were to blame for the oil, and that it would not take long for this toxic side-effect to disappear from the shore.

However, the real reason was different. Ship crews flushed their oily tanks with seawater, which they then discharged into the open sea in ports all around the globe. The floating muck was not from oil spills, wrecks, or sunken submarines but rather the constant cleaning procedures. Moreover, ships also pumped used oil overboard.

Four years after the guns became silent, the British Royal Society for the Protection of Birds (hereinafter RSPB) moved to solve the worsening problem. In its Annual Report bulletin of 1922, the Society observed that instead of fading away slowly with the ocean waves, the oil problem remained and had actually become even worse – it had "developed with alarming rapidity until now the cry is heard from all around our shores."[21]

[17] DANIEL YERGIN, THE PRIZE: THE EPIC QUEST FOR OIL, MONEY, AND POWER 86 (1991).

[18] For a discussion on the technological developments with regard to marine transportation, *see* SONIA SHAH, CRUDE: THE STORY OF OIL 9–10 (2006).

[19] 22.34%, to be accurate. *See* Rudolf Drost, *Die Oelpest und ihre Wirkung auf die Lebewelt des Meers*, 4 NATURFORSCHER 541 (1927–1928).

[20] Anna-Katharina Wöbse, *Oil on Troubled Water? Environmental Diplomacy in the League of Nations*, 32 DIPLOMATIC HIST. 519, 525 (2008).

[21] ANNUAL REPORT OF THE ROYAL SOCIETY FOR THE PROTECTION OF BIRDS 8 (Presented at the Annual General Meeting, Mar. 7, 1923) (London; 1922).

The RSPB, which would become one of the main forces behind the antipollution campaign, turned public attention (first in Britain) in the early 1920s to the problem at sea and on the shores. Since the exact details were not yet completely clear at that time, devoted NGOs[22] quickly worked to establish a link between the increase in marine transportation and the disturbing number of oil-covered seabird carcasses covering European and North American beaches. NGOs were also the first to warn the public that all it took was a small amount of oil to cause lethal consequences to both birds and their eggs.[23]

The RSPB spoke on behalf of the dying, poisoned birds, but the birds were not the only victims of the industrial-technological development. An eclectic coalition of interest groups was created in the 1920s, sharing the damages caused by oil refuse at sea.

Tourists and touristic business, for instance, complained in the early 1920s about the side effects of oily water. Fishermen and fisheries saw their properties badly affected by the pollution; so did civilian authorities with regard to public safety, given the danger of flammable sludge on shores under their responsibility. Insurance corporations were also worried: not because of the terrible agony of the birds, but because of the risks posed by the flammable marine-transportation stains and their financial costs. Landlords were concerned that the market value of their real estate would be damaged by these disturbing phenomena.[24] All of these parties had their own interests to protect in the anti-oil-pollution campaign, which can almost be seen as an early-twentieth-century version of a grassroots movement representing different voices. The collaboration between nature-protection associations, tourism businessmen, civil servants, and others[25] constituted a call to put an end to the pollution threatening what each held dear.

At first, as with other environmental challenges that troubled the interwar world,[26] different states tried to find their own, national solutions. As the use

[22] Especially British NGOs, but as I will elaborate also Dutch, French, German, and American nature-protection associations.

[23] A Dictionary of Birds, *supra* note 10, at 407.

[24] For a discussion on the collateral damage effect of oil pollution *see*, for instance, Sonia Z. Pritchard, Oil Pollution Control (1987). During the American Congress's discussions on the oil pollution problem, Congress elaborated on the variety of parties that threatened by the problem, including the "potential fire hazards, destruction of fisheries, and depreciation of seashore resort properties." *See* 42 Stat. 821–22 (Pub. Res., No. 65 of July 1, 1922) (quoted by Sweeney, *supra* note 5, at 187).

[25] Wöbse, *supra* note 20, at 526–27.

[26] Mainly, as the next chapter will uncover, the whaling dilemma.

of oil by shipping and industry dramatically increased, local authorities in charge of ports and parliaments in different states[27] took action by means of special port regulations to prohibit the discharge of oil in certain harbors.[28]

The first important versions of general legislation forbidding the discharge of oil in territorial waters were enacted in Britain in 1922 and in the United States in 1924. In Britain, the Oil Pollution Act of 1922 limited the common practice of discharging and washing oil from ships to a distance of at least three miles from the shore. At almost the same time, the United States enacted a similar law in 1924, thanks to the quasi-environmental lobby of the National Coast Anti-Pollution League.[29] The American Oil Pollution Act of 1924[30] was also based on the principle of banning oil discharge from ships within territorial waters.[31]

This phase of national legislation briefly described above would eventually pave the way (inadequately, as it turned out) for future developments. Although bills were passed by the legislator, there were already those who called to move beyond the limits of domestic legislation, as the issue had become an international problem. Already during the discussions on the American Act, Congress requested that the President convene an international conference of maritime nations to determine

[27] Iceland, for instance, was one of the first countries to enact a formal antipollution regulation of its own. It is also interesting to note that Iceland was a rather unique case with its maritime legislation. Compared to the whaling problem, it was Iceland, and no other nation, that first introduced early whaling law. *See* the following discussion in Sections 2.3.1 and 2.3.6 in Chapter 2.

[28] Sweeney, *supra* note 5, at 187.

[29] The National Coast Anti-Pollution League was a mainstream internal American network and public-political coalition of elected officials, public health activists and advocates, and devoted practitioners. Together, they formed this network in 1922 as they fought the nuisance along the Atlantic Coast. For a study that has focused on the role of this interesting activist group, *see* Bill Kovarik, *Oil Pollution and the National Coast Anti-Pollution League*, http://environmentalhistory.org/people/gifford-pinchot-and-the-anti-pollution-league/. Unless mentioned otherwise, all the relevant websites and online references were last visited on Sept. 1, 2020.

[30] 33 U.S.C. §§ 431–37 (1957) (originally enacted as Act of June 7, 1924, ch. 316, 43 Stat. 604).

[31] According to Sec. 3, "except in case of emergency imperiling life or property or unavoidable accident, collision, or stranding, and except as otherwise permitted by regulations prescribed by the Secretary [e.g. Secretary of War] as hereinafter authorized, it shall be unlawful for any person to discharge, or suffer, or permit the discharge of oil by any method, means, or manner into or upon the coastal navigable waters of the United States from any vessel carrying or having oil thereon in excess of that necessary for the lubrication requirements and such as may be required under the laws of the United States . . . ."

For a study on the American legal and environmental entanglements with oil pollution in that period *see*, for instance, Joseph A. Pratt, Black Waters: Responses to America's First Oil Pollution Crisis (2008).

effective means[32] to prevent pollution, so that the problem could be solved by tools of international law.

Moreover, apart from the need for international action, there was another problem. Although the American legislation did introduce some important restrictions,[33] no one really knew for sure at this stage how far the drifting oil could travel. Scientific data was still lacking and so the distance limits were based on general estimations.

As concerns piled up, public pressure and media coverage of the British NGOs' campaign put the problem of sea pollution on the agenda of national politics. Supportive politicians in Parliament promoted a discussion in the House of Commons.[34] This move demanded tougher legal measures that would directly affect the shipping industry.

Both the RSPB and another British civil society association working for animal welfare – the Royal Society for the Prevention of Cruelty to Animals (hereinafter RSPCA) – threw their weight behind possible stricter solutions. In their British campaign, these NGOs referred to a polluter-pays principle and argued that this principle should also be applied to oil-pollution cases. As such, these NGOs argued that in cases of oil pollution, ship owners would be held responsible for the pollution and its collateral damages.[35]

In addition to the polluter-pays principle, the campaign pushed for a techno-environmental solution. The main goal of the antipollution coalition was to use law to force ship owners to install a mechanical device on board ships that would prevent discharge of oil into the sea. This separator, which had already been introduced to the maritime industry before the public campaign started, could remove oil from wastewater before it was discharged from ships, thereby preventing water contamination and damage to the shore and coastal environment.[36]

However, as reasonable as this solution seemed in terms of technology and environment, it was not simple when it came to the industry's interests. As I will elaborate, the shipping industry claimed that a mandatory installation of separators was both technically unfeasible and, above all, too expensive.

The shipping industry was reluctant to agree to the proposed new restrictions and tried to dodge the domestic initiative in Britain. The

32 Sweeney, *supra* note 5, at 187.
33 Pritchard, *supra* note 24, at 6–7.
34 Wöbse, *supra* note 20, at 527.
35 For a discussion on private law questions of oil pollution damage *see* Sweeney, *supra* note 5, at 164–80.
36 *Id.* at 189.

shipping lobby – mainly represented by the Board of Trade – argued, for instance, that the suggested technology of onboard separators would cost too much to install and required too much room on board – something a luxury marine transportation vessel could not afford. The lobby further objected that compulsory installation of separators would create an impossible financial burden for the industry. Given the alleged costs standing before it, the shipping industry pushed for further discussion on possible stricter rules concerning zones in which discharging oil would be banned, instead of agreeing to the compulsory installation of separators.[37]

Indeed, unlike the doubts raised by the whaling industry in the parallel dilemma (on which I will elaborate in the next chapter) on whether or not whales might become extinct due to increased hunting, in this case the British shipping industry was willing to agree to several restrictions and did not move to reject them altogether. On the one hand, it was willing to discuss the cost of further restrictions on areas where oil pumping and discharge were prohibited. But on the other hand, the non-state actors involved, and especially the animal-conservation NGOs, claimed that there was actually no use in debating or even agreeing to the enlargement of restricted areas for oil discharge. The crucial issue, the RSPB argued back, was using law in order to enforce a mandatory installation of separators on board any ship. "The nations cannot, so to speak, sweep the oil into the middle of the oceans and leave it there," the formal bulletin of the Society noted in summer 1922.[38] This, the RSPB argued, was because the problem was now starting to be discussed publicly, which introduced an international dimension to the issue.

At this preliminary stage of environmentalism, several actors were fighting against the convention of treating the ocean as a common dumpster for hazardous industrial waste or modern waste such as oil.

1.2.2 The Transnational Phase: The 1923 Paris Conference, and the First International Conference on the Pollution of the Sea by Oil (Washington, 1926)

American and British coastal cities, communities, and nature-protection associations were not the only ones that were affected or concerned by drifting oil. Other countries also suffered in the early decades of the

[37] *See* the RSPB's description of the shipping industry's arguments – Royal Society for the Protection of Birds, 10 Bird Notes and News 18 (1922).

[38] *Id.*

twentieth century. In this section, I will briefly introduce the main principles of several regional and transnational frameworks that strove during the interwar period to prevent pollution of the sea by oil, in ways that did not take place under the auspices of the League.

In 1923, Paris hosted a nongovernmental international conference, the Congress on the Protection of Flora, Fauna, and Natural Sites and Monuments. Different nonofficial representatives of several associations convened in order to better coordinate their different activities. Led mostly by the RSPB (and other representatives of British NGOs), this transnational collaboration requested to take part in the new international governance that was created in the aftermath of the war.[39]

Like the RSPB, the Parisian congress served as a site for mutual collaboration between several national associations to fight the negative effects of oil pollution in the oceans on seabirds and migrating birds; such associations included the Dutch parallel organization Nederlandsche Vereeniging tot Bescherming van Vogels, or the American Zoological Society of New York, alongside similar French associations.[40] By the time the congress concluded, all representatives, although they had neither governmental nor official roles on behalf of states, had reached an agreed declaration. They agreed that their joint efforts at home – advocating in the public sphere for domestic legislation in the parliaments – should focus on the compulsory installation of separators, rather than on discussions over the size of the restricted zone for oil discharge.[41]

The Paris Conference was, however, still no more than a preliminary transnational collaboration – one that did not produce (if it ever intended to) any concrete "hard" legal instrument. At any rate, different environmental efforts, beyond national frameworks and borders, were part of a general trend at the turn of the century. Moreover, it seems that the role of NGOs in this intensifying conservationist transnational activity cannot be overlooked.

[39] On the 1923 Paris Congress *see* LYNTON K. CALDWELL, INTERNATIONAL ENVIRONMENTAL POLICY: FROM THE TWENTIETH TO THE TWENTY-FIRST CENTURY 50 (1996); ANN HIRONAKA, GREENING THE GLOBE: WORLD SOCIETY AND ENVIRONMENTAL CHANGE 35 (2014).

[40] For a description from the mid-1920s on the Paris Conference, *see* PREMIER CONGRÈS INTERNATIONAL POUR LA PROTECTION DE LA NATURE (Raoul de Clermont et al. eds., 1925).

[41] F.-E. Lemon & Keith Henderson, *Destruction des Oiseaux de mer par les d͏̀chets d'huiles de la navigation*, *in* PREMIER CONGRÈS INTERNATIONAL POUR LA PROTECTION DE LA NATURE 157–59 (Raoul de Clermont et al., eds. 1925) (quoted in Wöbse, *supra* note 20, at 528–29).

The next step, the special Preliminary Conference on Oil Pollution of Navigable Waters held in Washington DC in the summer of 1926, continued the growing international concern on the matter. Some scholars have argued that the Washington Conference came in the wake of an "aroused public interest"[42] that followed the political discussion on the American Oil Pollution Act of 1924. Congress requested that the President convene an international conference of maritime nations to determine effective means to prevent the pollution of navigable waters.[43]

Between June 8 and June 16, 1926, the delegations of twelve industrialized[44] maritime states convened in Washington for the first international conference focusing on oil pollution of the sea. The conference was attended by experts representing the interests of conservation societies, fisheries, shipowners, oil producers, and marine insurance underwriters.[45] The Washington Conference considered the causes of pollution, the classification and admeasurements of vessels, territorial zones, and enforcement measures.[46]

This time, unlike the Paris Conference three years earlier, most of the representatives were official agents and the delegations were formal – a reflection of the intensifying threat. Moreover, the Washington Conference ultimately managed to produce a legal document, not just a public transnational call for action as in the case of the 1923 Conference: the first International Convention on Oil Pollution. The fact is, however, that this agreement was not ratified by any state.[47]

Along with this legal product, the Washington Preliminary Conference marked two important steps forward. First, it marked a growing awareness of the nature of the pollution problem as a common international challenge, one that demanded international solutions rather than national or regional ones. Second, and compared to the central aim of the Paris Conference of 1923, the 1926 Washington Conference aimed to use legal measures to encourage the shipping industry to comply. The main issue was once again the compulsory installation of separators, a solution that the industry was deeply concerned about. It seems, however, that the

42 Sweeney, *supra* note 5, at 187.

43 *Id.*

44 Except for one – Japan – the rest were European or North American: Great Britain, Denmark, the United States, Canada, Germany, the Netherlands, Sweden, Spain, France, Italy, and Belgium.

45 Sweeney, *supra* note 5, at 188.

46 *See* Wöbse, *supra* note 20, at 528; Sweeney, *supra* note 5, at 187–89.

47 Anyanova, *supra* note 14, at 31.

shipping industry still had the upper hand and managed to block the initiative to introduce compulsory installation as a binding international standard. According to the conclusions of the Washington Conference, the installation was to be achieved by means of incentive legislation (of each state) to exempt the space required for separators from the ship's payment of tonnage dues.[48]

Moreover, the transnational framework in Washington allowed for some decisive suggestions, some of which served as a legal base for future discussions on these concerns and possible solutions. One of the central issues for discussion following the Paris Conference was the demand for the total prohibition of oil discharge at sea, no matter the distance from the shore or port. The states involved were not at all receptive to this suggestion. Just as with the whaling case, where maritime nations such as Britain and Norway resisted harsh international restrictions – often while denying that there was a real problem at all – Germany and the Netherlands[49] argued that the problem of oil pollution at sea did not actually exist.

Unable to reach a binding agreement on the controversial separators, the Washington Conference signed an international convention that focused on the alternative option favored by the shipping industry – the measure of restricted zones for oil discharge. The different delegations concluded that the zone should be extended to 150 miles.[50]

Following the Washington Conference and the preliminary transnational phase of the antipollution campaign, the efforts to ban oil discharge from ships and vessels did not cease just because the first international legal attempt had failed. Instead of letting go, activist parties looked for alternative institutional and international frameworks.

Indeed, though it would take some time for British unrest to reach the League's Secretariat in 1934, the international approach was already underway. In the next section, I will analyze how the oil pollution problem evolved, transforming from a transnational to an international issue, this time under the auspices of the League of Nations.

[48] Preliminary Conference on Oil Pollution of Navigable Waters (1926) T.S. No. 736-A, at 440.

[49] Wöbse, *supra* note 20, at 528.

[50] Prior to the 1926 Conference, in certain states the restricted zone covered no more than three miles. However, as I have mentioned, the NGOs that were involved rejected the restricted-zone mechanism given its inadequacy in real-time circumstances.

1.3 The League of Nations and the Antipollution Campaign

In this central part, I will explore the antipollution campaign under the auspices of the League. Having concluded Section 1.2 with a discussion of earlier transnational steps such as the 1926 Washington Conference, I will now move further along the historical timeline and focus on several landmark events.

In Section 1.3.1, I will discuss Britain's formal request to the League in summer 1934 to prepare an international solution for the oil pollution problem.

In Section 1.3.2, I will describe how the Communications and Transit Organisation, a special auxiliary body of the League, took control of the issue and summoned a special committee of experts. I will analyze the preparatory work of that committee between 1934 and 1935, and will elaborate on its decision to distribute a special questionnaire and a draft convention in early 1935 to the international community in order to get feedback on a possible new antipollution convention.

Section 1.3.3 will focus on the various replies and views the League received, all of which expressed different concerns: some in favor of creating new techno-environmental requirements that would (legally) force the shipping industry to fight pollution, and some against these kinds of measures. This section, however, will present not only the official stance and replies of various states, but also petitions and calls prepared by worried NGOs who were advocating for the protection of birds and nature, and urged the League to use international law to fight pollution. This section will analyze the legal procedure through which these NGOs identified the League as *the* – and not just *a* – relevant institution to carry out the antipollution campaign.

As I show, this advocacy "targeted" national authorities before it turned to the League – and to international law – for rescue. However, when these domestic measures failed, the NGOs' advocacy for the protection of birds began to turn away from domestic constraints and legislators, which mostly favored the shipping industry's interests, to the new forum of the League. This section will hence focus on the conceptual shift from national and domestic modes of activity to international modes. This shift saw interested parties appeal to the League to use its mechanisms to support the antipollution camp.

Then, in the last section (1.3.4), I will explore how the League, relying on its special committee of experts, intensively discussed new means of international regulation that aimed to fight oil pollution of the sea.

The second part of the chapter will conclude with the final arrangements of the special antipollution convention of 1935, and the compromise it reflected between the conflicting interests, perspectives, and agendas of the parties involved.

In general, this part will on the one hand uncover the vast support in reaching a binding convention against oil pollution and the different suggested means of preventing oil spills and discharge. But on the other hand, it will compare the contrasting positions of different states and bodies, which rejected most of the restrictions in favor of saving the shipping industry's interests.

1.3.1 The Save-the-Seabirds Campaign Reaches the League: A Special Committee of Experts Is Formed

Although it was an environmental collaboration of associations led by the RSPB and the RSPCA that first opened up a national discussion in Britain on the problem of oil pollution (which then moved into the transnational sphere), the issue was also tackled by another player of interwar internationalism. Just as in the case of the endangered whale, scientists were among the first to identify the oil problem and to turn to the League for rescue.

An American biologist, George Wilton Field, presented his petition in 1931 that urged the League to lead the charge against oil pollution in the oceans. Doctor Field was a pioneer in the field of shellfish aquaculture and water pollution and took an interest in different conservation issues.[51] Field addressed the Economic Committee of the League and shared with it his scientific findings[52] on the issue.

[51] On Field's role in the American conservation movement, *see* WALTER J. WILSON, GEORGE WILTON FIELD, 1863–1938: A PIONEER CONSERVATIONIST (1968).

[52] The scientific and professional expertise of different persons who approached the League and its auxiliary bodies became a central characteristic of the League's activity. Dr. Field gained his reputation as a leading biologist in North America, having joined the Bureau of Biological Survey of the United States Department of Agriculture in the middle of the 1910s, and having supervised the seventy-four national American bird and mammal reservations.

In a similar way to the international, or at least transnational, affiliation of other interwar scientists (advocating for and in front of the League), Field became a formal consultant to the government of Brazil in the early 1920s on matters of environmental conservation of birds and other species. His international prestige and field of expertise also afforded him the position of United State representative for international cooperation on water pollution control under the auspices of the League.

Doctor Field, as representative of objective science, seemed to be advocating for a set of different considerations. On the one hand, given the large number of seabird deaths, he urged the League to use international law, and its authority and influence, to fight against the pollution of the oceans. But on the other hand, he also relied on economic arguments. Dying birds (and their protectors among the conservationist NGOs) were calling on the League to rescue them from deadly poisoning; but this agonizing phenomenon also had negative economic impacts. People had to pay higher taxes and more money for increased food prices, and for the betterment of seaside leisure resorts and tourism businesses that were suffering from the consequences of oil pollution on the shore.[53]

The invitation that was extended to the League and "its" institutionalized international law did not only come from America. Even when NGOs (primarily in Britain) began to suggest a transnational approach, domestic pressure did not cease. The British NGOs had hoped that the delegations would agree on stricter solutions for the pollution problem back at the transnational conferences in Paris and Washington in the 1920s; with this in mind, the parallel political campaign at home continued, targeting the industry's reluctance to cooperate.

Conservationist or pro-conservation politicians encouraged the government in the early 1930s to promote suitable regulations outside British Isles. In 1931, in the House of Commons, Sir Alfred Cooper-Rawson, a businessman and Conservative Party Member of Parliament, officially supported an international move – of the League – led by Britain. Great Britain was, according to him,

> still the largest maritime Power in the world, and although Britannia may not rule the waves, there is no reason why she should not keep them clean, and set an example to other countries. If we set that example to other countries by passing legislation, we may at Geneva get other nations of the world to follow our example.[54]

In May 1933, Parliament discussed the dilemma once more. It instructed the Foreign Office to run a comparative legal investigation to study how other maritime nations were willing to discuss this issue at the League.[55]

[53] *See* George Wilton Field, Memorandum on Oil Pollution Presented before the Economic Committee of the League of Nations, Geneva 1931, Manuscript, Public Record Office [hereinafter PRO], Foreign Affairs [hereinafter FO], 371/15138 (A6902/2678/45).

[54] House of Commons Debates, July 29, 1931, Col. 2300f.

[55] Wöbse, *supra* note 20, at 529.

As environmental awareness rose in Britain, mostly thanks to media coverage and the public campaign of local-national NGOs, and as political pressure increased correspondingly in London, the British government decided to turn to further external frameworks and to approach the League[56] on this matter.

Given the cross-border nature of the problem, oil pollution challenged national laws that were inadequate. Moreover, faced with pressure from bird lovers, a sympathetic media, and a defensive shipping industry at home, the British government was hoping to dodge the issue of oil pollution by handing over any perceived responsibility to the League. On the one hand, both the government and Parliament were under growing public pressure to introduce tough new legislation that would focus on the industry. But on the other hand, the shipping industry lobby had a political power of its own at the Palace of Westminster.[57] Therefore, it seemed to the British government that the League was its best option to avoid legal and political confrontation with a powerful industry at home.

It should be noted that this was likely a strategic political maneuver on the British government's part. First, the government suggested that an external authority tackle the suggested oil-pollution regulation – particularly the demand for obligatory separators – since the problem, they argued, could only be solved by means of internationalism and not by domestic legal solutions.[58]

Concern about reluctant commercial parties at home also encouraged the government to turn to a superstate forum – this time to the one in Geneva. However, it did not only intend for the League to find a solution that would balance the competing interests (and concerns) of environmental associations and the shipping industry. To a certain extent, the League actually also functioned as a mechanism for adjusting (and easing) public and political pressure between the various political sides in Britain. "We should then be in a strong position in the public eye, having pressed for action and been prevented by the coolness of other

[56] Sweeney, *supra* note 5, at 189.

[57] On the political power of the shipping industry in British history, *see* Ronald Hope, A New History of British Shipping (1990).

[58] Compared to the almost exact opposite reaction of the British government in the case of the League's initiative for the progressive codification of the exploitation of the products of the sea (meaning, to initiate an international whaling law), and early British (with other whaling nations) reluctance towards any international supervision of whaling. I will discuss that in the following chapter.

[nations]," asserted one official on behalf of the Foreign Office in London in October 1933.[59]

On July 19, 1934, Britain officially presented the problem of oil pollution to the League. The British government called for international action to save the oceans from further pollution.[60] It seems that without the public pressure of civil associations such as the RSPB and RSPCA, there would have been no governmental initiative to begin with, and the League would not have been invited to solve the problem.

Regardless of whether the initiative stemmed from the government or an NGO, once the League had the opportunity to tackle the British government's request, it placed the pollution problem on its agenda and gave it a platform. The League's new institutional mechanisms and routine were well suited to the pollution inquiry, and it got its own legal-diplomatic process. Because of the technical nature of questions relating to marine transportation, the League's Communications and Transit Organisation took over. In what would become its familiar method of prioritizing bureaucratic-technical expertise in shaping early international governance,[61] the League took upon itself the task of negotiating the oil pollution problem.

In response to the British request, the Communications and Transit Organisation started to look into the issue and to prepare it for further international steps. Following the recommendation of "certain Governments" that approached the Organisation,[62] several experts were invited to form a special committee of experts in order "to study the question of the pollution of the sea by the discharge of oil." Meanwhile, the RSPCA, one of the original pioneers of the campaign, did not sit idle and hurried to send its communication to the League that summer of 1934, even before the committee of experts started its discussions. The Society enthusiastically offered its services to the League, and emphasized that it and its members would be happy to assist the League with any step in the fight against the pollution problem.[63] In the

[59] Note, Oct. 30, 1933, PRO, London, FO, 317/17329 (W 12231/7252/50).

[60] Sweeney, *supra* note 5, at 189.

[61] For a broader study on the raised status of technical expertise and professional bureaucracy in the creation of European modern continental governance, *see* Wolfram Kaiser & Johan Schot, Writing the Rules for Europe: Experts, Cartels, and International Organizations (2014).

[62] Confidential Summary of Proceedings of the Committee of Experts, Dec. 5, 1934, League of Nations Archives [hereinafter LoN Archives], C.C.T./P.E./2., 15326, at 1 [hereinafter Confidential Summary].

[63] Letter to the League of Nations, June 29, 1934, LoN Archives, Dossier 50/2625/2625.

following months of November and December 1934, the committee of experts discussed the problem during a series of special sessions.[64]

Despite the seemingly objective request, the proposed committee was leaning towards economic and industrial interests, as most of its members represented the shipping industry's commercial interests. The Italian representative to the committee of experts was, for instance, S. Giacchetti, a port captain, Head of the Mercantile Marine Division at the Ministry for Communication; the Japanese expert was also a captain, named Y. Ishikawa, probably much closer to his national shipping industry than to nature protection considerations. Likewise, the American representative, Captain Chester H. G. Keppler, was the Naval Attaché of the United States Embassy in Berlin. It should be noted that the Americans sent an expert of their own as an official representative, although the Wilsonian United States was never a member state of the League. His Danish peer, Captain F. V. H. Laub, the Director of the Port of Copenhagen, also brought his professional background in the shipping industry. France sent P. H. Watier, Counsellor of State and Director of Navigable Waterways and Maritime Ports in the Ministry of Public Works.[65] Among the different representatives who served on board the committee, it seems that the only member who was not inherently sympathetic to the interests of shipping and marine transportation was the second Japanese expert, M. Yokoyama, who was "merely" a diplomat, a Consul-General at Geneva.

In an intensive series of discussions in late 1934, the committee studied and compared the damage caused by oil pollution to birdlife, touristic resorts, fisheries, and communities on shore respectively. Its members analyzed the disturbing phenomenon, its implications, and impacts, and also suggested reviewing possible ways to solve the problem. However, compared to other professional committees established by the League, which included representatives of NGOs (such as from civil society and nongovernmental welfare associations),[66] it seems that this special committee mostly consisted of experts who were closer to the commercial needs of the shipping industry and its economic interests.

[64] Confidential Summary, *supra* note 62, at 1.

[65] Who was replaced later on as the discussion went on by C. Lemoine, another official who was much more familiar with the industry's interests (he served as Chief Engineer of Roads and Bridges in the French administration).

[66] *See*, for instance, the case with the special Committee of Experts' discussion on the problem of women and children trafficking in Paul Knepper's *The Investigation into the Traffic in Women by the League of Nations: Sociological Jurisprudence as an International Social Project*, 34 L. & Hist. Rev. 45 (2015).

But that does not mean that concerned NGOs let go of the issue. Opening the oil pollution problem to the pluralistic and accessible[67] forum of the League gave the signal to a variety of NGOs to step in. As I will show, once the committee of experts started to fulfill its duty, different NGOs asked to take part in its work. As in many of the humanitarian issues handled by the League, civilian associations with different national backgrounds turned to the League to facilitate their entry into the ongoing discussion.

1.3.2 The Committee of Experts Discusses the Pollution Problem and Prepares a Special Questionnaire with a Draft Convention

Following the British request, and once the League (through its the Communications and Transit Organisation) had organized the special committee of experts, the committee started to discuss the oil pollution problem. After a series of proceedings in November and December 1934, the committee concluded its preliminary work and prepared an official document that was to be sent worldwide. As this section will elaborate, the committee finalized both a questionnaire and a draft proposal for an antipollution convention.

As a matter of fact, as other parts of the League's environmental regime would demonstrate, this was a part of the League's routine diplomatic, institutional, and legal work, which followed the "usual procedure of the Communications and Transit Organisation"[68] and also of other performative bodies of the League.

During this preliminary stage, the British position appeared to be the dominant stance. As American public opinion changed and the demand for a solution to the oil-pollution problem slowly decreased, the United States was no longer officially involved in the campaign, at least not to the extent that it had been during the 1926 Washington Conference.[69] Likewise, other leading forces, such as France and Germany, avoided taking on a central role and generally preferred to defend their industrial and governmental interests.[70]

[67] And in many ways, much more democratic than other frameworks in which NGOs could have made their voice heard. I elaborate on the democratic characteristics of the League in Section 5.4 of Chapter 5.

[68] Confidential Summary, *supra* note 62, at 1.

[69] On America's involvement in the League's antipollution campaign *see* Sweeney, *supra* note 5, at 189.

[70] Unlike the French, Swiss, and German NGOs, who strove to influence the League on that matter.

Given that Britain's official representative to the committee of experts was C. H. Grimshaw of the Marine Department of the Board of Trade, and the expert that would serve as the committee's chairperson, the formal British agenda eventually elevated the industry's interests over those of the NGOs with their petitions, warnings, and demand for mandatory separators.

The committee, and the shipping industry as a whole, knew how damaging oil pollution was. Under the subheading "Damage to Bird-Life," the committee admitted in its confidential Summary of Proceedings from early December 1934 that in both Britain and the United States

> numerous cases of the destruction of sea-birds on the shores of these countries have been reported. The birds' feathers become saturated with oil, rendering them unable to swim, fly or dive and thus causing them to die a painful and lingering death of starvation. In Italy, societies for the protection of animals have made similar complaints with regard to bird-life.[71]

However, despite the reports of "damage to beaches," "injury to bathers," and "danger of fire in ports," as well as the serious threat that the oil problem posed to fisheries (it severely affected shellfish and submarine flora), the committee, on behalf of the industry, strongly objected to any measures made compulsory by international law. "It was evident from the answers given that the *shipowners in all countries* of which the Experts on the Committee are nationals, were opposed to the compulsory fitting of separators on their vessels . . . ."[72]

The committee tended to agree with the industry's representatives. Although birds were suffering and dying, the committee admitted that efficiency and economic concerns trumped the NGOs' advocacy of a binding international regulation to make separators on ships mandatory. The installation of such, explained the committee's Chairman Grimshaw, would result in "a heavy economic burden" on shipping. The committee felt that it had no choice but to favor the industry's interests over those of migratory birds. Otherwise, commercial disaster would threaten the future of the shipping industry, "which would make itself all the more felt in view of the bad economic conditions prevailing."

Moreover, during the preliminary stage of the committee's international inquiry, different national industries also complained to the

[71] Confidential Summary, *supra* note 62, at 1.
[72] *Id.* at 2 (emphasis added).

League about large ships that were equipped with tankers that would need separators with a capacity of at least 250 tons. In these cases, the technical fact was that no separators of this capacity "ha[d] so far been constructed."[73] However, even if the proposed new regulation were only to apply to new vessels that would be constructed in the future (rather than forcing all existing fleets to bear the burden of fitting compulsory separators), the industrial needs still had the upper hand. The American expert said that he thought there was a tendency "to instal [sic] such separators on war ships . . . as well as on passenger ships burning oil, but not on tankers." The parallel French position, however, concluded that French shipowners, like their peers from abroad in Europe, East Asia, and America, were opposed to the installation of separators on board new ships.[74]

Once the committee had removed the threat to industry, if not to the birds – at least for the time being – it was willing to further discuss other means on its agenda as an alternative. Instead of the "radical" solution of separators (to which the industry was strictly opposed), the industry suggested revisiting the discussion on prohibited coastal zones, within which the discharge of oil from vessels should be banned.

At that point, the British cemented their pro-industrial stance. Chairman Grimshaw, in his own proposal, pointed out the "advantages" of leaving international law as flexible as possible. He proposed a more general agreement that would leave "individual states" to establish their own restricted zones. According to Grimshaw's agenda, the exact extent of the restricted zone would vary "according to the needs of their respective countries."[75] As the stricter measure of separators was currently off the table, the industry attempted to maintain its momentum and to defend its interests. At this stage, Grimshaw was suggesting a mild solution with regard to international law. In the summary from December 1934, the focus was on countries' needs rather than on the environmental implications of the oil problem. These needs, he admitted, might change after a certain time, but the countries could nevertheless modify the width of their restricted zones from time to time – keeping, "of course," the other contracting states duly informed about these modifications.

However, in spite of their pro-shipping-industry backgrounds, other experts were firmly in favor of a stipulated width for the restricted zone.

[73] *Id.*
[74] *Id.* at 3.
[75] *Id.*

The American expert was the most progressive among them, and the United States suggested that the width should be set to no less than 150 miles; other experts (and states), however, called for a less demanding width than the Americans had.

The Danish expert explained that in view of "the conditions prevailing in Danish waters," his government would hardly contemplate the establishment of a zone as wide as the one suggested by the Americans. Moreover, the French expert supported a different kind of restriction, one that favored the creation of several smaller restricted areas (rather than one general zone) along those parts of the coast "where oil pollution ma[de] itself felt." The French representative to the committee cynically observed that with the English Channel, which stretched almost 21 miles to Dover and measured exactly 150 miles at its widest part, a 150-mile-wide zone might actually "cover the whole distance between the coastlines of two countries." Italy noted, however, that if the committee did indeed recommend a 150-mile zone, then special attention should be paid to the question of safety. Italian ships might be imperiled, for instance, if they were to empty tanks of ballast water 150 miles from the coast in bad weather, thereby threatening their safety.

Generally speaking, most of the experts rejected the British call to leave the issue of oil pollution to national-domestic considerations and legislation, and instead promoted relying on a binding international regulation. Arguing against the British proposal, most of the experts noted that the 150-mile limit seemed reasonable[76] since it was difficult to predict how far oil might travel. As scientific assessments had shown, this distance could vary significantly depending on conditions such as the weather and currents. However, no matter how much the experts argued about how wide this zone should be, NGOs remained totally opposed to this legal solution. From their perspective, no restricted zone could ever be wide enough to be truly effective. As the French expert put it, the problem with the solution of a restricted zone was that, eventually, "masters would prefer to discharge their oily water *outside* the zone,"[77] and the ocean would remain polluted.

All of the experts who presented their professional and national positions on these issues expressed a decisive objection to the compulsory installation of separators. The Danish representative stated that his government would not be inclined to impose such an obligation upon

[76] Except for the Japanese, who would agree to a zone that measured no more than ten miles.
[77] Confidential Summary, *supra* note 62, at 5 (emphasis added).

shipowners. The American expert explained that the United States' objection to this proposal was driven by the "present economic situation," which made it rather difficult to impose upon harbor authorities this kind of regulation.

The committee, however, tried to argue that from a technical perspective, it simply did not have the capacity to enforce the compulsory installation of separators. The Summary of Proceedings also detailed that according to most of its members, it was impractical to find suitable barges that could carry out this complicated technical-engineering task. The Italian member, for instance, stated that in his country, separating barges could only be found in certain military ports, but not in regular civilian ones. This was also the claim made by the United States; whereas in the case of Denmark and Japan, separating barges did not exist to begin with.

Both the reports handed to the League, and the reports of professionals who served on the committee of experts, indicate that priority was given to the shipping industry. Even so, the dangers of polluted water were becoming more obvious, even to the representatives on the committee. This likely had to do with the fact that the League's institutional routine tended to give scientists and scientific observations more room to be heard.

In its confidential report from December 1934, the committee took into account an anonymous warning that was mentioned during its sessions. Contrary to the shipping industry's claims that "[a]ccording to some statements made at Washington,[78] oil on the sea quickly evaporated," scientific estimations were different. According to one "recent report," "*only 10%* of oil or oily mixture evaporate at normal temperature." Moreover, "[a]n English scientific expert had ... stated that the asphalt which forms part of the oil mixtures practically *never disappears* ...."[79]

Moreover, although the committee (mostly) favored the shipping industry's interests, its work also meant, as Chairman Grimshaw suddenly realized, moving some of the legal terms and solutions away from domestic jurisprudence and sovereignty: "The Chairperson reminded the Committee that at Washington [i.e., the 1926 Convention], the question of exempting vessels from the proposed obligation ... was left to *national legislation*."[80] While now in the mid-1930s, the committee was discussing

78 That is, the Washington Conference of 1926.

79 Confidential Summary, *supra* note 62, at 7.

80 *Id.* at 6 (emphasis added). It seems that even Grimshaw was trying to persuade the committee not to turn to international regulation. In doing so, he also "reminded" the

possible solutions as a basis for binding international regulations on oil pollution of the sea.

In trying to place the League's antipollution campaign on a broader timeline that reflects the evolutionary process of shaping international environmental law, perhaps the League's own comments on the matter might assist. The experts assigned to the mission defined their initiative as part of an ongoing process. As the committee of experts concluded its proceedings and made preparations for a new antipollution convention through the League, it specifically referred to prior legal arrangements. Under the subheading "Revision of the Washington Draft Convention of 1926," a special committee acting on behalf of the League's Organisation for Communication and Transit was assembled to follow up on what needed to be fixed and improved.

Although most of the representatives to the committee were not keen to see the warnings delivered by NGOs and scientists make their way into the concluding text and recommendations, the revision process itself reflected legal – and environmental – development. This was, as Chairman Grimshaw expressed, an "opportunity" – and one that "should be taken" – to examine the provisions of the Washington Draft Convention, which had never been ratified. After all, legally speaking, the Washington Convention (which was created outside the League in the mid-1920s) served as the foundation for the improved convention that the League would soon introduce to the world. However, Chairman Grimshaw explicitly mentioned that if the League introduced a new convention, it would not be limited by earlier arrangements. He agreed that it "would be of advantage to record any suggestion of the kind, but he wished to make it clear that it must not be assumed that a Convention on the lines of that of 1926 was necessarily the form of Convention which might be considered by the League."[81] Likewise, despite the obstacles the League faced throughout its existence, this institution also offered many new opportunities. Unlike the earlier Washington Convention, which was limited by its scope, the League's new convention would be able to reach a much larger international community and garner greater

experts that the 1926 Washington Convention had avoided setting international restrictions like the ones being discussed by the League's committee. Back then, he said, for safety reasons, the discussants and the states involved had chosen not to enforce the restricted zone: they were reluctant to bind themselves and their fleets in the event of an emergency (as the crew might have to discharge oil within the restricted zone by the shore).

81 *Id.* at 7.

attention thanks to its institutional framework, routine, mechanisms of international law, and diplomacy.

The committee of experts revised the original 1926 Washington Convention (the one that was never ratified), taking into consideration the League's international reach. As a result, the first amendment to the convention reflected the League's framework, agenda, and institutional possibilities. Whereas earlier legal arrangements were built on transnational ground, the new forum of the League shifted the discussion – particularly the solutions – into the sphere of internationalism. The committee deliberated the professional, scientific, and technical considerations of the oil pollution issue, concluding that a new international agreement should be established to solve the oil pollution problem. Although the core technical and environmental articles in the 1926 Washington Convention remained an important component of the newer convention, this time it was the League (as an institution and not an ad hoc forum) that was going to introduce a solution to the problem.

However, as the League considered possible improvements to the 1926 Washington Convention, the issue of compulsory separators was put on hold.

> Regarding the compulsory provision of separators, the Chairman remarked this was a rather complicated matter . . . . There would, however, be an opportunity of discussing this subject later, when the replies to the questions relating to it which would be included in the . . . Questionnaire to be sent to Governments of maritime countries had been considered.[82]

Although at this preparatory stage the committee rejected the NGOs' demand for the compulsory installation of separators (and only supported their use in theory), the new draft convention introduced at the end of the Summary included several improvements. Given that oil pollution was an ongoing problem, several of the articles in the committee's new draft focused on improving the ineffective aspects of the 1926 Washington Convention through better legal framing.

Article V of the original 1926 Convention, for instance, used the words "vessels flying their national flag." The committee suggested that this wording, which enabled naval crews and vessels to dodge the restrictions simply by choosing another national flag (to avoid legal obligations), be replaced with more concrete language. Stricter legal framing would

[82] Confidential Summary, *supra* note 62, at 12.

minimize the instances of ships that were trying to evade legal responsibility by exploiting customary international law.[83] By reframing this article, the League showed that it spoke the language of international law and was aware of the shortcomings of the existing legal arrangements.

"The words 'vessels registered in any of their ports' have been inserted in lieu [of the former legal terms] . . . in order to define more clearly the vessels in respect of which each Government undertakes the obligations imposed by the Agreements." With this, the new, stricter articulation ordered that the "contracting Governments undertake . . . to take the necessary measures to render illegal the discharge of oil or oily mixture . . . within any area."[84]

This was also the case with several other articles from the original text drawn up in Washington. Article I of the original Washington text also underwent revisions that resulted in much tougher legal terminology. According to the suggested new articulation (Article III in the League's preliminary draft), the discharge prohibited in any area prescribed pursuant to the former definitions mentioned in the draft included crude, fuel, or diesel oil – or any mixture containing more than 0.05 percent to 1 percent of such oil. The committee added a remark explaining that it would be wiser to insert the wording "shall be prohibited" instead of "may be prohibited." The issue of prohibition was "so essential" a matter, the confidential summary argued, that "it would seem preferable to employ a mandatory than a permissive expression,"[85] especially considering this issue would be a keystone of what would eventually become the next international convention.

It seems that the main articles of the suggested draft were actually reclaiming the core issues of the Washington Convention. Only this time, the techno-environmental obligations were based on the authority of the League. According to Article III, the governments undertook to establish areas in waters adjacent to their coasts within which discharge of oil would be prohibited. And according to Subsection (a) of that article, the heart of the draft, in the case of coasts bordering the open sea, such areas would not extend more than fifty nautical miles from the coast.

[83] The use of flags of convenience ("Panlibhon"), primarily those of Panama, Liberia, Honduras, and possibly others, under which many foreign ships are registered in order to escape certain legal obligations, continues to be a central problem in international law and shipping. This example of the interwar period shows that international environmental law also dealt with these implications under the auspices of the League and tried to find an alternative legal solution. For a study on the issue *see, e.g.*, BOLESLAW A. BOCZEK, FLAGS OF CONVENIENCE: AN INTERNATIONAL LEGAL STUDY (1962).

[84] Confidential Summary (Annex 1), *supra* note 62, at 17.

[85] Confidential Summary, *supra* note 62, at 18.

In that sense, Chairman Grimshaw's original minimalist goal – leaving the width of the prohibited strip up to the states' considerations (and to their legal domestic arrangements) – had failed. Nevertheless, unlike the drifting oil on the seas, the campaign for obligatory separators seemed to be fading away as the committee officially turned down the proposed solution of compulsory separators on ships. In this dilemma, the committee was firmly opposed to forcing the industry (and the governments) to install separators on ships. According to Article VI of the committee's draft convention, the contracting governments agreed that "no penalty or disability of any kind whatever in the matter of tonnage measurement or payment of dues be incurred by any vessel by reason only of the fitting of any device or apparatus for separating oil from water."

The suggested draft was not perfect, but it managed to achieve a compromise between the contrasting agendas and competing interests of the shipping industry and pro-commercial supporters on the one hand, and those of nature-protection NGOs, scientific associations and societies, and independent actors fighting against the harmful effects of the pollution on their coasts on the other hand.

Having said that, although the committee seemed to be doing its best to overcome NGOs' advocacy and demands, this was still not the end of the campaign. The League's institutional framework was not homogenous, and at least some of the maritime powers would be surprised by the broad range of feedback and responses that would follow.

Concluding this stage of its professional work, the committee prepared the questionnaire and the draft convention for worldwide distribution in January 1935.

1.3.3 The League Distributes the Questionnaire with the Draft Convention; States and Organizations Reply

Concluding the work of the special committee of experts on behalf of the Communications and Transit Organisation in late 1934, the League took the next step of opening up its initiative to member states, other states, and relevant parties. The year of 1935, amidst the stormy geopolitical waters of the 1930s, was an important year for internationalizing possible legal and techno-environmental solutions to the oil pollution problem. Although the issue of mandatory separators did not receive the legal support that NGOs and scientists were hoping for in the former round of the committee's discussions, the League remained focused on reaching an international agreement that would solve the crisis of polluted seas.

This round of activity, however, had brought with it new participants and positions.

As part of the League's procedural routine, the next step was to introduce the initiative into the international arena. The Secretary-General, Joseph Avenol[86] communicated to the League's Council that the committee had informed him that the subject was ready for an international convention. On January 23, 1935, the Secretary-General presented a long list of states with the circulated questionnaire and the draft convention. Shortly thereafter, the League published its proceedings, explaining that

> [t]he Committee of Experts were agreed that some international measures should be devised so as to limit the evil as much as possible, and the Communication and Transit Organisation therefore recommended that efforts should be made to attain the conclusion of an international convention on the subject. The advantages ... are ... obvious, in that the damage which is now being caused to property in harbours, to the interests of seaside resorts, to bird life, and to fisheries, would very largely if not entirely be obviated.[87]

The mode of using special questionnaires as a mechanism to engage with international law received its golden age under the auspices of the League, as the interwar environmental regime reveals. There was a general feeling of optimism about this new type of internationalism. Technical communication had improved and, with it, access to the international community, largely as a result of the procedural and diplomatic possibilities that the League was able to offer as an institution.

Although Chairman Grimshaw assumed that only maritime powers would participate in the pollution issue or be the main drivers behind discussions on it, the questionnaire and the draft convention opened the issue up to a much broader and more democratic international discussion. More than seventy states, members and non-members alike,

[86] Joseph Louis Anne Avenol served as the second Secretary-General of the League of Nations (July 1933–August 1940). Even with the recent renaissance in the study of the League, the biographical genre of the historical persons who built and led the League in the 1920s and 1930s is still underdeveloped. One of the very few works in this genre is James Barros's survey on Avenol's role from the late 1960s. *See* JAMES BARROS, BETRAYAL FROM WITHIN: JOSEPH AVENOL, SECRETARY-GENERAL OF THE LEAGUE OF NATIONS, 1933–1940 (1969).

[87] Summary of the Replies (Part I), Series of League of Nations Publications, VIII. Transit 1935. VIII. 5, Pollution of the Sea by Oil (Communicated to the Assembly, the Council and the Members of the League), Aug. 15, 1935, LoN Archives, at 3 [hereinafter Summary of the Replies].

received the questionnaire, which focused entirely on the oil pollution problem. Among the list of states who responded were maritime powers such as the United States, the Soviet Union, Canada, and Germany, along with landlocked countries such as Czechoslovakia and Switzerland. The League sought to ensure that all would be able to take part in the legal-environmental proposal.

The survey that was distributed posed eight different questions. The different governments were asked to state whether they had noticed the effects of pollution or any other effects in their territories, and to provide detailed particulars under each heading.[88]

In spite of the committee's political, commercial, and pro-industrial affiliations,[89] the League soon saw that the questionnaire opened the question up to broader international consideration. As other case studies

[88] Furthermore, the survey specifically asked states for "scientific or other evidence regarding the extent of oil pollution at sea." All the member states were requested to report on the extent of oil pollution and the devices they were using to combat it. The first, and most important question, reflected the campaign's primary goal: it asked the states about the effects of oil on birds. Then, the states were asked to comment on economic and technical aspects, and to notify the League if they thought oil pollution might also affect fish and the fishing industry, public health, "the amenities of the beaches for bathing, recreation etc., and ... harbours ... ." (The League of Nations Communication and Transit Organisation, Pollution of the Sea by Oil: Summary of Additional Replies to the Questionnaire, LoN Archives, Aug. 1, 1936, A.20.1935.VIII.)

The third question challenged the relevant states, asking them directly whether or not they would be willing to agree to an international standard that would require the installation of separators on ships, "with or without exceptions in the case of certain vessels."

Most of the questions that followed, it should be emphasized, dealt directly with the burning question of separators. "Are you prepared," asked Question Number 4, "to agree to an international requirement that such separators should be designed for and fitted to all new ships which will carry or burn oil?". Perhaps anticipating that some maritime nations would object, the committee also added, "If not, please state reasons for declining to agree." The next question asked about the types of separators used by the shipping industry and how much would they cost. In another question, states were asked if there were port facilities to separate waste oil on shore.

The eighth, and final, question asked states for their opinion about enforcing the restricted zone for oil discharge (as previously mentioned, this solution was favored by both the shipping industry and most of the committee's members). Once again, the League and its bodies turned to scientific discourse: "It has been contended that oil and oily mixtures discharged from ships at sea may pollute the coasts after travelling, in certain conditions, distances more than 50 and even more than 150 nautical miles. Please supply any evidence, based on scientific or other observations made by your country, which may bear on this question." (*Id.*).

[89] Keeping in mind, for instance, the industrial and professional background of the members of the committee, as I explained earlier, together with their reluctance to consider the obligatory installation of separators.

will show,[90] these special questionnaires proved to be far "riskier" than traditional ones. After all, inviting outside parties to weigh in on international law allowed them to raise their own agendas and ideas that other powers – especially maritime nations with their own interests to protect – might oppose. The "neutral" (legal) tone the League used to communicate its ideas allowed various states and bodies to engage in the developing discussion in a more open and democratic way. Indeed, these conflicts of power had not simply vanished with the Paris Peace Conference, which delivered the League into the post–World War I era. Political interests and affiliations, alongside economic motivations, continued to affect international issues throughout the League's rule. However the ways in which international law worked and had progressed had changed. With the Progressive Era behind it, especially in the North Atlantic, the League based its activity on scientific knowledge and objective reasoning. As the environmental questions show, including of course those related to marine environments, science diplomacy played an essential role in defining these dilemmas, their reasons and sources, and possible solutions.

By summer 1935, although the League's Secretariat had not yet received all the replies to the questionnaire, it had received the majority of those from the leading maritime countries. The Secretariat set about compiling these responses in a special summary, in which it further listed the different victims of sea pollution in perceived order of importance: first and foremost birds, followed by fish and fisheries, touristic resorts, and harbors.[91]

As with other environmental concerns, many states – including both maritime powers and those states not directly affected by sea pollution – were eager to take part in the evolving discussion on oil pollution.

Having been exposed to environmental issues throughout its work alongside (primarily British) nature-protection agencies in the 1920s, the United States' reply did acknowledge the "extensive damage" to the Atlantic coast; however, the official American stance framed the problem as one that had run its course between 1919 and 1930. In 1934, the American reply argued that "reports from various United States coastal areas showed that pollution had disappeared or had greatly improved."[92]

[90] As in the case of the whaling regulation the League developed from 1926, in which it distributed a special questionnaire that related to the "exploitation of the products of the sea." *See* my discussion in Chapter 2.

[91] Due to the danger of fire on decks.

[92] Summary of the Replies (Part II), *supra* note 87, at 11. *See* Sweeney, *supra* note 5, at 189.

The British government, however – at least at this point – did not try to dismiss the problem. The official summary prepared by the League featured a rather heartbreaking description from Britain, rather than one that typically might have been more laconic or diplomatic in nature: "Numerous sea-birds are reported to have been observed dead or dying in lingering starvation in recent years on various parts of the shores. Their wings were saturated with oil, and they were unable to fly, swim or dive."[93] The Canadian report was just as emotive: "Thousands of sea-birds perish each year as a result of pollution of the sea by oil. . . . [I]n areas polluted by oil birds' plumage becomes saturated and they cannot dive or go under water for their food. They, consequently, cannot feed and slowly starve to death."[94]

But not everyone was so easily moved. Newfoundland assessed the effect of oil pollution on birds in a single word: "negligible." While the Egyptian government did not express a specific opinion on any of the questions relating to birds, in its response to the question relating to ports and lighthouse administration, it did admit that the discharge of oil "is doubtless harmful to them."[95]

One way or the other, concern for the suffering birds paved the way for scientific support, as the French reply shows. "The disappearance of sea-birds which has been noted for some time as a result of the increasing use of heavy oil . . . has been brought to the notice of the public authorities . . . ." The report drawn up by the French focused on cause and effect, scientific experiments, and professional observations and methodology as a basis for both international discourse and information sharing: "Professor Portier, Member of the Academy of Medicine, has studied the effects of the discharge of fuel-oil residues on such birds."

The report clearly relied on objective observations and scientific evidence in making its conclusions:

> The experiments recently made have been *absolutely conclusive* so far as concerns the harmful action of oil on sea-birds; the bird, whose feathers have been soaked in fuel oil, dies of cold, since the oil cuts off the air from the bird's feathers, and water penetrates, chills the body, and causes death.[96]

Moreover, the experiments carried out by a qualified scientist had also proved that birds whose feathers have been soaked in oil refuse to enter

[93] Summary of the Replies (Part II), *supra* note 87, at 11.
[94] *Id.* at 12.
[95] *Id.*
[96] *Id.* (emphasis added).

the water. Hence, the birds were damned if they entered the polluted sea, and damned if they did not: in the case of seabirds, not entering the water meant an agonizing death by cold and starvation, since they could not dive into the sea to find food.[97]

Compared to other interwar environmental problems, oil pollution seemed much less important in scale. Several nations, such as the Union of South Africa, Bulgaria, India, Iraq, Italy, Iceland, Latvia, and Turkey concisely stated in their replies that there was no evidence of the deleterious effects of oil pollution in their territories (and territorial waters). Likewise, the Commonwealth of Australia (which comprised the states of New South Wales, Queensland, South Australia, Tasmania, Victoria, and Western Australia, as well as ten federal territories) did not express an opinion on any of the points raised.[98]

Nevertheless, other states involved confirmed the existence of problems near their shores. Moreover, in their replies, these states challenged the pro-industrial agenda by explicitly focusing on the effect of oil discharge on birds and by relying on clear environmental observations.

Denmark, for instance, replied that "regular reports of the destruction of birds in certain localities and at certain seasons have been received by the Government";[99] whereas the Irish Free State reported that the "deleterious effects" on birds were noticeable, especially on its southeast coast. Norway pointed out that "although oil pollution has been rarely noticed, in many localities birds have perished from such effects"; and Sweden, which did not play any significant role during the League's environmental discussions, also stated that there was "evidence of a large-scale destruction of sea-birds in the vicinity of the Swedish coasts."[100]

These replies indicate that most states were convinced that oil pollution was directly responsible for the death of migratory birds. As a result, this became the central issue, more so than related concerns such as the effects of oil pollution on fish and the fishing industry, or the danger of fire in harbors.

Unlike the effect on birds, almost no clear evidence was reported concerning any of the other issues discussed. In its reply to the inquiry on the possible effects on fish and the fishing industry, Canada, for instance, stated that there was "no evidence that fish have changed their habitat as a result of oil pollution."[101] The Australian reply briefly

97 *See* the British reply (*Id.* at 11).
98 *Id.* at 13.
99 *Id.* at 12.
100 *Id.*
101 *Id.* at 17.

mentioned that with regard to other subjects badly affected by oil, the Government could only vaguely recall "one case" that was reported in South Australia "some years ago," of a fish that "had perished from the effect of oil pollution."[102]

Given this backdrop, the League understood that the issue at stake was the willingness to subscribe to an international regulation, but that it would have to base this decision either on a requirement for compulsory separators, or on favoring the zoning system – something the committee of experts had recognized early on. The British reply revealed this dilemma, which addressed both options. Speaking the language of the evolution and genealogy of international law, the British reply to the questionnaire attached the current dilemma of the mid-1930s to the *former* pillars in the legal struggle against oil pollution. In this way, the League's efforts pursued the measures achieved in Washington, and it worked intently to revive – and in some instances to fix or improve – the 1926 Washington Convention as a legal base. As a matter of fact, the very question of compulsory separators directly related to the solution that was brought to the fore in the mid-1920s; however back then, it lacked the authority, resilience, and devotion of the League.

The basic conflict prevailed. The remedy mentioned in the questionnaire – choosing between the progressive but strict solution of compulsory separators, and the establishment of limited dumping zones, carried with it extensive practical, industrial, legal, and economic implications. It was now up to international law, and the League, to decide the matter.

Earlier discussions that had been held by the committee of experts had taken into account only certain opinions (especially those of the shipping

[102] *Id.* at 13. Having said that, it should be noted that the French reply (which was an exception) raised some concerns regarding the damage caused by oil not only to birds, but also to fisheries and their equipment. France replied to the section entitled the "Fishermen's Calling" and explained that stress "should be laid on the damage caused to fishing-nets and tackle used in contaminated waters .... In certain cases, tackle has been rendered unfit for use, a very considerable loss being thus caused to the owners of the damaged material" (*Id.* at 17). Moreover, it had also complained that small coastal fisheries were seriously affected by polluted water, and that fish that were caught in places where such pollution was particularly serious very often had a "strong oily flavor," which rendered them unfit for consumption (*Id.* at 16). France also identified a link between pollution and economic consequences, as it warned that in certain cases, the impossibility of selling polluted fish had brought the fishing industry almost completely to a halt, as it needed to wait until traces of the contamination had disappeared. On several occasions, large quantities of dead, poisoned fish "were seen floating on the surface, which tends to show that pollution ... may lead to the wholesale destruction of fish" (*Id.* at 17).

industry). The broader forum of the Assembly, however, was more transparent as the British response showed when it referred directly to improvements made in the field since the last (failed) round of 1926:

> Societies such as the Royal Societies for the Protection of Birds and for the Prevention of Cruelty to Animals, and many local coastal bodies supported by a body of opinion are in favour of this remedy [separators], the advocates of which support their contentions ... by a statement that separators are much cheaper than they were in 1926 and that the oil recovered from them can be used again.[103]

Moreover, supporting the view of nature-protection associations, the British report admitted that any option other than separators would not do enough. The zoning solution was almost useless. The British believed that "the voluntary action by the shipowners ... in prohibiting the discharge by their ships ... within fifty miles of any coast has touched *only the fringe of the evil.*"[104] They went on to say that the RSPB "rejects entirely" any remedy involving the establishment of zones "on the ground [sic] that no 'zone' could be wide enough to be effective, since there is evidence that oily substances discharged at sea will float for very long periods, and drift many hundreds of miles."[105]

Hence, the role and importance of international law, and the League as its creator and representative, grew considerably: "[T]the action needed is ... legislation ... declaring that pollution by ... ships is prohibited everywhere and requiring that effective measures be taken for preventing pollution."

However, in its report to the League (and the international community), the British acknowledged that the shipping industry still needed to be considered. Britain's governmental report took into account perspectives other than those relating to nature protection and it mentioned the Chamber of Shipping and the Liverpool Steamship Owners' Association in this regard, as a counterexample to the role of the RSPB and the RSPCA. The Chamber of Shipping contended that the fitting of separators would be "impracticable" in the case of many vessels, and unnecessary in that of others, while it would impose upon the shipowners "a heavy additional financial burden which, in the present state of their industry, they could not bear."[106]

103 *Id.* at 18.
104 *Id.* (emphasis added).
105 Summary of the Replies (Part II), *supra* note 87, at 19.
106 *Id.*

Although the British reply emphasized the contentious issue of separators and the industry's explicit reluctance to accept them, Britain decided to step back from the task of finding an international solution – whatever it would eventually be – including ruling on separators as a progressive international regulation, and instead entrusted the League with this responsibility. "The . . . Government is prepared to fall in with any international scheme proposed by the League . . . ."

When other maritime powers tried to defend the industry, Britain's stance ultimately won out. Leading maritime powers such as Canada rejected the solution of separators on the grounds that this international requirement opposed industrial interests. The Danish argued that "the considerable financial burden which would be placed on shipping by an international requirement for the fitting of separators in ships which carry or burn oil is *out of proportion* to the advantages to be expected from such an arrangement."[107] France refused any obligation to fit separators, considering such act to be "far too burdensome" to French shipowners, "who [had] already been hard hit by the present crisis." They would be less willing to accept an obligation stipulated by international law, since the goal of this legislation could be obtained "by simpler and less expensive methods."[108] But between environmental concerns and the shipping industry's interests, Britain seemed unwavering in its support of the League's endeavor to find a solution to the problem of pollution:

> The effectiveness of any remedy will depend partly upon its merits but largely upon international action in applying it. The action of one or two countries alone could not be effective. While this is the general position of His Majesty's Government, it would . . . agree to an arrangement which made it necessary to fit separators in ships . . . .[109]

Britain's support for this progressive – and to the shipping industry, rather radical – solution of compulsory separators received the approval of a few others. Besides those lands under British influence, such as Egypt,[110] India,[111] and Iraq,[112] Spain, for instance, announced that it

[107] *Id.* at 19–20 (emphasis added).
[108] *Id.* at 20.
[109] *Id.* at 19.
[110] Which replied that its government "should support" the British agenda on the matter.
[111] Which added that it would support the use of international law for this purpose, provided that the fitting of such separators was not compulsory for small vessels.
[112] Which declared that its government "would be glad" to accept an international agreement of this kind.

too would support the League's international requirement,[113] as did several other states involved in the discussion.

Those states that rejected the solution, and what they saw as the harsh enforcement of international law, provided their own justifications for doing so. The Italian government, for instance, argued that Mediterranean countries, unlike the northern ones (and the North Atlantic in particular) had not suffered any serious damage from oil pollution. According to Italy, this was due to the fact that the geographical and environmental patterns of the Mediterranean Sea differ from those of other seas and oceans. In this case, the government argued, a modified antipollution regulation should be introduced (if any at all). This was because in Italian waters in particular, the regular currents in the straits (which Italy claimed were "the only ones of any importance") have an ebb and flow that tends to disperse the oil floating on the water, rather than to send it in any one direction (as in the case of the British Isles, Scandinavia, or the Baltic states).[114]

The variety of responses to this interwar environmental initiative supports the general claim of the unique characteristics of the crafting of international law under the auspices of the League. It is true that some traditional powers that had typically shaped diplomacy, and most of the world order prior to the establishment of the League, resented and explicitly objected to this move in international law: such as France or the Netherlands,[115] or nations like Norway[116] – with its vast whaling industry and shipping corporations – who had a clear interest in thwarting this new attempt to change shipping rules. However, *other* relatively new players – such as India, Bulgaria, Latvia, New Zealand, Japan,[117] and Turkey – encouraged the League to pursue its revolutionary techno-environmental solution.[118] Even the Irish Free State, despite its direct

[113] Summary of the Replies (Part II), *supra* note 87, at 25–26.

[114] *Id.* at 30.

[115] The Dutch government declared it too was opposed to the compulsory installation because of the difficult financial position of its shipping industry.

[116] Justifying its objection to the new regulations, Norway replied that oil pollution "cannot be effectively prevented even by a general ruling that separators be installed." Moreover, the Norwegian government announced to the League that it would not be willing to charge the national merchant marine the fee of ten million crowns, the estimated total amount needed to fit of all of its ships with separators.

[117] Which complained that oil pollution not only damages local fisheries but also affects the national production of algae and seaweed.

[118] Summary of the Replies (Part II), *supra* note 87, at 18–22.

interests in the shipping industry to strengthen its national economy, enthusiastically supported a compulsory international regulation "without exception."[119]

Hungary was one of the few states that distanced itself from the antipollution regulation giving as its reason that it was a landlocked state;[120] however, Hungary was an exception rather than the rule. Other landlocked countries, as well as states with no direct stake in an oil pollution regulation,[121] identified the antipollution campaign as part of a broader move: the right to become involved in the making of international law.

States, members and non-members alike, were not the only ones that took part in the League's antipollution discussion. Besides the RSPB, the organization that had started the save-the-birds campaign back in Britain, other NGOs from different countries identified the League's move as an opportunity to get their foot in the door of international law. In addition to the formal replies to the questionnaire, the League Secretariat received a variety of petitions, requests, and reports from nature-protection societies.

Moreover, many of these non-state actors relied on scientific discourse in their communications with the League. The variety of formal letters that reached Geneva used a common language: that of objective data and research. It seems that institutionalized international law, unfamiliar to some of the players in the post–World War I world, needed to be built on solid ground, and that ground was science. In the modern culture of the twentieth century, science had become a source of legitimacy.

Evidence of this came in the form of a report sent by a German animal rights association, the Hamburger Tierschutzverein von 1841.[122] This report gathered data on dying birds and oil pollution along the German coast. The report concluded that the only solution to the problem was the introduction of a world-binding regulation that would require the

[119] *Id.* at 21.

[120] *Id.* at 22.

[121] Such as Czechoslovakia, for instance, who also supported the proposed solution of mandatory separators "without exception." (*Id.*).

[122] Letter by the Bureau International Humanitaire Zoophile, Mar. 13, 1935, LoN Archives, 50/2625/2625 viii. The scope of the international and transnational cooperation between nature-protection organizations over the problem of oil pollution is exemplified by this statement. Originally, the database was put together and revised by the German association in Hamburg. The Swiss office of the Bureau International Humanitaire Zoophile, which itself was a part of the Animal Defence Society in London (with the Duchess of Hamilton and Brandon as its president) sent the organization's report to the League.

installation of separators. Two French associations reached the same conclusion on the need for separators: a hunting organization named St. Hubert, and la Ligue pour la Protection des Oiseaux.[123]

The RSPCA also promised to assist the League "with evidence and stuffed specimens of birds which have been so destroyed."[124] A similar offer of alliance came from the American Humane Association, an umbrella organization that combined more than 530 different animal rights and nature-protection societies across the nation. The Humane Association urged the League and its special committee, "to use [its] great power . . . to stop this whole, unnecessary pollution of the seas [and] . . . prevent this waste of bird life."[125] Another American environmental association, the Audubon Society of Illinois, also approached the League and asked to take part in the discussion on a new global law. The Audubon Society emphasized the genuine belief of its members, as well as of other NGOs around the world, in the League and its ability to bring about needed change for the suffering birds. "We are all sure with all your able workers, you will perfect an effective means of correcting the error."[126]

The League, as a new and unfamiliar institution, needed to satisfy some of its own institutional and political interests along the way. The League's quest for legitimacy and worldwide acknowledgment as a new power in international relations also became apparent in the oil pollution discussions. When the League revised some of these NGOs' petitions, it gave special attention to media coverage of the oil pollution issue. In response to the Audubon Society of Illinois' statement of support for the League, one of the high-ranking officials of the League replied, "Perhaps . . . you will yourself find ways in which the support of public opinion can be added to the efforts now being made by the League for the protection of bird and marine life."[127]

This environmental issue became a quid pro quo arrangement: the League would address the NGOs' calls for help and use its institutional means and power to save the fauna and flora of the planet. In return,

[123] Or the National Bird Protection League. A. Feuillée-Billot, *De la nécessité d'une entente internationale pour la protection des oiseaux de mer contre l'huile lourde et le mazout, in* Deuxième Congrès *international pour la protection de la nature* 155–162 (Abel Gruvel ed., 1932); *See* also Comte W. d'Adix, "Les oiseaux et le mazout" *Le Bulletin du Saint-Hubert Club de France* (Février 1935), LoN Archives, 50/2625/2625.

[124] Letter to the League of Nations, June 29, 1934, LoN Archives, 50/2625/2625.

[125] Letter to the Secretary-General, Jan. 8, 1935, LoN Archives, 50/2625/2625.

[126] Letter to the Secretary-General, Nov. 27, 1935, LoN Archives, 50/2625/2625.

[127] Letter to the Illinois Audubon Society, Dec. 11, 1935, LoN Archives, 50/2625/2625.

these NGOs would do their best to support the League's quest for legitimacy, international acceptance, and authority. In this way, the Western media's deepening affection for nature protection in the early twentieth century served both the NGOs' and the League's interests.

The significance of scientific data was also reflected in the procedural ways in which the League strove to shape international law. Almost every state that participated in the discussion on the pollution problem turned to scientific observations. The United States, for example, notified the committee of experts with a formal scientific observation entitled "Report on Oil Pollution Experiments: Behaviour of Fuel Oil on the Surface of the Sea": a comprehensive document prepared by an associate engineer from the Bureau of Standards, Department of Commerce.

As with other cases in its environmental regime, as I will demonstrate, the League actively encouraged scientific research.[128] "Certain scientific investigations have been undertaken on behalf of the United Kingdom Government," mentioned the British reply to the questionnaire.[129] Egypt's involvement in the discussion is another example of how the League's structure and methods broadened the stage of international law. Egypt delivered a special report prepared by the Faculty of Science of the Egyptian University, which described the ways in which oil discharge had affected the marine environment of the Red Sea. It concluded, however, that "[n]o effect . . . on the pearl industry was noticed . . . ."[130] Italy also sent conclusions gathered from different inquiries carried out by leading Italian research institutes specialized in marine biology.[131]

With its unfamiliar mechanisms and authority, the League posed a threat with its new antipollution regulation, pushing several traditional and pro-industry players to hastily improve their current positions. With the possibility that separators could soon become compulsory, concern about the potential economic and industrial consequences was reignited. Suddenly, other *prior* legal arrangements did not seem as frightening as they had only a couple of years earlier, before the rise of the League. Concerned about future developments in international environmental law, the government of the Netherlands was suddenly willing to embrace the former international agreement that it

[128] For a discussion on the link between global (environmental) governance and information sharing, *see* Frank Biermann & Philipp Pattberg, *Global Environmental Governance: Taking Stock, Moving Forward*, 33 ANN. REV. ENVTL. RESOURCES 277 (2008).

[129] Summary of the Replies (Part II), *supra* note 87, at 29.

[130] *Id.* at 30.

[131] *Id.*

had completely ignored since the mid-1920s. In its reply to the League, the Dutch government stated, "however ... [that it was] prepared to accept the draft Washington Convention which contemplates a study of the question. Already the Government voluntarily applies the stipulations of this draft Convention."[132]

The same alarm can be found in the reply of the Free City of Danzig,[133] which perhaps tells the entire affair as a developing story. The government of Danzig, whose city was an important port city of the interwar period, was initially reluctant to support the suggested stricter international regulations. Originally, the government questioned whether the issue of pollution called for international regulation at all. However, as the discussion evolved, some of the players in Danzig began to understand which way the wind of international law was blowing – at least at this point in the discussion. Hence, despite its skepticism of the need for "radical measures," the government was "prepared to accede to any international agreement adopted ...."[134]

1.3.4 Finalizing the Antipollution Convention, and the Bitter End

Despite the pro-industry agenda of the committee of experts, and although many of the involved governments had much to lose if the demand to install separators eventually became an international regulation, the League and the Communications and Transit Organisation moved forward with the antipollution initiative. According to the Communications and Transit Organisation's explanations, it seemed that the intensive participation of a variety of states in the international process of inquiry and consultation – and the strong sense of international support for compulsory installation – had been a deciding factor.

In one of the organization's reports from autumn 1935, the detailed replies showed that "the chief maritime countries ... are, on the whole, against this remedy, so far as it involves the compulsory provision of

[132] *Id.* at 22.

[133] The Free City of Danzig (now Gdańsk) enjoyed a unique legal status during the interwar period. Its strong German affiliation and its history, together with the terms of Article 100 of the 1919 Treaty of Versailles, created its status as a semi-autonomous city-state that existed between 1920 and 1939. For a study of this complexity (which was published shortly after World War II), *see* John B. Mason, The Danzig Dilemma – A Study in Peacemaking by Compromise (1946).

[134] Summary of the Replies (Part II), *supra* note 87, at 31.

separators on existing ships." While on the other hand, the countries that supported taking such a step by means of international law were "those which possess no mercantile marine or a comparatively small one."[135]

Taking into account that the League only started to tackle the oil pollution problem in summer 1934 (when the government of the United Kingdom first addressed the Secretary-General in July) – and compared to other international initiatives, environmental and otherwise, of the interwar period – the fact that it took no more than a year to introduce a complete draft for an international convention should not be overlooked.[136] This final draft was based on major parts of the 1926 Washington Convention, as well as on the different replies by the states from around the world. The suggested 1935 antipollution convention was quite similar to the one that had been published back in 1926 under the auspices of the League (although it had never been ratified). Moreover, this time, the environmental agenda was clear and specific (with the obligation of separators), and it was discussed by the League and its bodies.

But then, the oil problem was suddenly left behind. Following the vibrant international discussion based on the questionnaire and the work of the committee of experts, the Convention against the Pollution of the Sea by Oil was never actually introduced. Somehow, the sense of enthusiasm and urgency had dissipated. No serious follow-up discussions on the 1935 antipollution convention were recorded. In the years that followed up until the League ceased to exist as an institution, the new convention – and the oil pollution problem – lost their place in the League's ongoing agenda and routine.

What were the reasons for this? Some might argue that throughout the interwar period, the League was occupied with far more acute problems and challenges than pollution, especially since the international community and collective security were hanging by a thread with the rise of Fascism and Ultra-Fascism in Europe and in Japan.[137] This likely had

[135] Communications and Transit Organisation, Pollution of the Sea by Oil, Report on the 2d Session of the Committee of Experts, Oct. 21–25, 1935, C.449.M.1935.VIII., LoN Archives, at 3.

[136] The whaling dilemma, for instance, became an ongoing discussion starting from the mid-1920s and remained an open issue for intensive legal deliberations throughout the 1930s; it included the introduction of two international conventions down the road.

[137] One of the sources that was published during the war specifically referred to the possible link between the deteriorating external geopolitical situation and the feasible future of the convention, as Europe and other parts of the world were headed toward another battlefield. According to this observation, in 1936, when the new antipollution

a lot to do with the history of the late interwar period, and yet this explanation cannot stand by itself. As the interwar environmental regime shows, until its very end as an institution, the League worked intensively to find solutions for many other concerns, such as sanitation and rural hygiene in Eastern Europe and East Asia; the whaling dilemma; and the issue of timber trade and related concerns of deforestation. All of these issues occupied the League during the late 1930s and on the cusp of World War II.

Hence, perhaps we should look for other acceptable reasons. It might be that the League's already very busy schedule and routine in the second half of the 1930s pushed some of these problems aside (although certainly not all of them). Perhaps other environmental concerns seemed to be more worrying and urgent.

According to the common procedure of interwar international law, a special international conference was supposed to be convened in order to finalize the antipollution convention and to introduce it for ratification by the states. This time, however, it would be done with much stronger international support and commitment, unlike the 1926 Washington Convention from ten years earlier. However, external politics beyond the environment, the oceans, migratory birds, and oil pollution penetrated the dome of Geneva and affected some of its tasks besides maintaining collective security and peacekeeping. Key maritime powers, such as Imperial Japan, (already Nazi) Germany, and (Fascist) Italy dramatically withdrew from League at that stage. Due to the turbulent geopolitical situation, the League's relevant bodies (primarily the committee of experts) no longer believed it would be possible or feasible to promote the convention. Chairman Grimshaw, although unhappy with the section on separators (which featured in the final draft), nevertheless conceded in a letter to one of his colleagues: "[W]e apparently must take it as settled that there can be no International Conference before 1937, if the League . . . is in existence then."[138]

However, political instability did not halt the diplomatic activity aimed at the realizing the antipollution convention, and at putting an end to the oil pollution problem in the sea. In a letter from summer 1937 addressed to Grimshaw, it was mentioned that representatives of Canada, the

convention was handed in to the League's Secretariat, the League was still "brooding over the question [the antipollution convention], but worse things were in store for the League of Nations and no further word has been heard on oil pollution." HAYDEN, *supra* note 11, at 13.

[138] Letter by Grimshaw to Tombs, Apr. 21, 1936, LoN Archives, 50/18544/2625.

United States, and the Union of South Africa were still working on the possibility of organizing the conference, at which the new achievement of the League's environmental diplomacy could be publicly introduced. These representatives had maintained their belief in interwar international law and were "*anxious* that a convention should be concluded on this subject."[139]

But it seems that the League was on a course of decline as 1938 and 1939 approached. Some states were turning away from the League and its new mode of international governance, and retreating to mechanisms and frameworks that had preceded the League: more "traditional" systems or networks of bilateral mutual agreements and transnational arrangements. At this point, France, for instance, suggested an almost copy-paste bilateral or multilateral agreement between different states without the institutional framework of the League.[140]

And then, in the late summer of 1939, war arrived and put an end to this international collaboration that was so close to imposing a new and relatively progressive environmental regime on a reluctant industry in order to save the birds, the sea, and the shore.

1.4 Conclusion: Pollution, Seas, and the post-1945 Period – from Geneva to Stockholm and Back Again

As with other challenges handled by the League, World War II might have terminated the existence of the League as an institution, but it did not halt the course of environmental history. The League's role – and influence – in legal and other issues did not simply vanish.

As I briefly described in the introduction, some scholars have placed the pollution problem as a clear post–World War II issue. According to such descriptions, "public interest in the environment" got stronger, and coastal states' concerns about "increasing ship-source marine pollution and oil spills"[141] started to be heard after World War II. Edgar Gold has argued that the connection between incidents involving tankers and oil spills in environmentally or economically sensitive areas emerged[142] only in that period. However, the interwar antipollution campaign shows that the 1940s, and especially the 1950s, should be understood as bearing

139 Letter by Tombs to Grimshaw, Aug. 8, 1937, LoN Archives, 50/18544/2625 (emphasis added).

140 *See*, PRITCHARD, *supra* note 24, at 64–70; Wöbse, *supra* note 20, at 535.

141 Anayanova, *supra* note 14, at 29.

142 GOLD, *supra* note 15.

some connection to the League's effort, even if one believes that these later developments were not necessarily a direct continuation of the interwar period.

Like other environmental campaigns of the interwar period, the oil pollution campaign saw the emergence of certain technological developments, some of which, it could be argued, were responsible for the problem of pollution in the first place. In terms of periodization, the League was established at a time when new, faster ships that were equipped with different technical improvements began to change marine transportation and worsened the oil pollution problem as a result. Therefore, the role of the League should not be skipped in the evolutionary process of international environmental law. Overlooking the interwar period is not only unjustified in terms of environmental history, but could also lead to inaccuracies, to say the least.

This trend in scholarship not only means that a whole chapter in the evolution of environmental history is incomplete, but also that certain milestones in the genealogy of the international regulation of marine environment pollution are missing. The interwar period stands right between the Washington Convention of 1926 and much later legal arrangements, such as the Declaration on the Human Environment (Stockholm Declaration) of 1972, or transnational regional legal agreements – such as the Convention on the Protection of the Marine Environment of the Baltic Sea Area of 1992, and the parallel 1992 Convention for the Protection of the Marine Environment of the North-East Atlantic. The polluter-pays concept, for instance, was one of the principles at the heart of the Baltic Sea Area Convention.[143] This legal regime, which was based on tort law mechanisms and placed liability on shipowners, was already being discussed during the interwar period.[144] As this chapter has explored, important environmental concerns of the 1920s and 1930s took their place alongside other initiatives that occupied the League during this time.

Our understanding of the developing antipollution regime and the layered structure of international law would not be complete without an assessment of the interwar period. After all, it was during this period that, under the auspices of the League, mechanisms aimed at solving concerns regarding the transportation of oil and oil incidents were first introduced. The international nature of the problem and its effects upon nature and

[143] The Baltic Sea Area Convention was also known as the Helsinki Convention.

[144] See my discussion in Section 1.2.1 above.

communities brought together different bodies, all of whom were concerned about the deteriorating situation. The sea became a particular and turbulent site of common problems and international law at the same time.

The migratory nature and behavior of wild birds added an international dimension to the ongoing discussion, and made these creatures obvious subjects for international law. Migrating species of birds such as Audubon's Shearwater or Waxwings were seen as international creatures because they challenged the notion and capability of national or domestic sovereignty. Any measure taken by one state, progressive as it might be, could not be enough to solve the threats to the survival of birds or to prevent drifting oil from crossing borders, territories, and sovereignties. Therefore, the international nature of different species of birds invited the League to step in as a relevant power.

Ultimately, the League's actions in this regard were a disappointing failure. This study does not try to deny either the historical facts, or the significance of these legal and diplomatic discussions. As Ekaterina Anyanova, Edward Salter, and John Ford have argued, we can indeed trace a "comprehensive regulatory regime" on the prevention of marine oil pollution, and particularly oil spills from ships, however much earlier than the period to which these scholars refer. This regime, they claim, developed in international law "in the course of time."[145] These were important bricks that the League introduced and used to build antipollution regulation in the second half of the twentieth century (and, in some cases, also in the early twenty-first century). However, the role of the League continues to be overlooked in the literature. Some of the examples of the (more successful) post–World War II antipollution period show that several central issues on which the League focused prevailed and reappeared. Further studies into the primary sources would be better able to decide whether or not these issues continued, or were influenced by, the League's campaign.

As briefly mentioned earlier, the Helsinki Convention of 1992 once again highlighted the mechanisms of legal liability that were introduced during the interwar period. More generally, Principle 7 of the Stockholm Declaration,[146] which was the first overall declaration that covered a broad variety of issues relating to the responsibility of humankind for

[145] Anyanova, *supra* note 14, at 31; Edward Salter & John Ford, *Holistic Environmental Assessment and Offshore Oil Field Exploration and Production*, 42 MARINE POLLUTION BULL. 45, 49–50 (2001).

[146] The Declaration of the United Nations Conference on the Human Environment, 1972.

the environment, echoed legal terms that were used by the League. Principle 7 stated that "States shall take all possible steps to prevent pollution of the seas by substances that are liable to create hazards to human health, to harm living resources and marine life, to damage . . . or to interfere with other legitimate uses of the sea." This was basically a repetition of the wording that had appeared in the 1935 antipollution convention. Article II of the League's convention demanded that the "contracting Governments agree to take the necessary measures to ensure that their ... vessels shall take every possible precaution to prevent oil pollution."

As a matter of fact, the League's antipollution agenda, together with its legal ammunition, did not vanish when the League dissolved. Immediately after World War II, the Transport and Communication Commission (this time of the League's successor, the United Nations) reintroduced the concern about oil pollution of the seas in another ongoing international discussion.

Once again, the issue was revived. Reports signed by experts piled up (only this time in New York City and not in Geneva), and devoted environmental NGOs restarted their international advocacy. And, indeed, almost fifteen years later than the League was hoping for, the international conference on the issue of oil pollution of the sea finally convened. The British took the lead once more, since the British section of the International Committee for Bird Preservation had set up the independent Advisory Committee on Oil Pollution of the Sea[147] in the early 1950s. In 1953, this Advisory Committee had organized an international conference in London as a basic structure for the international network of non-state organizations working for the protection of birds. This time, without the distraction of a global war, the official diplomatic follow-up was not so late: in 1954, the United Kingdom convened an intergovernmental conference of forty-two nations.[148] On May 12, 1954, the different states agreed on the International Convention for the Prevention of Pollution of the Sea by Oil (OILPOL), which came into force four years later, in 1958.[149]

[147] Phyllis Barclay-Smith, *Oil Pollution of the Sea*, 7 BULL. INT'L COMMITTEE FOR BIRDS PRESERVATION 51 (1958).

[148] Indeed, this international cooperation was not under the auspices of the United Nations, but it gathered states that were responsible for 95 percent of the global shipping tonnage (*see* Wöbse, *supra* note 20, at 535).

[149] International Convention for the Prevention of Pollution of the Sea by Oil, 1954, The Center for International Earth Science Information Network (CIESIN), Earth Institute, Columbia University, http://sedac.ciesin.org/entri/texts/pollution.of.sea.by.oil.1954.html.

Unfortunately, the progressive provisions that the League had advanced in the mid-1930s, primarily the compulsory separators, were now replaced, much to the satisfaction of the shipping industry. The convention, however, returned to the safety of the restricted zone as a legal-environmental solution.

It should also be noted that Article 24 of the Geneva Convention on the High Seas[150] stipulated the obligation of states to draft national legislation on pollution prevention for ships, pipelines or seabed activities. Moreover, compared to the detailed discussions on specific sections of the antipollution convention during the League's period, the "umbrella convention" of the United Nations Convention on the Law of the Sea (UNCLOS), adopted on December 10, 1982[151] did not include detailed rules for the protection of the marine environment, only general provisions. These rules, proclaimed UNCLOS, would be implemented by means of "future regulations" of international law.[152] In other words, this example shows that the way in which the League dealt with the problem of oil pollution was, at least to a certain extent, more direct and explicit than later legal-environmental arrangements.

However, oil pollution, together with its tragic outcomes, was still on the global public agenda throughout the second half of the twentieth century.[153] Pollution of the sea[154] was still an urgent environmental concern, as it had been in the interwar period. All too often, media coverage of environmental disasters caused by oil discharge, which

[150] Convention on the High Seas, 1958. United Nations, Treaty Series, Vol. 450. P. 11, p. 82.

[151] And came into force on November 16, 1994.

[152] *See*, for instance, Ling Zhu, *Do We Need a Global Organization for the Protection of the Marine Environment*, *in* INTERNATIONAL MARITIME ORGANIZATIONS AND THEIR CONTRIBUTION TOWARDS A SUSTAINABLE MARINE DEVELOPMENT 157 (Peter Ehlers & Rainer Lagoni eds., 2006). Moreover, unlike the League's intricate attempts to create detailed legal definitions, UNCLOS provisions for maritime protection (which are contained in Part XII of the convention) were rather general, though they remain important globally today. The convention stipulates the general obligation of states to protect the marine and coastal environment and its resources (Article 192). Article 193, however, grants states the right to develop *their* natural resources (under the consideration of their natural environmental policy), and also stresses their duty to protect and preserve the marine environment. (However, it should be noted that the general provisions of Articles 192 and 194, which deal with the measures to prevent, reduce, and control pollution of the marine environment, are considered to be part of international customary law.)

[153] And, unfortunately, also at the dawn of the twenty-first century. For a discussion on the case of the BP spill in the Gulf of Mexico in 2008, *see* David Bond, *The Science of Catastrophe: Making Sense of the BP Oil Spill*, 3(1) ANTHROPOLOGY NOW 36 (2011).

[154] Especially from sunk ships and vessels.

severely affected marine life and creatures that lived on shore (mostly birds),[155] revived the call for tighter antipollution regulation and a stricter environmental regime. During the second half of the century, by which time the League had become a historical memory, NGOs – such as the RSPB, and a new and rather effective organization in town, Greenpeace[156] – played a "significant role in raising the salience of oil pollution, widening support, and pressuring lawmakers."[157]

To conclude, it seems that the current environmental regime still lacks strict and precise legal protection from oil pollution of the seas. In light of this, is it really fair to say that the League's legal endeavors "withered"?[158] In terms of legal history, the picture might be more complex. The central aim – a binding legal document that would mark a turning point in the evolution of environmental marine regulations – had failed, and the League ceased to exist before it could see its effort translated into any later legal arrangement. However, the ways in which the League discussed notions and solutions, which were close to being fulfilled in terms of international law, do deserve our attention.

The intensive interwar discussion surrounding the oil pollution problem serves as a vehicle with which one might journey into the past of modern environmentalism. First, this discussion shows that the reason why the oil pollution crisis of our time became an international issue is because it *was* already an issue of international law

155 Such as in the famous cases of the supertanker SS Torrey Canyon off the southwest coast of the United Kingdom in 1967, with an estimated 25–36 million gallons of crude oil spilled; Ixtoc 1 Oil Well (in the Bay of Campeche, Mexico) of 1979 with no less than 140 million gallons spilled; and the Castillo de Bellver (off Saldanha Bay, South Africa) of 1983, with 78.5 million gallons spilled. These and many other disasters that had a huge impact on birds and the marine environment, and which were caused by the discharge of oil or sinking ships, had an international legal and environmental legacy.

Moreover, one of the most famous illustrations of the Gulf War of 1991 was the devastating environmental outcomes of the oil spill – one of the largest spills in history – that occurred during this crisis. The pictures of dying, poisoned creatures on and near the shores of the Persian Gulf, and particularly those of dead cormorants and other birds saturated with thick black oil, disturbed the public. *See* Hosny Khordagui and Dhari Al-Ajmi, *Environmental Impact of the Gulf War: An Integrated Preliminary Assessment*, 17 ENVTL. MGMT. 557 (1993).

156 For a study on the rise of Greenpeace *see, e.g.*, John-Henry Harter, *Environmental Justice for Whom? Class, New Social Movements, and the Environment: A Case Study of Greenpeace Canada, 1971–2000*, 54 LABOUR / LE TRAVAIL 83 (2004).

157 Ronald Mitchell, *International Oil Pollution of the Oceans*, *in* INSTITUTIONS FOR THE EARTH: SOURCES OF EFFECTIVE INTERNATIONAL ENVIRONMENTAL PROTECTION 241 (Peter M. Hass, Robert O. Keohane & Marc A. Levy eds., 1993).

158 Wöbse, *supra* note 20, at 536.

during the 1920s and 1930s. As my examples from the many different agreements of the second half of the twentieth century show, at least some of the legal terms can be understood or interpreted either as an extension of, or influenced by, the League's endeavors to save the sea and its creatures. And second, the interwar pollution discussion challenges the common narrative of early environmentalism. The League's antipollution campaign reveals that early international environmental matters were *not* issues of Western empires and colonial powers alone, as mainstream environmental historiography often tells us,[159] but involved a variety of different states and bodies. These new players in the game of international law included states that were not considered to be central political powers of that time (such as Canada and Spain) and who took advantage of the new institutional opportunities the League had to offer, as well as NGOs from different states that identified this as a propitious time to advocate for their own conservationist agenda by using the League's procedures. The test case of the antipollution campaign serves as an example of an almost "united" environmental move from below. The original initiative started its journey through the grassroots agenda of NGOs, where it managed to find its way to the highest circles of institutional international law – all the while overcoming national political barriers and challenging conventional international patterns of state-to-state frameworks. Along the way, as League and interwar international law began to focus on the problem, certain traditional and maritime powers attempted to bury this call and to fight against solutions they thought would jeopardize their industrial and economic interests, and put unbearable technical and financial burdens on their shipping industries. Finally, although this convention ended as a failure in terms of applicable law, it nevertheless showed how the League enabled and practiced a democratic, open, and pluralistic process of crafting international (environmental) law.

Moreover, it is quite impressive that so many states, not to mention the League itself, were able to finalize a legal agreement aimed at protecting birds, while at the same time dealing with serious challenges that threatened collective security and stability in the 1930s.

[159] *See, e.g.*, ADAM, *supra* note 13; Mario Prost & Yoriko Otomo, *British Influences on International Environmental Law: The Case of Wildlife Conservation*, *in* BRITISH INFLUENCES ON INTERNATIONAL LAW: 1915–2015, 192, (Robert McCorquodale & Jean-Pierre Gauci eds., 2016); RICHARD H. GROVE, GREEN IMPERIALISM: COLONIAL EXPANSION, TROPICAL ISLAND EDENS AND THE ORIGINS OF ENVIRONMENTALISM, 1600–1860 (1996).

Taken together, the League's environmental and legal reflections throughout the antipollution campaign tell a story of environmental history with its own lessons to offer. Indeed, the bodies that chose to side with the League in the 1920s and 1930s are perhaps different from those who have played a role in recent (and current) environmental controversies in the international arena. And yet many of the same tensions remain: a reluctant industry that continues to oppose environmental campaigns that threaten its interests; states that refuse to accept or cooperate with initiatives of non-state actors in the international sphere; deteriorating nature; and devoted civil-society organizations and visionary dreamers that are quick to recognize new possibilities offered by the institutional framework and the formative period of the League.

2

The League of Nations and the Whaling Dilemma

> We think that in this way the League of Nations would be able, in a relatively short space of time, to solve one of the greatest problems for the future of humanity and achieve, in this respect, the noble aim for which it was created.[1]

2.1 Sea of Whales

2.1.1 Introduction

During the last week of January 1927, the Committee of Experts for the Progressive Codification of International Law, one of the special committees under the auspices of the League of Nations, sent a detailed memorandum to the headquarters in Geneva. After an extensive process of back and forth replies and suggestions between the League and different states (members of the League and nonmembers alike, as well as some other surprising bodies who showed an interest including several unique organizations, professional unions, and research institutions), the Committee approached the General Secretariat of the League with a list of measures that needed be taken as soon as possible in order to solve "one of the greatest problems" threatening mankind and its prosperity.

With interwar Europe, and many other parts of the world in the 1920s, facing acute and troubling concerns, such a phrase could refer to any number of issues – issues that might have arisen while redrawing European borders, or while supervising the implementation of one of the many disarmament agreements that postdated the bloody battles of World War I, or perhaps while handling the self-determination agendas

[1] Report by the Committee of Experts for the Progressive Codification of International Law. Received in the registry of the League of Nations on Jan. 1, 1927, League of Nations Archives [hereinafter LoN Archives], 19/55517/47284 (it should be noted that the Report referred to the problem of whaling).

of different minorities around the world.[2] However, this Committee, whose final report concludes with the optimistic quotation provided above, was a special (international) committee of diplomats and jurists that had dedicated its attention to the threat of extinction of whales at the beginning of the twentieth century. This Committee viewed the whale issue as an urgent and troubling problem the international community – and international law in particular – needed to face as soon as possible.

As I will argue in the following chapter, the study of the whaling dilemma of the 1920s and 1930s emphasizes both the humanitarian drive of the League, and its enthusiastic approach to issues and problems that seemed – at least to some statesmen and diplomats who preceded the rise of the League – to be completely beyond its jurisdiction, its original goals, and its authority. Numerous reports reveal the League's deepening involvement in such issues, including the threat to different species of whale, such as baleen, right, and gray whales. These reports express the League's belief that international law held the power and ability to fight the danger posed by extinction and to protect valuable parts of nature. The League served as a forum that integrated diverse and rival considerations simultaneously, such as international goodwill,[3] scientific expertise, international governance, commercial and industrial interests, environmental concerns, and pioneering notions of international legal authority and collaboration.

[2] Two other broader, classical and familiar accounts of the general history of the League of Nations during its two decades of existence are ELMER BENDINER, A TIME OF ANGELS: THE TRAGICOMIC HISTORY OF THE LEAGUE OF NATIONS (1975); and GEORGE SCOTT, THE RISE AND FALL OF THE LEAGUE OF NATIONS (1973; U.S. ed., 1974). Other important surveys are F. S. NORTHEDGE, THE LEAGUE OF NATIONS: ITS LIFE AND TIMES: 1920–1946 (1986), and John Mearsheimer's *The False Promise of International Institutions*, 19(3) INT'L SECURITY 5 (1994). For different examples of the humanitarian issues and other social aims and problems handled by the League *see*, among others, THE LEAGUE OF NATIONS' WORK ON SOCIAL ISSUES: VISIONS, ENDEAVOURS AND EXPERIMENTS (Magaly Rodríguez García, Davide Rodogno & Liat Kozma eds., 2016).

[3] IRIS BOROWY, COMING TO TERMS WITH WORLD HEALTH: THE LEAGUE OF NATIONS HEALTH ORGANISATION 1921–1946 (2009); STEPHANIE LIMONCELLI, THE POLITICS OF TRAFFICKING: THE FIRST INTERNATIONAL MOVEMENT TO COMBAT THE SEXUAL EXPLOITATION OF WOMEN (2010); Keith David Watenpaugh, *"A Pious Wish Devoid of all Practicability": Interwar Humanitarianism, the League of Nations and the Rescue of Trafficked Women and Children in the Eastern Mediterranean, 1920–1927*, 115 AMERICAN HISTORICAL REVIEW 1315 (2010); JEAN ALLAIN, THE SLAVERY CONVENTIONS: THE TRAVAUX PRÉPARATOIRES OF THE 1926 LEAGUE OF NATIONS CONVENTION AND THE 1956 UNITED NATIONS CONVENTION 31 (2008).

For those studying the League's environmental regime, the scope of the actors and forces that were involved in this cooperation extends well beyond "familiar" European borders and into the international arena. I will present and analyze campaigns and concerns that involved nations from (almost) every continent,[4] commercial corporations, early and emerging civil society organizations, and different bodies and departments of the League itself. As an international institution, the League was dealing with environmental dilemmas as they unfolded.

The seas were open to all. Although only a relatively small number of states took part in the intensifying practice of whaling, the urgent need for a legal regime that would regulate the different powers and their harvests had been discussed by different forums within the League, at conferences and special commissions. Rapidly developing exploitation of the treasures of the sea, as the League referred to it when it started to tackle the issue, caused fears of impending disaster. Thus, a variety of actors emphasized the necessity of law – any kind of law – and of professional diplomatic efforts, legal mechanisms, and proper solutions.

During the interwar period, this special committee of the League (followed by other bodies and agencies) addressed particular questions on international law, sovereignty, industrial needs, and nature. Although the committee was not originally created to review the possibility of establishing an international regulation for whaling, it was not long before a unique mode of operation and of international law "on-the-move" emerged – the dynamics of which led the Committee on an intensive journey toward what would become the first ever international whaling law. Experts who were involved were either invited during the League's ongoing discussions to contribute from their scientific knowledge and fields of expertise,[5] or were sent as delegates by various states; most expressed deep concern over the danger of an impending whale extinction. Some shared surprising, progressive observations of the problem and sketched pioneering drafts for a new international whaling law.

This chapter examines the interwar deliberations and the obstacles the League faced upon launching a fierce and intensive environmental, economic, political, and legal campaign. Besides the special Committee of Experts, other bodies and actors – including old empires, new

[4] In the case of the problem of whaling, however, attention was mostly given to the least national place on earth: the seas around Antarctica. *See* William Cronon's introduction to KURKPATRICK DORSEY, WHALES AND NATIONS: ENVIRONMENTAL DIPLOMACY ON THE HIGH SEAS, xix (2013).

[5] Among them were legal scholars, economists, and other professional experts.

emerging states, and independent organizations with their own agendas – became involved in dilemmas that brought to the fore early environmental issues, powerful commercial and industrial interests, and the increasing importance of scientific expertise. The chapter will explore the ways in which diplomacy and international cooperation were monitored by certain parts of the League, as well as the effort it dedicated to securing the survival of whales on the high seas by legal mechanisms. This chapter will also assess the role of the League and its contribution to the legal foundations of international ocean governance in general, and to the development and evolution of international whaling regulation in particular. To do so, I will use a timeline that tracks both the period before the League was established in 1919, and the period following its dissolution in the aftermath of World War II, when it was replaced by the new organization of the United Nations.

In order to place the story of whales and the League in a coherent context, I will open with a historical background. This section will include periodization, which will shed light on the interwar period as part of a broader timeline of the history of whaling and internationalism, alongside a general outline of the course of events.

Then, I will address the main historical narrative of the period under examination, which serves as the center of the study. As the historical narrative unfolds, I will focus on the role of the Committee of Experts for the Progressive Codification of International Law (hereafter referred to as "the Codification Committee") as a leader in intensive international discussions on the whaling problem, starting from the mid-1920s and throughout the 1930s. In this central section, I will analyze the various ways in which the Codification Committee, and different parts of the League, interacted with multiple players engaged in the battle on whaling: interwar-period powers and states; powerful and aggressive industries that feared any kind of external legal obligation or constraints on their economic and commercial activities; and activist NGOs, devoted scientists, and enthusiastic scientific associations who were concerned about the potential destruction of whale species at the hands of dramatic technological developments in the field of modern whaling. Importantly, I will also examine the interactions within the League itself, as a multilayered institution with its own routine, mechanisms, agenda, and interests in certain cases, such as that of whaling.

I will trace the landmark events throughout the complex interwar saga of trying to create international whaling law. These markers will draw on the international correspondence and interactions between bodies of the

League and other political, scientific, and commercial centers. The story is illustrated by numerous sources: the dozens of replies (including stern warnings) that were sent to the League on this issue; special reports made by and for the Codification Committee during its work; drafts of innovative international conventions that proposed some surprising solutions, and which were discussed and distributed across the (interwar) world; as well as internal negotiations and various unpublished documents that shed new light on the vibrant whaling discussion.

As the chapter weaves together the chain of events, challenges, and entanglements that took place during this complex period, I will also add a final summary of several different conclusions, following the historical narrative.

Although there is vast scholarship on the history of whaling, almost all of these studies tend either to overlook or to dismiss the role of the League. Mario Prost and Yoriko Otomo, for instance, said that there is "a wealth of scholarship on this topic [the conservation of whales], but . . . it is beyond the scope of this chapter to canvass the wide-ranging discussions on cetacean conservation."[6] Likewise, Gerry J. Nagtzaam, a historian of whaling diplomacy, almost completely omits the era of the League and its involvement in the issue of whaling, merely observing that "prior to the establishment of the IWC [International Whaling Committee] in the post-World War II period, there were earlier attempts to create a global whaling regime. The effort, however, was hampered by a lack of commitment from the relevant parties, despite ample long-term economic imperatives to do so."[7] Other scholars, such as Peter J. Stoett[8] or Anthony D'Amato and Sudhir K. Chopra,[9] view the early 1930s as the beginning of a turning point, when whaling nations began to recognize the need to regulate catching whales to prevent species extinction. However, they show very little interest in exploring the history during the "four years of negotiations between the states attached to the League of Nations . . . ."[10]

[6] See note 52 (at 206–07) in Mario Prost & Yoriko Otomo, *British Influences on International Environmental Law: The Case of Wildlife Conservation*, *in* BRITISH INFLUENCES ON INTERNATIONAL LAW: 1915–2015, 192, (Robert McCorquodale & Jean-Pierre Gauci eds., 2016).

[7] Gerry J. Nagtzaam, *The International Whaling Commission and the Elusive Great White Whale of Preservationism*, 33 WILLIAM & MARY ENVTL. L. & POL'Y REV. 375, 393 (2009).

[8] PETER J. STOETT, THE INTERNATIONAL POLITICS OF WHALING 57 (1997).

[9] Anthony D'Amato & Sudhir K. Chopra, *Whales: Their Emerging Right to Life*, 85 AM. J. INT'L L. 21 (1991).

[10] Nagtzaam, *supra* note 7, at 393. *See* also D'Amato & Chopra, *supra* note 9, at 30; and STOETT, *supra* note 8, at 57. Moreover, in his overview of the environmental history of the

As I will show later on, although some of these scholars do deal (however briefly) with the whaling problem during the 1920s and 1930s, they rather choose to assert that the League's shortcomings as an international institution had much to do with the failures of its evolving whaling regime. Perhaps, with regard to the League's success on the ground, these assertions are correct. However, a recent study of the modern history of whaling and international law suggests that even current international arrangements supervised by the United Nations are sometimes ineffective, largely due to a "lack of compliance and enforceability."[11] And yet scholars do not dismiss this period, despite its failures. Although this study does not aim to focus on the core issues of international legal studies of compliance and enforceability per se, I will nevertheless address (in the conclusion) some of the possible reasons why most of the legal solutions introduced by the League eventually failed or were not enforced. Here, I will also offer a new perspective on the influence of the League's involvement in the whaling dilemma on whaling regulations after 1945. I will also try to explain why some of these solutions were not ultimately accepted as binding international law.

Other chapters in this study look at the various ways in which the League addressed environmental concerns and pursued environmental goals. Here, I will show that the League went to great lengths to ensure the survival of whales on the high seas, through careful diplomacy and the monitoring of international cooperation efforts. What the biologist Garrett Hardin referred to in 1968 as "the tragedy of the commons"[12] was already a well-known and apt description of the reality of the creatures of the sea,[13] and the League and its organs were deeply involved in this international marine and legal dilemma. As I will discuss, the question of whaling, whales, and international law out in the open seas actually became one of the central, ongoing issues tackled by the League in the second half of the 1920s and throughout the 1930s. As a matter of fact, the League struggled with the dilemma until its last moments, a few months before Hitler's divisions would storm Poland.

twentieth century, stretching over almost 400 pages, J. R. McNeill mentions the League of Nations no more than once: in his discussion on whaling and fishing. See page 242 in J. R. McNeill, Something New Under the Sun: An Environmental History of the Twentieth-Century World (2000).

11 Cameron Jefferies, Mammal Conservation and the Law of the Sea, xx (2016).

12 Garrett Hardin, *The Tragedy of the Commons*, 162 Sci. 1243 (1968).

13 Dorsey, *supra* note 4, at xi (2013).

The League's long deliberations, transnational correspondences, scientific observations, legal discussions, and multinational negotiations highlight dilemmas that point to tensions between the scope of international law and international regulation of the sea on the one hand, and between international law and the sovereignty of nations on the other hand. It is clear that the League was facing a very pressing problem: the decrease of marine life and animals in general, and endangered whale species in particular. It was an issue upon which the League spent an enormous amount of time and diplomatic energy and deployed vast numbers of personnel. The League played a central role in drawing global attention to the problem, at a time when other parties and organizations stubbornly advocated against this cause.

I will reveal the complex historical course of the dilemma as it was discussed by different bodies under the auspices of the League, as well as between the League and external organizations that were involved in the issue based on different (and in many cases also conflicting) interests. In fact, the future of the whale and the threats to its survival – as outlined by many scientists and agents involved in the ongoing debate – actually became part of a broader discussion on national sovereignty versus international (environmental) regulation. Some of the states that participated in the interwar discussion used the whaling problem as a platform for legal deliberations, to tackle fundamental questions of international law and sovereignty.

Besides being a challenging environmental dilemma for global diplomacy and evolving international law, the whaling problem also served as the foundation for emerging institutionalized international law. As other historians have shown, early international environmental law existed well before the establishment of the League;[14] however, the framework of the League's organs, such as the Assembly, the Council, different special technical committees, and so on was rather new and full of anticipation, not only when it came to the problem of whales. In that sense, the League changed environmental law. The whaling problem[15] gained much of its intensity and energy during the interwar period *as an outcome* of the structure and diplomatic routine of the League as an institution. The League's move from ad hoc initiatives,

[14] *See*, among others, David Frank et al., *The Rationalization and Organization of Nature in World Culture, in* CONSTRUCTING WORLD CULTURE 82 (John Boli & George M. Thomas eds., 1999).

[15] Like other problems and challenges that were tackled by the League and its institutional structure.

which characterized earlier experiences in international environmental law, to a "constant" or prevailing diplomatic agenda, was more than just a technical shift. Communicating from its headquarters in the new capital by Lake Geneva,[16] the League's regime governed by transparency, fixed procedures, and a firm schedule, all of which were reflected in the general institutional mechanisms of the League.

The role of scientific expertise within the world of early international law has been exemplified in different studies,[17] and I will show that it can be viewed throughout the League's campaign for and against whaling regulation. However, in the context of environmental concerns, this scientific discourse played a central role in the vast attention the issue began to receive in the mid-1920s.

Moreover, the League proved to be "a welcome venue for environmental NGOs"[18] and other kinds of independent organizations[19] trying to play a part – and to secure their interests and agendas at the same time – by turning to the League and its mechanisms in order to promote their agendas.

The picture that is revealed as we remove the curtain includes different organizations, institutions, and interest groups, all playing some part in the fierce battle over whaling. Some states favored the progressive initiative that the League promoted, while others were reluctant, and some rejected it completely. Some NGOs and independent actors worked enthusiastically for the sake of saving the whale, while other transnational consortiums moved to secure industrial interests. And certain scientists and dedicated visionaries frequently acted on their own behalf and on conservationists' agendas, sometimes in ways that contradicted, or even

16 For an interpretation on the unique features of interwar Geneva, including religious ones, *see* Susan Pedersen, *Back to the League of Nations*, 112 AM. HIST. REV. 1091, 1112 (2007).

17 Liat Kozma, *The League of Nations and the Debate over Cannabis Prohibition*, 9 HIST. COMPASS 61, 63–64 (2011); Magaly Rodríguez García, *Child Slavery, Sex Trafficking or Domestic Work? The League of Nations and Its Analysis of the Mui Tsai System*, *in* TOWARDS A GLOBAL HISTORY OF DOMESTIC AND CAREGIVING WORKERS 428 (Dirk Hoerder et al. eds., 2015).

18 Anna-Katharina Wöbse, *Oil on Troubled Water? Environmental Diplomacy in the League of Nations*, 32 DIPLOMATIC HIST. 519, 522 (2008).

19 Such as commercial, industrial, and economic organizations with common interests and international cooperation. *See*, for instance, the leading role – as I will discuss later on – of the Copenhagen Council, an international consortium that had a direct interest in the whaling industry. Based on a specific resolution of the League Assembly in January 1928, the Copenhagen Council became a formal player in the negotiations and discussions on whaling regulation.

undermined, "their" nation's interests. We should also pay attention to the fact that the League itself was not, of course, a homogeneous body. In some instances, the Codification Committee drove the agenda; in other cases, the League's Council, or the Assembly (the more general forum of the League), was at the center of negotiations. At various times, each of these organs offered different perspectives and positions on both international law as a whole, and global whaling regulations in particular. The wide variety of actors involved had a direct effect on how the question of whales and whaling unfolded between the League and other parts of the world.

The history of international law and diplomacy, particularly during this new and unfamiliar kind of institutionalized international forum, is, in many aspects, centered on the League of Nations. It was in Geneva, as Susan Pedersen stated nearly a decade ago, that internationalism was enacted, institutionalized, and performed.[20] As this chapter will elaborate, the question of whaling became, from its very first moments, a fierce battlefield for different and unfamiliar players, traditional and imperial powers alongside emerging states, all wishing to be part of the creation of international law. All were looking at the League – some with a sense of great hope, but some with fear and growing dissatisfaction – as it tried to establish an internationally binding agreement on whaling that adequately represented different perspectives, interests, and perceptions of environmental issues, commercial motives, and international law all together. In recent years, scholars engaged in studies on the League have identified and compared its tensions, characteristics, and modes of operation, which have appeared in hundreds of documents from the League's archives. As such, the negotiations on international whaling law demonstrate the many intersections and interactions between individuals and organizations in the midst of early institutionalized international law. They highlight the rise of information sharing as a leading method of discussing and practicing diplomacy during the first half of the twentieth century. They reveal the tensions between state sovereignty and emerging abstract (and ambitious) international authority and governance. Finally, they underscore the leading role of scientific expertise as one of the League's most important means of enhancing (and perhaps even creating) the basis for its legal legitimacy in a world that was not yet familiar with this kind of superstate institute.

[20] Pedersen, *supra* note 16, at 1112.

The history of international law, and the environmental – as well as commercial – problem of the dwindling whale population began at the start of the twentieth century when people first became aware of the severe condition of whale populations,[21] prompting discussions about the need for worldwide regulation of the whaling industry. This was many years before the League was established in 1919, or its actions in the 1920s and the 1930s. However, we cannot deny that the League played a central role in how the whaling question developed in the first half of the new century; nor can we deny its influence on future international legal arrangements relating to whaling in the second half of the century and beyond. An honest account of legal history must necessarily evaluate the League based on both its achievements and its failures. In the case of whaling law, a study of the League's initiatives and its outcomes shows that most did not make it. However, I do not believe that determining the *immediate* success of these efforts is the only relevant criterion; especially from a legal history perspective that looks at the layers that create legal arrangements in the long run. The fact is that the League (and many states – members and nonmembers alike) invested huge amounts of time, resources, and diplomatic effort into this issue. In this way, the whaling problem became a continuous process of trying to shape international law, evolving diplomacy, and competing international relations in conjunction with environmental concerns, agendas of conservation and nature protection, and also of industrial and commercial interests. This mix of interests still colors many of the current environmental entanglements of the twenty-first century, and the ways with which earlier diplomacy and international law tried to deal with them are worth our attention.

Moreover, some of the ideas that the League raised did not manage to find their way into the final, legally binding and official documents it produced – at least not during its lifetime. As the evolutionary history and genealogy of (international) law – and environmental history – tend to show, some of these innovative ideas, such as restricted areas for whaling, seasonal moratoria, and defending either certain whale species or specific populations (females or calves), were ahead of their time. The diplomatic microcosms of the League stood, as I understand it, as an early experimental stage for pioneering ideas and mechanisms. Some of these were discussed, and nothing more; some were very close to being accepted and formulated into legal articles; and some – unfortunately

[21] Or at least of some whale species.

for certain species of whales – had to "stand in line" and wait their turn in the course of legal-environmental history. One way or another, the League served as a vibrant diplomatic laboratory for discussing, deliberating over, and consulting certain environmental ideas and fears that concerned parts of the interwar world. At least some of this interwar period has profound implications, and even lessons, for our twenty-first century world's pressing global environmental challenges.

2.1.2 General Timeline and Outline

This chapter will cover the turbulent environment in which international law had to operate in order to tackle the overexploitation of whales and to ensure their survival.

The chapter begins with the launch on March 22, 1926 of the Codification Committee's first special questionnaire. This legal document addressed issues focusing on various realms of international law. Question No. 7 in particular related to different options for "exploitation of the products of the sea," (in the words of the Codification Committee), and also to the future of a (possible) worldwide whaling regulation. I will first describe the legal-history context and backdrop of the Codification Committee, and the League's reasons for assembling it in the first place. Then, I will go on to explain the sources of the questionnaire, as well as its original intentions. Surprisingly, what was supposed to be no more than one section of an almost entirely scholarly discussion on issues relating to the possibility of starting a comprehensive codification of international law,[22] suddenly became an independent branch, gaining increasing attention, and filled with tensions and controversies.

I will follow the historical track of the questionnaire, and explore how it evolved into a microcosm of international relations, interwar diplomacy, economic and commercial interests, environmental concerns, and scientific warnings. I will go on to analyze different replies to the questionnaire that the League received from different states. I interpret these both in the context of international legal discourse, and against environmental reflections in a historical perspective. The chapter will also analyze the obstacles the League faced in its attempts to call a summit for a special international whaling conference in London. Then, I will discuss the main impressions of the 1931 Whaling Conference – as a direct

[22] Such as the problem of piracy and the role of diplomatic privileges and immunities in the twentieth century.

outcome of the first initiative of the 1926 Questionnaire – and its attempts to translate the League's legal work that had been carried out during the late 1920s into a binding international whaling convention.

The story will then move to a discussion of how the League revised the 1931 Convention in light of the developments and reactions in the international arena. In this section, I will focus on certain arrangements of the 1931 Convention that were considered inadequate to meet the rapid increase in whaling and changing hunting methods and technologies. Alongside several other international developments, including increasing scientific warnings and non-state actors' activities, the League's whaling campaign made relatively quick progress (especially given the geopolitical turbulence of the 1930s) and led to a second whaling conference, which was held in 1937. The whaling year of 1937 was one of the last major legal steps taken by the League, before the institution was made irrelevant by the outbreak of World War II, and Europe and the rest of the world were thrown into chaos.

Although World War II brought an end to the League as an institution, the League's story does not simply end there. As other environmental issues uncovered in this study show, the interwar period cannot be disconnected from the rest of environmental history and its continuing timeline. We cannot examine how environmental history develops, reacts, and evolves over time while ignoring the 1920s and the 1930s. Just as environmental historians tend to understand and interpret history as a chain of events rather than isolated incidents, so we should view the League's environmental initiatives as part of an evolving process, and situate them within a broader timeline. Hence, the historical story of the League might terminate on September 1, 1939 but its role, ideas, and the mechanisms it employed in response to the challenge of whaling did not suddenly vanish. In the final part of this chapter, I will suggest a more positive interpretation of the League's effects on the postwar whaling regime. Although environmental historians who study the entanglements of twentieth-century whaling tend to focus on the role and significance of the 1946 International Convention for the Regulation of Whaling as a cornerstone of whaling diplomacy, I will show why the League's conservationist efforts also merit a contextual study, one that sheds light on later legal arrangements. Moreover, although September 1939 marks the League's actual termination, I will not leave the story unfinished. Rather than presenting the whaling dilemma as an isolated event, frozen in time, I attempt to weave the entanglements of the interwar period into the rest of the story of modern whaling diplomacy.

In so doing, I suggest a more comprehensive notion of the League's role in the evolution of the international whaling regime both in the 1940s and in the latter half of the century.

2.2 Whales and Whaling: The Historical Background of Whaling in a Nutshell

The history of whaling and whales begins neither in the modern era nor with the rise of the League. The following section introduces key points in the common environmental historiography of whaling, to better situate this chapter in a continuously developing context.

Whaling as an activity has been carried out since the dawn of human history in many parts of the globe.[23] For centuries, humans treated whales as a "free resource," in the sense that they were considered a gift from nature to be enjoyed by anyone who could catch them.[24] However, until the development of more efficient harvesting technologies in late modern times, mostly starting from the 1860s onwards, as I will elaborate later, humans lacked the ability to catch pelagic whales in large numbers.

Therefore, overexploitation of whales was not recognized as a - problem.[25] Though some environmental historians cite the technological means of the eleventh century as proof of premodern proto-industrial whaling (which is thought to have originated with the Basques in the Bay of Biscay),[26] such whaling was initially limited to coastal shores and carried out only from small boats.[27] The British and the Dutch quickly

[23] Sebastian Oberthür, *The International Convention for the Regulation of Whaling: From Over-Exploitation to Total Preservation*, *in* YEARBOOK OF INTERNATIONAL CO-OPERATION ON ENVIRONMENT AND DEVELOPMENT 1998/99 29, 29 (Helge Ole Bergesen, Georg Parmann & Øystein B. Thomnessen eds., 1998).

[24] D'Amato and Chopra, *supra* note 9, at 28. It must be stressed that this notion of "treasures of the sea" – whales in particular – as natural resources belonging to humankind was still an influential one in the corridors and negotiation halls in Geneva during the 1920s and 1930s. Several representatives expressed this perception of whales and their habitats in response to scientific warnings against overexploitation. See, for instance, the specific comment made in the Roumanian reply to the League as discussed especially in Section 2.3.2.

[25] Oberthür, *supra* note 23, at 29. Industrial whaling refers to the commercial hunting of the larger of the migratory seventy-nine whale species, for example, the blue whale.

[26] *See*, for instance, the descriptions in ELIZABETH DESOMBRE, THE GLOBAL ENVIRONMENT AND WORLD POLITICS 150 (2007); or in D'Amato and Chopra, *supra* note 9, at 28–29.

[27] Nagtzaam has claimed that by the middle of the fifteenth century, Basque whalers were venturing further afield, even as far as the eastern coasts of Canada. *See* Nagtzaam, *supra* note 7, at 389.

adopted their rivals' techniques, expanding their own whaling activity to Newfoundland in the North Atlantic. As a result, Basque whaling had almost completely ceased by the end of the sixteenth century. Some historians argue that the danger of whale extinction had already begun to emerge at this time and that, in the following century,[28] an increase in premodern whaling threatened the future survival of right whales in the North Atlantic. By the seventeenth century, whaling countries ventured as far as the Arctic in pursuit of whales for meat and other products.[29] As the nineteenth century approached, and with the shift in international European power, the Dutch industry declined while the British whalers strengthened their control of the sea. With new whalers from France, Germany, and Spain[30] joining the (international) hunt,[31] other whale populations began to suffer. Greenland bowhead whales, the third largest whale in the major species, were nearing extinction, as was the Biscayan right whale during that period.[32] Between 1750 and 1870, whales were considered a lucrative and valuable natural source of oil, bone, and other products, such as perfume and clothing.[33]

[28] PATRICIA W. BIRNIE, INTERNATIONAL REGULATION OF WHALING: FROM CONSERVATION OF WHALING TO CONSERVATION OF WHALES AND REGULATION OF WHALE-WATCHING 66 (1985); EVERHARD J. SLIPJER, WHALES 17 (1962); NEIL A. MACKINTOSH, THE STOCK OF WHALES 146 (1965).

[29] In this period, English and Dutch vessels in the hundreds primarily hunted right whales – Greenland whales and nordcapers – in the Arctic, bringing untold wealth to their national treasuries. *See* COMMITTEE FOR WHALING STATISTICS, INTERNATIONAL WHALING STATISTICS II 4 (1931), LoN Archives [hereinafter COMMITTEE FOR WHALING STATISTICS].

[30] It should be noted that American whalers entered the industry in the eighteenth and nineteenth centuries. On the East Coast, for instance, whaling became a growing industry in the states of Connecticut, New York, and Massachusetts; while on the West Coast, gray and right whales were hunted off the California coast. In the years that followed, the symptoms of overexploitation, along with a local version of the *tragedy of the commons*, became apparent on that side of the Pacific Ocean, as American whaling continued to exhaust the West Coast's whaling population. Their expeditions moved far beyond coastal waters, reaching as far as South America and parts of Oceania (Australia and New Zealand). American involvement in whaling on the high seas in the nineteenth century (which at its peak amounted to 700 American commercial vessels) was negatively affected in the 1860s due to the Civil War and its aftermath. Nevertheless, it is interesting to note that when the petroleum industry was introduced into the American national economy in the last third of the nineteenth century, the involvement of American whalers in transnational whaling began gradually to decrease.

[31] *See* FARLEY MOWAT, SEA OF SLAUGHTER 210 (1989).

[32] SLIPJER, *supra* note 28, at 22; BIRNIE, *supra* note 28, at 68. Moreover, *see generally* G. JACKSON, THE BRITISH WHALING TRADE 3–156 (1978).

[33] *See* ALEXANDER STARBUCK, HISTORY OF THE AMERICAN WHALE FISHERY FROM ITS EARLIEST INCEPTION TO THE YEAR 1876 (1878).

Most environmental historians agree that the modern history of the industrialization of whaling begins around the early 1870s. The fact that the American fleet was on its way out of whaling (due to the evolving petroleum industry, as alternative source to whale oil) did not change much for the whale population, unfortunately. In 1870, a Norwegian seaman and inventor, Sven Foyn, presented a technological innovation that almost completely changed the cetacean industry and massively increased its brutal efficiency: an exploding harpoon fired from a canon.[34] The Norwegian invention enabled whalers to hunt larger, faster-swimming, rorqual whales such as blue, fin, sei, and minke whales.[35] Small, fast steamers called "catchers" joined the explosive grenade harpoon and the canon.[36] Late nineteenth-century technology changed the field of whaling, and the world of whales, making the fishing fleets from countries such as Canada, Norway, Japan, Denmark, Iceland, and even the United States (to a certain extent) more successful in their hunt for whales. With new and faster steel-hulled ships, equipped with steam (and later diesel) engines,[37] and with the devastating harpoon, "the biggest of all the Antarctic and Arctic whaling periods was launched."[38]

Steam vessels, exploding harpoons, and compressed air made the ocean much more accessible to whaling, as more and more whales entered into the hunting zone. These new whaling technologies and hunting methods enshrined exploitationist practices as the global standard.[39] As if that was not enough, another industrial-technological development was introduced at the turn of the century – a land station for processing whale products – which seemed to "complete" this new mass-production era in whaling and to further threaten the survival of whales. In 1904, Norway established its first Antarctic whaling station in Georgia; within a year, seven floating factories were operating. As World War I approached, by 1910, two land

[34] Francis Downes Ommanney, Lost Leviathan 95 (1971). Svend Foyn's first use of the harpoon gun, in approximately 1864, was not considered a great success, however. The story goes that he somehow managed to become caught in the line and was hurled into the ocean, but was rescued.

[35] Committee for Whaling Statistics, *supra* note 29, at 5. *See*, for instance, Ray Gambell, *The International Management of Marine Mammals*, *in* Conservation and Management of Marine Mammals 179, 180 (John R. Twiss Jr. & Randall R. Reeves eds., 1999).

[36] Ommanney, *supra* note 34, at 95–96.

[37] Larry L. Leonard, *Recent Negotiations Toward the International Regulation of Whaling*, 35 Am. J. Int'l L. 91 (1941).

[38] D'Amato and Chopra, *supra* note 9, at 29.

[39] *See* DeSombre, *supra* note 26, at 151.

factories and fourteen factory floating ships were in operation and supported whaling worldwide.[40] Combined, these new, turn-of-the-century technologies meant that whaling increased significantly and became successful on an industrial scale.

This hunting and producing revolution had a direct impact on the ground. In 1910 alone over ten thousand whales of different species were hunted; and in 1914–15, Norway alone caught no fewer than 14,917 whales just in the bountiful waters of the Antarctic.[41] The last historical event that should be mentioned before the League's appearance in the story is World War I, which drove whale harvesting into a steep decline (9468 were hunted in 1918–19). However, after World War I had ended, the whales continued to be at risk: as early as the first season after the war (1919–20), shortly before the establishment of the League, the industry was back on its feet with 11,369 catches. And in a little over a decade, hunting in the industry had jumped to no fewer than 43,129 catches in 1931,[42] despite the League's strong presence during this period.

And yet, in spite of these worrying numbers, the danger of extinction did not enter the public awareness until the early twentieth century, when it became apparent that commercial hunting was negatively impacting whale stocks.[43] Robert Ellickson has argued that prior to this point, there might well have been a material incentive for whaling nations to actually *continue* excessive hunting in order to prevent other states from exploiting this lucrative resource. This scenario rather quickly emerged as a living version of the tragedy of the (marine) commons.[44] However, some scholars have suggested that a balanced whaling regime preventing total exploitation of sea species could have been achieved without an international authority[45] like the League.

By the end of the nineteenth century, whalers had exploited whales so severely that whaling vessels were compelled to go further out into the oceans every year to hunt.[46] This led to the inevitable demise of the

[40] *See* D'Amato & Chopra, *supra* note 9, at 29; and N. Tønnessen & A.O. Johnsen, The History of Modern Whaling 178–82 (1982).

[41] Birnie, *supra* note 28, at 73 (note 26).

[42] Douglas M. Johnston, The International Law of Fisheries 398 (1965).

[43] Ommanney, *supra* note 34, at 92; D'Amato and Chopra, *supra* note 9, at 28–29.

[44] Robert C. Ellickson, *A Hypothesis of Wealth-Maximizing Norms: Evidence from the Whaling Industry*, 5 J.L. Econ. & Org. 83, 96 (1989).

[45] Nagtzaam, for example, asserts that this type of state interest "prevented a *conservationist regime* from being put in place, as states jostled to secure relative gains over other states." (Nagtzaam, *supra* note 7, at 390–91).

[46] Ellickson, *supra* note 44, at 96.

coastal whale, which by the new century had become extinct.[47] Already in 1913, six years before the establishment of the League, Sir Sidney Harmer, while serving as keeper of zoology for the British Museum (Natural History), warned:

> It is impossible to avoid seeing an analogy between what is taking place off South Georgia and the neighboring Antarctic localities and what has happened elsewhere in the world. . . . In southern waters, indeed, we are still in the period of prosperity. But, taking into consideration the more deadly nature of modern whaler's weapons than those have been almost successful in the extermination of the Greenland whale,[48] it can not be disputed that the present rate of destruction of whales in the south gives rise to grave anxiety.[49]

Thus, the story of whaling seems to have reached a critical point by the time the League came about. The League was beginning to emerge just when two camps, which would define the bitter politics and practices of whaling at the turn of the century, were on a collision course. On the one hand, the whaling industry was undergoing a "technological revolution"[50] that managed to revive and likely save the industry. After a boom for much of the nineteenth century, the industry then found itself in a certain crisis: commercial fleets had so severely overexploited the whale that this natural resource was all but depleted. However, new marine and economic opportunities were literally calling[51] to whalers from the depths of the Antarctic. The bowhead whale, native to Antarctic waters, carried much more blubber than fin whales, their relatively thin counterparts, which made them both more attractive and more lucrative. On the other hand, the first decades of the twentieth century were also the time when new and unfamiliar voices were advocating for the conservation of natural resources; and different parts of the Western world, especially Theodore Roosevelt's America,[52] had begun to promote the sustainable use of these

[47] David G. Victor, *Whale Sausage: Why the Whaling Regime Does Not Need to Be Fixed*, *in* TOWARD A SUSTAINABLE WHALING REGIME 292, 295 (Robert L. Friedheim ed., 2000).

[48] Meaning, in Harmer's words, right whales.

[49] Untitled excerpt, source unknown, Nov. 7, 1913, presumably transcribed by Remington Kellogg, Smithsonian Institution, Washington, DC, International Whaling Conference and International Whaling Commission, 1930–1968, (Record Unit 7165), Box 8, Folder I.

[50] DORSEY, *supra* note 4, at 3.

[51] For a painful description of a dying, crying hunted female whale during one of the expeditions, *see* the personal experience of the naturalist Farley Mowat, *The Trapped Whale*, *in* MIND IN THE WATERS 13, 28 (J. McIntyre ed., 1974).

[52] Early conservation ideas had started to appear in the American context in the last quarter of the nineteenth century. Figures such as Gifford Pinchot, an influential forester and ideologist of this new agenda toward nature, called for the efficient use of natural resources. According to this conception, which can also be seen in the early eco-

resources. In this tension between early environmentalism and economic uses, conservationist voices were pushing for restraint – which the League was able to offer as an institution of international law – in the use of the whale as a natural resource. These conservationist notions also followed increasing discussions about whaling as a dilemma, and as a battlefield for conflicting interests.

At the beginning of the twentieth century, and certainly throughout the 1920s and 1930s, whale oil was still a relatively cheap source of animal fat for industrial food processing. Changes in consumerism during that period, such as an increase in the popularity of margarine as a cheap alternative to butter, made the world's whale oil market one of the most important energy stocks.[53] By the new century, whaling had stretched beyond local-national markets (especially in the West) and developed into a global industry, with international companies[54] supplying the world economies with whale oil and other byproducts in vast and growing quantities.[55] A relatively short time before the interwar period, in the whaling season of 1904–05, newly developed whaler factory ships – which had no need of a home port to process the products of their catch[56] – reached the hitherto pristine Antarctic waters at South Georgia, demonstrating just how far the industry's reach had extended.

commercial discussion over whaling, a resource – such as the whale – should provide the greatest good to the greatest number for the longest time. This early conceptualization of *rational* use of nature by mankind, which was better framed and defined later on in the twentieth century as *sustainable*, referred at that time to renewable resources such as fish (and whales in particular) and forests. For a discussion on these early notions on the "rational use" of natural resources *see*, for instance, CHAR MILLER, GIFFORD PINCHOT AND THE MAKING OF MODERN ENVIRONMENT (2001). Likewise, see Emma Rothschild's work on the topic of sustainability: Emma Rothschild, *Forum: The Idea of Sustainability introduction*, 8 MOD. INTELL. HIST. 147 (2011).

53 Or as William Cronon, puts it: "[W]hale oil became margarine; whale meat became pet food." (DORSEY, *supra* note 4, at vii, x).

54 Nagtzaam, *supra* note 7, at 391.

55 COMMITTEE FOR WHALING STATISTICS, *supra* note 29, at 4.

56 The technological methods that the whaling industry developed in the late nineteenth and the early twentieth centuries took huge leap forward, with disastrous consequences for the whaling population on the high seas. The use of steam engines was succeeded by diesel-powered floating factories, as they were called, which allowed the ship's crew to improve their hunting efficiency. They were not only able to catch faster (and more lucrative) species of whale (such as blue, fin, humpback, and sei), but also to avoid wasting time towing carcasses to land-based factories on shore (which ran the additional risk of losing the carcass on the way). In 1923, another technological improvement that was highly beneficial to the whalers was building factory ships with a ramp at the stern to allow an entire hunted whale to be brought aboard in a matter of minutes. *See* COMMITTEE FOR WHALING STATISTICS, *supra* note 29, at 5, 14–15.

When the League finally did begin to discuss the whaling dilemma, it would be at a symbolic juncture in whaling and environmental history: there was no longer anywhere that whalers and their ships had not ventured,[57] and nowhere for them to hide.

While it is true that this was not the first time the League had introduced a conservationist agenda in a transnational arena or spoken about it in terms of international law, the rapid development of whaling techniques and equipment, and the high number of whales caught on the high seas in the early twentieth century, led to attempts to create some kind of transnational regulation earlier than the one the League would eventually introduce during the interwar period.

In the 1910s, early transnational negotiations were held in an attempt to find a unanimous legal solution to the whaling issue (although the war would bring them to a halt for several years). It was becoming obvious that whaling was a rapidly expanding global industry beyond the control of national governments working alone. A short time before the League was established, the Canadians and Americans formed the International Fisheries Commission in January 1918 to consult on regional challenges relating to the exploitation of marine fauna near their shores. Due to the impact of World War I, the difficulty in predicting migration patterns of whales, and the inability of any one nation to create and enforce regulations beyond its territorial waters, both North American nations agreed there was no other choice but for maritime nations in general to create an international convention to prevent the extinction of the whale and to support the survival of the whaling industry once the war had ended.[58]

The Canadian-American cooperation is a painful and vivid example of the perception that whaling could not be solved either by national action or domestic regulation alone. Imperial or transnational endeavors, in that sense, were not sufficient. The International Fisheries Commission, as a regional economic framework, aimed to discuss and attempt to solve the problem shared by these two countries. Although both countries agreed that whaling was a common issue, the joint commission concluded that whales' natural migration patterns, and the ex ante legal inability of any state to achieve authority beyond its territorial waters,

[57] *Id.* at 14.

[58] As mentioned later on in a letter from A. Johnston, Canada's Deputy Minister of Fisheries to Deputy Minister, Department of Trade and Commerce, Ottawa, Jan. 30, 1923, National Archive of Canada, RG 23, vol.1081, File 721–19-5[2] (Quoted in DORSEY, *supra* note 4, at 299).

meant any action that was not international in scope was doomed to failure.

It seems that the Canadian-American commission was aware of the impacts of the context of the late 1910s. The difficulties of that time and optimism about the possibility of a postwar international cooperation served as a backdrop for the rest of the story. The commission called for a convention of maritime nations once the war was over, where they hoped to find a common solution to the whaling problem and secure the future of the industry by preventing extinction.[59]

When the Canadians and Americans announced their intention to assemble a special whaling conference right after the war, other members of the whaling community were not so convinced. The British believed that bilateral treaties were adequate, especially since the scientific data about whales did not lend sufficient support to any kind of international attempt to regulate whaling. Actually, it seems that the British – just like the Norwegians and other whaling nations – were doubtful of the ability of any conference – and likely of the League of Nations later on – to tackle this issue. Any move to place responsibility for the supervision of whaling in the open seas in the hands of unfamiliar (international) bodies raised great concern – even at this early stage – among the Anglo-Norse whaling industries[60] regarding their interests. As this chapter will show, the League addressed these tensions and introduced some innovative legal mechanisms for the first time in order to solve them.

However, as I attempt to depict the whaling dilemma and the period in which it unfolded, it is important to remember that this was a complex issue for all parties involved. The local judiciary in South Georgia and the Colonial Office, for instance, could have called for severe restrictions on whaling on "their" side, but the Foreign Secretary would have been able, and likely, to dismiss the entire idea. Indeed, according to the Foreign Secretary, Britain should oppose the extinction of "rare and valuable species," but in the meantime the Empire should be satisfied with the practical[61] system of licensing.[62]

[59] A. Johnston, Deputy Minister of Fisheries, to Deputy Minister, Department of Trade and Commerce, Ottawa, Jan. 30, 1923, National Archives of Canada [hereinafter NAC], RG 23, vol. 1081, File 721-19-5[2].

[60] DORSEY, *supra* note 4, at 33.

[61] Compared to the enormous difficulties of any international agreement; insofar as its dealings with elusive creatures such as the whale.

[62] L. Mallett, Foreign Office, to Colonial Office, May 2, 1912, National Archives of Great Britain [hereinafter NAGB], Foreign Office [hereinafter FO] 371412/108, pt. I. Even when the German ambassador, Prince Lichnowsky, expressed a genuine fear that whales were

Generally speaking, in terms of legal documents, starting in 1918 several preliminary proposals for the international regulation of whaling were discussed[63] but did not translate into a binding convention. Some scholars have focused here on the whaling industry's own interests,[64] which were the motivation behind certain transnational attempts at regulation outside the League's framework. The entry of the League, however, changed the balance of powers, and enabled other voices and agendas to intervene in a more vigorous way.

Moreover, the absence of any international regulation, supervision, or enforcement brought the whale to the brink of destruction, according to scientific experts in the interwar period. Some scholars have argued that the late nineteenth and the early twentieth century were characterized by the concept of "frontier economics,"[65] with no oversight of whaling practices, which almost completely defined both the industry and the oceans. According to this presumption, whalers – and their national industries as well – assumed that the marine environment consisted of virtually unlimited resources and whale stocks on the high seas.[66] This unrestrained mode of operation, along with the already vulnerable biological reproduction of whales,[67] brought both the industry and nature to the threshold of catastrophe.

nearing extinction and suggested an international conference to address the matter, the Foreign Secretary ignored his proposal. (See Letter by Prince Lichnowsky, German Embassy, to Foreign Office, 27 Jan. 1913, and the reply from Mar. 10, 1913, both in NAGB, FO 881/10446, "Further Correspondence Respecting the Preservation of Whales").

63 D'Amato & Chopra, *supra* note 9, at 30.

64 D'Amato and Chopra, for instance, explain that the "Regulation Stage" of 1918–31 was actually an initiative of the hunting and fishing industries, realizing that their collective profits depended upon the availability of a sizable catch. The time that any whaling vessel had to spend on finding and capturing a whale might, in many circumstances, have strained the economic efficiency of the venture, and made it unprofitable. Hence, a transnational motivation of whaling industries for "setting up a licensing system imposing temporal and spatial restrictions" upon their activities was on the move (*Id.* at 30).

65 Stoett, *supra* note 8, at 48–49.

66 *Id.* at 48.

67 Which are slow to mature compared to "other" fish stocks in the ocean. Conservation, in that sense, is more critical for whale populations than for fish, given their long life cycle. Whales give birth to live calves and suckle their young. Female sperm whales take between seven and thirteen years to mature, while males take up to twenty years, and breeding often does not begin until the age of thirty. (Baleen, or toothless, whales are thought to generally follow the same biological cycle, but under reduced population conditions are able to reproduce five and six years.) *See* R. Harrison & J. King Marine Mammals 91 (1965).

However, it seems that telling the story of whaling and whales only through the lens of the *tragedy of the whales*[68] might be an incomplete story, or an explanation that overlooks and underestimates the complexity of the dilemma. Next to the industry, there were other bodies – such as NGOs – who played their role in the dilemma. Moreover, although the whale mostly lived in a non-territorial space, certain domestic legal arrangements had previously tried to capture its elusive nature.[69]

Therefore, skipping over the negotiations that created the first Convention for the Regulation of Whaling (of 1931) in Geneva, as well as the following conference in 1937, misses an important part of the legal-environmental history of whaling. For instance, these legal arrangements introduced many innovative principles, such as Article 9 of the 1931 Convention, which asserted that the Convention covers "all water," "including states' territorial waters" (Article 9). This suggested revision would also explain, for instance, the reasons and incentives for legal restrictions of certain whale species but not others. The exploration of the interwar period from an environmental history perspective can explain the source of all these ideas;[70] such as why coastal aboriginal peoples were exempt from these restrictions, and who based this international rule on the fact that they used "canoes, pirogues or other exclusively native craft propelled by oars or sails,"[71] and did not use firearms or canons as Western fleets did. At the same time, focusing on

[68] As a reaction to Cronon's argument; and *see*, for instance, the discussion of ARTHUR F. MCEVOY, THE FISHERMAN'S PROBLEM: ECOLOGY AND LAW IN THE CALIFORNIA FISHERIES, 1850–1980 (1986).

[69] After all, the prediction of impending exploitation caused concern among some of the traditional whaling nations, mostly in Northern Europe, which first turned to their jurisdiction and introduced early domestic-national whaling laws. As early as 1902, Norway, a country with one of the most productive whaling industries in the world at that time (also during its political existence under the formal rule of Sweden, which lasted until 1905), passed a law strictly limiting its whaling companies' activities for conservation reasons. Although Norway was by no means a great supporter of (international) whaling regulations, its law introduced obligations such as a restriction on the number of catcher ships each whaling station was allowed to have, and rules regarding the distance (fifty miles) between each whaling station (*See* COMMITTEE FOR WHALING STATISTICS, *supra* note 29, at 10). Another Nordic state, Iceland, was the first to introduce the principle of a moratorium on whaling: for twenty years, starting from 1915. *See* Chris Stroud, *The Ethics and Politics of Whaling*, *in* THE CONSERVATION OF WHALES AND DOLPHINS 55, 61 (Mark P. Simmonds & Judith D. Hutchinson eds., 1996).

[70] Both the successes and failures, when speaking of their enforcement on the open sea.

[71] Convention for the Regulation of Whaling, art. 3, Sept. 24, 1931, 155 L.N.T.S. 349. *Quoted in* Randall R. Reeves, *The Origin and Character of "Aboriginal Subsistence" Whaling: A Global Review*, 32 MAMMAL REV. 71, 72 (2002).

the League can also explain why certain whaling nations joined the 1931 Convention, for instance, while others, such as Japan, the U.S.S.R., and Germany,[72] did not sign it.

The following sections of the historical narrative will address these questions and more.

2.3 Interwar Diplomacy and the Rise of International Whaling Law

2.3.1 Preparing to Launch a Special Questionnaire

In many ways, the interwar period was an appropriate time to review the fragile situation of the whale. From different ports and locations across the globe, whalers set out on their transnational search for oil and meat, equipped with new whaling technologies and faster and stronger ships. However, decades of intensive hunting at the turn of the century made it harder to find whales.

Simultaneously, calls for the need for conservation in the industrial world were starting to be heard. Possible solutions, such as restrictions on the exploitation of natural resources, were discussed openly. The issues of the open sea were, by their very nature, supranational: "It is therefore in the urgent interests of all mankind to put an end to this state of affairs and discover a new scientific and practical method of exploiting these products [of the sea], which belong not to any one country, but to the whole world."[73] Although at first glance these kinds of scientific and practical concerns seem to be peripheral (at least compared to other – much more pressing – problems handled by the League), their environmental implications spoke volumes. After all, a changing environment, destroyed nature, and declining natural resources did not just happen overnight:

> The rapid increase of population in the various countries, which is out of proportion to the increase in the production of ordinary food supplies; increased and improved methods of transport; improvements in the refrigerating and preserving industries; the perfection and multiplication of all industries engaged in transforming the products of the sea and rendering them more available for human requirements; and, finally, all the other technical improvements which are stimulating . . . the consumption of sea products and a considerable rise in their commercial value.[74]

[72] As DeSombre notes, *supra* note 26, at 151–52.

[73] Report of the Committee of Experts of the Exploitation of the Products of the Sea, Jan. 24, 1927, LoN Archives (hereinafter LoN Archives), 19/55517/47284, at 106.

[74] *Id.*

As mentioned earlier, the challenges whaling was facing in the first decades of the twentieth century were discussed in different national and transnational fora before the League was established. As I will show in the sections that follow, the League continued to hold the transnational view that whaling could not be addressed by domestic measures alone, and began an international discussion to address the problem. The Canadian-American International Fisheries Commission's intention in 1918 to work together on a transnational base once the Great War had ended made for a practical starting point.

This was how the League came to accept the unofficial challenge that was thrust into its hands in the 1920s. At first, the League intended to deal with a broader perspective of what it saw as the need for a new codification of international law, not just in terms of whaling or marine fauna in general. Indeed, the whale had to wait a little longer than the Canadian-American Commission expected in January 1918, and until a bit later than the eleventh hour of the eleventh month of 1918, the exact time that the Great War ended. However, given that the League started to handle the question of marine fauna (or "products of the sea") as part of a larger ambitious initiative, the international discussion quickly evolved into one that focused more specifically on marine fauna – and the problem of whaling in particular.

With the start of a new era of international cooperation in 1924, the League's Assembly wished to revise several problematic areas of international law. On behalf of its member states, it asked the international community for recommendations and suggestions on which issues it should work to fix or improve using its new institutional capabilities.

On September 22, 1924, the Assembly – the most "public" and international body within the League's institutional framework[75]– requested that the Council "convene a Committee of Experts ... whose duty it would be, after consulting the necessary authorities ..., [to] report to the

[75] In comparison with the Council, the Permanent Mandates Commission (PMC) or the Permanent Secretariat (which was based on certain other political and international principles of representation), the Assembly stands out as an objective body in the framework of the League. The Council, for instance, began with four permanent members, based on the role of the global superpowers of that era: Great Britain, France, Italy, and Japan; and four non-permanent members that were elected by the Assembly for a three-year term (the first non-permanent members were Belgium, Brazil, Greece, and Spain). It should also be noted that in the course of time, the number of non-permanent members in the Council increased: in September 1922, for instance, it grew to six; to nine in September 1926; and finally to fifteen as the Soviet Union joined the Council (as a permanent member).

Council . . . which [questions] are sufficiently ripe and on the procedure which might be followed . . . to preparing eventually for conference for their solution."[76] Given the economic and commercial characteristics of some of the questions at stake (especially concerning marine fauna), and as with several other interwar issues that mixed economic interests – and had environmental reflections, too[77] – the League's Economic Committee was given the task of handling these issues while simultaneously reviewing inadequate areas of international law at that time.

In order to do so, the League's Economic Committee delegated the task of distributing questionnaires and other legal documents for information-gathering purposes to a special subcommittee named the Committee of Experts for the Progressive Codification of International Law (hereinafter the Codification Committee). In late 1924 and 1925, this special subcommittee of experts prepared different issues relating to international law for open discussion internationally.

The seven preliminary issues that were prepared for this joint open discussion were fairly eclectic, some of which related to the role of seas and oceans in terms of legal frameworks. These issues covered general questions on possible joint legal reform and codification of common matters, such as nationality (Question No. 1 on the 1926 Questionnaire), territorial waters (Question No. 2), diplomatic privileges and immunities (Question No. 3), the responsibility of states for damage done in their territories to a person or to the property of foreigners, and the problem of piracy. During the preparatory stage, several participants highlighted the use of marine resources – or the "exploitation of the products of the sea," as it was articulated in Question No. 7 – as a problematic issue that was equally deserving of international attention.

As the developing international discussion would soon show, the Codification Committee understood that the question of whaling was going to be central to the 1926 Questionnaire. At this early stage of inquiry, many states had already raised the issue of the use of marine resources, especially whales, and argued that it should be addressed by the League. New pelagic expeditions and their implication for the whale stocks of the Antarctic seas likely had something to do with this

[76] Report by the Economic Committee on the matter of Exploitation of the Products of the Sea: Note by the Secretariat – History of the Question, Memorandum from Oct. 14, 1927, LoN Archives, 19/62527/62527 (II).

[77] The Economic Committee, for instance, also dealt with the timber question and, during the developing discussion in the 1930s, also discussed the fear of deforestation. *See* Chapter 4.

intensifying international concern.[78] Therefore, during its preparations, this special subcommittee set out to establish a new whaling regulation, "with reference" to the existing treaties that dealt with the exploitation of the sea. After such inquiry, the Codification Committee was also supposed to consider "whether it is possible by way of international agreement rules regarding the exploitation of the products of the sea."[79]

While the questionnaire was being prepared, the Codification Committee decided that the ability to set a global regulation[80] on marine fauna and whaling should not be limited to the member states alone. The Committee believed that this question, given its international nature, should be open to comprehensive international inquiry from all state governments, "whether Members of the League or not."[81] The League took the opportunity to make its initiative as broad and global as possible.

Led by Professor José Léon Suárez, an Argentinian professor of law (and the dean of the Faculty of Political Science at the University of Buenos Aires),[82] the Codification Committee wanted to change the rules of the game. Though it had anticipated that at least some of the "maritime Powers" would resist any progressive initiative (as Professor Suárez noted), the Committee's aim should be to ascertain:

> Should not a special technical conference be convened, to draw up *immediately*, without regard to the extension or maintenance of maritime jurisdiction . . ., uniform regulations for the exploitation of the industries of the sea, whose wealth constitutes a food reserve for humanity, over the whole extent of the ocean . . . ?[83]

The Codification Committee understood from the outset that the whaling dilemma was a legal issue. Whaling strongly captured the inherent complexity of the geopolitical struggle to control and manage the

[78] DORSEY, *supra* note 4, at 34.

[79] This quote from the private meeting of the Committee of Experts for the Progressive Codification of International Law on Apr. 8, 1925 appears in the report by the Sub-Committee from Jan. 8, 1926, LoN Archives, 19/62527/62527, at 1.

[80] Alongside a few other possible regulations (on other issues included in the discussion on the new codification of international law), and depending on the states' opinions.

[81] Report by the Economic Committee on the matter of Exploitation of the Products of the Sea: Note by the Secretariat – History of the Question, Memorandum from Oct. 14, 1927, LoN Archives, 19/62527/62527 (II), at 1.

[82] And who would serve as the chair of the later Committee of Experts on the Question of the Exploitation of the Products of the Sea.

[83] A quote from the private meeting of the Committee of Experts for the Progressive Codification of International Law on Apr. 8, 1925, which appears in the report by the Sub-Committee from Jan. 8, 1926, LoN Archives, 19/62527/62527, at 1 (emphasis added).

global commons[84] (referred to here by the Committee as a global "food reserve for humanity"). Moreover, given the supranational character of the whale – which lives in no-man's-land and constantly crosses territorial borders – on the one hand, and the lack of sufficient legal arrangements, either domestic or international, to save the whale or to regulate its existence on the other hand, the Committee aimed to find a new, global whaling law.

A relatively early report by the Codification Committee from January 1926 identified inadequacies in the legal framework as it applied to seas around the world. "I am still awaiting replies to the request for information regarding international maritime legislation which I sent ... to various legations and institutions in order to acquaint myself with all the available data," mentioned Suárez. The existing legal arrangements, as international and transnational as they were in the mid-1920s, were limited and suffered from a fundamental deficit in terms of their authority:

> As international regulation has ... been of a limited and local character and has been directed not solely to the protection of species from extinction but mainly to establish police measures and to ensure reciprocity and commerce, regardless of biological interests, which in this case are *inseparable* from economic and general interests....[85]

The danger, the Codification Committee further warned, threatened first and foremost the future of the whale, but certainly not this species alone. The result of pursuing the existing international regulations of hunting and fishing at sea "has been [a] useful but by no means sufficient one of delaying, but not preventing, the extinction of some of the ... species."[86] However, compared to the pre–World War I legal regime regarding the economic-environmental exploitation of the high seas, the involvement of the League marked a basic shift from earlier legal attempts: this time, not only whales were the focus of intensifying regulation, but also other marine species that had previously gone unnoticed. The problem with the whale "has escalated lately even more," the Codification Committee stressed. It further warned that possible extinction of the whale might endanger "other animals" – the Committee understood that the ocean is a marine ecosystem:

84 *See* STOETT, *supra* note 8.

85 Report by Professor Suárez from Jan. 8, 1926, LoN Archives, 19/49113/47284, at 6.

86 A quote from the private meeting of the Committee of Experts for the Progressive Codification of International Law on Apr. 8, 1925; appears in the report by the Sub-Committee from Jan. 8, 1926, LoN Archives, 19/62527/62527, at 2.

> [W]e consider the life of all the species in the animal kingdom, [but] biological solidarity is even closer among the denizens of the ocean than among land animals, [hence] the disappearance of certain species would destroy the balance in the struggle for existence and would bring about the extinction of other species too.[87]

Both Suárez and the Codification Committee were talking in legal terms. Although the Committee did not only include jurists and diplomats, but also scientists and professional experts in industry and commerce from different states, the legal discourse – and the existing (lacking) framework of international whaling law – served as the common language for all.

As the League prepared to launch its initiative and to further study its implications worldwide, it addressed the environmental aspects – and the legal and political difficulties – it would face once the special questionnaire was distributed. In February 1926, a couple of weeks before distributing the questionnaire, the Committee sent a special internal report to the League's Council regarding Question No. 7[88] – it had anticipated early on that this would be a controversial issue. The Committee identified tensions between legal principles of state sovereignty, industrial-economic interests, and (alleged) international authority, which they had discussed during the preliminary preparations of the questionnaire.

One short note from the internal report (dated February 9, 1926), signed by Suárez, specifically referred to the overwhelming "new" whale stocks of the Antarctic. It states: "The riches of the sea, and especially the immense wealth of the Antarctic region, are the patrimony of the whole human race, and our [Codification] Committee is the body best qualified to suggest to the Governments what steps should be taken before it is too late."[89]

Though it was still "just discussing" the matter of marine fauna with other bodies within the institutional framework of the League, the Codification Committee raised rather progressive ideas. A novel example of this was to use an unfamiliar form of international governance to monitor a natural resource – the riches of the sea, and whales in particular – that was owned by the global community. According to that report, whales were from that moment on to be treated as an international

[87] *Id.*

[88] Communication to the Council, the Member of the League of Nations and other Governments, Feb. 9, 1926, LoN Archives, 19/49113/47284.

[89] *Id.* at 4.

common – and not merely as a lucrative source for any one specific nation.

The Codification Committee's conceptualization of the whale as a collective asset for all was intended to ensure and to promote international interests, common to the whole world. Though it was ambitious, however, the Committee also acknowledged some of the limits of its power, legitimacy, and authority in the face of legal and practical obstacles it met as a proxy of the League. The Codification Committee was aware of its lacking mandate compared with the other bodies involved, and that without the cooperation and solidarity of other states, its proposed measures and recommendations were unlikely to be realized and enforced:

> To save this wealth, which, being to-day the uncontrolled property of all, belongs to nobody, the only thing to be done is to discard rules of the existing treaties, which were drawn up with other objects, to take a wider view, and to *base a new jurisprudence, not on the defective legislation which has failed to see justice done but on the scientific and economic considerations* which, after all the necessary data has been collected, may be put forward, compared and discussed in a technical conference . . . . In this way a new jurisprudence will be treated of which to-day we have no inkling . . . .[90]

On its fourth page of the report to the Council, the Codification Committee spoke clearly on the challenges of the whale dilemma and of treating the open sea as international waters. Even at this preliminary legal-diplomatic stage, it was clear that the issue of whaling captured the inherent complexity of the geopolitical struggle to manage the global commons. As states competed with each other over natural resources, the lack of clarity regarding the territorial and legal boundaries with regard to whaling made the dilemma even more complex:

> M. Valette[91] . . . has described this process of extracting oil from whales, and it really seems impossible that the Governments interested in preserving so important a source of wealth should do nothing to prevent its extinction, which will be complete in five to ten years at the most. "This class of fishing", he says, "has reached such a point as to be a veritable butchery, which is the more deplorable when one considers the uniparous character of whales and the length of their period of gestation."[92]

[90] *Id.* at 4–5 (emphasis added).

[91] Luciano H. Valette was an Argentine expert involved in the discussion on whaling as the chief of the Fisheries Department of the Argentine Ministry of Agriculture.

[92] Communication to the Council, the Member of the League of Nations and other Governments, Feb. 9, 1926, LoN Archives, 19/49113/47284, at 4.

These experts involved in the preparatory work identified a dangerous turning point in environmental history. Modern sailing and new whaling technologies at the turn of the twentieth century had rapidly changed the nature of marine hunting, posing a great threat to whales. Suárez was very clear about this concern prior to the League's circulation of the special questionnaire. This is probably also one of the reasons why, following the distribution of the questionnaire worldwide in March 1926, so many states rushed to become involved in the developing international discussion. Perhaps many of them pointed out the importance of whales in the context of the 1920s because they had very quickly recognized what new pelagic expeditions undertaken by nations such as Great Britain, Norway, Argentina, and Canada would mean for the whale stocks of the Antarctic seas. Given that backdrop, national and domestic means of enforcement, practical as they might have been[93] before the technological big bang of whaling, became irrelevant, and it fell to international law to try to solve this acute problem:

> If [one of the former proposals for handling the whaling problem] as it stood were limited to existing treaties, *it would not cover the modern whaling industry*, which is rapidly *exterminating* the whale. To-day it is carried out with the help of a perfected form of weapon and special craft; but the great increase in its scope is due to the manner in which the animal is treated once it has been killed. The extraction of the oil, which previously had to be done ashore, is now done in floating factories, which accelerates the process of ten – or twenty – fold and *renders national control impossible*, since no action can be taken in the open sea, and the whalers have no need to touch land to extract the principal product from their quarry.[94]

Indeed, while there were some transnational regulations that referred to marine ecosystems, the Codification Committee recognized that none of them was adequate to address the new situation on the high seas, due to the industrial and commercial hunger for whale oil and other products. With these different agendas identified during the preparatory work of the Codification Committee's first initiative, it was ready to launch the controversial legal questionnaire.

In early spring of 1926, the questionnaire was distributed to the capital cities of a long list of states, both members of the League and nonmembers alike. The different articles, which were presented as separate

[93] Which they were not.

[94] Communication to the Council, the Member of the League of Nations and other Governments, Feb. 9, 1926, LoN Archives, 19/49113/47284, at 4 (emphasis added).

questions, were suggested as the basis for a future comprehensive international agreement, led entirely by the League.

2.3.2 *Replying to the League: States and Different Organizations' Responses to the Special Questionnaire*

A long list of states replied to the special questionnaire. Maritime superpowers such as Great Britain, Norway, and France, were quick to assert their leadership in the matter; however, many other states, some of whom were only indirectly involved in whaling, began to join the developing discussion – something the British administration had previously expressed concern about.[95]

Unlike other issues that the League had been "forced" to deal with, the whaling dilemma was one of the initiatives that the League undertook rather enthusiastically, employing the full scale of its diplomatic instruments. Thanks to the framework of the institution, international whaling law became pluralistic and democratic. Where, prior to the distribution of the questionnaire, whaling had been limited to a (very) closed club of whaling nations and maritime powers, other states with their own perspectives on and interests in the issue were now able to join this open discussion, under the new auspices of the League.

According to Question No. 7, the last question of the document, different parties were asked to ascertain what problems "appear to be ripe for international action . . . and whether it is possible to establish by way of international agreement rules regarding the exploitation of deep-sea fauna against the danger of extermination caused by uneconomic exploitation."[96] Just as the Codification Committee had predicted, a great majority of the states that answered the League's questionnaire had focused on Question No. 7 and the issues related to the exploitation of the products of the sea. The Committee received replies in support of introducing a new international whaling regulation from all over the globe, including from emerging states and some that had almost nothing

[95] The Foreign Secretary, for instance, dismissed the early idea suggested by certain officials at the Colonial Office, which called for severe restrictions on whaling on the British imperial side. Indeed, Britain was expected to oppose the extinction of "rare and valuable species," but in the meantime (1912), the Empire should also have been satisfied with the practical system of licensing. (L. Mallett, Foreign Office, to Colonial Office, 2 May 1912, NAGB, FO, 371412/108, pt. I).

[96] From the 23d Session of the League of Nations Council, Dec. 1927, LoN Archives, 19/62529/62529 (II).

to do with whaling, but were nevertheless interested in the condition of whales, such as Romania,[97] Albania, Morocco, Iraq, Hungary, Sudan, China, Poland, Egypt, and more. Just as the British feared, most of the states that answered the questionnaire had paid specific attention to Question No. 7. States that were very reluctant to allow international law to dictate the course of whaling also replied to the League. All in all, there were thirty replies covering a wide range of national legal interpretations. Of the dozens of comments, a large majority voted in favor of a whaling regulation to be established by the League. Only five governments explicitly opposed the initiative: the British, Japanese, German, Dutch, and Norwegian governments.

So much attention was given to the legal future of marine fauna – and whaling in particular – that many of the replying states actually sent their responses on this matter in a separate file. One of the formal replies left no room for doubt as to the necessity of making whaling subject to a new international regulation, given the environmental and economic circumstances: "[T]here can be no longer any doubt as to the desirability of the codification of international law" on that issue.[98]

In retrospect, the sheer range of actors from across the globe who were eager to tackle this matter is quite remarkable. What other scholars might dismiss as an "inexplicable footnote to the history of diplomacy,"[99] can rather be viewed as a true reflection of the evolution of international law – from discussions and arguments to the actual sketching out of the law – right at its institutional birth. The Codification Committee explicitly acknowledged this in its own words, noting that "[t]he many valuable memoranda which we have received from the Governments in replying . . ."[100] drove it to further discuss and develop the matter.

Although most of the states, members and nonmembers alike, had no real involvement in the whaling dilemma until after the turn of the century, it seems that almost every nation felt compelled to respond to the experimental environmental balloon launched by the Codification Committee. No fewer than twenty-nine states sent their agendas back to

[97] When quoting relevant primary sources, I will try to use spelling as it appeared in the historical texts themselves (such as in the case of Romania, which many of the original sources handled by the League referred to as "Roumania").

[98] Reply by the Government of Brazil to the Questionnaire of the Committee of Experts for the Progressive Codification of International Law, (undated), LoN Archives, 19/57699/47284.

[99] Dorsey, *supra* note 4, at 17.

[100] Report of the Codification Committee, Mar. 28, 1927, LoN Archives, 19/58475/47284.

Geneva.[101] Some states could have skipped the questionnaire entirely – and most certainly the oceans question – as the diplomatic procedure of the 1920s enabled them to do, but many states decided that the time was right to recruit governmental and legal energies, and to deliver their take on the legal, economic, and environmental issue at stake

The dozens of official government documents received at the League's Secretariat reveal a few central parties in the escalating dilemma. In the following section, I will present some of the key responses, divided into two groups: those (unsurprisingly) from the well-established whaling nations, such as Britain and Norway, which rushed to oppose the threat this new global regulation posed to their obvious interests on the high seas; and a second, rather larger group of parties that supported the League's initiative.

In their replies, most of the parties involved referred directly and explicitly to whales and whaling, paying little attention (if any) to other marine fauna. These voices from across the globe encouraged the League to work toward a new whaling law that would stop – or at least control – the brutal exploitation of whales.

Resistant whaling nations expressed their growing concern, specifically about Question No. 7 and its future implications for possible restrictions on international law. Denmark, with its well-developed whaling industry, sent the League a detailed and reasoned comment[102] of no fewer than eleven pages; Norway,[103] Finland,[104] and Estonia delivered similarly detailed replies stretching over more than eleven pages.[105] Great Britain mobilized its full energy to limit the scope and authority of the new body and its initiative. In a letter directed by Foreign Secretary Sir Austen Chamberlain, Britain informed Secretary General Drummond that His Majesty's Government considered the subject of exploitation of the sea as one which "is *not* a subject the regulation of which by general

[101] Report by the Economic Committee on the Matter of Exploitation of the Products of the Sea: Note by the Secretariat – History of the Question, Memorandum from Oct. 14, 1927, LoN Archives, 19/62527/62527 (II).

[102] 19/56881/51535; also has been cataloged under 19/56888/47284.

[103] 19/54946/47284.

[104] 19/54740/47285.

[105] Although Estonia could not be considered a power or a leading force in international relations during the interwar period, it still played a role in the whaling industry; and its geographical position on the eastern shores of the Baltic Sea contributed to its special interest and expertise in whaling. *See* Estonia's Reply to the League of Nations Experts for the Progressive Codification of International Law, Oct. 14, 1926, LoN Archives, 19/54843/47284 (also can be located in File 19/54836/51535).

international agreement is feasible."[106] The League's global approach (on that matter) was clearly rejected in London. Rather, the British government relied on tailor-made bilateral or multilateral solutions between a few relevant countries, where the conditions could be influenced more directly – "particular conventions relating to particular products and special areas." After all, it was a British tradition: in 1899, for example, Britain had successfully concluded a convention with Japan, Russia, and Canada on the protection of seal populations. Why broaden the circle of participants unnecessarily?

Since the very notion of legal restrictions on the free use of the ocean as a natural resource threatened Britain's interests – both at home and abroad – it strove to prevent any comprehensive move by the Codification Committee (or the League as a whole) in that direction:

> [F]or the reasons that the considerations upon which its [i.e., the issue of exploitation of the sea] regulation must depend are of *a technical rather than a legal character* and that the information at present in the possession of His Majesty's Government on the subject leads them to the conclusion that the exploitation of the products of the sea cannot be made the subject of any general convention . . . .[107]

As long as the Codification Committee targeted the whole marine environment as a space that required the defense of international law, Britain would try to gain control of the initiative. The British tried to ensure that there would be no general marine regulation (led by foreign powers and "irrelevant states" with regard to whaling interests), but instead one that dealt specifically with the problem of whaling. "[It] should be attempted rather by particular conventions relating to particular products and particular areas between the countries interested." In that case, Britain, like other whaling nations, would have the upper hand.

The British also called on other states to support them, including those who actually had a direct interest in whaling. The Dominion of New Zealand took the issue to the highest authority. In a direct statement from the Prime Minister's Office,[108] the state aligned itself promptly with the British stance: "[A]nd in reply [I] have to say that the New Zealand Government desire to associate themselves in this matter with the replies

[106] A letter to the Secretary General, Nov. 11, 1926, LoN Archives, 19/55536/47284.
[107] *Id.*
[108] Joseph G. Coates at that time.

forward to the League of Nations on behalf of His Majesty's Government in Great Britain."[109]

The League paid special attention to New Zealand, likely considering its role on the whaling map. As discussions over the replies became more intensive, an internal memorandum circulated between the Legal and the Economic Sections of the League revealed the special (and from a European view, distant) example of Oceania. In a document from October 10, 1927 the Secretariat pointed out to the Legal Section that "this question is of considerable interest of New Zealand, which, having jurisdiction over the southern waters within an angle of 60 degrees from the South Pole, has been much disturbed by the destruction of the whales by foreign whalers in this area." Given that the Codification Committee and the League were planning for a conference (followed by a convention) on this subject, "it would seem to be appropriate that a New Zealander should be appointed to such body . . . ."[110]

In contrast to Britain's expanding political and imperial influence on the whaling dilemma, the Indian reply stands as another interesting example. As an empire that had proclaimed its dominance of the seas, the British understood all too well – as the League did – that interwar whaling was no longer a game of privileged marine powers, but an international issue – one that was now being handled by a new and unfamiliar institution, whose agenda and growing authority was unlike anything the Empire had ever seen. It seems likely that the British used their authority, possibly by influencing India's response, to discourage the Codification Committee from advancing the League's initiative the way it wanted. The India Office replied to the Secretary General that India, in fact, has no real notice to add to the discussion on whaling regulation. "The Government of India have now stated . . . that there is no intensive exploitation of such products in India and that they have no observation to offer on the subject."[111]

Norway, one of the most important maritime powers and a leading whaling nation,[112] observed the League's progress with reluctance. Like

[109] Letter of Prime Minister J. Coats to the Secretary-General of the League of Nations, Feb. 26, 1927, LoN Archives, 19/58822/47284.

[110] A Notice by Joseph V. Wilson, a member of the LoN's Secretariat from Oct. 10, 1927, 19/62453/61453 (I).

[111] Letter from the Economic and Overseas Department at the India Office to Secretary-General of the League of Nations, July 28, 1926, LoN Archives, 19/52899/47284.

[112] The Codification Committee had mentioned that "[t]o such a pitch of perfection have the Norwegian whalers brought *their* [whaling] trade that one of the conditions imposed

Britain, in reaction to the League's "dangerous" agenda, Norway and other whaling powers put forward their best diplomatic efforts to minimize the scope of the ongoing initiative. Instead of a comprehensive and full regime over the seas, Norway and Britain called to limit the scope of the advancing international cooperation and appealed to the international community to turn from a general international agreement to a more specific one. Both the British and their Scandinavian co-partners claimed that "this is not a subject the regulation of which by a general international agreement is feasible." Since there were "various initiatives pending" on the matter of the exploitation of the sea, Norway declined the proposal. At the most, the Norwegian government agreed to organize a conference[113] to implement international rules for the exploitation of the sea.[114] In his official reply from March 21, 1927,[115] the Minister of Foreign Affairs explained that, as much as Norway was "interested to take part of the international initiative," the Codification Committee and the League must also acknowledge the importance of the sea resources for the Norwegian economy. As a sort of compromise that echoed principal features of the League's style of international governance, Norway suggested first obtaining a full and detailed scientific study on the issue.

Among both camps, there was a subgroup of countries that either opposed or supported the League's initiative, but for reasons other than whaling. Alongside those countries that were interested in whaling specifically and supported halting the hunting of whales for conservationist, economic, or environmental reasons, several other countries seemed to support the issue because of their interest in the sphere of international law. Some of the states, including those who were not member states of the League, identified the challenge of whaling as an opportunity to advance international law and internationalism as a whole. In that respect, they used the Codification Committee's transmission as a way to engage with the world of international law, although their role in the world of whaling and their inclusion in the institution were unclear.

Alongside those countries that wanted to use the exploitation of the sea as a test case for a new version of internationalism, there were those who, for reasons unrelated to whaling, opposed regulation. In contrast to

by the majority of insurance policies for this class of craft is that the harpooner and some of the crew should be Norwegian."

113 What the League would eventually do once the replies had concluded.

114 *See* Communication to the Council, the Member of the League of Nations and other Governments, Feb. 9, 1926, LoN Archives, 19/49113/47284, at 4.

115 Norway's Reply appears also in 19/54946/47284.

whaling powers who resisted the whaling initiative to protect their obvious and continuing industrial and economic interests, China's reply reflected a different objection to the dilemma. According to the Chinese, whales and whaling were not the central matter at hand, but rather the League and its involvement in shaping the world of international law.

The Permanent Office of the Chinese Delegation to the League, the official Chinese representative in Geneva, sent a detailed legal reply to the Committee.[116] A special Annex in this document was dedicated to the Chinese stance on Question No. 7 and the whaling dilemma. In China's view, the issue entailed much broader questions of international law and sovereignty. This is why China's reply is the only one that made changes to the wording of Question No. 7. While other states simply quoted it as it was, the Chinese Annex introduced a slightly different perspective, and right at the beginning:

> In connection with the question of Exploitation of Products *within the territorial* sea of any power, the Chinese Government is firmly of the opinion that such right shall exclusively belong to the territorial sovereign and shall in no wise be infringed upon by the nationals of any other power.[117]

China, which played a supporting role in the international arena at that time, was looking at the questionnaire holistically, as a base for negotiating the role of the sea in international law – rather than focusing specifically on the future of the whale:

> As to the special treaties by which one of the contracting parties grant within its territorial water the national of the other the right of fishing etc. it is a question of interest *only* to the contracting parties, and need not form a subject for settlement by progressive codification of international law.[118]

China, like leading whaling nations, was trying to prevent the whaling dilemma from becoming "too" internationalist, but the opposition camp's collective efforts were in vain. They failed to minimize either the scope of the future whaling regulation or the Codification Committee's enthusiasm. Both the wide range of states that supported the initiative and the Codification Committee's own agenda (and Suárez in particular) were in

116 Reply by the Permanent Office of the Chinese Delegation to the League of Nations, Aug. 8, 1927, LoN Archives, 19/61129/47284.
117 *Id.* (emphasis added).
118 (emphasis added).

favor of using Question No. 7 as the foundation for a more substantial legal arrangement.

The Codification Committee mentioned the French reply in this regard. "Among the favorable replies, mention should be made of that from the French Government, [which] emphasises the importance of an immediate international measure to prevent the extinction of marine animals in the near future, and put an end to the reckless slaughter reported from different quarters."[119]

Despite the many opponents, a long list of states decided that the future of the whales deserved their attention, and special treatment by international law. This included Yugoslavia, Czechoslovakia, Bulgaria, Cuba, the Netherlands, Spain, Belgium, Sweden, Poland, Portugal, and Greece among others.[120] Many of the replying states had no whaling fleet at all. Others had access neither to an open sea, nor to an ocean. Some had no serious involvement in whaling, while others (e.g., France) apparently did. And yet, these states all offered their opinion on how the law should be used to control the world of whaling. It should also be mentioned that those states who had "delicate" or complex relations with the League (and the international community at that time), such as Germany[121] during the Weimar Republic, were also eager to take part.

[119] Economic Committee – Exploitation of the Products of the Sea: Note by the Secretariat – the History of the Question, Oct. 14, 1927, LoN Archives, 19/62527/62527 (I), at 2.

[120] Yugoslavia's reply to be found in source 19/58351/47284; France's – 19/57810/47284; Czechoslovakia – 19/55697/51535; Bulgaria – 19/57481/51535; Cuba – 19/51535/51535; the Netherlands – 19/57271/51535; Spain – 19/57162/51535; Belgium – 19/55792/51535; Sweden – 19/55639/47284; Poland – 19/55868/47284; Portugal sent two replies, one signed by the Minister of the Sea to the League of Nations (dated Sept. 15, 1926, 19/54682/51535), and another letter from Lisbon on the same matter, from Oct. 7, 1926, 19/54684/47284; and Greece's reply – 19/5466/47284.

[121] 19/56117/47284; this document can also be located under File 19/56112/51535.

Putting aside the advanced environmental scientific and political views and initiatives in German society in the late nineteenth and early twentieth century, Germany had an elusive relationship with the League, both before and after Hitler and the Nazis came to power. After the war, and during the Weimar Republic, Germany was not allowed to be a member state of the League. Germany applied to join the League, and after a long and detailed process of international consultation with its member states on whether or not Germany should be allowed to join the organization, the League approved its admission in 1926. However, in October 1933, and once Hitler came to power, Nazi Germany announced its withdrawal from both the Disarmament Conference and the League. On early German environmentalism *see*, among others, FRANK UEKÖTTER, THE GREENEST NATION? A NEW HISTORY OF GERMAN ENVIRONMENTALISM (2014), or BERNHARD GISSIBL, THE NATURE OF GERMAN IMPERIALISM: CONSERVATION AND THE POLITICS OF WILDLIFE IN COLONIAL EAST AFRICA (2016).

Roumania's reply captured the crux of the whaling dilemma. Although it was not involved in the whaling industry – either in the late nineteenth or first decades of twentieth centuries – Roumania did have its own bitter experience with exploitation of the products of the sea. The country felt the burden of the tragedy of the commons in the absence of clear and firm regulations. In its reply on whaling, Roumania referred to a parallel phenomenon – the devastation of sturgeon populations as a result of overfishing in the Black Sea. It provided a bitter account of the damage inflicted on its local ecosystem and the sturgeon that inhabited it, and the resulting economic losses sustained with the disappearance of caviar from its (domestic territorial) waters. Perhaps it is precisely because Roumania was not a whaling nation that it was able to assess the dilemma objectively, using its similar experience as a reference.

The Roumanian reply was actually an open discussion about the tension between the risks that modern whaling posed, and demand. This reply used several terms and patterns that would seem familiar today in light of contemporary environmental dilemmas relating to the exploitation of natural resources, sustainability, nature conservation, and the role of international law. "Our aim should be a wider one," declared the Roumanian government, "to preserve intact the whole productive force of the riches of the sea, animal, vegetable and mineral, and by a *rational system of exploitation*. To make the sea permanently provide the human race with the quantity and quality of food and economic products of which it is capable."[122]

"Nature," concluded the reply, was "sending a warning to the effect that the vandalistic methods"[123] used by the industry could no longer be continued. Otherwise, extinction would be inevitable.

Spain, another supporter of a new whaling regulation, declared that it had no objection to the initiative. The Spanish government supported the call for an international conference, in which it would be able to contribute and to suggest international regularization based on former experience and study. The reply observed that, given the current situation on the high seas, it would be happy to consider initiatives that seemed attainable.[124]

The Brazilian reply correlated with the Chinese interpretation of Question No. 7 as having significant implications for international law. However, unlike China it was in favor of the new initiative. Like China,

122 19/55517/47284 (emphasis added).

123 Committee of Experts for the Progressive Codification of International Law, Question No. 7, C.196.M.70.1927.V, 223, LoN Archives.

124 19/57165/47284.

Brazil saw the move as a new step in internationalism, but also recognized it as an opportunity to enter what, prior to 1919, was an exclusive club of traditional powers.

The government of Brazil admitted that while it was no longer a member of the League, "the fact that Brazil has withdrawn from the League of Nations in no way implies that she [sic] should be held aloof from the work of coordinate international relations. . . . [T]his should not deter her from co-operating in the similar work now being undertaken in Europe."[125] Moreover, despite not having a large-scale fleet or whaling industry, as other powers did, Brazil insisted on having its opinion heard on whaling and international law.

The same Brazilian government also did not hesitate to push the Codification Committee, and the League, toward a strict and unmistakable set of rules for the ocean. The new regulation "must be founded on justice embodied in definite, clear rules and its ultimate aim must be to protect the *major interests of civilization*," the reply from Rio de Janeiro asserted.[126] Moreover, the broad international discussion on these issues also shows how early environmental law under the auspices of the League – compared to other forms of institutional international cooperation – enabled players that were not key states or historical powers per se (like Brazil), to take part in shaping (environmental) international law:

> The democratisation of the world, the equality of States . . . – these are the constituent elements of a new international order which necessitates the careful definition of reciprocal rights and duties. . . .
>
> America has long been engaged in patient effort to solve this problem. . . . These efforts have been continued at various conferences and it is not too much to say that the ground is now ready for the final work of construction.[127]

Brazil encouraged the Codification Committee, and the League, to fulfill the call to regulate exploitation of the sea and establish an international whaling law: "The report of the distinguished . . . Professor Suárez deals with this matter satisfactorily, without, however, preparing any rules for its settlement. He nevertheless defines the problem and indicates certain bases for its solution, which would be entirely acceptable."[128]

125 Opinion of Professor Clovis Bevilaqua, Legal Advisor to the Ministry of Foreign Affairs, Received on Feb. 28, 1927, LoN Archives, 19/57699/47284, at 2–3.
126 *Id.* at 2 (emphasis added).
127 *Id.* (emphasis added).
128 *Id.* at 4.

Whether for fear of a future version of the tragedy of the commons on the high seas, or wariness of the link between basic questions of international law and national sovereignty, from the mid-1920s many non-whaling states thought it would be better to deliberate the questionnaire not as a whole, but in parts and paragraphs. Many of these states also ignored all the other parts of the original distributed document and wrote to the Codification Committee *specifically* on the issue of exploitation of the sea.

Reviewing their various replies, it seems that the League inspired in them a strong belief in its ability to solve pressing problems across the globe, and offered them a new means of participation in the international arena. The whaling dilemma in general, and the questionnaire in particular, served as a mechanism through which different states, players, and organizations could discuss the language of international law in a way that was not available before. Some rushed to protect the whale from extinction, while some strove to limit the race to the bottom in order to make whaling more efficient and sustainable. And as these several examples imply, some entered the discussion due to other, more general, incentives relating to the framework of international law. The diplomatic routine of the League also attracted commercial and industrial consortiums and, as I will show later on, scientific boards of museums and research centers. Some of these, like the International Mercantile Marine Officers Association, replied directly to the 1926 Questionnaire and focused on Question No. 7. The association sent a special reply from its Head Office in Antwerp, in which its secretary suggested that the association's members had a direct interest in the evolving discussion on whaling and addressed the League in this regard. In his application,[129] the association's secretary asked that its perspective be included in the discussions and its conclusions.

To a large extent, it was in fact the reply that arrived from Venezuela that eventually set the course of the initiative. The new stage of internationalism at the League enabled other, perhaps more objective voices, to be represented. Dr. Pedro Itriago Charin, the Venezuelan Minister of Foreign Affairs, replied in a very practical manner. Although Venezuela was not one of the "maritime Powers," as the Codification Committee's Suárez had observed almost one year earlier in his first report,[130] the

[129] Letter to Robert Hass, Director of the Communication and Transit Committee of the League of Nations, Dec. 30, 1927, LoN Archives, 19/63331/63331 (III).

[130] Report by the Committee of Experts for the Progressive Codification of International Law (Questionnaire No. 7), from Feb. 9, 1926, 14/49113/47284, at 6.

ministry had given "due consideration to these questions." On the matter of the marine dilemma, Venezuela reached the conclusion that there existed a body of principles that had definitely secured international acceptance. The introductory stage of the League's whaling diplomacy was now ready to move on to a more "concrete" practice of international law. "These questions would therefore seem to be sufficiently ripe to be considered by international conference."[131]

2.3.3 *The Codification Committee Summarizes the Replies with a Sense of Urgency*

After receiving dozens of different replies from states from all across the globe, and seeing the urgency – according to an internal report from January 24, 1927[132] – they conveyed, the Codification Committee drew up its conclusions and suggested steps for the future. The Committee wrote quite a daring conclusion, which one editor (whose identity remains unknown) tried to make more moderate. This document sheds light on the struggle between the Committee's progressive and enthusiastic agenda – armed with its belief in science and in the capability of international law to overcome the environmental danger – on the one hand, and on other commercial and conservative approaches to the tension between states and international sovereignty in the interwar period on the other hand.

First, according to the Codification Committee, the need for regulation was obvious. It believed that this kind of regulation should and could be achieved by an international legal agreement, which seemed to be both "desirable and realisable."[133] Second, in addition to the need for an international legal solution was the need for the kind of inquiry the League had taken upon itself. Unfortunately, such a broad investigation was not feasible prior to the birth of the League. But, this need for inquiry "ha[d] long been manifest": given the awful condition of the whale, and following the technological improvements in the whaling industry, the League was just the right institution to conduct a broad, comparative, international inquiry of this nature, which began in March 1926.

[131] Letter from P. Itriago Charin, Republic of Venezuela Ministry of Foreign Affairs to Secretary-General, Oct. 6, 1926, LoN Archives, 19/55086/47284 I.

[132] Report on the Questionnaire of the Committee of Experts for the Progressive Codification of International Law, Jan. 24, 1927, LoN Archives, 19/55517/47284 [hereinafter Report on the Questionnaire].

[133] *Id.* at 101.

Third, the Codification Committee clearly articulated the complex perspectives, interests, and conflicts embedded in the whaling problem. The stark tension between the "rapacity" of commercial exploitation of the sea; nature protection, preservation, and conservation; and conflicting interests of whaling powers and other states, was explicitly reflected in the report:

> This is indeed a case in which action is necessary, for the problem is a vast one, is of the *largest importance for the future of mankind and can only be solved by international agreement.*
>
> For certain countries, including some in a very advanced stage of civilisation, the products of the sea constitute the main source of food supplies and revenue, in that they exert a decisive influence on national economy and general prosperity. In other cases, the products of the sea constitute a great reserve of future food supplies.
>
> Abundant though they are, these resources are in certain respects threatened by man's rapacity and the destructive methods employed. Certain species of aquatic animals of great utility which provide the raw material for great industries, have been almost entirely exterminated.[134]

In this respect, "the case of cetaceans," which the Codification Committee presented as the focal point of the discussion (and the problem), "is a conclusive one," and time was running out: "Of the ten to twelve thousand whales alive today, fifteen hundred are being killed annually. Consequently in ten[135] years' time they will have been completely exterminated."[136]

It should also be noted that the report and the concern it expressed were not restricted to the whale alone, but also to other creatures of the sea as part of an ecosystem. In its initial pages, the report also discussed the parallel, and disturbing, danger that threatened other species of marine fauna. A fairly large part of the discussion dealt with the more general version of the tragedy of the commons, this time in the case of the herring (*Clupea arengus*) "tribe,"[137] "which is also on the decrease owing to modern fishery."[138] This report struck a balanced conclusion, with a general overview of the current status of marine fauna in light of fundamental technological improvements in fishing (and especially

[134] *Id.* at 101.

[135] Originally, the report declares (p. 101) that in *ten* years from that date (meaning, from early 1927), there is a great and concrete danger that the whale will be extinct from the oceans.

[136] Report on the Questionnaire, *supra* note 132, at 101.

[137] The report used this term, and not species (for instance).

[138] Report on the Questionnaire, *supra* note 132, at 101.

whaling) methods. Although the Codification Committee seems to have been far more progressive (environmentally speaking) than other bodies of the interwar period – including within the League itself – its members did also consider other ideas, some of which competed with or contradicted one other. Whereas other bodies seemed more inclined to defend one view at the most and rarely took all aspects of the issue into consideration (whether commercial, economic, legal-political or environmental), the Committee considered the dilemma in a more balanced way. The report summarized the deep economic and commercial interests of several states,[139] while also drawing on increasingly valuable scientific data and research (on the migration and the general conditions of different migratory species),[140] to address the growing fear of the extinction of marine species.

Indeed, some of the voices and claims that were heard with regard to whales reflected clear conservationist patterns, too. However, unlike other marine fauna, whales were the only case (and species) that the parties involved discussed – the League and the Codification Committee in particular. The Codification Committee clearly distinguished between the whale and all the other creatures of the sea, warning of "years of national catastrophe,"[141] "progressive diminution of production which … has [caused] alarm,"[142] or simply that the situation was "disastrous."[143] Any concern for species other than whales was driven by commercial interests alone, and no one urged protection of this wildlife. Even the scientists who would later become part of the evolving discussion did not seem overly concerned about the survival of other species, as they were with whales, due to broad, historical, considerations. Science and scientists initially played a leading role in the commercial-industrial race to increase the number of successful catches, and they were working for the betterment of the harvest (and did not advocate limiting or regulating it). As such, they

> carefully studied the question of migration and the general conditions under which these fish live, in order to ascertain the place and depth at which they are to be found and direct the fishing fleets accordingly.
>
> The progress of biological research, which, by studying the whole migratory cycle of each species of aquatic animal, has made it possible

[139] It refers, specifically, to the "national economy of the Northern European peoples" (Report on the Questionnaire, *supra* note 132, at 102).

[140] Such as various eels or sardines (*Id.* at 103).

[141] *Id.* at 102.

[142] *Id.* at 103.

[143] *Id.* at 102.

> to determine the locality in which it is to be found at any given time of the year, so that it may be caught more easily.[144]

As will be described in the following sections, when it came to the matter of the whaling dilemma, scientists (and science) would find themselves in a very different position compared to the one they had held over questions concerning (other) migratory marine fauna.

The changing role of science in regulating commercial activity in the seas reflects the complexity of the issue. While the report, which drew heavily on scientific data and discourse, acknowledged how important successful fishing was to states that relied on it for their national economies, the report also highlighted the danger of using science to justify commercial initiatives. The successful use of science supported these states' fishing industries on the one hand, but also allowed for the over-exploitation of marine fauna on the other hand. "This intensive fishery, assisted by biological research and continual improvements in fishing apparatus, fishing-boats and the preparations of the products themselves, has now begun to produce results which may well prove disastrous; in any case, it is already causing a continual decrease in production."[145]

Either way, science and scientists were gaining more and more attention in international environmental issues, and scientists' concerns about overfishing were quickly becoming central to the discussion. Scientific discourse enabled more accurate observations and hence allowed for better conclusions to be drawn. Moreover, given its institutional capabilities, the League stood as a centralizing forum in which these kinds of considerations could get proper treatment. In this way, the League and its environmental regime marked a transition from earlier or parallel transnational and ad hoc frameworks to international and institutionalized ones:

> Most of these scientific data are already available. Some are being studied by oceanographical institutes, biological stations and laboratories; they have formed the subject of great scientific expeditions. Others are scattered throughout the economic, legal, political and social bibliography of the various countries. All available data must be prepared for such further research . . . by a special institute created for the purpose by the League of Nations. The problem is too vast and important a one to be treated empirically; it demands careful collaboration between the leading scientific institutes of all countries . . . .[146]

144 *Id.* at 102, 105 (respectively).
145 *Id.* at 102.
146 *Id.* at 108–09.

This kind of comparative look demonstrates the difference in the way the Codification Committee and the League discussed and dealt with the subject of decreasing marine fauna in general, and the whaling problem in particular. The issue of concern for other marine species, which raised international alarm during that time, involved mostly economic and commercial interests. However, when whales were discussed, the discourse shifted to include explicit environmental concerns regarding their possible extinction, alongside conservationist considerations. In the case of other species, when shoals of fish started suddenly to disappear from the shores of Newfoundland, Iceland, and the banks of the North Sea, the emphasis was almost entirely on the industry and its interests, and not necessarily on the different species of endangered fish. All of the actors involved, whether the Codification Committee, the League itself, or scientists and biologists, did their best to protect the industry's survival. Once special measures had been taken, the fisheries industry would be able to prosper once again:

> As soon as these shoals make their appearance [again], great fishing expeditions set out . . . in which all the fishing fleets of seafaring folk are part. The preparation of the catch affords employment for a powerful industry, with thousands of factories, cold-storage room and costly apparatus of every kind installed along the coasts of every continent. This industry provides work for millions of workpeople and contributes to the food supplies of populations in the interior, even in the remote districts.[147]

Embracing this comparative perspective, it should also be noted that in both cases – migratory fish and whales as well – at least some of the states involved decided there was an urgent need to turn to international law for help. While some made this decision based on the Committee's concluding report, others did so based on their former experience. Roumania, in that sense, stood as a successful example of a comparative case study that justified international law as the applicable legal framework, instead of local, national-domestic, and regional arrangements. In similar cases, these kinds of legal frameworks failed to protect other species of marine fauna. The report strengthened its focus on the need for international regulation and used an almost personal recommendation from one of its members, based on his nation's experience. He suggested turning to regional and transnational mechanisms (which were nevertheless in vain, as environmental history has shown):

[147] *Id.* at 103.

> As a Roumanian, I cannot refrain from quoting the case of sturgeon in the Black Sea ... which, in spite of all the protective measures applied by Roumania in and at the mouth of the Danube – measures which, by special convantions [sic], made binding on the four other Danube riparian states – nevertheless displayed an increasing tendency to disappear.[148]

The Codification Committee claimed that binding international regulation, rather than any national, regional, or transnational environmental-legal cooperation, was the only real and lasting solution to the problem. Certain states had already initiated previous campaigns that had struggled to protect their fishery industries, despite the different protective measures they attempted to implement "in their legislation,"[149] "including even artificial re-stocking." However, all of these solutions failed to protect marine fauna. Eventually, "these species [were] rapidly decreasing."[150]

It seems that the Danube experience, together with the difficulties and entanglements it revealed regarding the international nature of this issue, resulted in a better understanding of the policy needed to address the problem:

> The young sturgeon are exterminated, because the open seas are international water where there is no law to prohibit fishery. The result is that the full-grown fish ... are becoming increasingly rare, while the old-established fishing colonies engaged in the sturgeon fishery are being slowly ruined. Consequently, fishermen are everywhere complaining that the number of sturgeon is decreasing, while whales, seals and several other aquatic animals have already been exterminated.[151]

Once the Codification Committee had turned its attention to marine fauna and whales, the League's tone developed a sense of urgency. "The same dangerous symptoms are now appearing among other migratory species," declared the Codification Committee on page 103 of its special report, and continued further on: "[T]he path now being followed in exploiting the products of the sea is a highly dangerous one and may soon lead to the destruction of the greatest natural wealth placed by Providence at the disposal of man ... ."[152] The Committee used the same warnings when it explained that whales might suffer the same fate as the herring: as a result of modern fishing technologies, its numbers had

[148] *Id.* at 104 (emphasis added).
[149] *Id.* at 103.
[150] *Id.*
[151] *Id.* at 105.
[152] *Id.* at 105–06.

been depleted so drastically that the countries that relied on this species suffered from "years of national catastrophe."

This sense of alarm and the urgent environmental discourse are also exemplified by one of the concluding paragraphs of the report. It merged several principles that echoed different missions undertaken by the League: the severe situation of natural resources (some of which were also considered to be raw materials);[153] the need for rational, collective global action under the auspices of the League and by means of international law; the inefficient and reckless exploitation of nature (mostly by hungry industries); and the central role of science and scientists in the measures to be taken. Given the urgency, the League made nature itself a relevant player in the game of international law. Since nature was not capable of advocating for itself, the League did so on its behalf through the legal discourse:

> Nature is therefore sending out a warning to the effect that the vandalistic methods of fishing now being applied can no longer be continued, and must be replaced as soon as possible by rational exploitation based on a system of international protective measures dictated by science in accordance with the results of oceanographical and biological research.[154]

The Codification Committee reflected on a variety of perspectives relating to nature: from utilitarian conservationism to preservationism. Some of these notions were direct and explicit, while others had to be interpreted from the text and discourse. Revising the different replies and preparing its conclusions, the Committee came to view the ocean as one complete and vulnerable ecosystem. Therefore, the Committee aimed not to limit its authority to the issue of whales alone, but to promote a universal solution for the high seas – nothing more, nothing less:

153 *See* the general discussion on raw materials as part of the League's concern or interest in Section 4.2.1 of Chapter 4.

154 Report on the Questionnaire, *supra* note 132, at 105. The progressive approach with which the Codification Committee, one of many appointed to inspect international-environmental aspects, handled these issues can be clearly identified by the study of these different action-copy documents in the archives. As the Committee originally chose to write "*nature* is therefore sending out a warning . . .," the referee/s of the document circled (for the first and only time in this report) the word "nature," and put a bold question mark in the middle of the page, almost as if to ask why "nature" had been given a human role. For a similar (rather later) discussion on the role of nature and animals as legal players *see, e.g.*, David Boyd, The Rights of Nature: A Legal Revolution That Could Save the Planet (2017), in which Boys elaborates on legal discourses and moves that aim to provide nature and species legal entities, as well as rights.

> Above all, we must realise that our efforts cannot be directed solely to preventing the destruction of certain species of animals – quite apart from their relative importance – which man's rapacity threatens with extermination, such as the cetaceans and pinnipeds (whales and seals). Our aim should be a wider one – to preserve intact the whole productive force of the riches of the sea, animal, vegetable and mineral, and by a rational system of exploitation to make the sea permanently provide the human race with the quantity and quality of food and economic products of which it is capable.[155]

Finalizing its report, the Codification Committee prepared a detailed road map for the coming years to achieve the League's goals. The Committee did not limit its steps for action to a theoretical discussion, but recruited both the institutional energies and the capabilities of the League for the mission ahead. It recommended that the League carry out three specific stages: first, it was to convene a conference of experts "in applied biology, economists and international law experts of all States possessing maritime interests." Moreover, the discussion was not an abstract one and it did not hold steadfastly to the realm of law alone, but related specifically to the ways in which these necessary arrangements should be carried out with regard to the open sea. The Committee completed its report by saying that this special conference would establish "fundamental principles," a relevant program of "detailed inquiries" and "means of application," and the formation of a central research institute that would gather all the relevant necessary data. Moreover, this research institute was to collaborate with existing institutions of all countries such as zoological institutions, fishery services, and institutes of the social economy. Second, the League would need to support and inspect the work of this proposed central research institute, which would collect and coordinate data, carry out research, identify problems, and prepare "all material for the final solution." Third, and finally, a new conference would then be convened, based on the data gathered through the scientific work, in order to discuss and adapt "the final solution for the new body of law."[156]

The Codification Committee was setting quite a challenge for the League with this road map. While both the suggested meeting of experts and the international conference were achieved during the interwar period,[157] the objective research institution that the Committee had

[155] *Id.* at 108.

[156] Report of the Committee of Experts of the Exploitation of the Products of the Sea, Jan. 24, 1927, LoN Archives, 19/55517/47284, at 111.

[157] This meeting of experts took place in Paris in April 1927; the first international conference on whaling was held by the League in London in June 1931, and the second was also in London, in June 1937.

outlined turned out to be rather different than the one the Committee initially had in mind. When it came to the whaling problem, the powerful whaling nations, such as Norway, Britain, Finland, and Denmark promoted the Copenhagen-based International Council for the Exploration of the Seas, an international consortium of (mostly) whaling industries and governmental officials of several nations.[158] The Council served as a research organization, providing the League and its expert committees with necessary data and statistics. However, this Copenhagen Council was also closely affiliated with several whaling nations. It could therefore hardly be in the interests of the Council or its member states to open the floor to institutions like the League, which had already begun to widen the circle of participants. The Committee was intently focused on advancing collective action within the world of international law, and saw the need for a very precise practical solution to the crisis. In one of its conclusions, the Committee laid out the dilemma in legal terms:

> The aim of world legislation must be carefully determined. In the first place, we have . . . the 'mare liberum', that is to say, the whole ocean apart from those portions of the sea which constitute the territorial waters of riparian State. But it is those portions of . . . water [the mare liberum] which are often of decisive importance in the problem of protecting aquatic animals.[159]

Therefore, the Committee concluded that another general convention concerning marine fauna would not be enough. It understood its part in

[158] The Conseil International de Copenhague was a transnational body of marine states with central whaling industries, such as Norway, Great Britain, and Denmark. It worked on the basis of an informal gentlemen's agreement from 1902, and served as a forum for exchange and correspondence between interested parties and states involved in commercial fishing. Its main aim was to serve as a center for comparative biological and hydrographic data for the fishing industry. As I will elaborate, the Copenhagen Council took on a leading role in the whaling regulation negotiations, as a unique NGO, or as a transnational organization affiliated with several Western states (though not necessarily Western powers of that time). It was influenced by the spirit of internationalism in nature sciences at the turn of the century, but was not an autonomous institution, and persons that participated in its discussions represented the interests of their countries. Generally speaking, and throughout the whaling regulation campaign, the Council's interests were determined by the economic interests of Western states that were exploiting the sea. Besides the Copenhagen Council, the League also consulted and communicated with several other NGOs (or non-state agencies) on that matter, such as the International Mercantile Marine Officers Association (whose head office was located in Antwerp, Belgium). For the Correspondence between the League and the Association *see* 19/63331/63331 (III), dated Dec. 30, 1927.

[159] Report on the Questionnaire, *supra* note 132, at 109.

the context of an existing legal framework; however, it also recognized the shortcomings of this framework given that it lacked the necessary international reach (which the League seemed to be able to offer) to solve the problem. Thus, there was an urgent need for collective (legal) action specific to securing the whale: "[A] great many of the less migratory species of the inhabitants of the sea are adequately protected by the many bilateral and plurilateral conventions which exist and ... it would be a mistake to superimpose upon them a general convention relating to such species."

To the Committee, there was no doubt that whaling was a subject suited to the mechanisms of international law; it was also certain that the consideration of whaling should include not only whaling nations, but also other bodies. At this stage, and given the environmental context, the League exercised what one could call a *deep interpretation* of international law: it insisted that not only states but also other players, such as nongovernmental and external or independent organizations, should take part in the discussion. The League called explicitly to take scientific knowledge into account and to summon experts and scientists to assist in the creation of international law. The League intentionally promoted a supranational framework on the question of whaling. A simple paragraph (circulated by the League on behalf of the Codification Committee in the spring of 1927) from one of the papers detailing preparations for the special meeting of experts (held in Paris in April 1927), supports this interpretation:

> We therefore recommend that the Council should summon a Conference of technical experts of the problems involved; that these experts should be selected not upon a national basis but in such a way as to represent the different regions involved and the different kinds of species involved; that the assistance of the international organizations ... should be involved ....[160]

The Codification Committee specified exactly how this whaling regulation should be advanced to achieve blanket protection for all species of whale.[161] In many ways, one can interpret the battlefield of whaling within the world of international law as an ongoing campaign that

[160] Action Copy of Proposed Conclusions submitted by M. McNair on behalf of the Committee of Experts for the Progressive Codification of International Law, Questionnaire No. 7. (Products of the Sea), Mar. 27, 1927, LoN Archives, 19/58475/47284, at 2 [hereinafter Proposed Conclusions].

[161] The Committee was rather reluctant at this stage to limit or minimize the scope of the planned whaling regulation by making it specific to one species of whale.

stretched throughout the 1920s and 1930s under the auspices of the League. This campaign began with Question No. 7 and the numerous replies received from interested states, and was followed by preparations for the next step – summoning an international conference to deal specifically with the problem as an issue of international law.

In this twisting story, the Codification Committee did all that it could to widen the scope of international whaling law as far as the horizon allowed. It aimed first to break free from transnational arrangements (bilateral and multilateral) and, second, to move away from limited protection for only specific species of whale. When other players, with different interests and expectations of the future of whaling, struggled to limit the number of different species of whale at stake, the Committee deliberately suggested viewing the species as a whole:

> We recommend . . . that by the terms of reference of the Conference thus constituted the Conference should be requested . . . to give special attention to the case of whales of all kinds and . . . to draft a general convention or a series of plurilateral conventions for its conservation, and to consider and advise whether there are other species of the inhabitants of the sea whose conservation would be fostered either by general or plurilateral conventions, and, if so, upon the best method of achieving this result.[162]

In the case of whaling, the rule of international law differed from the cases of "other" aquatic animals. A comparison between the creatures of the sea, based on the League and the Committee's deliberations, might suggest that while other species were caught between jurisdictions, the whale was a pure subject of international law and did not fall into the domain of domestic law or national sovereignty at all. In the case of other species of marine fauna, especially fish and seals, the principle of mare liberum was often applied, with its promise that no national law would apply on the high seas. There were also "portions" of territorial water that were often of "decisive importance"[163] because fishing or hunting took place there. Great reserves and certain lakes along the sea coasts, lagoons, and harbors were of "paramount importance," particularly in the case of salmon and sturgeon.[164] Beyond the measures that the Codification Committee took to protect the whale, it was much less eager to confront sovereignty and the economic-political interest of other states: "These

[162] Proposed conclusions, *supra* note 160, at 2.

[163] Report on the Questionnaire, *supra* note 132, at 109.

[164] Roumania had warned of a similar problem in the case of the whales. *See* the discussion in Section 2.3.2 above.

measures will require careful consideration in order to avoid any action derogatory to the great interest of the various countries and their sovereign rights."[165] The whale, however, remained almost completely beyond the reach of any nation state's jurisdiction, which made it the target for other considerations and possible solutions.

Which measures ought to be adopted? After the Codification Committee had analyzed the different replies and agendas and discussed the implications of Question No. 7, its legal-environmental investigation led to a visionary proposal – one that imposed some daring limitations on a powerful industry that had been expanding almost completely without external restrictions prior to the League. These measures included rotating sanctuaries, closed seasons for whaling, and the articulation of the principle that all nations should be governed by a binding international convention. Many of these measures would become more familiar in *later* attempts to fight the threat against marine fauna and whales, and would be developed after the League was dissolved.

The preliminary report[166] also claimed that certain measures of the legal proposal should, "in the first place," supply certain definite requirements established by scientific investigation, such as encouraging reproduction amongst certain species, protecting fries, defining regions of seasonal protection, absolute or temporary prohibition of catching threatened species, and more.[167]

Although most of its focus was on what can be termed "law on the books," the League was both aware of and involved in concerns regarding law in action, and how these kinds of solutions should be enforced on the ground. The Codification Committee practically acknowledged that such progressive measures, which were defining a new spectrum of international law with regard to sovereignty and its limits, could not rely merely on acceptance and ratification by the states. The Committee discussed ways and tools that would enable the realization – and legal enforcement – of the suggested global regulation. The Committee concluded that special performative bodies would be established and made responsible for the effective application of these measures. However, fundamental difficulties with this global marine regulation emerged and continue to be the subject of contemporary discussions on international whaling law in the twenty-first

[165] Report on the Questionnaire, *supra* note 132, at 109.

[166] Meaning, the Report on the Questionnaire of the Committee of Experts for the Progressive Codification of International Law, Jan. 24, 1927, LoN Archives, 19/55517/47284.

[167] Report on the Questionnaire, *supra* note 132, at 110.

century. "What penalties could be levied on offenders, and in virtue of what right?" asked the Committee out loud:

> What are the obligations to which the various States could subscribe by means of an international agreement without, by so doing, sacrificing their legitimate interests, or without shouldering a burden too heavy for them to bear? These . . . are the questions of principle which the League must solve before any measures can be adopted for establishing a rational exploitation of the products of the sea.

In other words, these environmental questions also raised general considerations of international law per se. The environment, and the dilemmas it revealed, stimulated macro-questions that moved beyond the frame of a balance between preservation, conservation, and commercial interests.

Based on the core issues that the Codification Committee included in its concluding report, the League then moved on to presenting a complete draft for an international whaling law. The Committee felt at least some of the comments and replies accredited it with a mandate to push forward a joint effort. As the report of January 1927 recommended, the next step in the campaign was to convene a special meeting of a group of experts in Paris in April 1927, in the hopes of reaching a consensus on an advanced version that would form the basis for an international convention.

2.3.4 Toward the April 1927 Experts Meeting in Paris, and the British Interdepartmental Conference on the Question of International Control of Whaling (October 1927)

The Codification Committee was overwhelmed by the variety of replies and different interpretations of this question of environmental international law. Nevertheless, it maintained an optimistic view of the matter. Several of the Committee members saw the big bang over Question No. 7 not as a problem, but rather as an opportunity to expand the Committee's role and, perhaps, also to strengthen its conclusions.

After one year of receiving, collecting, and reviewing the different replies, the Codification Committee was satisfied that it had gathered enough support to push forward its initiative. In one of its drafts for proposed conclusions on Question No. 7 and the issue of the products of the sea, M. McNair, one of the Committee's members, concluded that these replies "are definitely favourable to the summoning of an

International Conference . . ., " something that was not completely true – at least as far as it depended on certain whaling powers, as I will elaborate. The Committee was intent on drawing a very specific picture from the replies – one that would support its conclusions and (mostly) back up its planned follow-up steps, and assist it with marking its territory vis-à-vis other players that had their own agenda:

> The many valuable memoranda which we have received from the Governments in replying seem to us to point to the [following] conclusions:
>
> (a) that this is a . . . matter in which it is possible to subordinate particular interests of a political and economic character to the world interest of conserving the natural resources of the sea;
> (b) that *the case of the whale* which by reason of its extensive migratory habits *seem to me more of an international animal* than most of the inhabitants of the sea demands special treatment.[168]

The Codification Committee left little room for a different interpretation of the replies as a whole. "This Report shows," the Committee decisively asserted, "that, generally speaking, the replies from Governments approve the conclusions of Professor Suárez, and nearly all the replies, even some of those which are unfavourable, recognise the importance of the question and the necessity of its regulation by means of agreement." The Committee also did not forget to include in its report to the Secretariat, first and foremost, the support of the French: "Among the favourable replies, mention should be made of that from the French Government, which emphasises the importance of immediate international measures to prevent the extinction of marine animals in the near future, and put an end to the reckless slaughter reported from different quarters."[169]

The fact that the French reply was the first mentioned in the Codification Committee's special concluding report was by no means coincidental. This probably had something to do with the leading role of France in the international alignment of the interwar period.[170] But besides that, the legal work of interpreting the replies and weaving

[168] Action Copy of Proposed Conclusions submitted by M. McNair on behalf of the Committee of Experts for the Progressive Codification of International Law, Questionnaire No. 7. (Products of the Sea), Mar. 28, 1927, LoN Archives, 19/58475/47284 (emphasis added).

[169] Economic Committee – Exploitation of the Products of the Sea: Note by the Secretariat – the History of the Question, Oct. 14, 1927, LoN Archives, 19/62527/62527 (I), at 2.

[170] And as a Permanent Member of the League's Council (*see supra* note 75).

(some of) them into one coherent document with legal instructions and implications, gave the Committee relative freedom to formulate a document that reflected its own agenda. Therefore, the tone and discourse that were used adopted – and echoed – Suárez's perspective. France, in that case, emphasized the importance of an "immediate" international solution to the problem.

The Codification Committee seemed to sideline the more reluctant approaches, such as those of Norway and Britain, with the "international consciousness" it was striving to shape. Instead of engaging with all aspects of the dilemma, the Committee preferred to draw a description of the evolving diplomatic and legal dispute in a way that better suited its agenda and goals: "Several Governments are of the opinion that preliminary enquiries should be made." Replies from states that were concerned that the League would create a new authority by promoting and enforcing a global whaling regulation, such as China for instance, were cautiously woven into the concluding report to the Secretariat. As such, strong objections, such as "requests for further inquiries," became far more muted in the report. Likewise, the report promoted replies that supported the desire to establish a whaling regulation, such as the Polish stance: "[T]he Polish representative stated that the question ... *was in fact that of protecting the valuable fauna of the deep sea against extermination by uneconomic exploitation.*"[171]

In April 1927, as recommended by the Codification Committee after it had concluded studying the replies, the League organized a special forum of experts, named the International Committee for the Protection of the Great Cetaceans. This was a meeting of whaling experts that convened in Paris to revise Suárez and his Committee's reports and preliminary proposals as a basis for international whaling law.

Thanks to Abel Gruvel, a French professor and government advisor, a treaty proposal was put forward for discussion in Paris. Originally, Gruvel had proposed a whaling regulation in 1913.[172] Although the French proposal forms part of a larger picture of early French involvement in nature protection or imperial conservation,[173] it seems that the

[171] Report by the Economic Committee on the matter of Exploitation of the Products of the Sea: Note by the Secretariat – History of the Question, Memorandum from Oct. 14, 1927, 19/62527/62527 (II), at 3 (emphasis in the original).

[172] DORSEY, *supra* note 4, at 34.

[173] The first campaign to restrict whaling had already begun in 1913 as it aimed to secure whale stocks in the waters of France own colonies. It seems that the French general policy had expressed a will to internationalize its own initiative. Hosting the 1927 experts

strong support for international law, which the Codification Committee had introduced in the preliminary stages, was somehow replaced at the Paris meeting by a gentleman's agreement. Unlike the concrete (though still preliminary) legal ideas the Codification Committee raised at the Paris meeting, Gruvel's proposal was based more on the concept of "mutual understanding" of powers than on obligations and restrictions governed by the new institutional authority (and energy) of the League. Compared to the practical solutions of rotating sanctuaries and the like that the Committee had proposed, those at the Paris meeting favored the French proposal, which was less progressive and also less demanding of whaling powers and their industries:

> France has thought that all the naturalists of the world should join together and come to an understanding, not to interfere with an interesting industry but to try to regulate the destruction of the animal species in the interest of Science in the first place and in the interest of the world industry in the second place.[174]

In some ways, the far more assertive method of dealing with environmental international law, which had been introduced only a short time earlier during the first round of the Committee versus the whaling nations, was replaced by a more cautious and hesitant one. Some might argue that this cautious approach was more diplomatic and balanced. Johan Hjort, the Norwegian representative at the experts meeting in Paris, mentioned with some concern that certain whaling nations might refuse to sign the new convention prepared by the League. Gruvel replied that it would hence depend on "the *honesty* and *goodwill* of the powers."[175] It seems that the time was not yet ripe to introduce a complete convention draft to the international committee; the Paris meeting of experts had certainly discouraged some of the progressive

meeting in Paris was perhaps based on the fact that the Empire introduced conservationist patterns in transnational contexts prior to the whaling dilemma. The International Convention for the Protection of Useful Birds was signed in Paris in 1902. In 1909, the first International Conference on Local Heritage and Landscape Protection took place in the capital as well. In 1923, the first public international congress for nature conservation was invited to France as a private initiative. *See*, among others, Diana K. Davis, *Eco-Governance in French Algeria: Environmental History, Policy, and Colonial Administration*, 32 J.W. Soc. for French Hist. 328 (2004).

174 Minutes of the International Committee for the Protection of the Great Cetaceans, Apr. 7, 1927, LoN Archives, 19/55517/47280.

175 *Id.* (emphasis added). Also appears in: Minutes of the International Committee for the Protection of the Great Cetaceans, Apr. 7, 1927, NAC, RG 23, File 721-19-5[3].

solutions and the agenda that the Codification Committee was considering at that time.

After the Paris meeting in April, the Codification Committee continued in its efforts. In a report to the Assembly from late September 1927, M. Politis, the Greek representative to the Codification Committee, stated that they had "carefully examined" different documents and had reached several conclusions on the questionnaire as a whole. Politis noted that several questions that had been introduced to the international community in the original questionnaire "by now appear ripe for Regulation by International Agreement,"[176] such as those dealing with nationality, diplomatic privileges and immunities, or piracy. However, given the deluge of replies and different perspectives on the issue of whaling, the Committee was firmly of the opinion that this issue "should be governed by a special procedure."[177] Despite the discontent leading powers had expressed at the Paris meeting, the Codification Committee seemed intent on pushing the League – from within – toward a revolutionary whaling regulation. In the process, the Committee dismissed opponents' claims that there was no danger threatening the survival of the whale, stating, "[t]here is no doubt that marine fauna is exposed to the risk of early extermination by exploitation which is opposed to economic principle." Moreover, given that no solution could be found in any domestic legislation, no matter how advanced it might be, "[i]nternational protection would fill a real need and at the same time meet the wish of all Governments concerned." Hence, with its legal mechanisms, the League was the most suitable and capable forum by which this kind of environmental arrangement could be delivered. "It would be well worth while to establish such protection by means of an international agreement . . . ."[178]

The planned regulations were based on the questionnaire and a comparative legal study of different maritime agreements. Suárez analyzed sixteen treaties that dealt with local or transnational questions relating to marine fauna.[179] In a report to the Secretariat, he indicated as the representative of the Codification Committee that it was possible to establish an economic "rationale" for the use of marine resources, based

[176] Report of the First Committee for the Progressive Codification of International Law to the Assembly, Sept. 23, 1927, LoN Archives, 62453 A. 105. 1927. V., at 1.

[177] *Id.* at 2.

[178] *Id.*

[179] Appendix to the Report on the Exploitation of the Products of the Sea: List of International Treaties on the Regulation of Maritime Industries (Rapporteur: J. L. Suárez), Jan. 8, 1928, LoN Archives, C.P.D.I.28.

on an appropriate legal framework. However, the existing multilateral treaties were all too brief.[180] Moreover, this partial legal framework was insufficient to address the fact that "[t]he wealth constituted by the creatures of the deep is not fixed in the sense of being confined to one region or latitude but varies from year to year according to the biological, physical and chemical circumstances affecting the plankton among which they live."[181] Therefore, any whaling regulation presented by the League would need to address four general principles: the establishment of protected areas, which would be used only in a rotation system; the development of protection periods and age limits for hunting; efficient implementation and fixed international supervision of the regulation; and agreement on how to ensure the accession of all maritime nations to a common legal framework.

The preliminary proposal was also holistic in that it reflected the latest findings in zoology. Suárez stressed the ecological importance of the continental shelf for the regeneration of fish stocks, upon which whales and other species were dependent. He pointed out that the disappearance of certain species would "destroy the balance" in the ocean and would bring about an "extinction of other species also."[182] The three-mile-wide shelf was where the nurseries of future food fish were located, and this basic physical condition had to set the framework for the new regulation. According to Suárez, the legal regime not only had to react to the new biological findings, but also had to be integrated into a humanistic educational concept. Whales appeared to him as actors whose needs had to be met through international law. Whales, in particular, were "happier in this than men, are ignorant of jurisdiction and national frontiers and observe not international law but internationalism; the sea for them is a single realm." The report interpreted international law as a living organism that needed to keep evolving. As an aquatic animal, the whale was essentially migratory and, given this characteristic, it should find "its counterpart in a legal solidarity in the sphere of international law in which we are working."

In a similar report, Suárez linked the need for legal solidarity to the geopolitical circumstances of that period. He portrayed the whales as "refugees" with an instinct for self-preservation, who were driven by whalers across the oceans of the world. In doing so, he purposefully

[180] *Id.*
[181] *Id.* at 2.
[182] *Id.* at 2.

established displaced individual rights, refugees, and peace as central tasks for the League.[183] During a time when central parts of the League were committed to protecting minority groups and communities in need, the Codification Committee, and Suárez in particular, deliberately staged the whale as an icon of persecution and exploitation – one whose protection depended on the League and its mechanisms of international law.

As expressed in many other discussions throughout its environmental regime,[184] the League was not actually satisfied with diplomats alone, but rather emphasized the role of experts – and of scientists in particular. The case of whaling drew heavily on, and gave special expression to, their expertise.

The Committee's conclusions seemed to oppose whaling powers. The conclusions appeared all the more daring since the Codification Committee and the League both had a very young history, and questionable authority compared to other nations sharing the same diplomatic space and capacity. The Codification Committee, young and inexperienced as it was, knew that in order to better promote the goal of whale conservation, it would need to keep the picture as *international* – and as *professional* – as it could. This meant not favoring competing commercial and industrial (and national) interests instead. Alongside "regular" diplomats, jurists, and statesmen, scientific experts were very welcome:

> We therefore recommend that the Council should summon a Conference of technical experts connected with both the economic and the scientific aspects of the problems involved; that these experts should be selected *not upon a national basis* but in such a way as to represent the different regions involved and the different kinds of species involved.[185]

This mode of international investigation also encouraged Suárez to promote his visionary proposal for a new whaling regulation, the main elements of which had been introduced in the concluding report as general

[183] Report on the Exploitation of the Products of the Sea (Rapporteur: J.L. Suárez), Nov. 2, 1927, LoN Archives C.196.M.70.1927, at 124.

[184] As well as others, including humanitarian and sociopolitical ones. *See* the discussion in Chapter 5, in which I elaborate on the role of experts in the daily professional diplomatic routine of the League. For a variety of studies on the central role of professional experts in the institutional work of the League *see, e.g.*, THE LEAGUE OF NATIONS' WORK ON SOCIAL ISSUES: VISIONS, ENDEAVOURS AND EXPERIMENTS, *supra* note 2.

[185] Action Copy of Proposed Conclusions submitted by M. McNair on behalf of the Committee of Experts for the Progressive Codification of International Law, Questionnaire No. 7. (Products of the Sea), Mar. 28, 1928, LoN Archives, 19/58475/47284, at 2 (emphasis added).

protection measures, which posed an almost direct threat to whaling nations and the industry. It seems that Suárez's role as an expert enabled him to obtain a leading position in drafting the whaling regulation. One can also assume that the tailwind of the previous round (with the support Suárez had found in the replies and the international concern for the future survival of the whale) served as a backdrop for introducing his advanced ideas and suggestions for a complete draft of a revolutionary whaling convention. After Suárez asked to dismiss all previous conventions as insufficient or too commercial, these suggestions for conservationist and preservationist solutions began to include ideas such as rotating sanctuaries, closed seasons for any kind of whaling, and a diplomatic principle by which all nations should be both involved in and subject to any new and unprecedented regulation.

International diplomatic and legal activity continued after the Paris meeting had concluded. At the time, whaling nations, and especially Britain, watched not without a certain concern as the League's initiative gained momentum. The questionnaire, its special focus on the issue of whales and whaling, the growing (and surprising) interest of so many non-involved states and agencies, and the fragile period as a whole required decisive action. The British government decided to call together a special (and in some ways competing) body to better deal with the emerging danger: not the danger threatening the survival of whales on the high seas, but rather the one that threatened British and other whaling nations' interests in keeping the oceans – and the whales – as a free, accessible common. Representatives[186] from eleven different government agencies convened in London at the beginning of October that year (1927), half a year after the Paris experts meeting was adjourned, for a pan-British discussion on the way the League was handling the question of whaling in terms of international law.

During the meetings and discussions of the Interdepartmental Conference on the Question of International Control of Whaling, a similarity emerged regarding the League's reliance on scientific observations and the British conference's use of data provided by professional experts. Both forums based their arguments and conclusions on experts and scientific discourse. Much of the British resistance to firm international regulations at that point was based on the support of different scientists and experts. With this kind of science-based discourse, the

[186] The special London committee assembled not only scientists and diplomats, but also high-ranking officials.

British governmental gathering[187] tried to promote and defend both commercial and imperial interests, and to maintain a much more "balanced" equation than the one sketched on behalf of the League with the Codification Committee.

In one set of its minutes, the British Interdepartmental Conference concluded that priority should be given to commercial needs and not to the conservation cause, stating that "the object to be kept in view was to safeguard the economic future of the industry, and ultimately to secure that the annual destruction of the whales should not exceed the natural annual increase."[188] As a counterattack to the dire forecast presented by the League prior to the British move, Stanley Kemp, one of the British officials, declared that fin and blue whales were actually "as numerous as ever"; he also claimed that humpbacks might just have been migrating differently on the high seas.[189]

Along with the Paris meeting of experts and the (British) London Interdepartmental Conference, 1927 also brought another important player to the whaling table. One of the important decisions made at the Paris meeting was the formal collaboration with the International Council at Copenhagen – the formal name of the consortium of leading whaling industries and governmental agencies that was based in Denmark.[190] Like other pro-whaling players in the 1920s and 1930s, the Copenhagen Council watched with great concern how the League's initiative was making its way toward what the Council saw as its oceans around the world. It seems that the fact that the Council also managed to obtain itself a formal role in the League's routine had a certain effect on narrowing the radius of the League's authority with regard to promoting relatively conservationist perspectives, and also regarding its chances of succeeding in its mission.

Efforts to engage the Copenhagen Council in the whaling dilemma had started prior to 1927. Throughout the long process of gathering replies to the questionnaire, whaling nations were lobbying the Copenhagen Council to come on board. Moreover, given the need for technical expertise, economic experts, on behalf of the League's Economic Committee (like

187 With officials of the Colonial Office, Foreign Office, India Office, Admiralty, Ministry of Agriculture and Fisheries, as well as several other administrative agencies.

188 Minutes of the Interdepartmental Conference on the Question of International Control of Whaling, Oct. 12, 1927, NAC, General Records of the Ministry of Fisheries, vol. 1081, File 721-19-5[3].

189 *Id.*

190 See in Section 2.3.3 above.

their jurist peers on the Codification Committee), were looking to the Copenhagen Council for assistance. In September 1927, the Assembly officially approved this approach.[191] In one of the following conclusions prepared by the Codification Committee, it concluded that it was up to the Assembly to determine that the Committee "study, in collaboration with the International Council at Copenhagen and any other organization specially interested in this matter, the question whether and in what terms, for what species and in what areas, international protection of marine fauna could be established."[192]

Although the League had collaborated with a variety of non-state actors throughout its two decades of activity, its cooperation with the Copenhagen Council – which several members of the League encouraged – actually turned out to be a problematic decision from an environmentalist or pro-whale perspective. Although the League often involved a variety of organizations (which sometimes had opposing views to its leading member states) to contribute to its initiatives, it tied its hands by recruiting the Copenhagen Council to its mission. Much of the Codification Committee's enthusiastic spirit to deliver change for the devastating world of whales became limited and supervised by the Copenhagen Council: indeed, though it was a non-state actor, which the League often favored, the Copenhagen Council supported a framework that decisively represented and promoted the interests of whaling nations and industries.

Whether the Codification Committee's initiative was progressive or not, the League's institutional framework and legal routine set a procedural example for others to follow. Members of the Committee, as representatives of the League, started to collaborate with the Copenhagen Council to comply with a resolution adopted by the Assembly on September 23, 1927, which additionally required them to reach an agreed international convention. "I have been especially entrusted with the matter," wrote Charles Smets, an official of the League Secretariat, to Adolf Jensen, Chief of the Department of Statistics in the Ministry of Finance in Denmark,

> and I venture therefore to ask if you could . . . approach people from the International Council . . . in order to find out if they have any ideas about what might be done, i.e. on what lines they contemplate such collaboration

[191] Work of the Committee of Experts for the Progressive Codification of International Law: Resolution adopted by the Council on June 13, 1927, LoN Archives, A.18.1927, at 7.

[192] Report of the First Committee for the Progressive Codification of International Law to the Assembly, Sept. 23, 1927, LoN Archives, 62453 A. 105. 1927. V., at 5.

> and for what species of animals *they think* that some kind of international protection is needed and could possibly be secured.[193]

In many ways, the League's collaboration with the Copenhagen Council – likely influenced by certain whaling powers' attention and the League's reliance on scientific and professional diplomacy during the interwar period – was akin to letting the fox guard the henhouse. The League – and not the Codification Committee – allowed the Copenhagen Council, a body with clear commercial interests and economic incentives, to supply data and to define part of the planned international policy. The expertise and cooperation the Copenhagen Council had to offer released the Codification Committee from duty. With Resolution E 346 of its September Session, the Assembly empowered the Economic Committee to investigate the issue, and the legal experts of the Codification Committee who had launched the initiative seemed to step aside. With them, Suárez's universal approach became weakened.

The late 1920s were a crucial time for the endeavor to protect the whale through international law. The Codification Committee and its questionnaire; the vivid responses of key players and new voices in the international arena; the preliminary suggestions for legal restrictions and limitations on whaling; the Paris meeting of experts and the London Interdepartmental Conference – all this and more heralded a new kind of internationalism. Suárez's initiative to summon a conference including experts in applied marine zoology, persons engaged in marine (and whaling) industries, and jurists marked an opportunity to overcome the powerful whaling and commercial lobby. Institutionalized as this move was, in many ways it was driven by Suárez's pioneering and Quixotic spirit; with his death, the conservation lobby became vulnerable in the tough world of interwar diplomacy. In 1929 Suárez passed away and, with him, part of the progressive conservationist agenda faded too, which removed the need for certain League departments.

In these uncertain times, the League, as a forum that aimed to promote scientific expertise, opened the door to other bodies besides the Copenhagen Council. As the Council continued to gain power in this fierce match, another scientific body joined the discussion. Zoologists from across the globe had been paying close attention to Suárez and the progressive attitude he and the League were advocating. In 1929 another scientist – this time from a non-member nation, the United States – wrote

[193] Letter from Charles Smets to Adolf Jensen, Nov. 11, 1927, LoN Archives, 19/63036/62524, at 1–2 (emphasis added).

to the League in the hopes of supporting the initiative. In the late 1920s, the conservationist lobby's loss of one of its main leaders[194] seems to have been offset by Remington Kellogg joining the discussion.

Kellogg was an American scientist and a doctor of zoology and paleontology, and a member of the American Society of Mammalogists.[195] As a leading American naturalist, Kellogg had already been concerned with conservationist ideas since the early 1920s, when he conducted the Biological Survey of 1921 based in Washington. His scholarship focused on marine mammals. When he compared databases that were created by previous expeditions, Kellogg became – much like his late South American colleague, Suárez – a true and passionate advocate of whale conservation. His position as a scientist whose field of expertise was whales (and whaling),[196] and the growing importance of scientific expertise in the work of the League, put him in an apt position to influence the institution's work to follow Suárez and the Codification Committee's path.[197]

It should be noted that Kellogg was not the only American scientist who watched the whaling scene with great concern. The fear of overexploitation was common among a small – but influential – group of prominent experts, who joined a lobby calling for more public attention to the environmental problem that humankind had created in the oceans. Starting in the late 1920s and early 1930s, the American Society of Mammalogists took up an important role in the League's international discussions.

Moreover, after addressing the League, Kellogg was invited by the Institution to speak at the special conference the League would soon assemble in 1931. During the second half of the short, but intensive, chapter of the League, Kellogg was appointed as the United States delegate to the International Conference on Whaling to be held in London in 1937,[198] which will be discussed later on.

[194] Professor Suárez died in 1929. In retrospect, his death was likely one of the key reasons for the lost battle to protect the whale during the interwar period.

[195] Later on he was also known for his position as the Director of the United States National Museum.

[196] Kellogg's PhD dissertation established him as an international authority on cetaceans.

[197] For a more detailed description of Kellogg's endeavors to protect whales in the open sea, *see* Frank C. Whitmore, Jr. *Remington Kellogg, in* BIOGRAPHICAL MEMOIRS: NATIONAL ACADEMY OF SCIENCES OF THE UNITED STATES OF AMERICA (VOL. 46) 155–74 (1975).

[198] Kellogg continued to serve the whale cause even after the LoN had collapsed. He was head of the United States delegation in two further conferences in 1944 and 1945 (which took place outside the League's auspices). Moreover, his prominent role in American

This specific American environmental advocacy played, at least to some extent, a role in the evolution of the whaling dilemma. The external involvement of nations such as the United States enabled engagement with diplomacy and international law – and not necessarily through formal and hierarchical channels. The League, with its in-transition framework, which in different cases was also driven by grassroots movements and initiatives from below, enabled – and even encouraged – this kind of participatory and practical international law during the interwar period.

But whaling powers, with the assistance of the Copenhagen Council, put up a persistent fight. With Suárez no longer around to courageously promote conservation efforts, anti-overexploitation agents appeared to be losing some of their hold on the campaign. As the 1930s arrived, the issue was passed on to the Economic Section of the League, which sought advice from the Copenhagen Council.

2.3.5 *The Early 1930s and the First International Whaling Convention*

The second decade of the League opened with new suggestions for solutions from the toolbox of international law. Some of Suárez and the Codification Committee's conservationist ideas managed to find their way in after being discussed in the diplomatic routine of the League, and were articulated in the legal documents that were eventually introduced as a product of the institutional process, while others were left aside.

While the leading whaling nations, particularly Norway and Great Britain,[199] were set on putting a spoke in the wheels of whaling diplomacy as they rushed to defend their industries, other forces – besides scientists and dedicated conservationists – were advocating for the protection of

diplomacy on this issue can also be seen in his appointment as the Chairman of the 1946 Whaling Conference, after which he became the United States Commissioner of International Whaling Commission between 1949 and 1967. He served as Vice Chairman of the Commission between 1949 and 1951, and as its Chairman between 1952 and 1954.

199 Side by side with Japan and France, both of which had been whaling close to their home shores and had commercial interests in expanding and developing their national whaling industries. Although the Codification Committee extracted some relevant material from the French reply to the questionnaire (see my discussion in section III.b. above) that fit its pro-conservation agenda, both France and (especially) Japan eventually displayed a growing reluctance toward the initiative of Suárez and the Codification Committee. The fact that at least two of the nations central to the establishment of the League of Nations – Great Britain and France – resisted the environmental aspects of the Codification Committee had a lot to do with the final results of this move, as I will show.

the whale. In the late 1920s and early 1930s, besides the support from non-involved states[200] to revise the status quo, states such as New Zealand and the United States – which had a direct interest and were involved in international whaling – embraced scientific warnings in support of the League's whaling regulation campaign.

Shortly before the League's Economic Committee took the next steps in the process of international consultation, and convened another meeting of experts in Berlin in the summer of 1930, the dilemma became more complex. A formal report from the New Zealand government weighed up the need to promote the conservation of the whale as a species against the maintenance of whale oil stocks as a global natural resource.[201] Almost simultaneously, it seems that the efforts and scientific advocacy within the American administration, which was carried out by the American Society of Mammalogists, bore fruits: the State Department favorably received anti-whaling petitions, as well as special public statements submitted by a new scientific NGO, the Council for the Conservation of Whales,[202] which was led by the American Society. In one of its reports, sent to the Secretary of State in the early 1930s, this environmental scientific-civilian organization urged the American leadership to take a central role in whaling diplomacy efforts, which the League sought to promote, and to save "these wonderfully adapted creatures, the greatest mammals that have ever inhabited the globe."[203]

New Zealand and the United States promoted a conservationist agenda and supported international regulation; however, the fact that they were not leading actors in the interwar diplomacy, and that the United States was not a member state of the League, meant that like Suárez, some of their influence and weight soon disappeared. This marked a certain shift between the two sides of the whaling equation.

200 Such as Roumania or Venezuela (as I elaborate in Section 2.3.2 above).

201 Whaling Industry and Ross Dependency: Historical Sequel of Incidents (October 1929), Archives of New Zealand, Records of the Ministry of External Affairs, ABHS 950/W4627, File PM 104/6/9/1, pt. 2.

202 The American Society of Mammalogists, watching with great concern how the whale faced the threat of extinction in the early twentieth century, established the Council for the Conservation of Whales, a scientific organization founded and organized by biologists and other scientists. In the period under investigation, its main agenda was conducting and promoting scientific studies, supporting quantitative databases, and establishing channels of communication with the American administration, and relevant regulation.

203 Clinton Abbott, Director, Natural History Museum of San Diego, to Secretary Stimson, Mar. 2, 1932, United States National Archives [hereinafter USNA], RG 59, File 562.8Fi.

Following the earlier discussions, the deliberations of experts, and the preparatory institutional work of the Codification Committee and the League, the second meeting of experts was organized by the Economic Committee and gathered in June 1930 in Berlin in order to create the whaling convention. At the meeting, representatives from most of the whaling nations pieced together a draft for a convention that would later be adopted in 1931, at the League's final formal convention. One of the reports from the Berlin meeting stated that the layout of the central articles used Norway's 1929 whaling law as a blueprint.[204] Moreover, although the meeting was meant to find ways to save the riches of the sea and "to help the whaling industry," the subtitle of the final report additionally emphasized the "protection of whales."[205] As it was still no more than a general layout for a complete convention, the preliminary proposal suggested more research to determine whether it would be wise to outlaw whaling, as planned, in tropical and subtropical waters.[206] As preliminary as the Berlin proposal was in legal terms, two of the British officials that were involved in the June meeting explained that it marked "the beginning of international regulation of whaling."[207]

Based on a mandate given by the Assembly, the Economic Committee had to investigate together with the Copenhagen Council "whether and in what terms, for what species and in what areas international protection ... could be established."[208] The Economic Committee was eager to present useful results, and quickly. The ambitious questionnaire and the steps that followed turned into a draft that referred exclusively to a single economically relevant species – baleen or whalebone whales – as agreed in Article 2 of the draft convention.

Common support for the Berlin proposal[209] paved the way for the full official document. Following the Berlin meeting, the League convened the London Whaling Conference in June 1931, which prepared the final

[204] Report to the Economic Committee of the League of Nations on the Question of Whaling, Berlin Meeting of Experts, June (undated) 1930, LoN Archives, RG 25, vol. 1543, File 455, pt. I [hereinafter Report to the Economic Committee].

[205] Report (by the Economic Committee) to the Council on the Work of the 32d Session, June 14, 1930, LoN Archives, C.353.M.146.1930.II, at 8.

[206] Report to the Economic Committee, *supra* note 204.

[207] P. A. Clutterbuck to A. W. Leeper, Nov. 27, 1930; and Leeper's reply, Dec. 1, 1930, NAGB, FO 371 14932 W382/50.

[208] Extract from Minutes of the 1st Meeting of the 55th Session of the Council, June 10, 1929, LoN Archives 19/41260/10950.

[209] Report (by the Economic Committee) to the Council on the Work of the 32d Session, June 14, 1930, LoN Archives, C.353.M.146.1930.II, at 8.

draft; and on September 24, 1931 it introduced its first full proposal for a binding international convention: the Convention for the Regulation of Whaling, 1931.

The 1931 Convention (or the "1931 Geneva Convention") was actually one of the first conventions achieved by the League. In legal terms, the 1931 Convention brought to the surface new and unfamiliar ideas regarding nature and enforcement. For example, it covered "all waters of the world," including both the high seas and states' territorial and national waters (Article 1). Although the open sea was no-man's-land prior to the establishment of the League, now the League's explicit jurisdiction regarding whales according to the convention stretched across all seas. Moreover, the 1931 Convention demanded that the signing states take "appropriate measures" to ensure both the application of its articles and the necessary "punishment" of their infractions.

The attempt to place the whaling industry under the supervision of international law was an ambitious move in the early 1930s. Article 8 demanded that all whaling vessels be licensed. International law had the chance, even if only on the books, as a legal source of authority to enforce what seemed to be a practical licensing system to monitor hunters out in the open sea.

Although Suárez was already gone, some of his ideas did prevail. At large, and though it was far from being a perfect solution to the whaling problem, the Geneva Convention aimed to protect the biological life cycle of at least some of the whales. Article 5, for instance, banned the killing of calves, immature whales, and female whales accompanied by their calves, a practice that was common among whalers. The importance of scientific expertise also continued to grow and it took on a central role in discussions on the dilemma: according to Article 10, all signatory states were obliged to create a quantitative statistical and scientific database within a central organization.

The League also used the Geneva Convention to battle certain economic incentives in whaling, which were sometimes more powerful than any legal restriction. According to Article 7, whalers were no longer to be paid solely based on the number of whales they caught. In this way, the Geneva Convention aimed to disincentivize the indiscriminate hunting of whales.

Moreover, the first whaling convention did not focusing on industrial whaling alone, which was considered the only real threat to the survival of whales. The Geneva Convention also took into account whaling carried out by native peoples. These traditional methods, so far removed from the explosive new hunting technologies and titanic floating factories used in commercial whaling, were exempted by Article 3. As long as coastal aboriginal peoples utilized "canoes, pirogues or other exclusively native craft propelled by oars or sails," and on the condition that they did not use firearms or employ non-aboriginal staff on their vessels, these traditional and autarkic methods were exempted from the 1931 Convention.[210]

And yet, it was not as conservationist a regulation as the Codification Committee would have liked to achieve. Despite the different restrictions, and apart from the species banned by Article 2, new international whaling law still allowed the hunting of (adult) whales with almost no restraint. New Zealand, for instance, complained about this very point during the final stages of the draft, when the new convention was about to impose "no restriction upon the number of whales that may be taken."[211] The 1931 Convention managed to secure only some of the dwindling species.

The Geneva Convention was opened for signature on September 24, 1931. It was to be completed by April 1, 1932. The League's initiative had a degree of international influence given that major whaling powers, such as Norway and Britain, had joined it (even though it contained several restrictions that had the potential to limit their industries). Norway, for instance, did not hesitate to sign. A few days earlier, King Haakon had instructed Foreign Minister Birger Braadland to sign the agreement on the day of the opening ceremony.[212] However, in general, the League found the whole process to be alarmingly slow. The Director of the Economic Committee, Pietro Stoppani, wrote to the entire team of experts who had advised the League on the draft convention. The experts needed to act as diplomatic bridgeheads and influence their home governments to sign the agreement quickly.[213] Stoppani relied on their direct influence, especially since the experts themselves had an interest in ensuring that their work was successful.

Charles Smets, the coordinator of the League, was afraid of a possible failure and moved to push the 1931 Convention forward. After three

[210] For a discussion on the sources of the ways in which the international whaling regulation acknowledged traditional and nonindustrial whaling, *see* Reeves, *supra* note 71.

[211] Governor General Bledisloe to J. H. Thomas, Dominion Affairs, Apr. 22, 1931, Archives of New Zealand, Records of the Ministry of External Affairs, File PM 104/6/9/I, pt. 2, "Whaling General" (quoted by DORSEY, *supra* note 4, at 47–48).

[212] Report to the League of Nations from the Government of Norway, Sept. 18, 1931, LoN Archives, 3E/31390/31270.

[213] Letters from Stoppani to the members of the Economic Committee, Oct. 12, 1931 and Feb. 1, 1932, LoN Archives, 3E/33029/31270.

months, only eleven countries – Canada, Australia, New Zealand, India, France, Norway, South Africa, Britain, Spain, Colombia, and Greece – had signed the agreement. Therefore, in November, Smets wrote to Lucius Eastman, who had represented the United States as an expert, about how important the Geneva Convention was for the United States in scientific and economic terms.[214] Smets referred to a March 1931 Senate hearing in which an initiative of American organizations called for intervention to protect whales and other marine mammals, which coincided with the convention's restrictions. Smets claimed that the convention directly served American domestic interests and offered solutions to the whaling problem, as mentioned in the Senate's statement: a win-win situation. Smets needed the Americans as a key player. The League needed another strong modern nation that would follow Britain, France, and Norway, to demonstrate how international solidarity could look beyond immediate commercial interests. International solidarity in the early 1930s could have been built on environmental challenges: "I hope that you will be able to convince your government that in signing the above Convention it will be giving evidence of solidarity which I am certain will not fail to constitute a most useful example."[215]

Not only the Economic Committee, but also the Council and the Assembly of the League repeatedly stressed that the convention had to be signed by as many states as possible, including those not directly involved in whaling. This was the precondition for preventing companies or individuals from practicing illegal whaling under the flag of non-contracting states. Soon afterwards, President Herbert Hoover had the Geneva Convention signed.[216]

But Smet's hope that the American accession influence other nations was not so easily achieved. Despite the American approval, the signing process stagnated and the Secretariat tried tirelessly to push the project forward. Smets was anxious to use the institutional capabilities of the League. He asked Gunnar Jahn, a Norwegian representative who had participated in some of the experts meetings, whether he could suggest in Oslo that Norway and Britain persuade those governments whose signature to the convention was still pending.[217] At the end of February 1932 – the end of the signing period was approaching – Smets, again in collaboration with the Norwegian

[214] A letter from Charles Smets to Lucius R. Eastman, Nov. 27, 1931, LoN Archives, 3E/33029/31270.

[215] *Id.*

[216] Report to the League from Mar. 16, 1932, LoN Archives, 3E/33029/31270.

[217] A Letter from Smets to Jahn, Dec. 14, 1931, LoN Archives, 3E/23031/466.

delegation in Geneva, wrote an urgent letter (to be sent by Britain and Norway) to the states which still had not acceded. The call stressed that the parties were dismayed at the low number of signatories and that only a universal recognition of the convention could prevent abuses of this source of wealth, "which remains at the disposal of all but which is seriously imperiled,"[218] in the future. As with the Americans, the letter appealed to the "sentiments of international solidarity" and urged nations to sign the convention as soon as possible.

The laborious process continued. By 1935, twenty-six states had signed the convention. International whaling regulation finally came into force on January 16, 1935. The League did not miss the opportunity to prepare a special press release and announce its success publicly. This was something the entire world should know about, since the convention was "a certain human interest."[219] At the same time, the League stressed the unfinished nature of the agreement, stating that the project would only be successful if all states signed it and that it "should be adopted by every country in the world, whether maritime or not . . . ."[220]

In fact, it turned out that the Geneva Convention was generally not very effective in reducing the overexploitation of whales either as a precious natural resource, or as an endangered species. However, the League had some success. Reaching an overall restriction on the number of whales that could be caught, even of certain species, put a new kind of legal discourse on the table. Certain parties who negotiated later whaling conventions or arrangements would rush to remove all trace of this conservationist agenda.

The 1931 Convention, imperfect as it was, promised a protective shield against intensive whaling – the first time such a thing had been implemented through mechanisms of international law. One can argue that it also had a macro effect in terms of external legal frameworks. A bilateral agreement signed in 1936 between Britain and Norway, in which both countries' whaling companies agreed to restrictions on the length of the whaling season of 1936–37, might have had something to do with the intense dynamism of whaling diplomacy led by the League.[221] If the 1931

[218] Note Draft: Convention for the Regulation of Whaling, (no date; probably late February), LoN Archives, 3E/35394/31270.

[219] Note by the Information Section, Oct. 28, 1934, LoN Archives, 3E/14201/4483.

[220] Communique No. 7240 by the Information Section, Jan. 22, 1935, LoN Archives, 3E/14201/4483.

[221] Excessive hunting in the Antarctic, and the intensification of whaling in the late 1920s, emphasized the *tragedy of the commons* syndrome. The growing demand for margarine in societies and industrial markets saw an increase in the number of vessels on the high seas, which brought the whaling season of 1930–31 to an unprecedented (and

Convention failed to push nations into this new world of conservation, the possibility of introducing the kinds of restrictions that these two leading whaling nations (with their mighty fleets and industries) took upon themselves was uncertain.[222]

And yet, these achievements that followed the 1931 Convention somehow stood in the shadow of continuing reluctance by important whaling powers. The Soviet Union, Japan, and Germany, all of which were prolific whaling powers,[223] refused to sign the convention. Germany was using whale oil to reduce its need to import edible oil; whereas, Imperial Japan was using the profits from exporting whale products to finance its imperial goals and missions in China and Manchuria.[224] Against this backdrop, given the competing interests, the story of whaling regulation certainly deserves the term "dilemma." Politics, commercial incentives, and ambitious scientific experts created a picture that could have ended differently. The Germans, for instance, were deeply involved in the whaling discussions, especially between the 1920s and 1930s. Berlin in the Weimar Republic was actually the city that hosted the experts meeting of summer 1930; however, Germany then decided to pursue its industrial interests entirely.

This is not to suggest that the 1931 Convention was "a collective failure" and "ineffective in its aims";[225] however, it does reflect the fact that several key players were absent as a result of their clear economic and commercial incentives. This is particularly relevant when taking into account that these three powers together accounted for almost 30 percent of international whale hunting in the period under investigation. The

dangerous) peak: no less than 3.6 million barrels of precious whale oil were produced by the different fleets. However, this eco-commercial race to the bottom actually created an oversupply in the markets, especially given the historical context of the Great Depression. Some historians claim that this was the major reason behind the 1936 special bilateral whaling agreement between Britain and Norway (*see*, for instance, D'Amato & Chopra, *supra* note 9, at 31). The fact is, it was actually the British-Norwegian agreement that was the first of its kind to introduce noncompliance with whaling regulation as an international offense. Further comparative research might reveal the ties between the 1931 Convention's spirit (and the Codification Committee's assertive agenda) and the progressive protectionist measures presented by such leading whaling nations in the middle of the 1930s.

222 This agreement, negotiated after both countries joined the 1931 Convention, strengthened several conservationist legal measures. For the first time, an international penalty was provided. In addition, the regulated area was increased and a sanctuary area between the countries was also introduced.

223 Nagtzaam, *supra* note 7, at 394.

224 DeSombre, *supra* note 26, at 151.

225 *Id.*

problems of implementing and enforcing international legal mechanisms – particularly during a preliminary stage of institutionalized international law such as the one during the interwar period – did not skip the complex and elusive issue of supervising a far-off activity on the high seas. In fact, the databases and the reports reveal that in the first year under the 1931 Convention, the number of whales caught worldwide was the highest ever recorded.

2.3.6 Toward the 1937 Convention: The Media Picks a Side

In many respects, the 1931 Convention and the difficulties that came with enforcing its new mechanisms led the League (and other bodies involved) to search for a more suitable solution.

Indeed, several players tried to come up with alternative transnational mechanisms. Some of the big whaling companies attempted to implement initiatives aimed at self-regulation in an effort to stabilize the phenomenon of overexploitation. For the whaling seasons of 1933–34, for instance, the major Antarctic whaling companies – which formed the International Association of Whaling Companies[226] – voluntarily agreed to restrict their hunting expeditions, in what might be called a "regime of mutual production restraint."[227]

However, in the mid-1930s, the 1931 Convention proved to be a problem in the whaling business. Not all of the parties involved were satisfied with the legal results and capacity of the convention. Japan, for instance, refused to sign it, and both Norway and Britain decided this act should not go unnoticed. They made a formal diplomatic complaint in Tokyo, urging Japan to join the treaty and to adjust its whaling law, just as the European powers had. It was not very successful. The Japanese Foreign Ministry formally refused to share the burden. Unlike its European peers, Japan's national whaling industry was still young and underdeveloped, the letter from Tokyo explained.[228] Hence, it still needed time to catch up with the rest of the whaling states.

The implementation of the 1931 Convention caused several states to revise their restrictions. The Japanese whaling expeditions (if not their

[226] The Committee for Whaling Statistics, International Whaling Statistics VI, LoN Archives, 1 (1935).

[227] John Vogler, The Global Commons: Environmental and Technological Governance 49 (2000).

[228] A Letter from Gaimusho to Royal Norwegian Legation, Oct. 31, 1935, NAGB, FO 371 19625 246/50, 10730.

entire industry) were best known in the West[229] for their unique method of extracting relatively little oil (compared to Western whaling techniques); their crews were chiefly interested in whale meat, and not in oil as the Europeans were. The result of this alleged culinary-cultural difference was a horrible layer of whale carcasses scattered across the surface of the oceans, especially in Antarctica. This was, in legal terms, a violation of the 1931 Convention; the only problem was that Japan had never joined it. A similar environmental and legal concern arose following reports on Japanese whaling practices. Diplomats in the West[230] presented evidence that Japanese whalers were hunting blue whales with calves, and demanded that Japan ensure its fleets comply with international standards and international law as articulated in the 1931 Convention.

In many ways, the 1931 Convention only strengthened the urgent need to build a broader and more comprehensive global whaling regime – especially in light of German and Japanese whaling fleets crossing the oceans and exacerbating the ruthless competition of the 1930s. After Suárez stepped down from international regulation, the League's Economic Committee picked up the baton. The period that followed the first convention can also be told through the lens of the mass media and increasing international public opinion on the issue of whales. Western media picked the League's side in the dilemma, identifying it as a central player – and more than that, the most suitable and competent – in this game of interests on the high seas.

By 1936, two years after the 1931 Convention had gone into effect, more than "just" scientists were concerned about what the future held for the whales. The *New York Herald Tribune*[231] wrote an investigative story about the whaling problem and the potential extinction of the species. The newspaper's Editor in Chief wrote to the League, identifying it as the most capable body to handle the dilemma and protect the whale. In this letter, the *Herald Tribune* complained about a new whaling fleet that had been built in Northern Europe, which seemed to be a violation of the 1931 Convention. In this way, the media gained a certain (noninstitutionalized)

229 Some scholars argue that some characteristics of the Japanese whaling technologies and preferences would last and affect international whaling up until the late 1950s. *See*, for instance, DORSEY, *supra* note 4, at 62–63.

230 Especially in Britain and Norway.

231 The *New York Herald Tribune* was a newspaper published between 1924 and 1966. It was created in 1924 when the *New York Tribune* acquired the *New York Herald*. It was relatively popular and competed with *The New York Times* in the daily morning market.

influence in the international battle on whaling, just as scientific expertise and NGOs had in the interwar period. Under the headline *The Passing of the Whale*, the popular American newspaper explicitly encouraged the League to take the lead as it "would do industry and science a good service if it were to interest itself in the future of an animal that has benefited men so much in the past."[232]

To the current staff of the Economic Committee, this was also a trigger for positive international public relations for the League. The game of establishing international law was, in many ways, mutually beneficial to the parties involved. NGOs, scientific associations, devoted professional experts, and even the media turned to the League for guidance, seeing the possibilities and opportunities this new institution offered. At the same time, as an institute literally under construction, the League was looking for new pathways to legitimacy and authority. Environmental fears, and the whaling concern in particular, called different agencies and voices to join the evolving turbulent discussion. The League's relatively flexible institutional structure, with its committees, subcommittees, and fora such as the Council and the Assembly (not to mention specific individuals and officials, sometimes with their own private agendas), created a broad base for taking part in crafting international law from scratch. The League sought worldwide attention and wished to drive the global public discussion. While it may not have initiated the many petitions, letters, and applications it received from so many different bodies, or the growing interest of the international media, it seems that at least in some cases the League took into account the institutional benefits it could gain from such involvement in environmental problems and discussions on possible solutions.

In the small note below the newspaper's petition, one of the Economic Committee officials laconically mentioned to his colleagues in Geneva:

> I think we might make a little propaganda by posting . . . our activities regarding whales, and by sending him the text of the Convention. Besides, as he says, *doing humanity good*, the whales might perhaps *do us a bit of good too*, in the shape of inspiring a laudatory article.[233]

The *Herald Tribune*'s interest was not the only time the media became involved in whaling and international law. Correspondence between

[232] Extract from the article "The Passing of the Whale" from the *New York Herald Tribune*, Nov. 10, 1935 sent to the League Secretariat on Jan. 9, 1936, LoN Archives, 3E/21971/4483.

[233] *Id.* (emphasis added).

representatives from South Africa and the League during the early 1930s also dealt with this issue. In November 1930, J. Willis wrote to the League on behalf of the government of the Union of South Africa. The government sent a letter from Durban with the title "Danger of Whale Exterminations,"[234] based on scientific data that it possessed. South Africa referred the League to an article that was published in *The Times* of London and warned of the coming danger. The South African official addressed two bodies that the government perceived to be relevant and competent: Initially, he wrote to the newspaper "for the purpose of focusing public attention"; but then, he also approached the League, sending a copy of the article[235] for its review and consideration.

The role of the media and public relations in the whaling dilemma became clear to diplomacy, and to those advocating for creating a progressive international whaling law in particular:

> Your Committee [the Economic Committee] will agree that this matter is of international importance and it is hoped that when sufficient data has been obtained, prompt action will be taken to prevent indiscriminate slaughter. Legislation by International agreement is *imperative* if the species are to be saved from extinction.[236]

Like the *Herald Tribune*, *The Times* was deeply concerned about the hunting fleet that was being built in both Norway and Great Britain. The South African government, collaborating with the League, approached the editor in London and furnished him with further details (as a follow-up to the article) taken from the Annual Report (1929) of the Principal Fisheries Officer for Natal. *The Times* and its readers needed to be aware of the danger of the "wiping out of certain species of whales," the diplomatic-media collaboration between South Africa and the League warned.[237] The increase in whaling throughout the late 1920s had set alarm bells ringing; in the special letter, the newspaper's editor revealed that the catch and output of whale oil "eclipses all previous records of the industry since operation on this Coast started in 1908."[238]

Particular concern was expressed about the humpback species, which was one of the main targets of the whaling industry and its vessels, owing

[234] Letter to the Secretary, Economic Committee, League of Nations, from J. Willis, Durban, Natal, Nov. 26, 1930, LoN Archives, 3E/24696/466 (I) [hereinafter Letter from Willis].

[235] The Letter was addressed to Pietro Stoppani, the Italian Chair of the Economic Committee during that time.

[236] Letter from Willis, *supra* note 234, at 1 (emphasis added).

[237] *Id.*

[238] *Id.* at 1.

to the high yield and quality of the whale's oil. The international media was aware that this species in particular comprised nearly 90 percent of the bulk of whales killed, "a fact that among protectionist circles [was] causing much alarm." As the industry turned its gaze on the new stocks in the Ross Sea, and especially in the Antarctic regions, some "great fears" were expressed regarding operations at the time set up by Norway and Britain. To the media, at least in the 1930s, the pressing situation presented an opportunity. While there was much to be done to combat these new threats using the tools of international law under the auspices of the League, almost as important was the fact that this environmental campaign would simultaneously rely on the internationalist media:

> The fleet, which consists of 23 Norwegian and 1 British whaling expeditions, with crews totaling 6000 men, is the largest number of vessels yet dispatched to hunt whales in these latitudes, that up to now have remained immune from operations of whaling ships. In addition ... there are several factory ships of between 12,000 and 13,000 tonnage, including the largest Transport afloat, the Kosmos, of 32,000 tons, which for scouting purposes is equipped with an aeroplane.[239]

The tensions surrounding the whaling question now also became more common within the whaling industry itself,[240] especially among the states. Despite some progressive solutions, the 1931 Convention did not manage to solve the core problems of the dilemma. Further steps – in terms of international law – had to be taken.

Ten leading states took part in the next whaling conference, held in London in the early summer of 1937. In fact, besides the Soviet Union and Japan[241] (which explicitly refused to take part in the second conference), most of the whaling forces took part in this event. Portugal, Canada, and South Africa sent their representatives as observers;

[239] *Id.* at 1–2.

[240] The whalers themselves had realized at this point that domestic measures, introduced by several active states, were just not enough given the depth of the problem. Indeed, Iceland (which despite its geographical size controlled a significant portion of global whaling in the first decades of the twentieth century) was first to legislate; Norway followed suit several years later with similar legislation. However, the databases and the numbers reported to the Committee for Whaling Statistics have shown, in real time, that these efforts did not change the overall picture.

[241] Japan was doing more than not taking part in negotiating international regulations. In early March, Japan's Minister of Fisheries and Agriculture announced to the Diet (Japan's national bicameral legislature) a governmental plan to expand pelagic expeditions. Estimations in the West predicted that no less than four new floating factories would sail toward the Antarctic, with eight planned expeditions for the 1938–39 season.

Germany continued its intriguing and ambivalent policy, participating in the 1937 Conference though it had never ratified the League's first convention. The issue was also important enough in the late 1930s for the governments of Australia, Argentina, the Irish Free State, New Zealand, and Britain to be involved. The Americans, it should be stressed, maintained their special role within the environmental dilemma of whaling[242] and, although the United States chose not to join the League itself, it did send an official delegation.

Continuing its role in the early 1930s, the United States even intensified its role in the international environmental issue. American scientists and civilian associations (in what can be termed "civilian diplomacy") became more involved, and the federal delegation to the London Conference of June 1937 officially declared America's special role in the matter.

The conclusions of the London Conference were articulated into a second convention, the International Agreement for the Regulation of Whaling, which was signed in London on June 8, 1937. In many ways, it responded to the problems of the Geneva Convention. First, it aimed to deal with the challenge of non-signing states, such as Japan and the Soviet Union. Second, it was attempting to keep pace with the rapidly advancing industry.

Using the momentum of international regulation, the pelagic whaling states succeeded in persuading countries that relied on land stations to additionally accept restrictions on waste, a minimum catch size, and seasons similar to those applied to pelagic whalers under the first convention. Just as the 1931 Convention had secured[243] the safety of right whales, the new 1937 Convention extended this protection to gray whales.[244] Other ideas, originally suggested by Suárez in the late 1920s, finally managed to find their way into a new agreement. Among them was the introduction of restricted hunting areas and limitations on the length of the whaling season. Article 7 limited whaling to the period from the eighth day of December to the seventh day of March. Moreover, the new London Convention reclaimed the protection of mothers with calves

[242] The United States was also the first nation to quickly and enthusiastically ratify the 1931 Convention (followed by Switzerland and Norway).

[243] Even if one can critically argue that these species were secured by international law on the books alone, but not in action. For a more general discussion on the question of the gap between formal law and law in practice, *see*, among others, Jean-Louis Halpérin, *Law in Books and Law in Action: The Problem of Legal Change*, 64 ME. L. REV. 45 (2011).

[244] *See* Article 4.

(Article 6), complete utilization of carcasses (Article 11), and mandatory collection of data from whaling expeditions for scientific monitoring (Article 17). A special professional inspector was allocated to each (factory) ship to ensure that restrictions on the size of the catch were adhered to for humpback, fin, sperm, and blue whales – the most hunted and popular species.

Like its predecessor from 1931, the London Convention had its achievements and failures. Its achievements, even if they were (for the sake of discussion) merely formal,[245] offered at least some legal protection for young and immature whales. The 1937 Convention also acknowledged certain problems regarding its own implementation. Since some whaling states were not part of the agreement, they enjoyed the unfair advantages that not signing afforded them. As a result, the London Convention aimed to ensure compliance as far as possible. For instance, signatory states were to prevent the transfer of whaling ships to any reluctant state that did not join the convention.

However, the second convention did not solve the problem. Far from it. Given Japan's absence, the whaling industry refused to accept the quota principle and continued to catch as much as it was able (of the nonrestricted species). One way or the other, during the murky years of the late 1930s, when fascist and ultra-fascist powers were on the rise, the League dedicated special attention and abundant institutional energy to the restless whaling dilemma.

Neither the London Conference nor the improved 1937 Convention was the final chord in the League's campaign. One year later, in early June 1938, a few months after Austria's Anschluß (annexation) into Nazi Germany[246] and almost three months prior to the Munich Agreement (of September that year), the League began to increase its pressure on the environmental problem. Delegates from leading whaling nations met (again) in London.[247] Besides the clear call to make the 1937 Convention as global as possible, and the wish to see other nations join and sign it, there was also an intention to fix the earlier agreements. On the legal agenda this time was the Protocol on Regulation of Whaling,[248]

[245] D'Amato & Chopra, *supra* note 9, at 31.

[246] Austria was annexed by the Third Reich on Mar. 12, 1938.

[247] The 1938 Conference had two parts: first, the delegations assembled in May in Oslo for preparatory discussions, and then returned to their countries; they reconvened in London in June.

[248] Protocol on Regulation of Whaling, June 24, 1938.

which was set to amend the original agreement (of 1937) and to prepare it for the future.

The short-term nature of the 1937 Convention made it unique: it came into force in 1938 and was originally set to apply for one year. Accordingly, the parties could then extend its duration and terms. They did so in London one year later, while diplomats were actually working on the next legal stage even before it had gone into effect, and before all the states had fulfilled their commitment by ratifying it.

The accession of France and Australia to the 1937 Convention contributed to the increasing momentum of international whaling law and the campaign. Politically speaking, the main aim in that summer of 1938 was to bring Japan and other states into the circle and, above all, to bind its whaling industry to the developing regulation. The partial enforcement of the former convention indicated – both to the League and to those parties that had studied its execution – that any whaling agreement must include all whaling nations, otherwise its effectiveness would remain in doubt. Many of the whalers who were bound by the 1931 Convention complained about their unfair situation: other whalers[249] were taking advantage of the fact that the new, hard-line regulations applied to their commercial opponents. Moreover, revising the earlier whaling agreements resulted in whaling states claiming – as Japan was doing – that they could not accept legal limitations that had not been mutually accepted by other states. Japan had argued, for instance, with regard to the North Pacific, that as long as the Soviets were not part of the equation, they would be at a distinct disadvantage.

The Japanese stance gained center stage that summer. Akira Kodaki, a formal official on behalf of the Embassy of Japan in London, attended the discussion.[250] At the time, Imperial Japan was building the whaling vessel Tonan Maru 3, the largest commercial ship in Japanese history, and two sister ships, which formed the backdrop of the international discussions in Oslo and London. Moreover, a glimpse of the interaction between environment and war can be seen in this issue.[251] The growing

249 Mostly Japanese, but also industries of other states. South Africa, for instance, was still on the fence in the summer 1937 and had not yet joined the 1937 Convention; other parties claimed this was equally unfair.

250 International Whaling Commission [hereinafter ICW]/1938/13, Minutes of the 2d Session, June 15, 1938, UNSA, RG 59, File 562.8F3, at 10.

251 For an example of studies that combine environmental history and military history *see*, among others, Natural Enemy, Natural Ally: Toward an Environmental History of War (Richard P. Tucker & Edmund Russell eds., 2004).

concern and resentment over Japan's lack of cooperation and its continued whaling activity intensified in the late 1930s: the threat of Japanese whaling and naval power was very real as Japanese officials discussed the possible military value of their whaling vessels.

From an institutional perspective, the League actually intended to strengthen its hold in order to better supervise and control the world of whaling. The new planned legal arrangement of summer 1938 was supposed to implement changes that some states wished to see come into effect, and to set the terms for the next whaling season of 1938–39. The American, German, British, Argentinian, and Norwegian representatives decided to support an extension of the existing deal of 1937. This intention probably had something to do with the sobering statistics: compared to the relatively "reasonable" figure of 9572 whales hunted in the season of 1931–32 that followed the first convention, the data of the late 1930s were overwhelming – more than 46,000 whales were hunted in the season of 1937–38.[252] Even more concerning was the dangerous shift in the species targeted: during the years of the first convention, the blue whale was the main target of whaling ships (roughly two-thirds of the 1931–32 catch); however, the numbers showed that their share shrunk to less than one-third during the 1937–38 season. Shrinking blue whale populations in the oceans meant that whaling expeditions started to chase other species instead, first and foremost the (smaller) fin whales. The delegations at the two-part conference in Oslo and London were aware of the economic-environmental implications of these data. "The question is not purely an economic one," noted one of the Norwegian representatives, Birger Bergersen,

> it is first and foremost . . . a biological question. [W]e have to think about the next generation. What will they think if we take the last whale? . . . I really think as a biologist that it is a shame, a terrible shame for our generation and for our time, if this wonderful animal, one of the most splendid existing, should disappear.[253]

The Protocol Amending the International Agreement of June 8th for the Regulation of Whaling continued the progressive line throughout that decade. Besides providing more accurate and precise legal definitions for some of the terms of the 1937 Convention (like the definition of a land

[252] Antarctic whaling: 1904/5–1938/9, Material in Connection with International Whaling Conference 1939, USNA, RG 59, File 562.8F3.

[253] Proceedings of the Morning Session, Preliminary Whaling Conference, Oslo, May 19, 1938, USNA, RG 59, File 562.8F3.

station in Article 18), the 1938 Protocol provided several additional protective measures. New conservationist ideas found their way into improved legal provisions. Other whale species received legal protection from the League, such as humpbacks (Article 1). And the 1938 Protocol expanded the basic concept of sanctuary that had previously been introduced to include the far southern reaches of the Pacific Ocean (Article 2). The intention behind these restrictions was to make the Antarctic waters between longitudes 70° and 170° west as secure as possible. The scientific observations introduced in the discussions admitted that there was still not enough data on the condition of whales in the late 1930s in that vast region.[254] However, given the growing specific interest in whaling expeditions in the Antarctic, principles of caution had the upper hand.

Moreover, the diplomatic process between Oslo and London served as an opportunity to bring other environmental ideas to the table, even though they were not ultimately included in the 1938 Protocol. These included fixed limits on the number of catcher boats per expedition and a call to legally restrict whaling to the use of electric harpoons (instead of explosive ones).[255] All in all, it seems that the discussions reflected a growing understanding that, besides the variety of proposed mechanisms, the effectiveness of any international whaling regime would rely on the number of whales that could be hunted during the whaling season. The global supervision of the number of barrels of oil produced was also suggested, and relied on the League's ability to uphold this kind of harsh regulation. Above all, the idea of a global quota in summer 1938 seemed inevitable, with the survival of the whale at stake. As Henry Maurice, a British fisheries official active on whaling matters and who participated in the discussions, asserted: "We all realize that ultimately if we are going to save the . . . whales we have got to get down to quantitative restrictions."[256]

More broadly, the 1937–38 discussions made room for the revolutionary idea of banning all whaling completely – perhaps the first time this was done so publicly and on such a scale. The whaling operations in the second half of the 1930s seemed to be somehow immune to the League's legal restraints – so much so that a radical (and controversial) idea was proposed. With whaling operations so excessive, and with numerous reports[257] warning of the danger of complete destruction of the species,

[254] ICW/1938/23, Report of the Sanctuary Committee, NSNA, RG 59, File 562.8F3.

[255] ICW/1938/25, Minutes of the 4th Session (afternoon), June 17, 1938, NSNA, RG 59, File 562.8F3, at 14.

[256] *Id.*

[257] BIRNIE, *supra* note 28, at 129–30.

it was suggested that the League completely withdraw its legal restrictions. This would allow "indiscriminate whaling" to continue until whale stocks had become so depleted that whaling ceased to be remunerative.[258]

Although not too many states supported this last move, the League was almost unstoppable; at least with regard to the whaling problem. Several other states, such as Germany, eventually came on board too and acceded to the 1937 Convention and the 1938 Protocol. Despite the turbulent atmosphere of the international arena in 1938, eight states ratified or complied[259] with the latest agreement, while another twelve countries were invited to join. International pressure, and perhaps a certain sense of urgency, resulted in another important victory: Japan declared in June 1938 that it too would accede to the convention in the following year.[260]

The campaign was not over yet. The officials and bodies striving for whale conservation were aware that they had still not fulfilled their promise of ensuring the future existence of whales. Like its legal predecessor, the 1938 Protocol did not represent the finish line for the whaling dilemma.

One year later, in August of 1939 – shortly before Hitler's armies would storm Poland – further modifications were made to the 1938 Protocol. Delegates met once again with the Japanese representative, Kodaki, who officially reported that Japan would accede before the next season started; Japan's leading whaling companies, however, opposed the move. During this (last) session, delegates extended the protection offered by the 1937 and 1938 Conventions to include a ban on the hunting of humpbacks, and the addition of a second inspector to each factory ship, in an effort to strengthen compliance and enforcement.[261]

While these improvements may not seem that significant compared to the milestones of the 1930s, the legal-environmental additions of 1939 – along with legal measures promoted since the mid-1920s – emphasized the League's leading and pivotal role in the saga. Encouraged by Japan's positive response to its efforts, the League prepared for the next steps a couple of weeks before September 1, 1939. Optimistic as whaling

[258] Johnston, *supra* note 42, at 400.

[259] Compared to the nine that signed the 1937 Convention, and twenty-six that signed the 1931 Convention.

[260] Kodaki, the Japanese delegate, also mentioned that this acceptance relied on the agreement of the other delegates to open whaling in the North Pacific. *See* ICW/1938/29, Minutes of the 8th Session, June 23, 1938, UNSA, RG 59, File 562.8F3, at 4–5.

[261] Minutes of International Whaling Conference, 2d Session, Aug. 17, 1939, NAC, RG 35, vol. 1823, File 112, pt. 1.

diplomacy was under the auspices of the League, the states agreed to meet again in the new year.

However, the significant progress achieved since the Codification Committee's original initiative and the preliminary questionnaire of March 22, 1926 was about to be put on hold.

2.4 Conclusion

The conclusions of this discussion are multifaceted. Regarding the *effectiveness* of the outcomes of the whaling legislation, it is true that the various legal frameworks proposed by the League could neither save the whale nor solve the problem. As some scholars have claimed, the agreements of the 1930s largely failed to achieve their state objectives. As Patricia Birnie summed up, this was due to the "inadequacy of the scope of regulations; inadequate scientific data; non-cooperation by some major whaling nations; poor enforcement of arrangements and no international supervision or control; and lack of global interest."[262]

But putting aside relevant questions about the enforcement of international law and the problems this entails (including nowadays),[263] it seems that we can also view the role of the League in a broader context. In order to better understand the evolving legal history of whaling regulation – and the role of the League *within* the complex history of whaling – the interwar whaling regime deserves special attention, whatever its practical outcomes were. Even if, for the purpose of this discussion, all the League had done was introduce an inadequate environmental-legal framework, at least some of the ideas and solutions that were raised merit legal study and analysis. After all, the very nature of legal discussions and considerations, including those of our time, is based on the notion of a constant exchange of ideas, mechanisms, and legal drafts.

Environmental ideas, and especially solutions – whether about reducing carbon dioxide emissions in the late twentieth century, or drinking reclaimed or recycled wastewater and sewage – do need, as environmental history shows us, a few dialectic moves before they can achieve at least some of their aims. The League was doing much more than simply airing

[262] BIRNIE, *supra* note 28, at 129–30.

[263] For an examination of the mechanisms that currently exist to enforce international environmental agreements (especially treaties), including a discussion and an illustration of various shortcomings of the current international legal framework, *see*, among others, Andrew W. Samaan, *Enforcement of International Environmental Treaties: An Analysis*, 5 FORDHAM ENVTL. L. REV. 261 (2011).

differences of opinion and putting new ideas on the table. Its 1931 Convention reflects an evolving process in which different states, scientific associations, and commercial bodies were able to engage with one another on their competing interests. In legal terms, the convention brought to the surface new and unfamiliar ideas. Article 9, for instance, covered "all waters of the world," including both the high seas and states' territorial and national waters. This principle alone reflected the legal notion China had completely rejected during the first round of the 1926 Questionnaire.[264] Some of the articles marked an evolution in the world of international law. Although the open sea was no-man's-land prior to the establishment of the League, now the League's explicit jurisdiction regarding whales stretched across all seas.

Not all of the ideas that the League gave a voice to were included in the final drafts and legal arrangements. One such example was a total commercial whaling ban,[265] which was a revolutionary idea in the mid-1920s. Another was the shift from protecting several species in a *positive* legal manner (which both the 1931 and 1937 Conventions achieved for right whales, baleen or whalebone whales,[266] and grey whales),[267] to a general protection of whales in the 1946 Washington Convention; here, the law explicitly named those specific species that from now on were *allowed to be hunted*, and not vice versa.[268] However, in many ways, the League's existence served as an opportunity, or a laboratory, to process these ideas and present them to the international arena.

International law immanently needs time; and this seems to be particularly true of environmental international law. Thanks to the intensive role taken on by the League, the interwar period marked an important phase in the genealogy of whaling regulation, especially its layered structure. The League identified most of the central tensions in this dilemma and at least some of the necessary solutions. Still, only a small portion of

[264] *See* China's resistance as I have discussed it in Section 2.3.2 above.

[265] It was actually the International Whaling Commission that voted to introduce the moratorium on commercial whaling in 1986, once it became apparent that the numbers of whales being killed were unsustainable and jeopardized the whale population.

[266] *See* Articles 2 and 4 of the 1931 Convention.

[267] *See* Article 4 of the 1937 Convention.

[268] One of the first opening remarks of the International Convention for the Regulation of Whaling, signed in Washington on December 2, 1946, asserted "[r]ecognizing that in the course of achieving these objectives, whaling operations should be confined to those species best able to sustain exploitation in order to give an interval for recovery to certain species of whales now depleted in numbers" (The Introduction to the 1946 Washington Convention).

these found their way through the obstacles of international law and diplomacy. In addition to the usual difficulties involved in crafting international law, these solutions also had to navigate international relations, powerful commercial interests, and the growing fear – and sometimes even resentment – of leading political forces, some of which were actually the founding forces behind the establishment of the League as a post–World War I international institution. The League played a vital role in raising innovative ideas and progressive solutions, even if some of these did not ultimately find their way into final drafts and official agreements.

Moreover, almost the entire historiography of environmentalism refused to interpret any noncommercial motivation or perspective in an effort to face the challenge of whaling in the interwar period. John Vogler, for instance, argued that the behavior of the whaling companies was motivated "by the need to maintain and support oil prices in a depressed market [of the Great Depression] rather than any concern with long-term sustainable management."[269] Others have explained that the regulation led by the League from 1918 to 1931 was actually an initiative of the hunting and fishing industries. However, at least some of the norms that were reflected during the complex negotiations included preservationist ideas and calls for sustainability. Arguments such as the claim that the negotiations were "limited to merely protecting the long term viability of the whaling *industry* rather than the welfare of whales,"[270] seem inaccurate, to say the least.

Throughout these discussions, one encounters noncommercial environmental terms and definitions that featured strongly in the legal and diplomatic discourse of the League. Of course, the powerful whaling industry maintained a strong influence over the whaling problem and its suggested solutions, and the early chapters of the dilemma reveal both the measures the industry took and its involvement in the battle over international environmental law. And yet, the industry, as powerful as it was, was not the only significant player in this battle. Scientists joined marine biologists; concerned states approached the League and asked that the whales be rescued; and NGOs fiercely tried to convince the League and its committees to recruit international law for the conservation of the whale.

[269] Vogler, *supra* note 227, at 49.

[270] Gerry J. Nagtzaam, The Making of International Environmental Treaties: Neoliberal and Constructivist Analyses of Normative Evolution 162 (2009) (emphasis in the original).

The League played a significant role in unmasking many of the players. Don Manuel Malbran, the Argentinean delegate to the June 1938 London meeting concerning the 1938 Protocol, cynically stated, "I am inclined to believe that each delegation is taking into consideration, above everything else, the interests of each country . . . . We could not accept any agreement limiting the activities of the existing land stations, nor any commitment which could prevent us from establishing new land stations."[271]

As Britain suspected before the Great War, the League changed international whaling law not only in terms of routine, legal mechanisms, and procedure, but also in terms of who got to play the game of international law. Unlike earlier attempts to regulate whaling, the League shattered the closed doors of the traditional diplomatic club – or at least enabled its transformation. States, diplomats, scientists, jurists, whalers, and bureaucrats all turned to the League as an institution with which they could bargain and share their agenda.

The League also changed the framework of international environmental law as it enabled nontraditional players to step in and participate in crafting different arrangements. Instead of only traditional powers making the decisions, the League opened the door to nations less familiar, but no less relevant or legitimate, such as Roumania, China, and Brazil, all of which took on an active role in the campaign and in the legal discourse. In that sense, certain states used the whaling dilemma as a way to establish a place for themselves in the discussion on internationalism in general, and not necessarily because they were concerned for the survival of the whale (at least not in the long run). Explicit declarations – such as those of Brazil, for instance – support my claim that environmental concerns, such as whaling, actually enabled these (relatively) new voices to get their foot in the door. "The democratisation of the world, the equality of States," mentioned the government of Brazil as it dealt with the question, "are the constituent elements of a new international order which necessitates the careful definition of reciprocal rights and duties."[272]

Opening the issue of whaling to international discussion, as the League had begun to do in the mid-1920s, invited new voices and different perspectives – rather than favoring or protecting the obvious British,

[271] International Committee of Whaling Archives, Cambridge, England, 1938/21, Minutes of the 4th Session, June 17, 1938, at 15–16, UNSA, RG 59, File 562.8F3.

[272] Opinion of Professor Clovis Bevilaqua, Legal Advisor to the Ministry of Foreign Affairs, received on Feb. 28, 1927, LoN Archives, 19/57699/47284, at 2–3.

Norwegian, Japanese,[273] and other whaling nations' interests in keeping their industries intact and beyond any kind of international interference, whatever its form. Given the League's intensifying involvement, it seems that the traditional whaling nations were slowly losing their grip on an industry that they had dominated for a long time.[274] The British, for instance, concluded a short while before the introduction of the League that a call for large-scale international involvement would simply invite other states to develop their own whaling industries. Moreover, right after the League had started to investigate this issue, the British government argued that any agreement that did not include all the great maritime powers would be "rendered futile" by those powers.[275] Thus, despite its eventual collaboration with the League, Britain – with its special attitude toward whaling – was pretty cautious about any drive toward international whaling regulation[276] in the near future.

The structure of the League enabled the belief that it has the ability both to solve different problems across the globe,[277] and to literally shape and create international law. The modes of operation and mechanisms the League employed, such as open-for-discussion questionnaires and legal documents, were unfamiliar to most of the players who took part in the League's new international, legal, and diplomatic activities. Distributing a draft of what might become a relevant base for further discussion – not to mention for legal articulation by a new convention (as the Codification Committee promoted) – seemed to be an opportunity

[273] Though Japan claimed all throughout the 1930s (probably intentionally and in order to dodge any international limitation by regulation) that its whaling industry was still "young" and underdeveloped in comparison to the Western nations (especially Norway and Britain).

[274] However, other scholars, such as Dorsey, have claimed it was the industries' own concern for the survival of "their" natural resource that stimulated the move toward international regulation. *See*, DORSEY, *supra* note 4, at 58–59.

[275] Minutes of Interdepartmental Conference on the Question of International Control of Whaling, Oct. 12, 1927, NAC, RG 23, vol. 1081, File 721-19-5[3]. Perhaps one of the reasons for Britain's suspicion of any international action on the issue was the acknowledgement that any conference on whaling would also have to include certain Latin American states, especially rival Argentina, which would endeavor to make an issue out of British control over the Falklands.

[276] John W. Field, "Proposed International Action for the Protection of Whales," Jan. 9, 1926, National Archives of Australia, MEA Records, Series A981/4, File WHA 9, "Whaling and Sealing – Regulation International Measures. To 15.4.30."

[277] For a broad overview of the different tasks and missions the League took on (rather enthusiastically), *see* THE LEAGUE OF NATIONS' WORK ON SOCIAL ISSUES: VISIONS, ENDEAVOURS AND EXPERIMENTS, *supra* note 2.

that almost none of the states wished to miss, regardless of their ties to the matter at hand.

These new modes of operation, and the new world suggested by institutionalized international law, also enabled other bodies to step in and to influence international law directly and precisely. The "spectacular gathering"[278] of the world's statesmen, jurists, experts, and scientists of different fields revived and inspired the international engagement not only of neutral non-state actors, but also of certain players that wisely identified the new forum as a new opportunity for various kinds of NGOs – from commercial and industrial consortiums to scientific boards of museums and research centers. Many of these, like the International Mercantile Marine Officers Association, felt that they were also a genuine part of international law. The association's secretary at the head office in Antwerp believed that its members had a direct interest in the evolving discussion on whaling, and wrote an application[279] asking that their perspective be heard and included in the discussions and conclusions. Through this environmental discussion on the future of whales and whaling, many of these NGOs and non-state actors[280] "re-imagined themselves as actors in global governance."[281]

The replies of at least some of the states – most certainly those that supported international interests over the commercial interests of whaling nations – and the League's new format, which for perhaps the first time in modern history gave new states a voice equal to that of stronger and richer powers, all backed up Suárez and "his" Codification Committee. The international evidence, reaching to the League's Secretariat from different corners of the globe, supported the hope (at least of some of the League's officials) of achieving a new convention that would save the whale from disaster. Given the involvement and concern of member and nonmember states alike on the issue, the Codification Committee developed a source of authority, in a sense, to further develop this initiative.

278 Wöbse, *supra* note 18, at 521.

279 Letter to Robert Hass, Director of the Communication and Transit Committee of the League of Nations, Dec. 30, 1927, LoN Archives, 19/63331/63331 (III).

280 In that sense, and while discussing nontraditional players, it seems that the media should also further be studied as a new kind of non-state actor, but a rather different one than NGOs. Just like scientific expertise and NGOs, the media gained a certain noninstitutionalized stake in the international battle on whaling.

281 Steve Charnovitz, *The Emergence of Democratic Participation in Global Governance (Paris, 1919)*, 10 IND. J. GLOBAL LEGAL STUD. 45, 77 (2003).

As whaling nations intently watched the League's efforts to create an international whaling law, most of them realized that this ship had already sailed. No matter their reluctance to regulate whaling, they surely did not wish for it to be subject to the League's voices and agenda – especially given that the League was using its new institutional power to invite many new and unfamiliar players (all with their own perspectives, interests, and ideas of how international regulation *should* look) to become involved. Other powers and interest groups were almost "forced" to become involved in the ongoing discussion. Otherwise, the new rules would have left them behind.[282]

The League also served as a suitable space for some of the internal discussions, and also controversies, among the whaling powers themselves. The discussions on the 1938 Protocol revealed this tension. As the years went by, and as regulation moved ahead, the interests of pelagic whaling powers on the one hand, and states with land stations on the other hand, began – in a technological era of floating factories[283] – to conflict. Traditional whaling powers, such as France and Argentina, complained bitterly to the League that their industries could not survive with so few catches, particularly when Norway and Britain's emerging whaling fleets had enhanced their vessels and used floating factories to process their whale products out on the open sea. In London, in the early summer of 1938, the pelagic powers used international law as a warning (and deterrent) that once new obligations had been placed on whaling, they would demand new restrictions for land stations too, given the fact that these sites disrupted the breeding of humpback whales in particular. In any event, no more than a couple of months before World War II, the League managed to convince most of the players that whaling had the genuine ability not only to eliminate the

[282] Indeed, one of the main problems – and failures – of the interwar whaling campaign was the fact that some of the leading whaling powers were notably absent. Japan, for instance, consistently refused to acknowledge any authority the League claimed to have on this issue. But it seems this behavior was a response to the resilience the League had been showing, and the role it had assumed, for more than a decade. In the period almost post League of Nations, and actually in the midst of World War II, a series of legal agreements were negotiated and also signed. The most prominent at the time was probably the 1945 Protocol, which was signed by a long list of whaling nations, such as Norway, Canada, the United States, the Union of South Africa, the United Kingdom, Denmark, France, Mexico, the Netherlands, and more. As the 1945 Protocol was about to come into force in 1947, the Soviets saw the growing international awareness and joined as well. This series of legal arrangements warrants, I believe, further study in the future.

[283] Which obviated the need for regular factories to produce products out of the hunted whales brought to the shore.

shore stations and factories, but to destroy the worldwide whale population rapidly, unless the industry and the different players were regulated, supervised, and monitored.

Another concluding remark focuses on the central role of scientific expertise throughout the different discussions and suggested solutions. Scientists influenced early international agendas as a whole, and environmental aims and concerns in particular. They operated in the orbit of international organizations, whether it be the American Association of Mammalogists, urging the League to act due to the danger of the whale's coming extinction, or the International Conseil of Copenhagen, advancing different data of the whaling industry. Scientific expertise was therefore instrumental in constructing the intersection of the international, environmental, and industrial spheres.

It was the League that enabled scientific warnings to be heard. Other scholars argued that although developments had been achieved in whaling, it seemed impossible that "a few men on a remote speck of land could affect the whale population of a vast ocean."[284] However, the discussions this chapter uncovered show how and to what extent scientific experts, and their alarming concerns, stimulated the interwar period discussions over the dilemma.

It is true that scientists had long warned of the potential extinction of whales. The Canadian scientist William Wakeham, for example, concluded several years before the League's establishment that whaling on the North American east coast of Canada had maybe one more season before the whales were all chased away or driven to extinction due to the big bang in modern whaling.[285] Moreover, in 1911, diplomats and scientists discussing the status of the North Pacific fur seal agreed that other sea creatures would be fruitful subjects,[286] and relevant ones, of diplomacy. Once these parties had reached a multilateral solution on the seal dispute,[287] some of them also made early suggestions regarding the "maintenance" of whaling. Already at this point, ideas and recommendations for legal measures – such as a ten-year closed season, or a ban on the use of floating factories in the open sea –[288] had been heard.

[284] Tønnessen & Johnsen, *supra* note 40, at 183–84.

[285] William Wakeham to Fisheries Secretary, July 26, 1913, NAC, Records of the Ministry of Fisheries, vol. 1081, File 721-19-5[1].

[286] Dorsey, *supra* note 4, at 31.

[287] For a discussion on the 1911 Sealing Convention, *see* Thomas A. Bailey, *The North Pacific Sealing Convention of 1911*, 4 Pac. Hist. Rev. 1 (1935).

[288] On right and bowhead whales.

However, these scientific and legal inspirations toward a binding international law still needed a suitable and lasting institutional framework. Already in the 1910s, for instance, the British had taken the lead on collecting data on catches made by whaling ships under their jurisdiction. In the meantime, early voices within the British administration overseas started to express concern about problems that had begun to develop in the case of whaling.[289]

With this comparative perspective, a double conclusion can be noted. First, these earlier (mostly scientific) voices that had warned of a coming extinction prior to the League also acknowledged the *lack* of a practical or feasible solution to address this concern. The British government understood that monitoring and controlling whaling on such a large scale on the high seas posed a unique problem. The Colonial Office mentioned that this issue was ultimately[290] one that would have to be solved internationally.[291] However, at the turn of the century, and during the first two decades, the farthest-reaching solution that the British had in mind was an abstract transnational agreement with their Dominions, Norway, and several whaling states from South America.[292]

And second, the ongoing reluctance of certain parts of the scientific community to support intensifying whaling, which can be traced during the turn of the twentieth century, places the role of the League on a developing historical timeline. The interwar period saw certain trends develop, such as the growing awareness of the dangers of whaling; the League bridged the gap between early ideas and preliminary solutions from before 1919, and current institutional frameworks, which allowed for these early ideas to be transformed into "real" international legal agreements.

289 On South Georgia, for instance, J. Innes Wilson, the stipendiary local magistrate, reported back to Lord Harcourt, the Secretary of State for the colonies, that the whalers had a difficult time separating males from females out in the open sea. However, what is even more interesting at this point in the discussion is Wilson's rage against the British whalers, who admitted in front of him that they are hunting calves in order to capture their mothers, who rushed to protect their young. Wilson, far away from London Metropolitan, was calling for (British) regulations to halt this practice (J. Innes Wilson to Lord Harcourt, Apr. 8, 1912, NAGB, FO 371412/109, pt. 2, "Correspondence Regarding the Preservation of Whales").

290 Dorsey, *supra* note 4, at 32.

291 H. W. Just, Colonial Office, to Foreign Office, Apr. 20, 1912, NAGB, FO 371412/108, pt. I.

292 *Id.*

Analyzing the role of scientific discourse during the whaling dilemma invites additional ideas within that context. The role of Kellogg and the American Society of Mammalogists illustrates the indirect ways in which American involvement in the League's activities became quite prominent. Although the United States was not a member state, it seems that scientific expertise in general – and environmental science in particular – enabled both American individuals and associations to take part in the new institutionalized internationalism the League was promoting.

This specific American environmental advocacy did play, at least to some extent, a role in the evolution of the dilemma.[293] The external involvement of nations such as the United States enabled engagement with diplomacy and international law – and not necessarily through formal and hierarchic channels. The League, with its in-transition framework, which in many cases was also driven by grassroots movements and initiatives from below, enabled – and perhaps even encouraged – this kind of practical and participatory international law. However, other historians have so far tended to overlook this involvement, or refer to it only laconically.[294]

Indeed, not all the scientific facts and claims that were presented in the 1920s and 1930s were accurate or complete. As a matter of fact, the players who resented the League's aspirations of creating a new and promising international whaling law often pointed to the lack of useful scientific knowledge,[295] or accurate and reliable databases on which to base such important decisions (especially when it came to their commercial interests and their sovereignty). Perhaps these claims were true; and maybe no scientist in the first decades of the twentieth century could have known for sure how old or large a great whale had to be before it could reproduce, for example, or what whales' real migration patterns were like. And yet, the rise of the League, and its leading role in *trying* to solve the whaling dilemma, became possible thanks to the unique role of scientific expertise in this institutionalized internationalism. Acting on behalf of

293 I take into account the continuing involvement of the United States in regional arrangements of whaling regimes. Both the US and Canada already had a common history of promoting the conservation of marine resources, starting with the 1911 North Pacific Fur Seal Convention, and followed by the joint agreements with Canada on fisheries in the 1920s.

294 Dorsey, for instance, mentions the American involvement very briefly, while other historians such as Stoett or D'Amato and Chopra skip it altogether: "Because this was a league effort, it also drew attention from nations with no direct stake and from some that were not league members, like the United States." (Dorsey, *supra* note 4, at 40).

295 *Id.* at 50.

the League and its committees, and also on behalf of different scientific associations and research institutions, scientists were instrumental in navigating this dilemma during the interwar period. As a matter of fact, one cannot tell the story of whaling under the auspices of the League without describing the influential voice of science and its representatives in interwar international law.

Though the League failed in the end (as those critics or historians who dismiss its role tend to point out), it seems the history of the period owes at least its sense of urgency to the League. It was the League, and no other institution, that stirred the international community to action over the future survival of the whale. Posing counterfactual assumptions is often discouraged in history studies; nevertheless, it seems that without the League's leading role (and that of its committees in particular), the discussions on whaling would have been conducted very differently, and the solutions likely would have been similarly different. The sense of urgency created by the intensive work of NGOs and non-state actors, and scientific discourse as a reliable source of legitimacy, also had a lot to do with the fact that the League managed to include considerations of nature protection and conservation in the creation of international law at its birth. Certainly, these moves were not always successful with regard to the final, practical legal outcomes, but they did have an important influence on the *future* course that international environmental law – and environmental diplomacy – would take in the years after the League was dissolved.

Despite its obvious imperfections, the League wisely used its institutional framework to overcome obstacles. Some of these obstacles were tied up with the "natural" difficulties of applying (international) law on the open sea; but at least some also had to do with the open political suspicion of leading forces in the interwar period regarding any intervention in "their" whaling businesses. The League had tried to use its own institutional structure to meet these challenges by turning, for example, to the more open stage of internationalism. In this dilemma in particular, the League allowed players who were not as attached to commercial-industrial interests as certain whaling nations were, to become involved; however, it did not allow for any party's reluctance toward the further development of international law to hamper its activities.

Moreover, its institutional structure also responded to the constant need for investigation, monitoring, and surveillance – something the League's committees and scientists fiercely argued about given the deterioration of the ongoing whaling dilemma. Indeed, many of the problems the League had to deal with required immediate action and swift solutions. While the League, as a complex institution, was not always able to respond to issues immediately, it did manage to address them eventually. In the ongoing case of whaling, the League relied on a systematic routine and thorough methods to deal with various problems (using both its committees and scientific databases to inform its decisions), to ensure that the dilemma did not remain unresolved. Unlike with other initiatives that preceded the establishment of the League, this time international law was not entirely reliant upon the "good will" of the parties involved, and did not rely on ad hoc initiatives. The new interwar international law had a different foundation: a core institution in Geneva, devoted personnel with a fixed routine, and an organized agenda. Simply put, the Codification Committee set its own schedule and handled its missions (almost) independently. To an extent it perhaps needed the cooperation and the good will of the different states involved, but once the League was assembled, it carried out at least some of its initiatives on its own.

All in all, the whaling diplomacy of the League, and its obvious use to international law, also had other results on the ground, besides specific legal articles. The intensity of the ongoing discourse on the dilemma created other pressures besides explicit or formal agreements. When Japan was considering its position on the 1938 Protocol, for instance, it was caught between two positions. On the one hand, it was reluctant to agree to any central international whaling regulation. But on the other hand, Japanese manufacturers also feared possible boycotts of their products in the West[296] as a public response to their uncooperative whaling policy, the same one led – successfully or not – by the League.

One of the most important conclusions of this retrospective of whaling diplomacy, perhaps, relates to the fact that at least some of the tensions concerning whales and whaling lasted after World War II, continuing into the second half of the twentieth century and beyond. Some Western powers hoped that the axis whaling vessels would be lost in the conflict, but Japan got back into whaling, and international whaling regulation, as soon as 1946;[297] these tensions and rivalries influenced whaling diplomacy for the rest of the century.

Placing the interwar period on a broader timeline – rather than an isolated one focusing on the interwar period alone – reveals that the League engaged with earlier ideas for transnational solutions to marine

[296] *Id.* at 79.
[297] *Id.* at 69.

problems concerning natural resources. This was also followed by later international regulations concerning the oceans in that respect. At least some of the legal ideas that were developed during the interwar period laid the foundation for later arrangements post–World War II. As a matter of fact, some of these also served as a basis for legal discussion during the war.

In January 1944, a special conference was held in London to update the 1937 Convention – a sign that the League was revising its legal procedures as part of its diplomatic routine. The London Conference of 1944 not only saw discussions intensify, but it also marked a shift in the central conceptions on whaling. The catastrophic conflict and humanitarian hardship had led to a general policy of austerity, and a shortage of raw materials and food. The severe fat and oil crisis in particular pushed many parties to ask the League to ease its restrictions on whaling. In a broader perspective, this conference also marked a geopolitical shift: the next stage of international law would be governed by the Americans with the 1946 International Convention for the Regulation of Whaling. The 1946 ICRW was not signed in Europe, but in the American capital in early December, 1946, in order to "provide for the proper conservation of whale stocks and thus make possible the orderly development of the whaling industry."[298] As earlier discussions under the auspices of the League had indicated in the late 1930s, the post–World War II whaling regime would be carried out by a special international organization that would regulate whaling, relying on an international convention to give it legitimacy and authority. The International Whaling Commission (IWC) is a global agency set up by the terms of the ICRW (according to Article III).[299]

One can also track some of the League's proposed legal solutions at several points in the post–World War II era. This is the case, for instance, with the solution to place a global cap on the number of whales that could be taken (instead of a closed season, as the conventions of the 1930s asserted). Applying and enforcing this idea, which was known in the interwar period as a global or Antarctic quota, as a legal mechanism was not a simple task at all, especially given the huge distance between the Antarctic and other regions. But it was seen during the 1930s as one of the only possible and practical ways to ensure that only a set number of

[298] Preamble to the International Convention for the Regulation of Whaling, with Schedule of Whaling Regulations, Dec. 2, 1946, 62 Stat. 1716, 161 UNTS 72.

[299] For a review of the Commission *see*, for instance, Nagtzaam's discussion, *supra* note 7.

whales was caught. Other delegations rejected this legal solution in 1937, but it would later reappear as one of the key elements in the postwar regulation. Subparagraphs 8(a) and 8(b) of the Schedule of the 1946 International Convention for the Regulation of Whaling, for instance, set a fixed number of baleen whales that could be caught. According to this arrangement, no more than sixteen thousand blue whale "units" were to be hunted during the open season.[300]

However, some fundamental problems remained, such as the ongoing resentment of certain whaling nations, which accepted – or had no choice but to follow – the League's restrictions in international law, particularly regarding the "tricky" role of Japan.[301] One might claim that the general view of Japan as an irresponsible player in the game of whaling in the early twenty-first century had its roots in the League's intensive efforts.

A comparative analysis of the legal history reveals that several states relied on a similar discourse to avoid restrictions introduced by international law. Japan, for instance, argued that its whaling industry – and its whaling vessels in particular – deserved special treatment since it was (allegedly) so far behind its Western peers in terms of whaling technologies and equipment. Given this gap, which unfairly benefitted whaling nations in the West in exploiting the products of the sea, Japanese whalers should not be expected – even with regard to the 1937 Convention – to abide by the same legal and technological standards as the more developed whaling fleets. The legal implications of discrepancies in development history, technologies, and environment are also evident in the case of China. It rejected restrictions on emissions, which were proposed by Western countries during early discussions about creating an international industrial emissions policy as part of the global climate regime. The fact that Western economies had completed "their" Industrial Revolution – at the expense of nature and the environment – made the claim that China needed to restrain its industrial development unjustified and biased.[302]

[300] For the purpose of subparagraph 8(a), blue whale units were calculated on the basis that one blue whale equals two fin whales, or two and a half humpback whales, or six sei whales (see subparagraph 8 to the 1946 Convention).

[301] In many ways, Japan saw no benefit in joining any international move that would result in limitations on its fast-growing whaling industry. However, the interwar period also tells of an ambivalent whaling politics, as Japan asked – and also acceded – to be informed of the discussed legal mechanisms and arrangements, though it did not sign them.

[302] *See* THOMAS L. FRIEDMAN , THE WORLD IS FLAT: A BRIEF HISTORY OF THE TWENTY-FIRST CENTURY 411 (2005).

Moreover, the League's whaling diplomacy had also emphasized that partial agreements, even if they applied to most of the central players on the global map (as the 1937 Convention did), were just not good enough. Since the agreements did not apply to the Japanese fleets, other whaling industries, frustrated by their limited yields, felt that the League's international law had unfairly restricted them. Hence, the post–World War II legal arrangements in the field of whaling were based on the League's experience at the time. During and after the war, a different concept of whaling regulation emerged: it was more important to achieve an overall international agreement, even if this strategy involved agreeing to far less progressive solutions.

Indeed, the League had many weak points from the outset. Some of these, such as the problem of reaching a common solution in a polarized world, or the huge obstacle of enforcing the legal arrangements the League had finally managed to reach in the 1920s and 1930s, were also projected over the course of the whaling dilemma. However, the unique challenge of whaling, with its wide range of commercial, industrial, national, legal, and environmental considerations, also highlighted some of the League's strengths. Whalers might have sailed far from any source of authority, but they could not escape the League or *its* international law. It was the League that used an environmental challenge as the basis for international collaboration. It strove to expand the circle of states that would sign the 1937 Convention, to include the United States, France, and Norway. Pro-regulation forces within the League believed that this would demonstrate how international solidarity could look beyond immediate commercial interests. International solidarity in the early 1930s was built around environmental challenges: "I hope that you will be able to convince your government that in signing the above Convention it will be giving evidence of solidarity which I am certain will not fail to constitute a most useful example."[303] One way or another, the recorded discussions during the interwar period reflect much more than a "comment" that "might compare to a modern environmentalist position," as had been said of the League's whaling policy.[304] The League provided an innovative space in which to tackle this complex dilemma, one that still troubles international environmental law today,[305]

303 A letter from Smets to Lucius R. Eastman, Nov. 27, 1931, LoN Archives, 3E/33029/31270.

304 *See* Dorsey, *supra* note 4, at 73.

305 In December 2018, for instance, Tokyo announced it will join Iceland and Norway and quit the IWC next year, and resume commercial hunting of whales in its territorial

introducing an interpretation of international law that enabled a variety of players to become involved in its creation in real time.

waters and exclusive economic zone starting in July of the following year. International parties were furious. *See* Ahmet Salih & Sena Güler, *Under Fire, Japan Joins Whalers Iceland and Norway*, ANADOLU AGENCY (Dec. 30, 2018), https://www.aa.com.tr/en/asia-pacific/under-fire-japan-joins-whalers-iceland-and-norway/1352052.

3

Sanitation, Spreading Diseases, and Environmental Concerns: The League of Nations' Campaign for Rural Hygiene

> "[W]e are not going to lay down rules and principles with a view of stabilizing an existing state of things, but that we are going to *change the existing state* of things is so far as we are able to do so and to promote progress."[1]

3.1 Introduction

In the aftermath of World War I, the interwar world was facing a variety of acute problems. Despite these pressing global challenges, the League of Nations invested a huge amount of time, institutional energy, and effort in tackling sanitation risks and environmental threats in rural areas. In fact, throughout its activity, the League worked to combat a variety of "rural hygiene" issues on an increasing scale during that period. Different organs of the League[2] were deeply involved in efforts to promote solutions for sanitation and public health concerns, which concurrently raised environmental questions and sought direct environmental outcomes.

In order to respond to the various aspects of sanitation that posed local, national, and global public health risks, the League worked on revising policies that could deal with these challenges. To do so, it relied heavily on scientific and professional expertise and comparative data. Although these suggested policies were discussed in terms of international law, the League did not necessarily intend to apply and enforce them itself; instead, it meant for states and government authorities to take charge of issues pertaining to "rural hygiene." These issues focused mainly on the eradication of a variety of environmental sanitary risks and spreading diseases that the League believed to be plaguing the countryside. The international community's concerns included the need to protect water resources from human and nonhuman pollution; treating refuse; fighting the spread of disease, particularly in rural and

[1] Gustavo Pittaluge, Opening Address of the European Conference on Rural Hygiene, Vol. II, Minutes, C.473.M.202.1931.III, at 19 (emphasis added).

[2] And especially the League of Nations Health Organisation.

peripheral areas; controlling breeding flies and rats, and other pests; and more. The League identified these concerns as threats to local, national, and international communities in an attempt to justify the measures it suggested: the League conceptualized agricultural peripheries in both Europe and in Asia, as well as a rural frontier, from which humanity could protect itself, using means such as sanitary engineering, special medical services, and political awareness.

Exploring how the League, as the first institution of its kind, was involved in trying to solve sanitation risks and environmental threats in rural peripheries allows us to look into the different political and legal layers that shaped policies concerning public health, nature, and sanitation in the changing world of the 1920s and 1930s. The League's continuing campaign for rural hygiene was entangled in the webs and political structures of imperialism, colonialism, and early international institutional law. Moreover, my analysis will show that this campaign was one of the League's most central missions, right until its bitter end.

Therefore, this chapter will study the rural hygiene campaign as a test case with which the history of international law and environmental history can be revised. Scientists, professional experts, jurists, diplomats, and various representatives considered the periphery – both in terms of rural areas and the *East* as a space – as a dangerous and important challenge for the West, as well as for local communities. Since these spaces posed both regional and international threats, the League treated rural sanitation as a central brick in its efforts to create and enforce *a global system of security*. The growing fear of the surrounding environment – first across the periphery, and then from this rural front into the urban centers of these regions – did not stop at Eastern Europe or East Asia alone: the League and the international community were concerned that the pathogens present in the rural margins of the global village would infiltrate the West as well. No need to be mentioned that the current colossal impact of COVID-19, and the ways in which it spread from (relative) peripheral areas in China to the rest of the world, shed a special (comparative) light on the interwar campaign.

As this chapter will show, the sanitation campaign reflected a different mode of internationalism and international law that the League was developing. Unlike the other routines in its environmental regime, it would be rather difficult to identify concrete suggestions for formal conventions or binding legal agreements with regard to this campaign. This phase of international environmentalism relied mostly on international cooperation that was triggered and promoted by the League. The League organized two main international conferences at which delegations, League officials, scientists, and professional experts discussed and revised different mechanisms to solve rural hygiene and sanitary problems.

This chapter will explore these two conferences, which were keystones of the League's campaign for rural hygiene, and will also study their environmental perspectives as they were developed. Moreover, in order to illustrate the campaign as a developing story, the chapter will also analyze the preparatory and the follow-up stages of each of these conferences.

Obviously, the interwar period was not the first time that humanity had struggled with sanitary risks and crises. As I will elaborate in the historical background I offer, the historical context might also have played a role in the reasons for the intensive campaign. In the aftermath of the Spanish flu, the epidemic that devastated the globe in the late 1910s at the end of the Great War, awareness seems to have been heightened about the danger that deteriorating environmental sanitary conditions and the surrounding nature posed to population centers. Therefore, in terms of the developing historical timeline, the chapter will place the interwar discussions on spreading diseases and their environmental risk factors alongside earlier steps that focused on lacking environmental conditions as a source of sociodemographic danger.

In early summer of 1931, the League organized its first international conference on the issue of "rural hygiene." As most of the issues of the first conference, the 1931 European Conference on Rural Hygiene dealt with sanitation and environmental risks, it focused on Eastern European countries, where these issues were prevalent. This conference was not a singular event. The institutional capabilities and the diplomatic routine of the League meant the first conference in 1931 did not function as an ad hoc initiative. It was followed by another international joint cooperation, even larger than its predecessor. In summer 1937, during one of the tensest periods of the interwar period, dozens of delegations from different countries convened under the auspices of the League for the special Intergovernmental Conference for Rural Hygiene in Far Eastern Countries (the second rural hygiene conference).

Like its predecessor, the second conference of 1937 also turned to tools of international governance, information sharing, and other modes of international law. By using these tools, the goal was to eradicate environmental and sanitary risks. Similar medical, environmental, and social concerns that occupied European minds had also become concerns among policymakers and political elites in different countries in East Asia. However, it should be noted that Java (in what is today Indonesia), which hosted this second conference in the City of Bandoeng,[3] was at that time under Dutch rule. Moreover, most of the countries that took part in the second conference were part of colonial and imperial networks of the British, French, and Dutch. Within this context, discussions on breeding flies and comparative studies on flea control took place alongside power relations between hegemonic Western powers and "Far Eastern" countries. This chapter not only analyzes the different sanitary challenges and rural hygiene problems across this huge geographical space, but also tackles these political dimensions.

Moreover, I will show that the League considered the mission of sanitation, especially in rural areas beyond the Western geocultural hemisphere, as part of its broader ideological paradigm. Although the context was not entirely colonial or imperial as it had been with regard to earlier transnational initiatives,[4] there was something of the "White Man's Burden" narrative in discussions between the League and different delegations on technological improvements and sanitary concerns. Indeed, the League's international cultural duty to spread the benefits of technological progress cannot alone explain why it became so intensely involved in the rural hygiene campaigns. Likely, the League's involvement was also attributable to growing fears over the environmental, social, and financial costs of disease spreading across the new "Cordon Sanitaire" at a time when ships were crossing international waters much faster than they were able to prior to the jump forward in modern shipping. But it seems the there was also, at least to a certain extent, an intention to promote general environmental-sanitary conditions in rural areas that Western progress had not yet reached. While exploring these two special international conferences, the chapter will discuss the different, and sometimes confusing, layers of colonialism, imperialism, and modern progress alongside the role the League took upon itself.

In addition to environmental concerns, colonial influence, and scientific endeavors, the study of the interwar period reveals unique historical patterns. Both of these international conferences discussed problems that were not only far beyond the scope of the core aims for which the League was established, but which also reflected different concerns about the danger that the environment and nature posed to humankind. As I move

[3] Nowadays spelled Bandung, the Capital of West Java.

[4] Besides the interest of colonial or imperial systems in sanitation, sanitation was also a central aim of other transnational frameworks. The International Institute of Agriculture, for instance, which was founded years before the League (in 1905), developed an interest in rural health matters in the 1920s. *See* RAPLH W. PHILLIPS, FAO: ITS ORIGINS, FORMATION AND EVOLUTION 1945–1981, 3–4 (1981).

toward the conclusion, I will compare how and to what extent this agenda concerning nature and environment was different than other nature-related initiatives the League promoted.

Moreover, one should also consider the historical context of the campaign. The second conference in Bandoeng took place two years before the outbreak of another global war, when the geopolitical situation in East Asia was already in crisis after Imperial Japan invaded Chinese Manchuria. This period was filled with conflict, from increasing fascist threats in Southern Europe and Asia to the intensifying of ultra-fascist powers in Germany, not to mention the long and difficult recovery from the financial and economic crisis of 1929. Given these numerous challenges, it seems surprising, to say the least, that the League's interest in the link between polluted environments and sanitation was growing – including in specific issues such as "the Fly Problem in the East," which the second rural hygiene conference addressed.

This chapter comprises three sections in addition to the introduction. First, in order to place this analysis on a broader and continuing timeline (rather than an "isolated" one), I will give a general background and a historical survey, starting with a brief introduction to the main historiography of the links between sanitation and environmental concerns. As in the other chapters of this research, this survey will also demonstrate that, despite the growing body of sanitation studies (including those conducted in conjunction with environmental studies), a study focusing on the role of the League with regard to environmental concerns and sanitation has not yet been introduced.

In the second section (which provides the historical narrative), I will trace the steps taken by the League to construct its campaign for rural hygiene. This section mainly explores the two international conferences that the League organized to tackle these issues: the first conference in 1931 (held at Geneva), and the second rural hygiene conference in 1937 (held in Bandoeng), which focused on East Asia. Delegations at both conferences included a variety of professional delegates, including physicians, engineers, public health experts, and officials. The various delegations consulted with one other and compared policies, measurements, and other relevant techniques, including the purification of sewer effluent and disposal of garbage for example, as key steps in fighting deteriorating sanitary conditions and the spread of diseases and plagues.[5] This

[5] League of Nations European Conference on Rural Hygiene, June 29–July 7, 1931, Geneva, League of Nations Archives [hereinafter LoN Archives], C. 473. M. 202. 1931. III.

section will discuss and compare the recommendations of these conferences. The primary focus of this section is on the warnings and advice provided by scientific observations, committees of experts, detailed reports, and comparative information gathered from different countries and authorities, Western and non-Western alike. Together, they show that the League directly and explicitly addressed the outcomes of environmental flaws in peripheral areas, as well as the means to solve them. As this story will show, the League had two aims: On the one hand, it strove to prevent infectious diseases from spreading outwards from rural areas, mostly as a result of poor environmental conditions. On the other hand, the League also ascribed itself certain characteristics as an agency of modernity and cultural and scientific progress. In that sense, overcoming mass epidemics through an alliance between science and international law became a central aim of the interwar period.

This chapter will conclude with the third section. Here, I will briefly address the main arguments of the chapter. Moreover, in placing the League's environmental concerns about sanitation on a broader historical, timeline, I will also provide a current overview of the role of the interwar period compared to later discussions and steps taken in the field of sanitation within the sphere of international law and international governance, including the second half of the twentieth century and recent years.

Taking into account that the League's cross-border campaign mostly did not progress beyond being law on the books, this discussion's main argument is that the hidden story of the interwar period can nevertheless also be viewed in terms of sanitation and environment. Whether the sanitation campaign was successful or not, applicable or too naïve, the institutional energy the League applied to it was quite significant compared to other initiatives in the 1920s and 1930s.

This assessment also holds when one takes into account the League's involvement in the eclectic variety of humanitarian issues and progressive aims during that period. Therefore, the primary focus of the historical narrative here is the different ways in which the League, the international community, and the various players and parties involved viewed the environment and nature. Unlike in the cases of the polluted oceans, endangered whale, or shrinking forests, this time nature was the cause of danger to society at a rural-peripheral, urban, and then a global level. Here, the League, as a representative of the global greater good, strove to mobilize different means of international law, not to conserve the environment, natural resources, or species from extinction due to human activity or expansion, but to defend society from the dangers that lurked in water and on land.

"[F]rom the point of view of leprosy propagation, the part played [by one's] dwelling is no less important in Asia and Africa today than it was in Medieval Europe. . . . [T]he resistance of exposed subjects must not be weakened by diseases which chiefly occur in rural surroundings."[6]

3.2 Background and Historical Survey: A Brief Introduction to the Historiography of Sanitary Efforts and Environmental Concerns

The shift from hunting and gathering to producing food around 10,000 BC marked a fundamental change in the ways human populations were organized in terms of public hygiene. Permanent settlements challenged traditional patterns that had existed for thousands of years and led to the need for improved technologies to adequately handle ancient sanitary and waste disposal requirements. In certain rural areas, at least until late modern times, on-site dumping and natural decomposition were common disposal methods before public health concerns became less tolerant of rural habits.[7] In this section, I will give an overview of the historiography of studies that have focused on the links between sanitation and environmental factors.

In my examination of the main bodies of literature, I will show that there are few studies that explore these links during the interwar period in general, or during the role of the League in particular. Certain scholars who have studied the dense history of the League's Health Organisation have dealt with some of the issues this chapter explores;[8] however, the lenses through which these analyses were carried out chiefly focused on issues of public health, and medical and scientific concerns. Yet the broad, intensive campaign that the League led in remote peripheral areas can be analyzed not only as an important part of the League's international health governance, but also as part of the developing field

[6] Preparatory Papers for the Intergovernmental Conference of Far Eastern Countries on Rural Hygiene, LoN Archives, 6098/8A/29782/8855, at 101 [hereinafter Preparatory Papers].

[7] Martin V. Melosi, Garbage in the Cities: Refuse, Reform, and the Environment 3 (Rev. ed., 2005).

[8] Iris Borowy, Coming to Terms with World Health: The League of Nations Health Organisation: 1921–1946 (2009).

of environmental history. This shows that the sanitary challenge of the interwar period can be studied as more than "just" a health issue.

As this chapter will reveal, the League's Health Organisation took on a central role during this campaign. Likewise, the organization's first manager, Dr. Ludvik Witold Rajchman,[9] had an ongoing role as the campaign developed. Rajchman was a Polish physician and bacteriologist, and the driving force behind the Polish National Institute of Hygiene in Warsaw. Thanks to his active role in the fight against several waves of the typhus epidemic, which was devastated East European countries in the late 1910s and early 1920s, he was noticed by the professional administration of the burgeoning League. In 1921, he was therefore appointed to set up a special Health Organisation within the institutional framework of the League.

However, that does not mean other departments and bodies within the League were not involved in the discussion too (although they took on a secondary role). The International Labour Organisation, for instance, also participated in the discussion and stressed the importance of health insurance funds in order to improve rural hygiene status and to overcome sanitation problems.[10]

The following brief exposition will place the study of the environmental concerns, those that triggered the start of the League's (rural) sanitary campaign in the 1930s, in a historiographic context. In so doing, this exposition will sketch a relevant timeline for the League's efforts.

Within the interdisciplinary scholarship of environmental studies as a whole, it seems that one can quite easily trace the development of the history (or histories) of sanitation. In many ways, it stands as one of the richest and most diverse fields in the world of environmental history. The interplay between the ways in which human populations used to treat their waste, sewage, and disposal with regard to surrounding nature has been reflected and analyzed in a variety of studies.

These studies have focused on different periods across the Anthropocene and on eclectic geographical areas. As Martin V. Melosi put it, compared to other issues of environmental history, the history of sanitation, disposal, and the environment is one of the first fields that environmental historians

[9] *See* MARTA A. BALINSKA, FOR THE GOOD OF HUMANITY: LUDWIK RAJCHMAN, MEDICAL STATESMAN (Rebecca Howell Trans., 1998).

[10] *See* the resulting report "Sickness Insurance as a Factor in Rural Hygiene," report submitted to the European Conference on Rural Hygiene by the International Labour Office, (undated), C.H. 1045, LoN Archives, European Conference on Rural Hygiene, Vol. II, Minutes, C.473.M.202.1931.III., at 161–79 [hereinafter European Conference].

focused on both in antiquity and modern times. According to Melosi, the reason for this special interest is the fact that, since "human beings have inhabited the earth, they have generated, produced, manufactured, excreted, secreted, discarded, and otherwise disposed of all manner of waste."[11]

This might not be the right place to try to summarize the history of sanitation. After all, sanitation and environmental fears have had different impacts on human societies at different times – from ancient times[12] to the Industrial Revolution – and in different circumstances: local, regional, and national. Environmental historians have studied sanitary concerns and technical methods with which ancient powers fought against environmental threats.[13] Both the Roman Republic and the Roman Empire, for instance, had to overcome sanitation risks unheard of by the Greeks. Given the geographical size and their much denser population, the Romans developed impressive sanitation systems.[14] Historians have also connected deteriorating sanitary conditions in medieval times with the catastrophes of the period.[15]

The historic and the historiographic pictures change dramatically with the start of the Industrial Revolution. This is probably also the reason why such a large proportion of the scholarship on environment and sanitation tends to focus on urban centers. With the end of medieval times and the reemergence of populated cities during the Renaissance, early modern Europe did not undergo a fundamental demographic, urban-centered, transformation. All this changed in the late eighteenth and early nineteenth centuries, when the old order – mostly agrarian – was dismantled by rapid new urbanization. Environmental history of the Industrial Revolution tracks the tremendous environmental change in cities as both residents and urban systems were forced to confront

[11] MELOSI, *supra* note 7, at 1.

[12] *See* LEWIS MUMFORD, THE CITY IN HISTORY: ITS ORIGINS, ITS TRANSFORMATION, AND ITS PROSPECTS 75 (1961). It should be noted, however, that Mumford's scholarship is nowadays seen as controversial.

[13] On ancient sanitary methods *see* GEORGE ROSEN, A HISTORY OF PUBLIC HEALTH (1938). Furthermore, scholars have also explored the Jewish laws of cleanliness as patterns of early public sanitation. *See* E. S. SAVAS, THE ORGANIZATION AND EFFICIENCY OF SOLID WASTE COLLECTION, 11–13 (1977).

[14] As a matter of fact, most of the scholars argue that sanitation in ancient Rome was a complex system similar in many ways to modern sanitation systems. *See, e.g.*, Emily Gowers, *The Anatomy of Rome from Capitol to Cloaca*, 85 J. ROMAN STUD. 23 (1995).

[15] A variety of studies use the Black Death plague as a symbol for a failure of human sanitation and medicine. *See* D. E. Davis, *The Scarcity of Rats and the Black Death: An Ecological History*, 16 J. INTERDISC. HIST. 455 (1986).

massive pollution in many forms – drinking water, sewerage, and living conditions. Compared to earlier periods, these kinds of studies tracked the ways in which sanitation, spreading diseases, refuse, and environmental threats emerged as severe social and political problems.[16] The inability to house such a rapidly growing working-class population in industrial centers led to severe overcrowding, as well as sanitary and environmental problems. Different studies have added additional layers to Charles Dickens' dark description of industrialized England – they have analyzed the period's reflections on stinking water, spreading "urban" diseases, ear-shattering noise, waste, filthy streets, and deteriorating sanitary conditions.[17] Since then, with the unfamiliar difficulties and accumulating waste that modern lifestyles have produced, the environmental living conditions of an average urban resident have formed the focus of a variety of sanitary studies exploring neglected sanitation and inadequate waste collection and disposal facilities.[18]

Sanitation studies, it should be emphasized, are primarily urban studies. Unlike cities and towns, which are limited by space and densely populated, agrarian societies throughout history have successfully avoided solid waste and sanitation pollution. Therefore, the different ways in which cities and towns faced sanitation challenges and environmental threats have been of interest to most scholars.

In trying to evaluate the various aspects of the rich historiography of sanitation, it seems one can point to several general assumptions concerning the existing scholarship. First, historians, including environmental ones, have so far mostly been interested in the implications of lacking sanitation systems, environmental risks, and spreading diseases for societies and their structures over a range of time periods, inasmuch as these implications occurred in cities, towns, and urban centers in different civilizations. Second, this kind of environmental historiography is less interested in policy studies in terms of legal interpretations and discourse,

[16] For a (partial) bibliography on the Industrial Revolution in terms of environmental concerns, *see* PETER N. STEARNS & JOHN H. HINSHAW, THE ABC-CLIO WORLD HISTORY COMPANION TO THE INDUSTRIAL REVOLUTION 299–310 (1996).

[17] *See, e.g.*, ASA BRIGGS, VICTORIAN CITIES (1963); Eric E. Lampard, *The Urbanizing World*, *in* THE VICTORIAN CITY: IMAGES AND REALITIES 1, 19–22 (H. J. Dyos & Michael Wolff eds., 1973).

[18] On the emphasis on modern evolution of sanitary regimes and official policies *see* R. M. Hartwell, *The Services Revolution: The Growth of Services in Modern Economy*, *in* THE INDUSTRIAL REVOLUTION: 1700–1914, 364 (Carol M. Cipolla ed., 1976); ANTHONY S. WOHL, ENDANGERED LIVES: PUBLIC HEALTH IN VICTORIAN BRITAIN (1983).

and is generally closer to the disciplines of social sciences, engineering studies, geography, and so on. Third, taking into account the neglected realm of the interwar period and the contextual focus this study suggests, viewing the 1920s and 1930s in terms of sanitation and international law issues contributes to the existing literature by shifting the lens from urban surroundings to rural landscapes and their environmental threats. Fourth, though there are studies that focus on sanitary and environmental risks and human surroundings in terms of policymaking and legal frameworks, these works largely deal with regional, domestic, and national legal arrangements, but overlook certain conjunctions of sanitary issues and different modes of international law – such as those the League offered throughout its campaign.

Moreover, the historiography of spreading diseases with regard to inadequate public hygiene, insufficient sanitation, or environmental risks is also relevant to colonial lands and imperial contexts. The study on cholera in Colonial India, for instance, is a relatively rich field.[19] However, although scholarly discussion on the changes in history in terms of disappearing borders, floods of refugees, and problems of sanitation is prolific, neither the role of international law nor the League's endeavors on the matter have been thoroughly studied. The more familiar discussions exploring the protection from epidemic threats by means of sanitation have focused on domestic and national levels, but did not place sanitation (and rural sanitation in particular) at the center of a study of international law. Moreover, as this chapter will detail, the interwar period not only presents new territory for sanitation studies of non-Western areas in between international law and national-domestic dimensions of sovereignty and jurisdiction, but also provides a unique opportunity to examine rural sanitation – and not urban – as a primary focus.

In many ways, both in Europe and on other continents – at least with regard to the countryside in remote areas – the interwar period marked a turning point in the awareness of the need to introduce new means of sanitation to rural areas. Western empires had already dealt with concerns about populations and space either through direct control or indirect influence, and these concerns were articulated in transnational and imperial policies and legal regimes. However, these criteria were not

[19] *See*, among others, Sheldon Watts, *From Rapid Change to Stasis: Official Responses to Cholera in British-Ruled India and Egypt 1860 to c. 1921*, 12 J. WORLD HIST. 321 (2001); MARK HARRISON, PUBLIC HEALTH IN BRITISH INDIA: ANGLO-INDIAN PREVENTIVE MEDICINE: 1859–1913 (1994).

yet international (at least not in the way that the League was working toward) and did not cross, or intend to cross, national borders or imperial territories per se.[20]

With this overview, it should also be noted that the sanitary regime the League was promoting was not the first to consider environmental concerns in transnational terms. Transnational cooperation on the matter of the links between deteriorating sanitary conditions and the outbreak of diseases had begun a (relatively) long time before the League was announced.

The common history of (modern) transnational sanitary cooperation can be divided into three different periods, as suggested by Iris Borowy.[21] The first period is marked by the first International Sanitary Conference of 1851. This conference was organized by the French government in order to standardize international quarantine regulations against the spread of cholera, plague, and yellow fever. This collaboration symbolized the general awareness of European and North American political, scientific, and social elites that epidemic threats, in spite of their direct implications for domestic national populations, were a challenge that had to be faced with transnational cooperation. With faster and denser means of transportation in the age of railways and transoceanic ships, and with the pollution of shared water sources such as rivers and lakes as a result of lacking or defective sanitation systems, national borders and customs checkpoints were no longer efficient barriers against spreading epidemics.

The 1851 Sanitary Conference was the starting point of a series of fourteen more conferences that followed its original agenda over the years. During the second half of the nineteenth century, different official governmental delegations discussed the possible means to address sanitation threats.[22] This series of conferences continued until 1938, and

[20] *See, e.g.*, Muhammad U. Mushtaq, *Public Health in British India: A Brief Account of the History of Medical Services and Disease Prevention in Colonial India*, 34 Indian J. Community Med. 6 (2009).

[21] Borowy, *supra* note 8, at 12.

[22] This series of conferences was a reaction to the outbreak of the second cholera pandemic in 1829. This pandemic encouraged several European governments to appoint joint medical missions to investigate the causes of the plague. Different expert expeditions were sent in June 1931 to Tsarist Russia, Prussia, and the Austrian Empire. Following these expeditions, France also promoted a survey on the sanitary regulations of Mediterranean countries. This survey (officially published in 1834) pointed to the different types and policies of quarantine requirements among the countries, and called to better organize and monitor national standards. The call to convene an international conference that would eventually introduce border-crossing quarantine regulations against "exotic diseases," at least some of which were spreading because of insufficient

different scholars have argued that it played a major role in the formation of the World Health Organization (the successor of the League of Nations Health Organisation) in 1948,[23] and also in the realization of a permanent fixed institutional framework.[24]

According to this common periodization of international health cooperation and its focus on sanitation, the second period starts in the 1910s and relates to the international sanitary conferences that continued into the 1940s, and after the League was dissolved. This second wave differed from the former by the growing awareness that ad hoc meetings were too slow, too inflexible, and too amateurish to deal with recurrent epidemics at a time of rapidly evolving scientific knowledge. This realization of the early twentieth century motivated a preliminary institutional shift, with the founding of a series of international health organizations. Historians of international health and medicine tend to characterize the second period as a transition phase between the early and global phases of international cooperation. This second phase was terminated by World War II, from which the World Health Organization emerged.

And the third period (starting with the establishment of the WHO after World War II had ended) studies the endeavors of the current international institution of the WHO, today one of the most powerful agencies of the United Nations. These studies have explored different issues related to the central role of the WHO as the leading institution for all worldwide health concerns.

The focus this chapter suggests, however, revisits the traditional historiography. Up until now, most historians have tended either to overlook the story of the Health Organisation of the interwar period, or, inasmuch as they have studied it in detail, to skip its environmental aspects in terms of the meeting points and interplays between sanitation, environment, and public health. Moreover, the interwar international community expressed a growing sense of concern about sanitary crises that emerged not from urban centers, but rather from the periphery and rural areas where modern means of sanitation were lacking. As with the rural hygiene campaign, the League dealt intently with numerous health

means of sanitation, became real in the form of the (first) 1851 Sanitation Conference in Paris.

[23] On the series of sanitary conferences *see, e.g.*, Valeska Huber, *The Unification of the Globe by Disease? The International Sanitary Conferences on Cholera, 1851–1894*, 49 Hist. J. 453 (2006).

[24] Norman Howard-Jones, *The Scientific Background of the International Sanitary Conferences: 1851–1938*, 1 Hist. Int'l Pub. Health (1975).

issues and (mostly medical) prevention protocols during this time. However, its central conferences in Geneva and Bandoeng in the 1930s were different, as they identified the countryside (both in Europe and beyond) as a dangerous source of infection and pollution. Due to the central involvement and leading practical role of scientists, experts, engineers, and medical doctors, the League was able to establish a link between serious outbreaks of disease, lacking sanitation, and environmental conditions, all of which play part in the distribution of pathogens.

Here, one might recognize a similarity to the historical-environmental "cordon sanitaire," the geographical (and geopolitical) belt that represented a shield protecting Europe against the spread of diseases – or from political ideologies. For instance, Georges Clemenceau, the French Prime Minister, warned of the need to defend Western European borders from Soviet Russia and Eastern Europe.[25] Similarly, the Austro-Hungarian Empire tried to "defend" its walls in Vienna against the epidemic threats posed by the Ottoman Empire.

> I am sure that this first European Conference on Rural Hygiene will mark an epoch in the history of hygiene in agricultural and rural districts. For the first time on so large a scale and with so much authority, practicing physicians, health officers, administrators, agriculturists, engineers and organizers of agricultural associations have met together for the thorough study of those questions which are most important for the improvement of conditions of life in rural districts from the standpoint of sanitation .... It will not be the last time. There is still a long road to be travelled, but this Geneva Conference, convened by the League of Nations, marks a starting point on that road ....[26]

3.3 The League of Nations, Rural Hygiene, Sanitation, and Environmental Threats

Prior to the establishment of the League, revolutionary improvements had begun to emerge in mass transportation, such as trains and ships, which connected global spaces more efficiently. However, as other issues with environmental dimensions showed, such as modern whaling

[25] In a formal public announcement in March 1919, he referred to the dangerous (Communist) frontier beyond the border of Western Europe, and the danger posed by its liberal-democratic regimes.

[26] Technical Recommendations by the Preparatory Committee, Extracts from the Report of the Preparatory Committee, C.H. 1045, LoN Archives, European Conference on Rural Hygiene, Vol. II, Minutes, C.473.M.202.1931.III., at 71.

technologies and evolving shipping and naval transportation,[27] the League's period of activity intensified these phenomena. As the world became smaller and closer thanks to new and faster means of transportation and communication, and with old borders changing dramatically after World War I, spreading diseases also crept closer than in earlier decades – at least in the public mind.

The transmission of diseases between non-Western areas and the West (mostly in Europe) was not a new phenomenon either in the early twentieth century or in the interwar period. The fact that the end of World War I also marked the breaking down of old borders across vast areas in Europe set new patterns of mass migration in motion all across the Continent. In many cases, refugees and migratory populations carried epidemic threats with them; or, at least, that was the common impression.

Cholera, for instance, had already begun to threaten the West long before the League had even been conceived of;[28] but when the distance between Eastern Europe and East Asia started to shrink in the 1920s and 1930s, other diseases – mostly those that spread through poor sanitation – increased the perception of the West's new fragility[29] in a period when technological improvements were increasingly changing the world (and more dangerously).

Just like international trade, commodities, and ships, different diseases profited from modern technologies, which made their geographic distribution much easier and faster than ever before. The movement of trains, steamships, and people across larger distances within much shorter times made the League realize that sanitation and rural hygiene had suddenly – unexpectedly – become one of its main international missions.

[27] From a historical perspective, international trade grew remarkably in the second half of the nineteenth century, especially around the turn of the twentieth century. After a long period characterized by persistently low international trade, over the course of the nineteenth century, technological advances triggered a period of marked growth in world trade (what historians of economics usually refer to as the "first wave of globalization").

However, the interwar period is rather ambivalent. The golden years of the mid-1920s gave way to a halt in growth, which was eventually reversed in the first half of the 1930s following the Great Depression. *See*, among others, A. G. Kenwood & A. L. Lougheed, The Growth of the International Economy 1820–2000 (4th edition) (1999).

[28] *See*, for instance, Anne Hardy's assessment that in nineteenth-century British society, cholera was perceived to be a dangerous invader moving toward the British Isles: Anne Hardy, *Cholera, Quarantine, and the English Preventive System*, 37 Med. Hist. 250, 250 (1993).

[29] Huber, *supra* note 23, at 455.

To complete the historical context of the common fear of spreading diseases in the first decades of the twentieth century, one should keep in mind another threat that caused a deep sense of alarm: the Spanish flu. Although this pandemic was not directly related to the Great War, the unfavorable wartime conditions between 1914 and 1918, in which soldiers spent extended periods in the dense trenches in close quarters, suffering from malnourishment and poor hygiene, contributed to its overwhelming reach. As a result, during the interwar period, an entire world was still terrified by the enormous effect the pandemic had upon public health and society. Thus, at least some of the reasons for the international interest, if not paranoia, in improving sanitation, public health, and rural hygiene in the 1920s and 1930s can be traced back to this pandemic. The virus, or "La Grippe," was extremely violent and caused a death toll of biblical proportions;[30] it was undoubtedly a global disaster.[31]

Though the exact reasons for the outbreak are still unclear, some historians have argued that "Patient Zero" can likely be traced back to the overcrowded trenches of the Western front in World War I. However, other scholars have claimed that since this virus was found to be a mutation of avian flu, it is more likely that its geographical origin was East Asia. Here, different species of domestic birds (mostly poultry) and humans shared much closer quarters on a daily basis, thus creating the ecological conditions that could allow the transmission of avian flu to humans.[32]

[30] Until the early 2000s, experts presented estimations of between twenty-five and forty million deaths. However, a study from 2002 revised the recorded impression and claimed the real numbers were much more severe: perhaps fifty million. However, these scholars have also added that even this dramatic number could well fall short of the actual death toll. One way or the other, the pandemic killed more people than all the battles of the Great War together, and it was cited as the most devastating epidemic in recorded history: more people died of influenza in a single year than in four years of the Black Death (Bubonic Plague) from 1347 to 1351. *See* Niall Johnson & Juergen Mueller, *Updating the Accounts: Global Mortality of the 1918–1920 "Spanish" Influenza Pandemic*, 76 BULL. HIST. MED. 105 (2002).

[31] Several studies are: JOHN M. BARRY, THE GREAT INFLUENZA: THE EPIC STORY OF THE DEADLIEST PLAGUE IN HISTORY (2004); RICHARD COLLIER, THE PLAGUE OF THE SPANISH LADY: THE INFLUENZA PANDEMIC OF 1918–1919 (1974); ALFRED W. CROSBY JR., AMERICA'S FORGOTTEN PANDEMIC: THE INFLUENZA OF 1918 (1976).

[32] One can point to increasing interest from scholars, from social historians to historians of medicine, in the study of the Influenza Pandemic. Several examples include JOHN M. BARRY, THE GREAT INFLUENZA: THE EPIC STORY OF THE DEADLIEST PLAGUE IN HISTORY (2004); THE SPANISH INFLUENZA PANDEMIC OF 1918–19: NEW PERSPECTIVES (Howard Phillips & David Killingray eds., 2003).

While the exact origin of the virus may be in question, what is certain is that in a very short time, local cases of the epidemic dramatically transformed into a worldwide pandemic. The League did not directly handle the outcomes of that crisis, but it did understand that health and sanitation issues posed a direct threat to the well-being of the entire international community. It was this realization that prompted its focus on preventing future pandemics.

To citizens in the second half of twentieth century, and most certainly those of the twenty-first century, the role of international law and of its institutions – such as the UN and the WHO – in preventing and confronting diseases seems almost obvious. However, to people during the interwar period this evolving institutional cooperation was new and unfamiliar. Besides the "conventional" threats of global security and the dangers of another battle in Europe, both the turn of the twentieth century and the interwar period reflected other causes for public concern. The Spanish flu, which in fact was much deadlier and more extensive than World War I, posed a huge threat to states and communities – in the public mind, pathogens and poor sanitary conditions came to be seen as being as dangerous as rifles. Given that another fatal wave of spreading disease might be on the horizon, feasible actions based on international cooperation and global governance had to be considered.

The following sections (3.3.1–3.3.4) will describe the keystones of the League's evolving campaign for sanitation and the fight against spreading diseases. As the historical narrative will show, environmental perspectives formed part of many of the central discussions and recommendations the League introduced by means of international law. First, Section 3.3.1 will focus on the first cooperation on rural hygiene that the League promoted: the Interchange Program of 1928, which mostly studied and compared different states' procedures for treating public health in remote and rural communities.

Then, the following sections will explore the more "organized" phase of the campaign and the ways in which it evolved. Section 3.3.2 will discuss the first rural hygiene conference assembled in Geneva in summer 1931. Sections 3.3.3 and 3.3.4, which make up the central part of the chapter, will elaborate on the second international conference, the Intergovernmental Conference on Far Eastern Countries on Rural Hygiene, which convened in Bandoeng, Java, in summer 1937, and which followed up on and responded to the first conference of 1931. Both of these sections will also draw attention to the many subsequent discussions that unfolded between the two conferences themselves. In particular, these sections will analyze the main environmental concerns regarding public health and sanitation that were discussed in Geneva and Bandoeng, as well as several parts of the special and detailed Preparatory Papers – the official reports and surveys that were sent to the League Secretariat in preparation for the conferences and different sessions. Together Sections 3.3.1–3.3.4. will sketch the thread linking these sets of professional recommendations, both of which tackled environmental concerns alongside public health interests and goals. During this journey, the League invested a great deal of effort into promoting international standards of sanitation services in rural areas. This agenda was entangled with environmental concerns – from waste collection to protective measures against pests, flies, and rats as generators of disease – particularly in the countryside. These concerns and fears served as a common base for international cooperation and information sharing, and engaged professional scientists, medical doctors, and different experts.

Although the League primarily developed mechanisms of international law to be used as practical tools on the ground, its efforts to combat sanitation issues and environmental threats often relied on tools other than conventions or official agreements, which characterized much of its activity. For instance, when it came to tackling sewage concerns and waste collection in rural areas, or deciding on the best way to handle the problem of flies and rats in East Asia, the League turned to methods that seemed even more lenient than what is usually referred to as "soft international law." The following sections will mainly explore other interpretations of international law: instead of circulating drafts for an international convention, or proposals for binding resolutions by the Council or the Assembly, the rural hygiene campaign relied on elements such as information sharing, distribution of knowledge, and comparative study. In this way, the League appeared to be developing other techniques of international governance as it expanded the reach of international law during the interwar period.

Obviously, this is not the place to start an ongoing discussion on what constitutes soft law – the domain of soft law is still tenuous (especially in terms of international law), and scholars continue to argue about what the generic term means. Finding a good, or even accepted, definition of soft law remains difficult, since there are those who deny its existence as a legitimate field of international law, and those who consider it a new source of international law (as valid as any other common source).

Though its characteristics are variable, and (very) negotiable, it seems that scholars tend to agree on at least some common features. The term encompasses "soft" reflections of international law that have not been developed (if they were ever intended to) into formal binding treaties and conventions. In that sense, soft international law covers nonbinding or voluntary resolutions, recommendations, codes of conduct, and standards. Dinah Shelton, for instance, has defined it as "normative provisions contained in non-binding text."[33]

Although it was not called "soft law" during the interwar period, this term refers to quasi-legal instruments that do not have any legally binding force, or whose binding force is perceived to be weaker than that of traditional law, which is often referred to as "hard law."

The terminology of "soft law," and perhaps even its definition, remains somewhat controversial because certain (formalist) legal views (still) reject its existence. Other views are still confused as to its exact status – and role – in the realm of law. However, for most international practitioners, the development of soft law instruments is an accepted part of the practical routine of international legal systems. Because it usually takes a relatively long time and a great deal of institutional resources to achieve formal, binding hard law in international affairs, soft law mechanisms facilitate and guide the routine work undertaken within the multilayered world of international law.[34]

The sections that follow will trace the primary developments that took place during the League's rural hygiene campaign, dealing almost exclusively with interpretations of soft international law[35] with regard to these issues.

3.3.1 Early Steps and Preparations: The Interchange Program (1928), and the Budapest Conference (October 1930)

In order to deal with sanitation concerns, the League first focused on the periphery in Eastern Europe, and only then dealt with farther areas in East Asia. The 1930s were a feverish decade in terms of international law. As mentioned in the historical background, the interwar period began when the Spanish flu, and the fear of its reoccurrence had overwhelmed

[33] COMMITMENT AND COMPLIANCE: THE ROLE OF NON-BINDING NORMS IN THE INTERNATIONAL LEGAL SYSTEM 292 (Dinah Shelton ed., 2000).

[34] On the relations between these two branches of international law *see* Allison Christians, *Hard Law, Soft Law, and International Taxation*, 25 WIS. INT'L L.J. 325 (2007).

[35] For an overview of the basic questions of soft international law *see, e.g.*, Jean D'Aspremont & Tanja Aalberts, *Symposium on Soft Law*, 25 LEIDEN J. INT'L L. 309 (2012); INFORMAL INTERNATIONAL LAWMAKING (Joost Pauwelyn et al. eds., 2012).

the public. In this section, I will describe the initial steps the League took to face the rural hygiene challenge.

As this section will show, while the idea to communicate sanitary information and epidemiological data began before the establishment of the League, and can be traced as early as the mid-nineteenth century,[36] much of the rest of these data were discussed and developed by the League between the two world wars.

This section begins with the early stages of the discussion on rural hygiene in European countries, when the League started to address these issues in its Interchange Program in 1928. The remaining parts of the discussion will focus on the two special international intergovernmental conferences organized by the League during the 1930s. These early moves, which the League made in anticipation of its involvement in the rural hygiene campaign, expressed a shift in the League's and the interwar period's focus on public health. As the historical review above described, prior to 1914, issues of public health, sanitation, and the prevention of environmental risks were primarily addressed in the context of urban surroundings. The League approached these issues from a different direction, which up to that point had not received much attention – certainly not in terms of transnational or international law. It identified the rural periphery as a dangerous and challenging space in the battle on public health: both in local communities and worldwide.

As this chapter will illustrate, what began as a modest internal program offered by the League in 1928, quickly developed into a rich and detailed international discussion on the ways in which environmental threats could be handled. Indeed, some of the methods the League suggested – for instance the joint international collaboration of statesmen and professional experts – were similar to those that other transnational frameworks (primarily the International Sanitary Conference, as previously mentioned) had built. However, unlike these frameworks, the League had already developed systems, routines, and procedures of information production and sharing (not necessarily with regard to environmental concerns, but rather as a general practice) that supported and encouraged the evolution of the rural hygiene campaign.

Moreover, the League's institutional framework also demonstrates how and to what extent environmental sanitation issues developed under the auspices of the institution. At first, the League addressed these issues as part of its interchange program in the late 1920s. But

[36] Borowy, *supra* note 8, at 12.

then, thanks to the requests made by delegates of several countries (such as Spain, India, and Portugal) at the Assembly,[37] the League placed rural hygiene at the center of two big international conferences that directly tackled these concerns and engaged a variety of professionals and official agencies.

The Interchange Program of 1928 started when the League (and the international community) became aware of certain dangers in the countryside that threatened general public health. Although the political, financial, cultural, and social centers of the West were located in urban areas, according to interwar period demographic surveys, the majority of the population in most countries still lived in a rural surrounding.[38]

However, compared to earlier generations, interwar rural life felt much closer (alarmingly so, especially during sanitation crisis) to densely populated cities. Villages, both in the West and in other regions, no longer seemed like the isolated places they had tended to be during earlier periods: easier to regulate – and also to place under different quarantine regimes – in times of dangerous epidemic outbreaks. Rural populations were now more physically connected to urban centers by railways, accessible roads, automobiles, modern waterways, canals, and other means of transportation.

At this time, the League began to discuss the changing impression of the countryside in terms of international law. Typical romantic descriptions of village life and the countryside as pure, quiet, open, and close to nature contrasted with the foggy and industrial city. The interwar period, however, offered alternative visions of the countryside. Reports that reached the League's Secretariat depicted rural areas also as a source of dirt, disease, and pollution, particularly with regard to water sources such as lakes and rivers that were contaminated with untreated human sewage.

This was not the first time that rural areas had been identified as a source of pollution and environmental threats. In the late nineteenth century, sanitation studies, germ theory, and bacteriology had encouraged this

[37] League of Nations Annual Report for 1928, A.8.1929.III (C.H. 788), Apr. 18, 1929, LoN Archives, at 5.

[38] A report written by the Health Organisation reviewed the proportion of rural populations in different countries. These data have shown that in the 1930s, with the exception of certain Western countries (such as England, with 20 percent rural population), the proportion of agricultural-rural sectors was high. In Yugoslavia, Turkey, and Roumania, for instance, the numbers pointed to approximately 80 percent of the entire population. *See* Second General Report on Certain European Schools and Institutes of Hygiene, C.H. 1247 (I), LoN Archives, Oct. 5, 1937, R 6099/8A/28718/8855, at 3.

negative stereotype of the countryside.[39] However, the League shed new light on the discussion on rural hygiene as a source of danger, revealing it to be an issue that also related to international governance. The fact that these concerns were discussed at a forum based on international law, rather than one that relied on local or national considerations, placed the rural hygiene issue in a different context. Diseases, pollution, lack of water, rat control, and inadequate sanitation in rural areas did not just present a human or social tragedy;[40] these were also issues of global security, given that this was a time when environmental threats at the local level could travel rapidly and over great distances.

When the Health Organisation started to focus on rural hygiene as one of its interests, it used skills the League had already introduced and developed during its institutional activity. As was typical, the League's involvement began with a professional review based on information collected from various countries about their own national policies, protocols, and the ways in which legal-sanitary regulations were carried out on the ground. The Interchange Program of 1928 mostly aimed to learn about and compare these different procedures.

At first, the League was mainly concerned about "clear" public health concerns in the periphery. One of the first professional reports that paved the League's way into the complex field of rural hygiene was actually a statistical study.[41] The study targeted mortality rates in different rural areas across Europe and reflected at least some of the humanitarian motivations that triggered the interest of the state, and also of international community, in the birth rate and demographic stability[42] in the countryside. While the comparative survey did not mention sanitary factors specifically, its general conclusion was that according to available data, the rural mortality rate was higher than the urban mortality rate in different states (such as Germany, Belgium, Sweden, Bulgaria, Norway, and Switzerland). Moreover, infants and young children were the most

39 *See, e.g.*, Steven Cherry, *Medicine and Rural Health Care, in* HEALTH AND MEDICINE IN RURAL EUROPE: 1850–1945, 19, 21 (Steven Cherry & Josep Barona eds., 2005).

40 BOROWY, *supra* note 8, at 327.

41 Knud Stouman, Mortality Conditions in Rural Europe, (undated; probably July 1931), LoN Archives, R 5917/8A/23882/22408.

42 For a study on the ways in which the devastating cost of human lives in World War I have changed certain perceptions of public officials and politicians during the interwar period with regard to the importance of demographic strength (including of rural populations), *see* Iris Borowy, *International Social Medicine Between the Wars: Positioning a Volatile Concept*, 6 HYGIEA INTERNATIONALIS, no. 2, 2007, at 13.

vulnerable age groups in rural populations, likely due to inadequate medical services and sanitation in the countryside.

Following this report, in autumn 1930, two member states addressed the Health Committee of the League, and proposed that the League convene a conference for the study of rural hygiene in Europe. The Spanish government wrote to the League in September 1930,[43] followed by Hungary, which sent a similar suggestion in October.[44] From this point on, the League, encouraged by formal appeals, would be robustly engaged in rural hygiene issues.

The Health Committee did not need long to consider the proposal. Before the autumn of 1930 had ended, the Sixteenth Session of the Committee adopted the proposal and ordered two institutional steps: a special European conference on rural[45] hygiene,[46] and a subcommittee that would organize the international gathering. Moreover, as different tasks carried out by the League had already shown, the rural hygiene campaign was going to be a professional rather than a political campaign. The League agreed that the conference should target experts from various technical fields, such as physicians, engineers, hygienists, biologists, civil servants of public health departments, and others. One of the main topics the subcommittee handled was how to find effective and efficient methods of improving rural districts through sanitation.

Though it did not focus entirely (or even chiefly) on sanitation, the conference on health centers in rural areas – which was held in Budapest at Hungary's request in October 1930 – set up an institutional framework that would serve as a basis not only in Europe, but also in other activities organized by the League later on. Health centers – in essence, big rural clinics that were smaller than a hospital but larger than a simple state-run clinic – were the most efficient method of organizing health services in

[43] Proposal by the Spanish Government, C.H. 917, Sept. 16, 1930, Annex 5 to Minutes of the 16th HC Session, 29 Sept. to 7 Oct. 1930, LoN Archives, C.527.M.248.1930.III, at 106.

[44] The Hungarian Ministry of Health wanted the League to support its new health center, and the Secretary for State of Health, Kornel Scholtz, suggested that the festive occasion be accompanied by a special conference of professional experts, to be organized by the League and thanks to its capacity. Letter from Kornal Scholtz to Ludwik Rajchman, Sept. 12, 1930, LoN Archives, R 5930/8A/23115/10183.

[45] The League used a working definition for "rural": "an area or district where agriculture is the chief or even the sole industry, and where all other industries are of small importance, and in the main dependent upon agriculture" (Memo for the 2d Session of the Preparatory Committee, LoN Archives, C.H. 948, Nov. 29, 1930, at 5) [hereinafter Memo for the 2d Session of the Preparatory Committee].

[46] Minutes of the 16th Health Committee, 29 Sept. to 7 Oct. 1930, C.527.M.248.1930.III, LoN Archives, at 9–10.

rural districts. Moreover, the scheme that the League introduced for a structured rural health system, to be offered in various parts of the world including East Asia, would serve as prototype for interwar sanitary regimes. This structure was based on a hierarchy of the urban centers and periphery. At the top of this structure was an institute of hygiene or central health administration, and a central staff of sanitary engineer directing the secondary and local health inspectors in the countryside. On the local level, in the village, the proposed scheme placed sanitary inspectors, in charge of routine rural hygiene supervision.

The Budapest Conference served as an introduction for the rest of the rural hygiene campaign to follow. Although this institutional scheme for rural health did not introduce any "practical" or tangible legal outcomes, such as a convention,[47] its importance lay in defining sanitation as an *international* problem – and not just a local or national one. One of the main conclusions of the Budapest Conference was the need to introduce modern sanitary systems in rural areas. Moreover, the League had identified water supply, housing, and sewage disposal as principal issues of international cooperation.[48] It seems that the League's international initiatives in the early 1930s secured it a place as a key player in rural health and sanitary care. Unlike earlier and other bodies, both on the national-domestic level as well as the transnational level (such as the series of the International Sanitary Conferences), the League was able to contribute its institutional framework to this issue.

Rather than relying on domestic forums alone, the Budapest Conference started an international discussion on rural hygiene that encouraged different reports from a variety of communities concerned about improper sanitation. Different civil society groups used the conference and the discussion to encourage the League to become involved in issues that previously had typically been dealt with by national institutions. This was the case, for instance, with the Austrian Association of Workers in Agriculture and Forestry,[49] which appealed to the League shortly after the Budapest Conference. The association complained that its members were suffering from poor sanitary and environmental working conditions: their

[47] As did certain other interwar conferences, including in terms of environmental problems, and as I will elaborate in Chapter 4 of the comparative discussion.

[48] Memo for the 2d Session of the Preparatory Committee, *supra* note 45.

[49] Die Wohnverhältnisse der landwirtschaftlichen Arbeiter Österreichs, Bericht des österreichischen Land- und Forstarbeiterverbandes, Feb. 26, 1931, LoN Archives, R 5927/8A/275438/26690.

sleeping quarters were too close to their livestock, and were plagued by smoky air and vermin. The association asked the League to look into these problems and to support its endeavors to promote a hygienic working environment for its members.

A committee of experts within the League applied itself to this matter. It understood that improved sanitary conditions in Austria depended, first and foremost, on domestic political power and suitable legislation. The international forum of the League considered and discussed the issue as part of *its* own mandate, as an institution shaping international governance.

Several other discussions by experts on rural hygiene under the auspices of the League in the early 1930s focused on technical data (gathered from different states) on drinking water, the dangers of polluted water sources, waste, and on the advantages of different methods of water purification. As it prepared the agenda for the first rural hygiene conference, the League identified these issues, including water supplies, sewage disposal, and rural housing as principle topics.[50]

The parties involved, including both the League and the representatives, were well aware of the complexity involved concerning the League's alleged authority and the national sovereignty of states with their domestic laws. Interestingly, whereas in other areas, the League had come into conflict with states in its attempts to achieve sovereignty and power, the sanitary campaign actually allowed the League to strengthen national sovereignty in this instance. When the experts acting on behalf of the League discussed sanitation and how it might best be improved, the Polish delegate, for instance, asserted that it would be rather disappointing if the League issued less severe (and demanding) sanitation standards than his government back home.[51]

In May 1931, following an intensive period of deliberation by the committee of experts, the League presented a report at a general meeting of the Preparatory Committee, a body whose responsibility it was to organize the next steps on the matter of rural hygiene, and to convene an international conference on this issue. The way was now open for another international conference on rural hygiene in the summer – this one much bigger than the preliminary conference that had been held in Budapest.

[50] Memo for the 2d Session of the Preparatory Committee, *supra* note 45.

[51] Minutes, Sous-Comité d'experts en matière d'assainissement des regions, May 12, 1931, LoN Archives, R 5927/8A/58564/26690.

3.3.2 *The 1931 European Conference on Rural Hygiene*

The Preparatory Committee, setting the agenda and framework for the (first) international conference scheduled for summer, saw sanitation as a central concern that it – and different (at this point, European) governments – should be focusing on. One of the League's first instructions to governments, which had both the formal authority and ability on the ground, was to introduce a sanitation system in the countryside. Sewage, the League asserted, should be disposed of by means of water carriage systems, piped from private households. Where installation of the modern sewage system was not possible, open drains could be used; but, it was advised that these should not transport excreta for public health reasons. The League's recommendations warned against polluting water sources, and explained that sewage could be permitted to flow into rivers and lakes, "if necessary," and only after a process of controlled purification.[52] At any rate, the League warned that surface soil and subsoil water had to be protected.[53]

The League, striving to improve sanitation systems on the ground, understood that unlike in other fields where environmental issues were discussed, its legal and practical capacity with regard to sanitation was much more limited. It therefore focused on international legal discourse to articulate its recommendations.

Other recommendations of this kind focused, for instance, on flies. The League suspected that these insects were responsible for the spread of epidemics and therefore posed a threat to the natural environment. Hence, flies needed to be kept away from sewage, and the League sought technical engineering means to ensure this. The committee also claimed that manure needed to be stored in watertight pits so that flies could not get to it. As the following sections will show, the fear of flies as an environmental and sanitary threat can be found in future steps taken in the rural hygiene campaign.

Solid waste and its disposal were also key issues handled by the committee. In order to prevent pollution and environmental hazards, it recommended implementing a garbage disposal protocol or policy in the

[52] Other means of purification were also possible: leaching cesspools, subsoil or surface irrigation, receptacles in fly-proof superstructures, pails or open pits.

[53] Technical Recommendations by the Preparatory Committee, Extracts from the Report of the Preparatory Committee, C.H. 1045, LoN Archives, European Conference on Rural Hygiene, Vol. II, Minutes, C.473.M.202.1931.III., at 142–61 [hereinafter Technical Recommendations].

countryside. Garbage was best handled through a systematic routine of collection. The League considered other more conventional or traditional methods, such as feeding garbage to pigs or dumping it, to be unsuitable options.

Moreover, the committee, and the League as a whole, turned to practical means of (international) law in action. For instance, the League explicitly recommended the construction of new institutions and technical systems. In order to prevent general water pollution and the contamination of drinking water and soil by sewage, the League asserted that rural communities should get their water supply from a central, regulated, system. Water should only obtained from natural sources such as lakes, springs, wells, or local cisterns as an alternative if strictly necessary. The Preparatory Committee's report emphasized that all water had to be strictly supervised by the state.

This sanitation protocol did not stop there. The committee also identified poor conditions created by rural housing, and their effects on lacking environmental sanitation. According to the preparatory report, rural housing in particular was in urgent need of improvement and required adequate means of sanitation. Besides overcrowding, lack of sufficient ventilation, and exposure to the sun, sanitary facilities, dampness, and protection from insects were major problems in the countryside in different parts of Europe.

As the League discussed practical and technical means to prevent sanitary dangers in the periphery, it was also doing something else, essential to the role of the state. With its suggested policies, protocols, and measures the League was pushing the state to exercise its authority and to be more responsible about tackling sanitation in the countryside. In this way, the League pushed a modernist, centralizing, state-based agenda.

Speaking of legal regimes, it should be also noted that although the League was a forum of international governance, it most certainly did not recommend decentralizing medical or sanitation services: both these things had to be rationally planned, regulated, and coordinated by the state and its agencies. In that sense, despite the tension over the question of the self-proclaimed authority of international institutions (and the League as a whole), the League explicitly supported reinforcing the state's authority, and rejected solutions that encouraged decentralization and promoting local agencies.

The bonification of rural Europe, concluded the committee, depended mostly on fixing sanitation – something that needed to happen in the countryside as well as in urban spaces, both problematic areas that were likely to suffer from exposure to spreading diseases due to environmental conditions. Existing conditions in too many parts of the continent posed a threat – both to the local communities in the countryside, and to other populations as well. In that sense, the first rural hygiene conference expressed a discourse of a different type of global security. The League had dedicated much of its institutional energy to peacekeeping and global security. The ways in which sanitation was considered to be part of securing international social welfare shed light on the League's environmental regime. This regime enabled the League to recruit other realms of international law to promote global security. In that sense – along with the framework of disarmament treaties, or enforcing and reinforcing new borders in the post–World War I world – proper sanitation and fighting hazardous flies and other pests were part of the new multilayered system of security and stability.

So much had to be done, asserted the professional committee. When it came to environmental and sanitary challenges, almost everything had to be repaired. In addition to drainage, a solid general infrastructure had to be established – including water supply systems for housing, and sewage and solid waste disposal systems in particular. In addition, the betterment of housing conditions, farming practices, and other daily systems and routines primarily relied on the introduction of modern means of sanitation that had been adjusted to the rural landscape, its natural geographical features, and environmental characteristics. As a representative of global security, the League was concerned about the possibility of the further spread of disease and pushed governments to formulate, in the midst of the Great Depression and economic and industrial pressures, a "complete sanitary reconditioning of the land."

Although the first (European) rural hygiene conference was chiefly intended to focus on necessary improvements in health and medical services in these regions, the experts who had studied the different conditions on the ground understood that in order to introduce a comprehensive, efficient, and practical regime in rural areas, environmental and sanitary issues had to be fully explored.

The 1931 European Conference on Rural Hygiene, which was held for eight days in Geneva, did not go far beyond these recommendations suggested by the Preparatory Committee.[54] This probably had a lot to do with the diplomatic and institutional routine of the League: the fact that the

[54] It should be noted, though, that the League distributed more than one hundred reports on a variety of issues that served as the basis for the first conference.

intensive preparatory work that preceded the conference in Geneva lasted nine months, made the work (and mostly recommendations) of the conference much quicker and more efficient. On the ground, the 1931 conference mostly considered the recommendations and comments made by the Preparatory Committee. The fact that these recommendations were not particularly binding in nature – either in terms of international law or national obligations – probably aided the fact that all the resolutions were eventually adopted by the foreign delegations unanimously.

Most of the European countries (twenty-four in total) sent their delegations. In addition to representatives from states such as France, Turkey, Great Britain, Roumania, and Portugal – and although the conference focused on European rural issues – the international framework of the League also brought other countries to the table, all of which were interested in ways to combat and overcome environmental threats too. Delegations from Latin and Central America (Bolivia, Colombia, Cuba, and Mexico), North America (United States), and Asia (China and Japan) also attended. The shift from transnational frameworks, which had dealt with the realm of sanitation prior to the League,[55] to international and institutional frameworks can also be seen in the other participants who took part in this collaboration. The conference brought together not only European and non-European states, but also a range of NGOs and bodies that looked at the League as the center of both international law and international governance. Several different associations and professional societies also took part in the discussions, among them the International Labour Organisation (ILO), the International Association of Medical Officers, and (of course) the Health Committee of the Health Organisation itself.

Moreover, the overall format used to discuss sanitation and rural hygiene was shaped by the variety of professional and technical expertise the conference brought together. Public health officers, agricultural experts, biologists, medical doctors, diplomats, and insurance experts all saw rural hygiene as a central issue that both the League and international law needed to address. Gustavo Pittaluga for instance, a professor from the National School of Health in Madrid and the President of the first conference, recognized the legal, diplomatic, and historical significance of the conference, and the League's role and contribution in making it happen:

> I am sure that this first European Conference on Rural Hygiene will mark an epoch in the history of hygiene in agricultural and rural districts. For

[55] The series of the International Sanitary Conferences from 1851 to 1938, for example.

> the first time on so large a scale and with so much authority, practicing physicians, health officers, administrators, agriculturists, engineers and organizers of agricultural associations have met together for the thorough study of those questions which are most important for the improvement of conditions of life in rural districts from the standpoint of sanitation .... It will not be the last time. There is still a long road to be travelled, but this Geneva Conference, convened by the League of Nations, marks a starting point on that road ....[56]

3.3.3 *Following Up the 1931 Conference and Preparing for the Second Intergovernmental Conference on Rural Hygiene*

The sense of optimism that guided the conveners and different participants who attended the 1931 European Conference on Rural Hygiene did not fade away quickly. Already during the closing sessions, Dr. Witold Chodźko (former Minister of Health), acting on behalf of the Polish delegation, called explicitly and enthusiastically for another international cooperation under the auspices of the League on these pressing challenges. According to his remark, another follow-up conference should be convened in "some years' time."[57]

Moreover, as it revised the recommendations of the first conference, the League's Health Section urged researchers and experts to engage with other bodies: peasants' associations, media and press, agrarian cooperatives, and more.[58] Once again, the League not only stepped beyond earlier initiatives of rural hygiene and public health (including transnational ones), but actually offered and positioned itself as a relevant institutional partner to various groups beyond (their national) governments, sometimes effectively bypassing their domestic authority.

Thanks to the League's efforts, sanitation and rural hygiene had transcended domestic, national, and transnational frameworks (and policies) and gained an institutional and international dimension. Other

[56] Technical Recommendations, *supra* note 53, at 71.

For a detailed chronicle of the conference *see* F. R. Morote, *La Conferencia de Higiene Rural en Budapest*, in GUSTAVO PITTALUGA, LA CONFERENCIA INTERNACIONAL DE HIGIENE RURAL CONVOCADA POR LA SOCIEDAD DE LAS NACIONES (29 JUNIO 1931) 43 (1931). For a study from a history of medicine perspective, *see* Josep L. Barona, *The European Conference on Rural Hygiene (Geneva, 1931) and the Spanish Administration, in* HEALTH AND MEDICINE IN RURAL EUROPE: 1850–1945, 127 (Josep L. Barona & Steven Cherry eds., 2005).

[57] Technical Recommendations, *supra* note 53, at 68.

[58] *See* Letter from Vacel to Ludwik Rajchman, Report on the Progress of the Rural Hygiene in Czechoslovakia, (undated), LoN Archives, R5932/8A/30078/30078.

representatives and experts agreed that the first rural hygiene conference's recommendations served as a test case in which international cooperation between professionals, scientists, and experts could unite different states and their respective national perspectives, policies, and agendas.

In addition to the recommendations the League published and distributed when the conference had concluded, it suggested that the follow-up conference deal with environmental concerns as well. In a report in the first issue of its Bulletin in 1932, the Health Organisation identified concerns such as the epidemiology of typhoid fever in rural districts and the sanitary improvements needed to overcome it; methods of treating garbage (and manure) to prevent fly breeding; and, in particular, methods of testing and analyzing water and sewage with a view to possible standardization in terms of international criteria.[59]

The League's institutional framework, together with its emphasis on information gathering and sharing, led the institution to not only accept this invitation for further collaboration, but actually encouraged it. Within weeks, the League received updates on planned sanitary projects in different countries, including (local-national) data on typhoid incidence,[60] suggested studies on the sanitary system from the hygiene school in Zagreb,[61] or on water management in different areas.[62]

When autumn of 1931 arrived, more than ten different institutions that were involved in sanitation and public health issues joined the League and engaged in its international campaign, following the summer conference. The League took it upon itself to coordinate[63] these different initiatives and make them coherent.

Although there was a period of intense activity surrounding rural hygiene in the wake of the first conference of 1931, this sense of urgency seemed to dissipate in the mid-1930s and onwards. However, it should be noted that the follow-up period's focus on fly control did manage to

[59] Report of the Health Organisation for the Period Jan. 1931 to Sept. 1932, Bulletin, Vol. I, 1932, LoN Archives, at 400–01.

[60] Letter from Gustavo Pittaluga to Otto Olsen, Aug. 20, 1931, LoN Archvies, R5932/30087/30078.

[61] Letter from Andrija Stampar to Otto Olsen, Sept. 8, 1931, LoN Archvies, R5932/8A/30088/30078.

[62] Letter from Jacques Parisot to Otto Olsen, Aug. 26, 1931, LoN Archvies, R5932/8A/30080/30078.

[63] Letter from Otto Olsen to Jacques Parisot, July 23, 1931, LoN Archvies, R5932/8A/30080/30078.

rekindle this urgency to an extent. The League, and most certainly the different experts who provided it with scientific observations and warnings, was particularly concerned by the environmental-sanitary threat that flies posed to rural health.

This issue was discussed at a special meeting of entomologists that was organized by the Health Organisation and held in London in 1935. The purpose of the meeting was to discuss a plan of experimental research to ascertain what part the housefly played in the epidemiology of diseases of the intestinal tract. This difference in the aspect of the "fly question" in Europe and in the East was emphasized and earmarked for attention by the rural hygiene conference in Bandoeng, which would follow the conference of 1931 several years later. Moreover, it seems that this special focus was not mentioned merely as a general and nonbinding declaration for the protocol. A program of research "appropriate for the East" was then drawn up by a special expert[64] and communicated to certain entomologists of Asian countries, who agreed in principle to undertake this research.

Flies were not the only insects being scrutinized by the League. During their discussions on leprosy, in which delegates shared progress on the current scientific research, they expressed particular concern about the part played by the mosquito and the phelbotmus (the "sand fly") in the transition of the disease. They were also of the opinion[65] that the surrounding environment was a relevant object for discussion and recommended measures.

On the ground, however, this burst of energy that followed the conference suffered from institutional difficulties of its own. The studies that were supposed to be carried out all across Europe did not go as planned. Often, the relevant preparations were more complex, expensive, and time consuming than they had at first seemed. Professional investigations suffered a lack of funds to support their research projects, bureaucratic obstacles, and more.[66] One formal report from summer 1934, for instance, complained that following the achievements of the first conference, only a single institute had started investigations into

[64] Professor B. A. R. Gater of Singapore.

[65] F. R. Morote, *La Conferencia de Higiene Rural en Budapest, in* Gustavo Pittaluga, La Conferencia internacional de Higiene rural convocada por la Sociedad de las Naciones (29 Junio 1931) 96 (1931).

[66] Letter from Bohumil Vaček to Ludwik Rajchman, Report on the Progress of the Rural Hygiene in Czechoslovakia, (undated; probably Oct., 1932), LoN Archives, R5932/8A/30078/30078.

the standardization of methods for testing water and sewage. However, no attention at all had been paid to the training of sanitary engineers.[67]

This is not to suggest that the research completely ceased on the ground; or that the League suddenly stopped receiving data from different states[68] as part of its information-sharing methodology. Several field studies that were sent to the League focused, for instance, on the drastic increase in typhoid in rural areas in Denmark, Roumania, Poland, Bulgaria, Czechoslovakia, Hungary, and Yugoslavia. Though the epidemiology of typhoid plague was yet unclear in terms of full scientific observation, the joint international campaign – under the auspices of the League – had identified several environmental factors that were assumed to be connected with the spread of the disease. Several of these reports concluded that flies were among the main generators of disease, due to field observations indicating the connection between their frequent visits to manure heaps in the countryside and the spread of illness.[69]

But it seemed that the focus on Europe was about to be placed on hold. The special International Exhibition on Rural Housing (and Hygiene) of summer 1937, which was organized in Paris in June by the French government (and supported by the League),[70] marked the endpoint of the League's focus on the European countryside,[71] which only regained prominence at the next international intergovernmental conference the League put together in August 1937. This time, however, attention had shifted to a vast area stretching from Japan to the western parts of India – this was the focus of the Intergovernmental Conference of Far Eastern Countries on Rural Hygiene, held in August 1937.

67 Report to the Council on the Work of the 21st Session of the Health Committee, June 7, 1934, LoN Archives, C.233.M.97:1934.III, at 5.

68 Most of the data in the mid-1930s referred to different tools that various countries were using to cope with typhoid fever, to handle the disposal of manure, or to fight against fly breeding in their rural territories. Report to the Council on the Work of the 25th Session of the Health Committee, May 1, 1937, LoN Archives, C.219.M.159.1937.III, at 10.

69 Typhoid Fever in Rural Areas: Results of the Enquiries So Far Effected in Pursuance of Recommendations of the European Conference on Rural Hygiene, Oct. 25, 1937, LoN Archives, C.H. 1276; or Draft Report of the Sub-Committee on Rural Typhoid, Nov. 26, 1937, LoN Archives C.H./Hyg.rur/Typh./13.

70 All participating governments used the 1937 Paris Exhibition to present their achievements and to give a purely positive description of rural life in their countries, sending photos and plaster models of villages, farms, and rural health centers. *See* exhibit plans and programs of participants, LoN Archives, R 6094/8A/26064/8855.

71 A letter from Parisot to Minister of Agriculture, Mar. 31, 1936, LoN Archives, R 6094/8A/26064/8855. On the preparations for the June 1937 conference in Paris *see* Note on the International Exhibition on Rural Housing, C.H. 1221, Nov. 20, 1936, LoN Archives, R 6094/8A/26064/8855.

3.3.4 *The Intergovernmental Conference of Far Eastern Countries on Rural Hygiene, Bandoeng (Java), August 1937*

Concerns about different environmental and sanitary threats did not only apply to Europe. These issues also affected regions beyond Europe's borders. East Asian countries, most of which were under the direct rule or influence of European powers, were particularly relevant destinations for international inquiry and cooperation, since they were overwhelmingly rural and suffered from the same problems that the first rural hygiene conference had identified.

The League had first started to view East Asia as another target of its rural hygiene campaign in late 1930, in light of post–World War I large-scale migration and intensive transportation between Europe and other continents.[72] At the 1932 Assembly, the Chinese and the Indian delegations both proposed that the League also organize an intergovernmental conference on rural hygiene for eastern countries, which encouraged the League to push forward this initiative. A couple of years later, in spring 1936, the League accepted another invitation, this time from the Dutch government, to hold a conference in the Netherland Indies in 1937.[73] At first, the focus was supposed to be chiefly on the availability of medical services and professional staff in rural areas. A special questionnaire was sent all around the world,[74] proposing a draft agenda for the planned conference.

Many governments expressed an interest in participating in the conference, which was scheduled to take place the following summer in 1937. The primary focus of the conference was to be on prevention methods, such as proper sanitary systems and securing water resources, as these were considered even more important in East Asia than in Europe, given the demographic differences between the two continents. The League reports, as previously mentioned, ascribed central importance to rural hygiene particularly in Asia, since 90 percent of the population lived in rural areas, and even urban or semi-urban centers were (according to the League's observations) often rural in character.[75]

[72] Minutes of the 16th Health Commission Session, Sept. 29 to Oct. 7, 1930, LoN Archives, C.527.M.248.1930.III, at 26–28.

[73] Report to the Council on the Work of the 23d Session of the Health Committee, May 2, 1936, LoN Archives, C.198.M.124.1936.III, at 3–4.

[74] As this was also the common technical procedure in other initiatives of the League.

[75] C. D. de Langen reports to the Conference on Rural Hygiene in the Far East, Sept. 3, 1936, LoN Archives, R 6095/8A/26762/855.

The second rural hygiene conference took place within a largely (though not solely) colonial context. The League used professional and technical expertise as a foundation for international law and governance, and it seems this general policy also guided the League in this case. In order to prepare for the conference, the League asked for reliable data, as it had also done in preparation for the first conference. However this time, professional expertise and data were a product of colonial knowledge and were part of the power relations of imperial networks and frameworks. In other words, information gathering, in the context of the second conference, was conducted rather differently.

The League mobilized professional experts, most of whom came from colonial backgrounds, to serve as commission members.[76] Ludvik Rajchman, for instance, in preparation for the conference, specifically looked for "a prominent Britisher possessing wide experience in the administration of rural regions and a thoroughly sympathetic attitude towards the native population . . . ."[77]

The League also appointed experts with an obvious professional background in colonial and imperial administration.[78] However, despite this imperial context, the conference also suggested drawing on the expertise of parties whose observations were more neutral, and not merely reflections of dichotomous relations between the hegemonic West and subordinated Eastern populations. Prior to the conference, a special tour across East Asia (held between April and August 1936) was organized in order to establish contact with relevant governmental departments that were directly or indirectly involved in health and sanitation matters. The aim of this tour was to motivate local Asian authorities to become involved in the League's campaign, and to spread the news on the upcoming conference.

[76] The commission, which visited in different countries in South East Asia (such as the Philippines or Ceylon) between spring and summer 1936, met local government officials and gathered data and statistics on rural hygiene. On the expedition *see* Summary of the Tour of the Commission in India, (undated; probably May–June 1936), LoN Archives, R/6093/8A/15110/8855.

[77] Letter from Ludkik Rajchman to Thorwald Madsen, Nov. 5, 1935, LoN Archives, R 6093/8A/15110/8855.

[78] This was the case, for instance, with A. S. Haynes, who was appointed as the Chairperson of the special Health Committee for the second conference, after his service as (former) Colonial Secretary of the Federated Malay States; and with Dr. Willem Theunissen, the Deputy Director of the Health Services and a "tropical hygiene" expert from the Dutch Indies.

In most respects,[79] the Asian conference followed its European predecessor, and most of its issues were directly drawn from the first conference of 1931 – including water regulations in terms of purification and supply, modern means of sanitation, and more. In a broader sense, most of the conclusions of the second conference echoed those of the European one. In the late 1930s, when the global geopolitical situation had become significantly worse than in the early 1930s, the League focused on ensuring rural hygiene in East Asia and recommended adopting those same principles that had proved to be beneficial in European cases. Throughout the discussions and sessions, the League recommended that governments focus on sanitary engineering, and strive to overcome environmental threats such as those to housing and the drinking water supply, as well as those threats posed by latrines, manure and household refuse, fly control, and more. The League further asserted that the implementation of modern improvements in these realms would function as measures to combat dangerous diseases in rural districts,[80] such as malaria, plague, yaws, and leprosy. Once again, the League used the rural hygiene campaign to promote modernization and centralizing tendencies, just as it had with the European delegates of the first conference.

Although the second conference was obviously modeled on the previous conference and used comparative methods, it also served as an opportunity to broaden the scope of the concept of rural hygiene in general:

> Rural hygiene, especially in Eastern countries, tends more and more to become only one of the aspects of the wider program of rural reconstruction. Therefore the Commission endeavours to investigate nutrition, agriculture, education, cooperative movements, for they are all factors that cannot be overlooked in any scheme of rural improvement . . . .[81]

[79] LoN Information Section: Far Eastern Rural Hygiene Conference, Aug. 1937, LoN Archives, R 6098/8A/28718/8855. One of the central differences in the agendas of the two conferences relates to the strong emphasis of the second conference on medical staff and its training in rural medicine and rural hygiene. The need for local native personnel was urgent, but also problematic in terms of colonial politics. Western colonialism did not favor higher education among the local population and rejected the idea of creating and supporting qualified intellectual and professional elites. These elites, apart from being efficient and contributing to the everyday life of indigenous communities, also had the potential to gain political power and eventually threaten Western rule.

[80] League of Nations Information Section: Far Eastern Rural Hygiene Conference, Aug. 1937, LoN Archives, R 6098/8A/28718/8855.

[81] Statement, (undated; probably Sept. 1936), LoN Archives, E 6093/8A/25509/8855.

Once again, using its tools and institutional reputation, the League organized an international forum that represented a variety of voices in a way that was hard to imagine before the League came into being. Almost all the political units of East Asia at that time sent their delegations to Java for the ten-day conference in early August 1937: North Borneo, Burma, Ceylon, China, Fiji, the Gilbert and Ellice Islands Colony, the New Hebrides Condominium, Hong Kong, British India (and four Indian States), the Netherlands East Indies, French Indo-China, Japan, British Malaya, the Philippines, Siam, the British Solomon Islands Protectorate, and Tonga. Among these countries, only three were independent: Japan, China, and Siam.[82]

Like its European predecessor, the second conference relied (mainly) on a variety of experts, including medical and health officers and doctors, sanitary engineers, and experts in agricultural hygiene. Following the aims that the first conference had declared, the delegations in Bandoeng were completely aware of their historic mission.[83] In one of the preparatory documents, the Health Committee reported to the Council that this kind of occasion also "[held] an opportunity to improve" living conditions across the region, and to bring prosperity and progress by means of better hygiene in the countryside.

The second conference also followed the recommendations of the first conference by emphasizing the technical means needed to create a more hygienic[84] environment for rural people to live in. The conference affirmed that rural hygiene policies should take into account the value of preventive activities. Like the European conference, it realized that these measures, such as modern means of sanitation, fly control, etc., were crucial to overcoming the environmental risks posed by pollution. The recommendations pointed to the need for clean water, ensuring the safety of water sources, and efficient waste disposal in rural areas, and called for further intensive study on flies as suspicious generators of disease in rural landscapes.

The analysis that follows will focus on several specific examples of rural hygiene and environmental concerns targeted by the conference. Moreover, these examples from the conference's agenda will show how

[82] Nevertheless, and despite their official independence, both China and Siam were at that time subjected to powerful foreign (Western) political and economic influence.

[83] Report to the Council on the Work of the 25th Session of the Health Committee, May 1, 1937, LoN Archives, C.219.M.159.1937.III.

[84] Report of the Health and Medical Services to the plenary meeting of the Conference (by Dr. J. L. Hydrick), Aug. 10, 1937, LoN Archives, R 6107/8A/37714/8855, at 4.

and to what extent the technical and professional discourse on rural hygiene in East Asian countries was based on security concerns. First, I will describe the conference's interest in protecting water resources as a primary issue. Second, I will focus on the connection between the disposal of human-organic waste, pollution, and environmental risks, and examine how this connection was discussed by the League and the delegations. Third, I will introduce the discussion on fly and rat control (as part of the goal to improve rural housing). And fourth, I will provide the example of ancylostomiasis and several other "rural East-Asian" epidemics that were described by the second conference.

Protecting water sources and ensuring the supply of pure drinking water, for instance, became one of the conference's central concerns. The 1937 conference studied the different methods of purifying water in each of the represented countries. In many ways, protecting water sources became a test case for addressing the interactions between pollution, sanitation, and environmental risks as issues for international governance policies. The different reports that the League received from these countries all identified water purification as a problem that was worthy of the attention of state authorities: the general government, the local governments, and different health authorities.[85]

The League's comparative study of these reports, which involved different agencies of the state, revealed the complexity involved in implementing water purification methods on a broad scale. To achieve this roll out, different districts across the rural periphery demanded not only financial support for their budgets, but also the collaboration of scientists, government officials, public health experts, and medical doctors.

Whereas delegations did not always agree on the issues discussed at the conference, they reached consensus on the matter of purified water given the direct implication of water management and environment on the (rural) public:

> Indeed, contrary to certain opinions which are based on purely superficial observations, the [ordinary individual] of the poor classes appreciates water that is clear, limpid, fresh, tasteless and odourless. Though he sometimes blames the water of the pipe system for hardening the rice, for making it less white, for blackening the tea or for destroying its aroma (when the water comes from deep-lying levels and contains iron), he nevertheless very soon becomes accustomed to it and the throngs of

[85] Preparatory Papers, *supra* note 6, at 51.

> water-carriers around the street hydrants furnish sufficient proof of the success of the water-supply systems established.[86]

However, the conference emphasized the difference between urban centers and the rural periphery. In the villages, inhabitants still preferred rainwater as their primary water source. Rainwater was stored in earthenware jars or in cisterns, or (in case these methods were not available) drawn directly from shallow wells or rivers. However, changes in climate and the surrounding environment made sanitary concerns increasingly likely. During the dry season, water ran out frequently in these shallow wells and other basins, becoming "nothing more than sheets of mud. This water is used for bathing, for washing linen and for drinking purposes."[87] One report from Indo-China revealed that in some of the villages, a small purifying plant with a reservoir of treated water had been set up – but without any distributing system. In other villages, the League noted with concern, rural communities were using unpurified water from wells, rivers, or irrigation canals. Given that these were the major natural sources of fresh water, particularly in rural areas,[88] the conference asserted that such water systems in the countryside urgently needed to be improved.

The conference also understood that rural hygiene was essential for the well-being of the environment. As water regimes changed due to pollution, unstable rural environments overwhelmingly began to affect the everyday routines of both local inhabitants and livestock. Therefore, proper water management and sanitation became clear and urgent requirements for local populations: "Live-stock has then to be moved elsewhere, and, when the family reserves in the jars are exhausted, the householder must buy fresh water from the water-sellers . . . frequently from great distances, from the fresh-water zone."[89]

Though most of the recommendations pointed to (modern) European techniques to improve rural hygiene conditions, the second conference also recommended using methods that had been common before modern times. The duration of the dry season in certain areas in East Asia (when brackish water affected the freshwater zone), for instance, tended to vary according to the specific rural region, and generally lasted at least fifteen days: "[T]his has made it possible to assist waterless districts by

[86] *Id.* at 59.
[87] *Id.*
[88] *Id.* at 61–62.
[89] *Id.* at 63.

means of a procedure which is merely a modernized form of the old method of solving the problem by making ponds." When fresh water was obtainable, the reservoir was not used and the water needed for consumption was pumped directly from the river and throughout the freshwater area. However, the conference emphasized, whenever water was obtained – either from the river, or from the reservoir – it always had to be treated before it was distributed. That way, the community was able to remove the environmental-sanitary risk, or at least to minimize it.

The issue of brackish water became an important point in the discussion. Although the duration of the brackish period changed from area to area, it was considered a problem common to the (entire) region. Both the League and other representatives were concerned that brackish water would endanger other water resources if it seeped into the reservoirs. On this issue, for instance, the experts recommended coating the reservoirs, and other nonnatural methods, to cope with the problem.[90] These recommendations exemplified the League's ability to serve as an information center which, although in some cases did not produce any new legal arrangements, did use its institutional capabilities and techniques to gather information and to "export" it to other parties.

In this way, problematic rural environmental risks such as brackish water allowed for the direct participation of locals, which challenged imperial networks and power relations. The rural concerns in East Asia show how fundamental the League's mission was, given that it had to change the conceptual thinking of that time. The campaign's focus had evolved from issues of colonial medical care systems to recommendations for the comprehensive development of Asian societies. These were environmental issues that changed the original goal of developing strategies to align subservient populations with European interests, to strategies that developed local Asian societies according to their own needs (just as European needs had been developed in Europe). In this way, the discussion of sanitary problems in the countryside created a more equal arena for a more pluralistic variety of voices.

The discussion on polluted water sources engaged sanitary and public health concerns, as well as considerations that took into account the need

[90] One of solutions recommended by the League was to build a special plant that would be installed in all the rural centers affected by the problem. The so-called "Cochin-China type" plant was installed in different agricultural areas, and the conference encouraged large rural centers and towns in the provinces – both in the freshwater and brackish areas beyond Cochin-China – to be equipped with a drinking-water system based on this model.

for the involvement of the local population. In most cases, the water supply in rural areas was distributed for consumption only after it had been treated through a process of water chlorination; however, the conference had identified risks posed by the margins of these regions. Unlike chief towns in the rural provinces, the conference observed that villagers generally obtained their water either from wells, ponds, or from irrigation canals. In all cases, the problem was that "[t]his water is always impure."[91]

When it came to the issue of water supply, the conference explained that the "most reasonable solution" would be to protect the safety and sanitation of the wells. This could primarily be achieved by placing a cover, fitted with a pump, on each well. However, "the purchase of a pump involves expenditure which the peasant will often not be able – or prepared – to afford not being convinced of the need for pure water."[92] The League was aware of this reality, and further acknowledged that rural wells, which were a notoriously poor source of sanitation, were not soon going to disappear from these parts of Asia. Still, the League did what it could to improve the local conditions on the ground using tools and discourses of international law and international governance. The conference suggested certain practical ways in which rural wells could be better treated, based on the typical model used in Annam.[93] This model required wells to be fitted with a reinforced concrete cover, which had a manhole leading to a ladder. The concrete protected the well from the immediate risk of contamination, and the well was further protected by a fence that surrounded it.

The delegations also dealt with the connection between the disposal of human-organic waste, pollution, and environmental risks. The conference suggested two sanitary solutions that could be used to decrease the danger of polluted water in the countryside. Both solutions were introduced based on the results of a comparative study and information sharing. The first recommendation was the use of rectangular pits (as latrines), such as those used in Antipolo.[94] It was unlikely that the use of

[91] Preparatory Papers, *supra* note 6, at 69.

[92] *Id.* at 52.

[93] Annam was a French protectorate encompassing the central region of what is today Vietnam. Before the protectorate's establishment, the name Annam was used in the West to refer to Vietnam as a whole. The Protectorate of Annam became a part of French Indochina in 1887.

[94] Antipolo was a small town in the Philippines, where these latrines were in use at the time of the conference.

these pits would lead to pollution of the subsoil water since, "according to experiments made . . . in 1921, the vertical infiltration from latrines does not exceed a depth of from 1–1.5 meters, while horizontal infiltration is negligible."[95]

The second solution that was suggested was a bored hole latrine, which had a deep hole (between three to six meters) instead of a pit. The conference observed that this option was "well known to all hygienists thanks to the efforts made by the Rockefeller Foundation,[96] which had invested a large sum to ensure the standard use of this model of latrine worldwide. "This type has a certain number of advantages," the conference recommendations detailed, "such as long life, absence of smell and of flies and the possibility in consequence of sinking the hole in the immediate vicinity of dwelling."[97]

These models that the League suggested, especially the second (the bored hole latrine), were based on experiments[98] and practical knowledge that had been gathered from other locations. They demonstrate how and to what extent this mode of international governance relied on methods such as information sharing and distributing.

Most of the contact with local inhabitants was conducted through the colonial authorities. However, the preparations for the conference, and the conference itself, made room for perspectives that reflected a different set of needs in the geopolitical situation of East Asia, which at that time was mostly controlled by Western imperial powers and colonial networks. Local East Asian authorities were asked to provide information on these topics to help shape the conference agenda,[99] and a large number of papers from these countries detailing their needs and problems arrived in Geneva.

The League also emphasized the importance of involving the local peasant population in implementing the environmental-sanitary measures

[95] Preparatory Papers, *supra* note 6, at 53. The conference conclusions state that this was only true for soils of low porosity. Further research should be undertaken with regard to infiltration in other types of soil such as sand, chalk, or marl, where infiltration could be far more extensive.

[96] On the involvement of the Rockefeller Foundation, *see* Josep L. Barona, *The League of Nations and the Rockefeller Foundation: International Activism in Public Health*, *in* The League of Nations' Work on Social Issues: Visions, Endeavours and Experiments 61 (Magaly Rodríguez García, Davide Rodogno & Liat Kozma eds., 2016).

[97] Preparatory Papers, *supra* note 6, at 53.

[98] Such as the experiment with the second model, which was carried out in Singapore in 1929.

[99] Report to the Council on the Work of the 25th Session of the Health Committee, May 1, 1937, LoN Archives, C.219.M.159.1937.III, at 10.

of the campaign. These two types of latrine "can be constructed by the villagers themselves," the conference recommended.[100] Moreover, the tools required to dig the holes "should be lent to them by the local authorities or by the health centers," so that the peasants would not be burdened with the cost of purchasing them. Considering the magnitude of the rural sanitation project that the conference was calling for, it was the government and the imperial authorities that would need to bear most of the financial burden. As I have mentioned earlier, the League displayed centralizing tendencies in this matter and used the campaign not necessarily to strengthen its own authority, but rather to support local authorities.

The League was thus aware of the delicate balance it needed to achieve between sanitary-environmental needs and practical considerations. Apart from environmental concerns, the discussions on relevant solutions also emphasized the economic burden on the local population. Therefore, the League's experts also mentioned that the relevant models had been decided on after "much thought," "and are now produced on a large scale at a low price."[101]

In addition to the pollution of water sources, the problems of manure and household refuse were considered acute problems in rural environments. Both conferences, and the second conference of 1937 in particular, focused on the study of this area of countryside hygiene. The second conference particularly dealt with the ways in which "Eastern peoples"[102] used to handle their different types of refuse. The diplomats' and experts' main concerns related to the environmental and sanitary effects of the conventional uses of manure in different parts of the countryside in East Asia.

While in some of these countries, the rural population tended to use manure as a fertilizer, others used it as fuel. In either case, the League was concerned about the sanitary and environmental risks posed by these traditional methods of treating refuse, and it was especially concerned that water resources would be polluted as a result:

> In either case [using the manure as a fertilizer or as a fuel] the manure is stacked in the immediate vicinity of the house, whereas it should be dumped with the household refuse, in a pit some distance away from

[100] Preparatory Papers, *supra* note 6, at 54.

[101] *Id.* One can claim that the League expressed a progressive agenda in its environmental effort. This early understanding took into account that there was a need not only to incorporate with the local population, but also to introduce practical and above all affordable environmental measures.

[102] Preparatory Papers, *supra* note 6, at 54.

> the house and the well. The health authorities and rural construction officers should explain to the inhabitants how important this is.[103]

The League was well aware of the need to present practical solutions, and not simply strategies that might be interpreted as being too "Western" in nature. The compromise it encouraged (although it was not a perfect method given the conditions in the countryside) was the use of incinerators to destroy household refuse. In larger communities, however, incinerators were less popular due to their environmental effects and because of the agricultural value of manure as fertilizer, which is was lost if the manure was burned. Therefore, "it might be more economical to treat . . . household refuse together by the 'compost' method."[104]

Like other sanitary concerns on the rural frontier, the problem of manure did not involve public health or environmental aspects alone, but also had an economic dimension, "which is of even greater importance." In countries such as India, for instance, where the soil had become poor from a lack of sufficient nitrogenous fertilizer, stable manure should be "spread on the fields instead of being used as fuel."

Both conferences may have discussed the different environmental risks separately, but that does not mean the League or the delegations treated the issues as if they were isolated from one other. The discussions reflected that these issues were part of a broader picture of the rural environment, which had to be protected from different hygienic risks. Flies and the risks they posed to public health also appeared repeatedly in the discussions on the recommended improvements to rural housing, and vice versa.

First, the delegations exchanged data on rural housing and how certain features (such as the location of houses) contributed to the fly problem in the rural periphery. This part of the second conference focused on an observation introduced by one of the French geographers, who warned of the "apparent illogicalities in the distribution of types of houses in Indo-China." According to this view, certain communities built their houses in the damp deltas on the ground level, directly on the foundation of beaten earth "where they are constantly befouled by the stagnant water."[105]

There environmental aspect of rural housing served as a basis for comparison by the League. The experts focused on the traditional method of building houses on piles. This was, the report concluded, "a

[103] *Id.*
[104] *Id.*
[105] *Id.*, at 51.

hygienic type of dwelling for tropical countries."[106] The report did admit that the stabling of animals underneath the house had certain (environmental) disadvantages such as attracting flies, but stated that this seemed to involve "no serious danger" – perhaps quite the opposite. "It may even be some kind of safeguard against malaria."[107]

Fly control was not the only issue to come up with regard to housing. The conference raised the importance of housing (or rehousing) as a part of an environmental and spatial redeployment while combating generators of disease. Attention to (environmental) improvements was necessary as part of the fight against diseases, "and should not be underestimated."[108] Rats, for instance, which constituted part of a larger rural-agrarian ecosystem that threatened the human population, were also discussed: first in the countryside, and later in urban centers.[109]

Given the vast undertaking ahead and the huge financial resources it would require, the League acknowledged that international law or transnational cooperation alone would not provide sufficient solutions. However, that does not mean the League disengaged from the problems at hand. The optimism surrounding international law in the interwar period was evident in the discussions on the possible solutions that legal mechanisms could offer: "If the past cannot be obliterated, it may, however, be possible to try by legislation to safeguard the future by, for instance, requiring all new buildings to be rat-proofed."[110]

The rat problem was of particular concern to the conference delegates, and they saw a great need for environmental measures that could cope with the severe threat of plague in rural areas and densely populated cities. In some cases, the environmental measures were neither easy nor practical, as it was not always possible to pull down and rebuild the rural infrastructure, simple though this infrastructure was. "In such circumstances," recommended the League, "the procedure . . . is to clean up the 'desas.'[111] The inhabitants have to build huts outside the village, and live in them while the rats in their houses are being destroyed and the most

[106] *Id.*, at 58.

[107] *Id.*

[108] *Id.* at 92.

[109] The conference proposed that the rat problem could be beaten in two ways: through housing (and proper hygiene and sanitary) improvements, and through vaccination. In both cases, and especially on the former, "gigantic efforts" had already being taken and the League supported and promoted these methods long after the conference had concluded. *See Id.* at 79.

[110] *Id.* at 79.

[111] The local villagers' houses.

urgent improvements made."[112] Using comparative data gathered by the League, the experts mentioned that in Ceylon for instance, the villagers temporarily had to relocate to the country, where they were fed for five days free of charge.

Given the social aspects of the rat campaign in Asia, the League encouraged governments to consider other areas that might be directly or indirectly affected. On the one hand, the League recommended that the state carry the economic burden of the different required tasks. But on the other hand, local citizens in the countryside were also encouraged to take action on the matter. In this way, international law acted – or proclaimed to act – as a mediator and as a policy generator.[113]

Once again, information sharing proved to be crucial. The delegates and experts compared the different measures that various countries had taken as part of their own rat-control policies. One of the cases discussed was that of Madagascar,[114] which drew attention to the risk posed by the rat, X. cheopis,[115] as the primary vector for bubonic plague (and murine typhus).

With its rural hygiene campaign, the League introduced a vertical or three-dimensional perspective. Rural hygiene issues had to go through three different layers of authority at the same time: the League itself, the states, and local communities and authorities. Unlike other missions (including environmental ones) that it promoted, the League used an almost direct approach toward local residents when it prepared this campaign. Some of the discussions and recommendations show that the League wanted to extend its collaboration so it would include local residents in these countries. The actions of locals were essential in responding to the cross-border threat of plague carried by rats. Once sanitary measures had been taken, rehousing had to be followed by a "greater use of order and cleanliness on the part of the occupants" themselves, and the League called for a special initiative aimed at educating rural populations. One might also interpret the League's call as an acknowledgement of its officials that international law, with its different modes, was not omnipotent. In order to achieve common aims, international law had to rely on local cooperation and other domestic measures – legal and nonlegal alike.

112 Preparatory Papers, *supra* note 6, at 79–80.

113 The details of the proposed rat-control campaign were elaborated in Preparatory Papers, *supra* note 6, at 81.

114 *Id.* at 80.

115 Or the Oriental rat flea (Xenopsylla cheopis).

The discussions during the ten-day conference in summer 1937 brought together proposals on environment, sanitation, and medicine. Both the League and the delegations were aware that medical and sanitary issues could not be considered in isolation, and environmental measures also needed to be taken into account. This was evident in the rat campaign, where a medical and scientific solution alone – that of vaccination against bubonic plague – was not enough. It had to be undertaken alongside environmental and sanitary actions. In the case of combating ancylostomiasis,[116] another issue that was raised through information sharing at Bandoeng, the conference's recommendations expressed a similar perspective: "On the showing of past experience, it may by asserted that ancylostomiasis cannot be eradicated by treatment alone. The construction and utilisation of adequate latrines are the essential corollary of treatment."

The discussion on the dangers of ancylostomiasis is another example of the different legal perspectives that shaped the campaign. The conference's participants were uncertain as to which practical legal measures to take. Should the special recommendations remain a nonbinding document of international law? Or was there a need to translate them into hard domestic legislation? In this case, unlike with other environmental challenges the League struggled with, participants chose soft international law: "It remains to be decided whether such constructions should be made compulsory or remain optional," as "[b]oth systems[117] have their adherents and it would be useful if they could state their views . . . ."[118]

Nevertheless, the League strongly encouraged ongoing environmental and sanitary supervision. In fact, the League itself offered to carry out this supervision and to monitor national and local rural hygiene efforts. This conclusion was based on certain countries' experiences. In Ceylon for instance, authorities were able to successfully treat ancylostomiasis thanks to the League's supervisory efforts. The local rural campaign, which was initiated in 1916, reached peak success in 1934 with nearly

116 Ancylostomiasis is an infection caused by Ancylostoma hookworms. The parasite can cause an iron deficiency by sucking blood from the host's intestinal wall. In the West, it is common in mine workers. Control of this parasite should be directed at reducing the degree of the environmental risk posed by contamination, or improved access to sanitation (especially regular toilets); efforts should also include convincing the local population to maintain sanitation infrastructure so that it is clean and functional, and thereby conducive to use.

117 Meaning both the compulsory and the optional solutions suggested.

118 Preparatory Papers, *supra* note 6, at 84.

two million cases treated. The conference did, however, acknowledge that the success of the Ceylon campaign also relied in part on the operation of a special ancylostomiasis control service "which [sent] its squads[119] all over the island to make microscopic examinations, apply treatment and compile statistics."[120]

The rural area as a whole, and the Asian village in particular, seemed to be epidemiological ground zero: it needed to be handled with caution, controlled and supervised. Leprosy was another "rural disease" that the conference identified as a pressing issue. Urban centers and towns were highlighted as "the places where lepers gather," but were not "the foci of the disease," as lepers were seen to "*come from the villages*."[121] Hence, the conference recommended specific legal measures: "[P]reventive activities should be decentralized and that epidemiological work, prevention and treatment should be directed to the promotion of rural hygiene."[122] Once again, the League gave recommendations to local authorities, and referred to the legal and procedural ways in which Asian countries should carry out these missions. This time, however, it was not necessarily the central government who would carry out these measures, but rather other agencies and local authorities. The conference concluded that the organization of ways to prevent rural and environmental dangers that posed a risk to urban populations should extend into "the remotest country districts like the capillaries into the tissues."[123]

Historically speaking, after the second rural hygiene conference, the League continued to promote its recommendations. Besides the "regular" step of using its institutional capacity and means of communication to distribute the recommendations worldwide,[124] the League also mobilized the Health Organisation to implement some of the assignments that had been agreed on. The Organisation was ordered to supervise the international

119 Once the League began to address environmental-sanitary issues, it sometimes used what can be interpreted as a military discourse. While fighting ancylostomiasis, the state sent special squads across the infected area; relevant help (such as teachers who could educate the population to better its habits) was enlisted for the mission.

120 Preparatory Papers, *supra* note 6, at 84. Next to ancylostomiasis, a long list of diseases threatened "Far Eastern" countries, among them smallpox, cholera, malaria, typhoid, and tuberculosis. All were treated as rural endemic diseases and, as such, the League concluded that "the only hope of . . . eradication lies in a sanitation, housing and food policy." (*Id.* at 90).

121 *Id.* at 99 (emphasis added).

122 *Id.*

123 *Id.*

124 Which it had done in October 1937.

study of malaria, plague, fly control, and other environmental threats that had been discussed in Bandoeng, and to promote further international collaboration.

But, as with other initiatives carried out by the League, including environmental ones that dealt with challenges that knew no sovereign borders, the instability of the late 1930s eventually affected this campaign too. First, Imperial Japan's aggression against China escalated in summer 1937 into a full-scale invasion, effectively ending the League's rural hygiene campaign in that country. And then, as the entire region sank into chaos of World War II, the entire campaign was put on hold.

3.4 Conclusion

The conclusion of this chapter is multifaceted. With regard to its effective outcomes on the ground, most of the rural hygiene recommendations suggested by the League remained just that – recommendations. Or, they were considered a reflection of soft (some might say too soft) international law. However, today, and also throughout the COVID-19 pandemic, international law is still attempting to navigate different environmental sanitation crises using some of the same methods that the League used: predominantly international frameworks to share information.

In a special poll taken in 2008 among readers of the British Medical Journal, the sanitary revolution of introducing piped water and water-borne sewerage to people's homes in nineteenth-century Europe was voted as the most important medical milestone since 1840, beating the discovery of antibiotics and the development of anesthesia.[125] According to UNICEF and the World Health Organization, well over a century after this breakthrough in modern sanitation, it is estimated that at least two billion people – nearly 32 percent of the world's population – were still lacking access to basic sanitation in 2015.[126]

Just as the League encouraged all those years ago, international governance still works to promote proper sanitation as vital for health, and to overcome environmental risks in the second decade of the twenty-first century. Whether we consider the hygiene campaign successful or not, the League identified sanitation, and especially sanitary threats transferred through environmental means, as an essential part of global security. After

125 Quoted by Peter A. Harvey, *Environmental Sanitation Crisis: More than Just a Health Issue*, 2 ENVTL. HEALTH INSIGHTS 77, 77 (2008).

126 UNICEF/WHO Progress on Drinking Water and Sanitation: Special Focus on Sanitation (2008).

all, in terms of periodization, it is also worth noting that the League started its campaign in the midst of the Great Depression. While the world – and the League – tried to cope with the effects of the crisis on the global economy, the League simultaneously took on the task of securing wells and other water resources from contamination in rural peripheries. Moreover, at a time when international stability – both in central Europe, and especially in East Asia – was deteriorating as tension rose with the growing power of Imperial Japan, the League dedicated much of its attention to the control of rats and flies as prime factors of pollution and disease.

And perhaps this background also supports the following claim: all in all, this campaign demonstrated the interwar period belief in international law and international governance.

When it focused on rural hygiene efforts in remote areas that suffered from recurrent plagues, the League expressed a genuine belief in the power and capacity of international law to overcome these dangers. Indeed, one might argue that the campaign introduced another embodiment of the narrative of the "white man's burden." However, as this chapter claims, alongside other familiar expressions of Western hegemony outside of Europe, when it came to this field of international law, the campaign did not always match the portrayal of Western institutions as subversive, or as the only power striving for progress. As different parts of the campaign show, the League, the officials, and the experts all expressed their own belief in international law, and they trusted in the League's ability to transform Asian societies for the better.

As early as the 1930s, the League considered the rural hygiene campaign to be a bright, brave, and necessary humanitarian part of the League's agenda. The League did not act alone in this ongoing effort. Other institutions and initiatives joined the wave of anti-epidemic campaigns that focused on rural areas; for instance, the League emphasized the founding of the International Center for Research on Leprosy in Rio de Janeiro as part of a general international movement. This network of different institutions, funds, and research centers, however, looked to the League – and the Health Organisation in particular – as the institution that was best suited to monitor and coordinate different tasks and aims – something both the rural hygiene conferences (and the ongoing international and procedural work they entailed) showed.

As briefly mentioned, unlike the European part of the campaign, the East Asian part should be placed (historically speaking) within a broader perspective – one that takes into account that most of the Asian countries who participated in the second conference were not fully independent.

Imperial regimes that participated in the campaign[127] reflected Western powers' interests, since they considered a variety of technological and environmental tools with which sanitation threats could be tackled within this huge region.

This is not to argue, however, that whenever the League advocated for improving sanitation or striving to fight environmental dangers, it was operating as part of an imperial or colonial network. Even as this chapter explores the role of the League – and of international law – in the context of Western hegemony in East Asia, it simultaneously shows that the historical picture on the ground was more complex than that. Indeed, colonialism and imperialism did not suddenly vanish – Western delegates worked hand in hand with local representatives, experts, and authorities, as discussions on the colonial medical care systems in rural areas revealed.

The assimilation of colonial and imperialist tensions into this campaign followed unique patterns. Some of these depict the imperial world not as a simplistic bipolar or dichotomous system, but rather as a multilayered universe. The environmental issues entangled with rural hygiene in the remote Asian countryside portrayed a rather different picture than the one we would usually expect to find in this kind of context. The topics that the second conference of 1937 focused on were, ultimately, quite similar to those that the first conference of 1931 tackled,[128] and environmental and sanitary concerns in rural areas had actually highlighted the similarities between East Asian and European (rural) environments (though these could hardly be considered identical). At least to a certain extent, rural hygiene issues served as a common ground between these two hemispheres.

This picture has two sides. On the one hand, the fact that the world was growing at an unprecedented rate due to new means of transportation enabled the West to establish and expand profitable colonial networks. But on the other hand, colonialism was also increasing the vulnerability of the West, since its merchant navy used remote ports to dock its ships, which exposed crews to infection in the event of an epidemic. Sailors, tourists, modern merchants, exporters and importers, and colonial officials traveling between different destinations and the metropolis all became possible carriers of infectious diseases. Imperial powers spread to vast regions and penetrated different countries; but this was not a one-

127 Such as the British Empire and Dutch rule.

128 Though the second conference also added nutrition and specific diseases to its agenda.

way street. Vulnerable countries in East Asia also posed environmental and sanitary threats to the West, which raised concerns that these dangers would harm Western sovereignty and put its metropolises at risk.

These tensions, which reveal the complexity of the power relations between Western countries and "their" protectorates in East Asia, were also evident in earlier attempts to overcome spreading sanitary treats.[129] However, the League's tendency to favor a more open, democratic, and pluralistic mode of international law shows that these unequal relations were not entirely transplanted into the sanitation campaign.

Loyal to *its* own way of organizing international law, the League seemed to turn away from traditional diplomacy in the discussion on fighting the spread of diseases. Compared to earlier forums, it seems that local problems in East Asian countries were not only viewed through a Western lens. For instance, the League also appointed experts with an obvious professional background in colonial administration.[130] However, despite this political context, the second conference also suggested some alternative options. A special tour across East Asia between April and August of 1936 was organized to establish contact with relevant governmental departments that were directly or indirectly involved in health and sanitation matters. The aim was to encourage and motivate Asian authorities to participate in the League's campaign, and to spread the news on the upcoming conference.

Indeed, the professional experts who were sent by the League seem to fit the common (critical) description of Western ways in which the East had been "explored" and subordinated.[131] And yet, the bipolar model that usually characterizes historical studies on the relations between Western imperial powers and non-Western communities might sometimes miss the complexity of the historical picture. Yes, rural hygiene issues exemplified power relations in the "Far East," but they also showed how and to what extent local communities were involved in health, sanitation, and environmental concerns. These issues also describe how

[129] *See, e.g.*, Ira Klein, *Death in India, 1871–1921*, 32 J. ASIAN STUD. 639 (1973).

[130] This was the case, for instance, with A.S. Haynes, who was appointed the Chairperson of the special Health Committee for the second rural hygiene conference after his service as Colonial Secretary of the Federated Malay States; and with Dr. Willem Theunissen, the Deputy Director of the Health Services and a "tropical hygiene" expert from the Dutch Indies.

[131] *See*, for instance, Edward Said's theory – EDWARD SAID, ORIENTALISM (1978); and/or his huge community of scholars who have followed his arguments, as described in DANIEL M. VARISCO, READING ORIENTALISM: SAID AND THE UNSAID (2007).

the League as an institution encouraged and motivated a variety of voices to become involved in the international campaign, and to strive for improvements of and within their agrarian societies. In that sense, it was a more elusive context than the narrative of "The White Man's Burden."

As in the case of the campaign, the discussion should be approached as more complex and layered than "bad" or "good" colonialism, and other familiar patterns of postcolonial studies. On the one hand, we can see "familiar" descriptions of the difference between the Western world and other parts of the globe, when rural hygiene served as a lens through which this gap was reflected. For instance, one of the experts who traveled to this region during the tour in April–August 1936 mentioned in his report that rural areas in India appeared to have remained largely "untouched by any western influence except the revenue collector and the itinerant vaccinator."[132] However, perceiving Asian societies as distinct and separate from Europe, he pointed out the similarity between Asian rural hygiene concerns, and European ones.[133]

Although this is not the place for a general discussion on the political ways in which the League challenged Western hegemony in terms of colonialism, at least some of the characteristics of the rural hygiene campaign – especially in its Asian version – place the League as an agent of change. It is true for instance, that for the most part, the West continued to serve as a model for the entire non-Western world, including in terms of sanitation and rural hygiene. But together with the mandates system, Asian rural hygiene introduced more than merely conventional patterns of Western hegemony. The mandates system called colonialism[134] into question by placing mandates under the tutelage of traditional European powers on the one hand; on the other, it stipulated that these special legal regimes had to be strictly temporary, and their intended aim was the eventual independence of those mandates.[135] The majority of delegations in Bandoeng opposed the idea that Western principles and methods – with regard to the entire

132 Letter from Emilio J. Pampana to Ludvik Rajchman, Apr. 14, 1936, LoN Archvies, R 6093/8A/25509/8855.

133 For a study on the imperialist character of international health campaigns in this vast region *see, e.g.*, Sunil S. Amrith, Decolonizing International Health: India and Southeast Asia – 1930–65 (2006).

134 Borowy, *supra* note 8, at 355.

135 On the concept of the interwar Mandate system *see, e.g.*, Anthony Anghie, *Colonialism and the Birth of International Institutions: Sovereignty, Economy, and the Mandate System of the League of Nations*, 34 N.Y.U. J. Int'l L. & Pol. 513 (2002).

rural culture – should be imposed onto Asian environments and nothing more.

Revising familiar patterns of Western influence and Eastern subservience, the rural hygiene conferences challenged some of these perceptions. On the one hand, the second rural hygiene conference's recommendations emphasized the need for cooperation between different groups within the country and the population. Not only the civil administration, public health authorities, and the Public Works Department had to work together, but the League was also in favor of a "close conjunction"[136] between architects, engineers, and health specialists. On the other hand, this "essential" collaboration was not always assured in every case, and the environmental consequences were visible: "It is but necessary to instance the case of irrigation works, which produced numberless mosquito-breeding sites." The recommendations also warned of drawing inspiration from overly simplistic Western systems, "which came under our observation [and] may serve to strengthen the argument" against a copy-paste pattern:

> The schools in a certain tropical area were housed in buildings of the local type, well lit, clean, ventilated and, above all, economical. The Public Works Department, having decided to replace them by masonry buildings, erected structures ten times as expensive, where the light was dazzling and the temperature high, while the sanitary installations were done cheaply, and the wells were not even sanitary.[137]

This is not to claim that the (familiar) tension between East and West was absent from other parts of the League's discussions. Some effort was made to improve wells (and sanitation) and to fit them with curbs and platforms, "but that is only a half-solution of the problem, so long as users of the well draw the water in buckets of dubious cleanliness."[138]

Whereas the Great Depression had a palpable influence on most other environmental dilemmas on the League's agenda – such as the issue of whaling regulations, the campaign for the convention against the pollution of the sea by oil, and fears of deforestation – its presence was almost entirely absent from the interwar sanitation campaign. As a matter of fact, one of the only times the economic crisis is mentioned in the context of the sanitation campaign is when the Health Organisation discussed the need to accommodate improved sanitation in rural areas (in order to

[136] Preparatory Papers, *supra* note 6, at 51.
[137] *Id.*
[138] *Id.*

prevent diseases). A couple of months after the first conference of 1931 concluded, one report mentioned that the initiative had revealed the extent to which rural hygiene had suffered during the economic crisis. The report went on to say that the League therefore had a responsibility to present reasonable and efficient (affordable) reform strategies.[139]

Even more important than the absence of the Depression is the role of nature in this campaign. Throughout this intensive campaign, the League viewed the environment in a completely different way than it had in other environmental initiatives. Here, the League did not recruit international law and international cooperation to save or protect certain landscapes (such as forests) or endangered species (such as whales or migrating seabirds). This time, the environment was viewed as a source danger, a realm from which the global community had to protect itself. The campaign depicted nature as inherently dangerous, though it also acknowledged that nature needed to be protected from problems like pollution. The discussions in Geneva and Bandoeng reveal that the League and the Health Organisation explored ways to protect rivers, lakes, and springs from harm so that these water sources did not become a danger to the human community, not because they considered these features to have intrinsic value.

To promote its cause, the League used a discourse of security. Unlike in previous periods in modern times, as the historical background in this chapter has briefly explained, it was the League that depicted the rural periphery as a dangerous environmental and sanitary space and a source of a *global* concern. The hope of both conferences, and of the whole campaign, was to change rural sanitation and hygiene, first in Europe, and then the rest of the world – as the broader geographical perspective of the second conference showed. The League's (and other agencies') use of the security discourse on the matter of sanitation bridged the gap between its more conventional activities and its environmental initiatives. After all, when it came to peacekeeping in general and global security in particular, the League was supposed to confront "real" threats, not polluted water, rats, or breeding Asian flies.

There are several possible reasons for this kind of policy, some of which likely have to do with the general *spirit* of the League.[140] Others are related to the assumption that discussing sanitary threats as part of

[139] Allgemeine Betrachtung der zu untersuchenden Fragen d. Ländl. Hygiene, Sept. 8, 1931, LoN Archives, R5932/8A/30088/30078.

[140] Susan Pedersen, *Back to the League of Nations*, 112 AM. HIST. REV. 1091, 1113 (2007).

a security framework was probably more convenient and efficient for those who developed this ongoing discourse. This kind of framework and its terms might also justify the mobilization of resources, energy, and budget. Another possible reason is a rather simple one: the West used its influence to mobilize the League because it was afraid of the East, and viewed spreading diseases as a direct threat to entire populations and their stability. Local East Asian urban centers were not the only sites threatened by rural surroundings in this sanitary-environmental context, the League argued. During the different sessions on water resource protection, sanitation, fly control, and other means of prevention in the countryside, another fear was made known: that the rural environment and its diseases would soon spill over into the world beyond the borders of Eastern countries. For instance, the second conference warned certain countries of the danger of a leprosy revival: "China, whose Government realises that it must make itself responsible for a task with which the missions are no longer able to cope, has not only *its own internal problem but, owing to emigration, also an external problem to solve.*"[141]

This view of the environment as a source of danger was all the more challenging given that the League and the international community were simultaneously dealing with *other* contemporary geopolitical threats – and in the same (vast) geographical space of the Far East. With Japan and China engaged in the bitter Second Sino-Japanese War, the League invested much of its institutional energy in tackling water supply problems in remote rural areas, the same regions that had been affected by the bloody conflict between these two regional powers. The League was naturally concerned about the regional geopolitical crisis, but it was also aware of the necessity of protecting valuable water sources.

Was this just a naïve policy on the League's part? Was the control of flies, rats, and fleas in East Asia in 1937 the right move in terms of international law and international stability, given our historical retrospective? This issue remains open for discussion. Rural hygiene in general and the measures human societies undertook to fight environmental-sanitary risks in particular were by no means the main goals for which the League was established. Rural hygiene does, however, appear to be the largest – and most important[142] – ongoing project of the League's Health Organisation. In many ways, one can also argue that the rural hygiene

[141] Preparatory Papers, *supra* note 6, at 103 (emphasis added).
[142] Borowy, *supra* note 8, at 325.

campaign determined the League's institutional profile with regard to public health concerns.

Indeed, based on the Covenant's description of the League's primary aims, issues such as polluted water sources or inadequate sanitation systems in rural areas were not supposed to gain as much attention as they eventually did during the interwar period. Concerns that were deemed to be peripheral or secondary by their nature eventually gained so much traction that they resulted in two special international conferences that were convened specifically to overcome them.

Moreover, although neither of the conferences concluded with a binding legal document (such as a convention), or even with (legal) articulation of the common environmental perceptions, these events were still valuable. First, they enabled a thorough discussion by professional experts on rural hygiene and sanitation. Second, at least some of the issues, recommendations, and possible solutions tackled at these conferences would eventually find their way into later discussions and international consultations on sanitation and prevention policies.

The campaign reflected different layers of soft law, and illustrated several practical instances of law in action. For instance, in addition to the recommendations the League published and distributed after the first conference had concluded, it sent out further inquiries that focused on environmental concerns. The Health Organisation reported on the first of these concerns in 1932, outlining the epidemiology of typhoid fever in rural districts and the sanitary improvements needed to overcome it; methods of treating garbage (and manure) to prevent fly breeding; and, in particular, methods of testing and analyzing water and sewage with a view to possible standardization in terms of international criteria.[143]

Although neither of the League's sanitary campaigns introduced many practical solutions, this mode of international law should not be overlooked. These campaigns relied on the expertise of professional experts, and encouraged them to deliver their proposals, plans, and recommendations for the improvement of sanitation and public health. As I have shown, this practice was not a solution that had been invented as a professional reaction to epidemic crises (including the COVID-19 challenge) in the early twenty first century, but rather as an interwar routine, led by the League.

[143] Report of the Health Organisation for the Period Jan. 1931 to Sept. 1932, Bulletin, Vol. I, 1932, LoN Archives, at 400–01.

When the World Health Organization, for instance, led the fight against the SARS virus in 2003, one of the routines that allowed the organization to overcome this global danger was the activation of its special Global Outbreak Alert and Response Network protocol (GORAN). GORAN had been established as a fixed protocol in April 2000; it connected numerous institutes and professional laboratories, scientists, and policymakers from a variety of states, all of whom worked together to establish guidelines for a rapid and efficient response to the epidemic.[144] Although the professional committees and staff that had convened back in the 1930s did not have the same technological tools and means of communication, the basic logic and framework was the same even then.

The League's environmental and sanitary initiatives in the rural peripheries were far more modest. Unlike the SARS experience, the League did not have the means and resources, such as a vast network of eleven professional laboratories in ten different countries (like Goran), at its disposal; nevertheless, it did engage different experts from a variety of fields – such as biology, chemistry, civil engineering, public health, and sanitation – in an evolving and ongoing effort to identify the flaws in the sanitary status of different countries in the 1930s. This mode of information producing and sharing was also a feature of other League initiatives, including environmental ones; however, given the obvious technical and professional aspects of sanitation issues addressed, the role of comparative data was particularly valuable in this case. Like their much later historical equivalents, the League's networks introduced and shared their pooled data very openly: their different policies, possible solutions, difficulties, and results. They used all the mechanisms and institutional possibilities that international law was able to offer, and they used the language of international law and global governance to face threats.

Indeed, the degree to which international cooperation was able to tackle environmental threats to public health is even more impressive in the late twentieth and early twenty-first centuries. Both the speed and the technological capabilities of the powerful professional bodies of the UN were much more advanced than when the WHO, the successor of the League's Health Organisation, and the international community fought against SARS. However, the cooperative approach and the belief in

[144] For an overview of the GORAN protocol and program *see* http://www.who.int/ihr/alert_and_response/outbreak-network/en/.

international law as a tool with which to overcome common (in this case environmental) problems were intensive and diligent.

After all, the League provided an opportunity to the international community to bring together a range of scientists and experts and to coordinate their efforts, instead of having them compete with one another. Today, when it comes to threats to sanitation, environmental concerns, and public health, we no longer underestimate the value of joint efforts or take international initiatives for granted. The experiences of the interwar period laid the institutional and conceptual foundations in this regard. Each individual component can be tracked (with the relevant differences) during this interwar campaign: the distribution of sanitary information and practical knowledge and experience; the sharing of laboratory findings and clinical experience; discussions on national schemes to fight environmental dangers; public health initiatives on these issues; and, above all, the coordination, monitoring, and supervision of one central institution offered by the League.

Whether one considers the League's endeavors to be successful or completely in vain, one cannot deny the significant work the League carried out in terms of *dealing* with rural hygiene and environmental risks in Europe and Asia. Both conferences (and the intensive follow-up institutional and interinstitutional work that continued once official discussions had concluded) expressed a general commitment in Europe and beyond to the improvement of rural hygiene and to the fight against environmental risks as a fundamental part of international governance. The League did not undertake this complex campaign because it was forced to do so, but rather because it believed in international law as an essential part of collective security, and that solving environmental challenges was key to achieving stability and prosperity.

This belief in international law alone, however, was not enough. As in later periods, the League emphasized the need for cooperation with the local civil population as well. Moreover, the shift from local to regional approaches to these issues is intriguing. This is not just a contemporary observation, but rather a perspective that was raised by figures of that period: "The problem in this form is not purely a problem of individuals; it is a collective problem."[145]

The variety of issues that the League promoted to achieve stability along the rural frontier is a clear indication of the connection it saw between rural hygiene and international stability. Otherwise, it would not

[145] Preparatory Papers, *supra* note 6, at 51.

have invested so much energy in these concerns. And it did not just address one or the other concern, such as sanitation, the installation of latrines, or fly control – the League understood that the entire rural environment acted as one system. Flood protection for the delta lands, for instance, was also part of the broader picture, as were the issues of water supply for agriculture, drainage and drying of low waterlogged ground, and irrigation of high ground when the soil was too dry.

Understanding these concerns as part of ensuring security echoes other perceptions of promoting security during the interwar period, which had little (or nothing) to do with supervising the international disarmament accords after World War I. As other studies have suggested, some of the League's activities focused on promoting international cooperation as a whole – and more specifically in the wake of the Great Depression and the uneasy international relations of the 1930s, when fascism was gaining more and more power.[146]

The League promoted an early concept of environmental security through tools of international law. In that context, this environmental-sanitary discourse also corresponds with contemporary literature that links other global environmental concerns and (broader or more elusive) definitions of security, whether they relate to climate change,[147] energy security[148] or water security,[149] facing the ecological crisis.

In a broader perspective, this concept of linking natural hazards caused by environmental factors with threats to local, national, and international security drew on the idea of the need for a new "cordon sanitaire." The interwar period introduced another phase in the evolution of this historic term. First, the use of "cordon sanitaire" to refer to a protective shield started as a tool with which spreading diseases from the East could be kept away from the West's frontiers. Then, during the interwar period, the French borrowed this term to describe their system of bilateral

146 Patricia Clavin, for instance, identified a link between supporting economic affairs in general, and assisting states in financial crises, as another dimension in the League's commitment to global security. *See* PATRICIA CLAVIN, SECURING THE WORLD ECONOMY: THE REINVENTION OF THE LEAGUE OF NATIONS, 1920–1946 (2013).

147 Jon Barnett, *Security and Climate Change*, 13 GLOBAL ENVTL. CHANGE 7 (2003); Matt McDonald, *Discourses of Climate Security*, 33 POL. GEOGRAPHY 42 (2013).

148 Marilyn A. Brown & Michael H. Dworkin, *The Environmental Dimension of Energy Security*, *in* THE ROUTLEDGE HANDBOOK OF ENERGY SECURITY 176 (Benjamin K. Sovacool ed., 2011).

149 Janos J. Bogardi et al., *Water Security for a Planet under Pressure: Interconnected Challenges of a Changing World Call for Sustainable Solutions*, 4 CURRENT OPINION IN ENVTL. SUSTAINABILITY 35 (2012).

alliances in the face of political dangers emerging from the (Soviet Communist) East; finally, the League transcended the term, using its connotations of security to portray severe problems of rural environment and public health.

As the League wrapped up the first conference of 1931, it concluded that the bonification of rural Europe depended mostly on fixing sanitation, but also on adjusting it to suit the needs of the countryside (not only urban spaces), as problematic areas that were more likely to suffer exposure to spreading diseases due to difficulties of the environmental conditions.

In that sense, the first rural hygiene conference expressed a discourse of a different type of global security. The League had dedicated much of its institutional energy to peacekeeping and global security. The fact that sanitation was considered an important part of ensuring and securing international social welfare sheds light on the League's environmental regime. This regime enabled the League to recruit other realms of international law to promote global security. In this way, like frameworks for disarmament treaties or reinforcing new borders in the post–World War I world, the issues of proper sanitation and pest control were important elements of international stability and prosperity.

4

Raw Materials, the Timber Crisis, and Fears of Deforestation during the Interwar Period

> Deforestation was one of the perils threatening mankind, and it was all the more to be feared because it always corresponded to a period of intense civilisation.[1]

4.1 Introduction

This chapter will uncover the entanglements of timber trade and deforestation in the interwar period as seen through the lens of international law and governance. As the chapter will explore the story of timber and trees during the period, it will show how certain voices claimed that the West (and other regions as well) had never experienced this scale of deforestation prior to the establishment of the League, and to which extent the League became concerned about the exploitation of forests.

As the chapter will show, forests and timber merged two intertwining threads. First, as an international forum for industrial cooperation and economic prosperity, the League, together with other bodies, was focused on ensuring efficient global production of a variety of raw materials. In the case of timber, the Great Depression of 1929, together with certain timber export policies of the Soviet Union, put other national timber industries at risk. Second, at that point, the interwar story of timber reflected a sort of harmony between the League, other international industrial frameworks, and Western nations' commercial interests. With their profits severely reduced, these players (including the League) wished to protect timber industries and to stabilize dropping prices by means of international law and international governance. The League, driven by certain agendas of

[1] Records of the 19th Ordinary Session of the Assembly: Minutes of the 2d Committee (Economic, Financial, and Transit Questions), Special Supplement No. 185, Sept. 22, 1938 League of Nations Official Journal (1938), League of Nations Archives [hereinafter LoN Archives] Annex 1, A.64.1938.II.B., at 26–27.

some of its own institutional bodies, first and foremost the Economic Committee, wished to support and assist in managing the supply of the timber market by restricting production in order to prop up prices and thereby ensure the survival of the industry. With the merging of these threads, environmental considerations were woven into the plot (even if during its relatively late phases), adding another layer to the economic incentives, and coloring the dilemma with urgent calls to limit forest harvest in order to stop deforestation from expanding.

As I will show, the timber issue placed the League in a complex position. Though it was primarily concerned about economic issues, the League did allow for environmental considerations in its continued process of discussion and consultation. In the timber story that I will tell, these environmental considerations – for which the League had no express or original mandate – were also expressed in the economic-industrial realm, and through economic institutions: both those within the League, as well as external independent ones.

As the independent organizations' and the League's economic-industrial agenda intensified, another concern began to emerge and added to this framework. This time, the concern was not about dropping prices alone. Voices that warned of spreading deforestation were gaining more and more attention in the League. Worried calls contended that forests were disappearing from regions around the world at an alarming rate, changing the landscape and causing dangerous erosion in vast regions in Europe, Soviet Russia, North America, and other regions. These voices found common ground with the desire of international bodies to govern natural resources and curb the exploitation of forests by managing timber trade with means pulled out of the toolbox of international law.

By the late 1930s, deforestation had become an issue for international deliberation, largely due to technological, economic, and industrial changes, and also because of the immense transformation in media and other forms of human communication. Due to the rise of mass-printed books and popular newspapers and their effect on landscapes, the discussion in the League painted deforestation in a very worrying light. Timber, cellulose, and other industries were as eager to protect their own natural resources as whaling companies were during the interwar period.[2] Like these industries, the League was "seriously concerned"

[2] As Chapter 2 describes, and as the League was pushed by scientific calls that urged to prevent the extinction of the whale, it developed in the 1930s the first international whaling law. *See* KURKPATRICK DORSEY, WHALES AND NATIONS: ENVIRONMENTAL DIPLOMACY ON THE HIGH SEAS 2013.

about the "steady decline" of "their raw materials."[3] As with the case of the increasing exploitation of different species of whale, counterefforts – such as monitoring, regulation, and supervision – were far behind the rapid consumption of trees by these industries.

Indeed, the timber campaign did not remove the threat of deforestation. Still, by the end of that period, advocators for the cause motivated the League to present deforestation as a global issue – one that needed to be solved by international law. However, as I will demonstrate in my conclusions, this was one of the last times in which international environmental law discussed deforestation as a problem that can be solved by global legal actions. In 2020, for instance, data from Brazil's national space research institute INPE shows that 830 square kilometers of rainforest was cleared in the "Legal Amazon," Earth's largest rainforest, during the month of May 2020 alone, bringing the total clearing since August 1, 2019 to 6,437 square kilometers, an area larger than Delaware.[4] Although a broad popular reaction across the globe against the actions or failures of the Brazilian government, and even when the rise in deforestation troubles scientists who fear that the combination of forest loss and the effects of climate change could trigger the Amazon rainforest to tip toward a drier ecosystem, international law – as a complex machine – was not recruited for the mission. Most of the calls focused on "private" domestic commercial actions (such as a ban on Brazilian timber), but not using international law (both hard and soft) as a policy.

Some voices advocating in the League, however, identified a pressing need for collective international environmental action to fight against this outcome of industrialism and modernization. Therefore, any relevant action had to turn away from domestic-national means in favor of international law led by international organizations. As the League's official records put it, "reafforestation was not proceeding as rapidly as the contrary process, and those industries alone consumed huge forests every day. The problem was at once an economic, a social and a human one."[5]

As the timber question discussion evolved, the League was definitely not the only agency involved. Different bodies, transnational commercial (private or semiprivate) consortiums, and international organizations

[3] Records of the 19th Ordinary Session of the Assembly, *supra* note 1, at 27.

[4] Rhett A. Butler, *14 Straight Months of Rising Amazon Deforestation in Brazil*, MONGABAY, (June 12, 2020), https://news.mongabay.com/2020/06/14-straight-months-of-rising-amazon-deforestation-in-brazil/.

[5] Records of the 19th Ordinary Session of the Assembly, *supra* note 1, at 27.

were also paying close attention to timber. However, the League played a unique role in the diplomatic activities. During the interwar period, the League served as one of the centers for international and legal consultation. This was not a one-way street but rather an ongoing reciprocal relationship, as the League cooperated with these organizations too, and followed their work.

Throughout the chapter, I will track the interplay between the League and other organizations that were involved in the timber question. First and foremost, I will describe the role of the Comité International du Bois (or the International Timber Committee). The Comité was an international consortium (founded in 1932) of private and semi-state central timber-exporting organizations. The timber plot also includes the involvement of the International Institute of Agriculture (IIA), which was established before the League (in 1905), and worked from its headquarters in Rome. The main focus of the following sections will not be on these bodies specifically; however, the story would not be complete without taking into account their role and significance.[6]

Moreover, in addition to these external independent bodies, different experts, diplomats, and committees of the League took part in the discussion on a global timber regime. It should be noted however that although the chapter refers from time to time to the League as a whole, the institutional structure on the ground was obviously more complex. The League was not, neither in the timber question nor in any other mission of its environmental regime, a single, unified entity, seeming to possess knowledge and will of its own. Therefore, in relevant places, the chapter will differentiate the views of the League's various organs (or individuals or groups within those organs).

Despite the eclectic studies that have been carried out on forestation and deforestation, these multiple endeavors – economic, industrial, and

[6] Several studies dealt with the three organizations and their effort from different angles, *e.g.*, Birgit Karlsson, *Cartels in the Swedish and Finnish Forest Industries in the Interwar Period*, *in* MANAGING CRISES AND DE-GLOBALISATION: NORDIC FOREIGN TRADE AND EXCHANGE, 1919–39, 188 (Sven Olof Olsson ed., 2010); ELINA KUORELAHTI, THE POLITICAL ECONOMY OF INTERNATIONAL COMMODITY CARTELS: AN ECONOMIC HISTORY OF THE EUROPEAN TIMBER TRADE IN THE 1930S (2020); Martin Bemmann, *Das Chaos Beseitigen: Die internationale Standardisierung forst- und holzwirtschaftlicher Statistiken in den 1920er und 1930er Jahren und der Völkerbund*, 57 JAHRBUCH FÜR WIRTSCHAFTSGESCHICHTE / ECON. HIST. Y.B. 545 (2016); Martin Bemmann, *Cartels, Grossraumwirtschaft and Statistical Knowledge: International Organizations and Their Efforts to Govern Europe's Forest Resources in the 1930s and 1940s*, *in* GOVERNING THE RURAL IN INTERWAR EUROPE 233 (Liesbeth van de Grift & Amalia Ribi Forclaz eds., 2017).

environmental – have not yet been studied as part of the history of the League. Furthermore, although timber issues have been studied at both the domestic-national level as well as at the imperial level,[7] it should be noted that the League was the first international institution to turn to legal mechanisms as solution. One way or the other, fear – either of a wood shortage or of the global destruction of forests during the interwar period – is missing from our textbooks. This absence is even more intriguing when we turn to a comparative perspective. In comparison with other fields within the world of environmental history, it seems that the scope of studies on forestation and deforestation is far broader, richer, and more eclectic.[8]

Prior to the establishment of the League, there were already early transnational discussions about cooperation between timber-producing countries and parties. However, the League joined this discussion and encouraged it thanks to its fixed diplomatic routine and relatively intensive institutional mechanisms. Moreover, in the late 1930s, as the environmental costs of timber production started to become clear, the League stepped forward, motivated by the French delegation to Geneva. As this chapter will show, and side by side with the ambition to participate in the discussions on a global timber policy, the League was asked to promote an open and ongoing discussion to find an international solution to the pressing problem of disappearing forests.

[7] Scholars were also interested in the interplay between imperialism and forestry policies. As different studies have argued, it is likely that French- and German-trained foresters, for instance, had carried forestry policies with them as they traveled across the French and German empires, and especially into the British imperial forestry-trained and professional community. *See* Ravi Rajan, *Imperial Environmentalism or Environmental Imperialism? European Forestry, Colonial Foresters and the Agendas of Forest Management in British India 1800–1900*, in NATURE AND THE ORIENT 324 (Richard H. Grove et al. eds., 1998).

In that sense, the richness of this part in historiography of deforestation does not focus on modern imperialism alone. Christof March, for instance, outlined the role of forests in different cultures across history (such as the Venetian empire's hunger for wood) – CHRISTOF MAUCH, THE GROWTH OF TREES: A HISTORICAL PERSPECTIVE ON SUSTAINABILITY (Katie Ritson trans., 2014).

[8] Forestation and deforestation are no strangers to environmental history. Environmental historians are particularly interested in the ways in which human activities have damaged nature, causing deforestation and other phenomena such as erosion and overgrazing over vast areas since antiquity. *See, e.g.*, J. Donald Hughes, *Ancient Deforestation Revisited*, 44 J. HIST. BIOLOGY 43 (2011); David Schorr, *Forest Law in the Palestine Mandate: Colonial Conservation in a Unique Context*, *in* MANAGING THE UNKNOWN: ESSAYS ON ENVIRONMENTAL IGNORANCE 74–75 (Frank Uekötter & Uwe Lübken eds., 2014); Andrew K. Jorgenson, *Structural Integration and the Trees: An Analysis of Deforestation in Less-Developed Countries: 1990–2005*, 49 SOC. Q. 503 (2008).

This chapter has four parts. Following this introduction, the second part covers the question of timber in the interwar period. This second part is further divided into several sections. In order to better situate the discussion of the League within the issue of timber, Section 4.2.1 will give a short introduction on the League's special interest in the concept of monitoring and coordinating the production and trade of different raw materials. Section 4.2.2 will cover the ways in which the League and other organizations started to handle the timber question, and how and to what extent the League treated timber as an essential raw material during that period. Compared to other raw materials, the League focused its attention on timber, examining policies to regulate timber production and trade. The last Section, 4.2.3, explores what I call the *timber wars* of the 1930s, which echoed both the Great Depression and the dumping policy of the Soviet Union in the late 1920s and early 1930s. During this stage, and given the outcomes of the Depression and the Soviet reaction, different leading timber-producing countries challenged the Soviet Union's timber policy.

Section 4.3 explores how the League was confronted with concerns of deforestation in the late 1930s. This part is divided into two sections: 4.3.1 will examine the League's (and the Economic Committee in particular) campaign for international timber regulation, which supported the industry. Section 4.3.2 reveals the ways in which environmental concerns were added to the League's discussion. The primary focus of Section 4.3, and of the chapter as a whole, is the emergence of *other* environmental, conservationist, and economic voices that joined interwar discussion on global timber regime. These voices strove to draw the international community's attention not to the price of timber alone, but also to the environmental cost of forest harvesting for development, industry, and commerce. Through their advocacy, these parties wished to make the League aware of the environmental outcomes of the timber industry, and openly discussed the issue of producing timber as the primary cause of deforestation that was sweeping the globe. This part of the chapter will draw on discussions and correspondence that highlight the League's role as a central institution – one that led environmental challenges while simultaneously supporting a certain economic agenda – in an unstable world. Moreover, all of this shows how and to what extent environmental concerns, like deforestation, were woven into the crafting of international law.

As I will further show, although the call for caution and action came primarily from the French, the League continued the deliberations even after 1938. However, World War II put a swift end to this initiative exactly one year later. Unlike other interwar environmental initiatives – which had at least some expression in international environmental law in the post–World War II era – it seems that the fear of spreading deforestation had not had, at least up to that point, a chance to gain sufficient international attention in terms of using international legal mechanisms, as they did during the interwar period.

Indeed, compared to other concerns that involved environmental aspects and were handled by the League, it seems that the timber question tells us relatively little about the law that applied to timber trade and deforestation in the interwar period. However, the discussions did reveal a certain place that has been given to international law, preliminary and not yet fully developed as it was during the 1930s. Moreover, the timber and forests question illustrates the emergence of norms such as precautionary principle or sustainable development, and therefore it justifies in my view this kind of analysis.

In the conclusion, I will wrap up the discussion with a broad comparison of post-World War II policies, and identify those ideas that started to emerge in the 1930s and which persist today.

4.2 Timber in the Interwar Period

> The developments of modern civilisation and of the numerous uses to which cellulose was put – newsprint in particular – constituted a terrible danger to forests throughout the world.[9]

The following part will trace the main challenges that timber-producing countries and the League experienced during the interwar period.

To better situate the interwar timber discussion, Section 4.2.1 will first give a short introduction on the League's involvement – and the Economic Committee[10] in particular – in trying to coordinate, monitor, and modify the production and trade of different raw materials.

[9] *Supra* note 1, at 27.

[10] The Economic Committee was an internal unit of the Economic and Financial Organisation, one of the League's auxiliary bodies (next to the Permanent Court of International Justice or the International Labour Organisation, for example). The Covenant of the League specified that additional bodies should be established to deal with questions of technical nature. The League created a group of such bodies, which worked under its auspices and within its parameters, but also had a certain independence. On the League's multilayered institutional structure *see, e.g.*, F. S. Northedge, The League of Nations: Its Life and Times – 1920–1946 (1986).

Section 4.2.2 will then go on to address how the League and other international organizations started to handle the timber question in particular. This section will show how and to what extent the League viewed timber as an essential raw material – more essential, in fact, than other materials that were discussed during that period.

I will also claim that it might be that the main reason the League engaged with the future of forests to begin with was its special interest in raw materials. The League was engaged in the exploitation of natural resources from its earliest stages. As research into the economic functions of the League is only now emerging, scholars have recently suggested[11] that the League strove to facilitate an international governance and monitoring of raw materials. The League's predominant assumption was that recovering industries' access to raw materials was necessary to ensure international recovery after the war. Stabilizing timber industries and keeping a reasonable and efficient price will become central aims of this campaign.

Section 4.2.3 will briefly describe how the turbulent timber trade of the 1930s was shaped by two major intensive phenomena: the Great Depression, and a Soviet dumping policy that followed it. I will discuss the economic and political reactions of some of the timber-producing parties involved, and the ways this tension was reflected in the League's activity.

4.2.1 A Short Introduction to the Special Interest of the League in Raw Materials

Before the League started to view the issue of timber trade and mostly its difficulties, it was already busy with a task that would soon become one of the main aims on its agenda. Although only a fraction of its formal legal foundation, the Covenant of the League of Nations, referred to economic matters,[12] the League invested much of its energy into promoting the idea of international supervision and monitoring of the production, trade, and constant supply of precious raw materials that were needed for the insatiable postwar global economy.[13]

[11] *See, e.g.*, Michael Fakhri, *The 1937 International Sugar Agreement: Neo-Colonial Cuba and Economic Aspects of the League of Nations*, 24 LEIDEN J. INT'L L. 899 (2011).

[12] Article 23 (e) of the Covenant called for equal treatment for the commerce of all the members of the League.

[13] In the center of the debates on timber markets stood the League's economic bodies. As Patricia Clavin has shown, these bodies had different members and sometimes they followed different logics than "the" League (or other part of the League): PATRICIA CLAVIN, SECURING THE WORLD ECONOMY: THE REINVENTION OF THE LEAGUE OF NATIONS, 1920–1946 (2013).

As the Allies suffered during the war from a severe shortage of raw materials due to the difficulties of warfare and naval blockades, they worked together to create a series of temporary legal-economic transnational agreements.[14] Ad hoc organizations worked to secure shipping purchases for the armed forces and (later) also tried to control commercial supply for civilian needs at the rear.[15]

When the war was over, the League encouraged the regularization and improvement of these temporary arrangements.[16] Though the League did not have the institutional power to fulfill that aim, the structure of the League enabled its member states, and not only postwar powers, to better coordinate their efforts to organize the constant supply of primary commodities even during peacetime.

The League believed that rationalization of the production and trade of these materials was needed to stabilize and control economic conditions of distribution and consumption in a way that would ensure economic efficiency.[17] Two special trade agreements, articulated (later in the 1930s) under the direct auspices of the League, subjected sugar and wheat, for example, to international regulations.[18] The League promoted the notion that a stable market for global raw materials was a necessary part of building a new peaceful international community.[19]

[14] MARTIN HILL, THE ECONOMIC AND FINANCIAL ORGANIZATION OF THE LEAGUE OF NATIONS: A SURVEY OF TWENTY-FIVE YEARS' EXPERIENCE 14–18 (1946).

[15] For an analysis of these kinds of economic Cooperation under fire *see* J. A. SALTER, ALLIED SHIPPING CONTROL: AN EXPERIMENT IN INTERNATIONAL ADMINISTRATION (1921).

[16] *See*, for instance, the role of James Arthur Salter. Salter was in charge of the interallied economic-industrial coordination activities, and appointed to carry out his mission under the auspices of the League as the head of the Economic and Financial Section (1922–31). *See* Susan Pedersen, *Back to the League of Nations*, 112 AM. HIST. REV. 1091, 1111 (2007); HILL, *supra* note 14, at 109; W. M. MCCLURE, WORLD PROSPERITY AS SOUGHT THROUGH THE ECONOMIC WORK OF THE LEAGUE OF NATIONS 66–74 (1933).

[17] For a discussion of this kind of rationalization as key to international stability in the interwar period *see* Jo-Anne Pemberton, *New Worlds for Old: The League of Nations and the Age of Electricity*, 28 R. INT'L STUD. 311 (2002).

[18] On the 1937 International Sugar Agreement and the 1938 Wheat Agreement *see* GEORGE W. BAER, INTERNATIONAL ORGANIZATIONS 1918–1945: A GUIDE TO RESEARCH AND RESEARCH MATERIALS 159 (1981).

[19] The World Economic Conference: Geneva, May 1927 Final Report, LoN Archives, 51. Likewise, the assumption behind the League's discussions on oil, coal, sugar, wheat, and timber was that future postwar rapprochement depended on good and reliable economic relations that were based on raw materials as a source of wealth (*see* Economic and Financial Section, Report and Proceedings of the World Economic Conference, Vol. I [1927], LoN Archives, 149). The access to these materials seemed as a central aim in

The League supported a concept of control of production and distribution through mechanisms that were far removed from the principles of free trade and the laissez faire economy; for instance, quotas and the granting of monopolies[20] in relevant industries in order to best regulate the flow[21] of materials. As such, using various means of (mostly, soft) international law and governance – such as committees, conferences, information collecting and sharing, setting international standards – to rationalize raw materials, a production quota system[22] between importer and exporter countries has been negotiated.[23]

The enthusiastic thought was that once the commerce of raw materials during the transition stage after the war and the financial crises of the 1920s would be ensured and modified, then "regular" and unregulated trade could occur normally between states around the world.[24] Different official reports and surveys arrived at the League's headquarters from all over the world,[25] articulating the production quantities of a variety of raw materials on different countries' national soil.

In the context of recovery from the war in terms of infrastructures and building, timber was essential, and everyday life was acutely affected by fluctuating timber supply and prices. Therefore, one can understand some of the reasons behind the international will and advocacy for securing timber production. The following discussion will focus on timber as one of the central indicators of the League's involvement in environmental

ensuring peace, stability, and global recovery after 1918 (*See, e.g.*, Preparatory Committee for the International Conference, Report on the 1st Session of the Committee 7–9 [held at Geneva from Apr. 26 to May 1, 1926] [1926], LoN Archives).

[20] K. Wiedenfeld, Cartels and Combines: Memoranda Released for Publication for the Preparatory Committee for the World Economic Conference 1927, LoN Archives.

[21] G. Cassel, Recent Monopolistic Tendencies in Industry and Trade: Being an Analysis of the Nature of Causes of the Poverty of Nations, Memorandum Released for Publication for the Preparatory Committee for the World Economic Conference 1927, LoN Archives.

[22] Fakhri, *supra* note 11, at 903.

[23] On the importance of raw material commodities in the interwar period *see, e.g.*, Patricia Clavin and Jens-Wilhelm Wessels, *Transnationalism and the League of Nations: Understanding the Work of Its Economic and Financial Organisation*, 14 Contemp. Eur. Hist. 465 (2005).

[24] *See, e.g.*, Secretariat of the League of Nations, Ten Years of World Cooperation (1930), LoN Archives, 178–206; Arthur Salter, *Contribution of the League of Nations to the Recovery of Europe*, 134 Ann. Am. Acad. Pol. & Soc. Sci. 132 (1927).

[25] *See*, for instance, the report of the Office of Census and Statistics, Union of South Africa, from July 8, 1925, in which the Director of Census and Statistics wrote to the Economic Intelligence Service of the League on the production of iron ore, copper, lead, and zinc: Letter to the League Economic Intelligence Service, July 8, 1925, LoN Archives, 10.44366.44346.

junctions as it wished to see the establishment of a monitored international economic regime.[26]

4.2.2 *Striving for a Global Timber Regime: International Bodies Apply Institutional Energy to International Timber Production and Trade*

In this section I will introduce the main developments of the complex timber market in the interwar period, and the intensive involvement of the League, exporting and importing countries and other involved parties. These various parties were concerned about the market's unstable condition in the interwar period for several reasons, as I will further elaborate.

In the early 1930s, the Great Depression threatened to collapse the Northern Hemisphere's timber industry interests. At that point, a group of bodies was working to coordinate and increase cooperation between different timber industries and to support them during hard times. The Comité International du Bois (or the International Timber Committee), together with the International Institute of Agriculture (IIA), marked the first steps in transnational cooperation in the field of forestry and timber trade.[27]

The International Institute of Agriculture – an independent body that was involved in the timber question – was established in June 1905 in Rome, almost fifteen years before the League. As it was founded and financed by governments, and based on cooperation between experts, professionals, and nations, this professional institute in Italy worked to create an international chamber of agriculture, an institution that would be best suited to tackle agricultural crises that crossed borders and national sovereignties. With the Depression affecting the global production and commerce of raw materials – and timber in particular – the role of the IIA became more essential in mapping timber trade and communicating between industries and policymakers in different producing countries.

[26] Moreover, while discussing timber, the League was also dealing with a tobacco inquiry (*See* the documents relating to the League of Nations Tobacco Committee of Mar. 20, 1933, and to the Tobacco Inquiry [under the Economic Relations section] between the years 1932–33, LoN Archives, 10A/362362). In this respect, further research, including from an environmental perspective, might be relevant.

[27] The knowledge on these organizations is still as rudimentary as it is on the timber related debates within the League. Yet the economic situation of timber industries and trade in the 1930s is analyzed by a number of studies, *e.g.*, Egon Glesinger, *Forest Products in a World Economy*, 35 AM. ECON. REV. 120 (1945); Martin Bemmann, *Im Zentrum des Markts. Zur Rolle Großbritanniens im internationalen Holzhandel der 1930er Jahre*, 99 VIERTELJAHRSCHRIFT FÜR SOZIAL- UND WIRTSCHAFTSGESCHICHTE 141 (2012).

In 1926, the IIA convened the International Forestry Congress in Rome.[28] The Congress recommended establishing a separate department or international body that was to focus on forests and timber. During the 1930s, the IIA's special bureau gathered information on forests, timber production, and trade and distributed regular surveys on these matters through its publications.[29]

Similarly, in spring 1932, as the interests of the timber industry neared collapse, the League's Economic Committee decided to convene an international conference of timber experts in Geneva. Shortly afterwards, the Comité International du Bois was created, with its headquarters in Vienna. The Comité was a body of private and semiprivate central timber exporting organizations of five central (though not the most important) exporting countries. Originally, it gathered representatives from Roumania, Yugoslavia, Poland, Austria, and Czechoslovakia.

Moreover, although the Comité was a separate institution, its members still saw themselves as a co-organ of the League and part of its international agenda, at least to a certain extent; or, "a child of the League of Nations," as the Comité's president himself, Krystyn Ostrowki, declared in 1936.[30]

The main focus of the Comité was on economic and industrial data relating to timber production. Its chief assignments were to collect and disseminate statistics that dealt with timber supply and demand; to coordinate technical research; and to collate and publish information on the utilization of wood.[31] Though organizations from the main exporting countries such as Sweden, the Soviet Union, and Finland never acceded (next to representatives of the biggest importing countries Great Britain and Germany), they still used its data.

This momentum, led by the League, the Comité, and the IIA, is a sign of the evolving international professional and bureaucratic community.

[28] On the history of international forestry congresses see Christian Lotz, *Expanding the Space for Future Resource Management: Explorations of the Timber Frontier in Northern Europe and the Rescaling of Sustainability During the Nineteenth Century*, 21 ENVTL. HIST. 257 (2015).

[29] *Publications of the International Institute of Agriculture: International Trade of Wood – Statistical Figures for the Years 1925 to 1939* (1944).

[30] Anonymous, *The Timber's "League of Nations": 21 Countries Represented at the London Conference*, 137 TIMBER TRADES J. 8 (1936). It should be noted, however, that the original quote also included the wording "but a very independent child."

[31] On the Comité's history *see* EGON GLESINGER, NAZIS IN THE WOODPILE: HITLER'S PLOT FOR ESSENTIAL RAW MATERIAL (1942); or ROBERT K. WINTERS, THE FOREST AND MAN 302–04 (1974).

This community of experts and commercial players sought to unify, or at least modify, national and domestic modes of operation and manufacturing to become a much more coordinated and efficient economic-industrial framework. In order to do so, both with regard to raw materials in general, and timber in particular, the League and other bodies involved turned to the discourse of international law and economic governance. This policy also supported the later conception of the League as an institution that formulated new modes of superstate professional bureaucracy.[32] In its own words, one year before its historical role came to an end, the League assessed its contribution as follows:

> The League of Nations was doing increasingly important work in such questions .... Reference should also be made to the economic studies made by the competent section of the Secretariat, as a result of which the League ... had become an *information centre* where the countries concerned could exchange their observations and conclusions on economic questions.[33]

Like wheat, coal, grain, cotton, and sugar, timber became an important and sought-after commodity during the interwar period. The main players were those countries producing timber as a core part of their national industry: mostly Scandinavian states (Finland and Sweden in particular) and Canada. Nevertheless, when Soviet Russia started to recover from the devastating outcomes of the Civil War and Military Communism, the USSR secured a key role in the global export of timber.[34]

The demand for timber was not limited to Europe alone, but extended further. Economic data from the interwar period actually show that timber's value exceeded that of oil or coal exports worldwide.[35] At the end of the 1920s, about forty million cubic meters of sawn timber – the

[32] For a similar move on the role of experts, professional bureaucracy, and international integration *see* the special volume in the series Making Europe: Technology and Transformation: 1850–2000: Wolfram Kaiser & Johan Schot, Writing The Rules for Europe: Experts, Cartels, and International Organizations (2014).

[33] (Draft) Report on the 48th Session of the Economic Committees held at Geneva, July 4–9, 1938, Oct. 19, 1938, LoN Archives, 10A/34675/1952 (E.1046), at 17 (emphasis added).

[34] On the capacity of the Soviet timber industry and forestation *see* Peter Blandon, Soviet Forest Industries (1983); Brian Nongomme, Forests, Peasants, and Revolutionaries: Forest Conservation and Organization in Soviet Russia, 1917–1929 (2005); Stephen Brain, The Song of the Forest: Russian Forestry and Stalinist Environmentalism, 1905–1953 (2011).

[35] *Comité International du Bois: Year-Book of World Timber Trade 1938*, at 2.

most popular product at this time – were exported worldwide per year.[36] The vast majority of this quantity came from the Northern Hemisphere. The Scandinavian countries,[37] Canada, France, and (after a decade of absence) also the Soviet Union were the central exporting countries.

Before the Great Depression, international consumption was on the rise, with different industries and markets using timber as a raw material – such as for building infrastructure, and in the pulp and paper industry (supporting the printed newspapers in a world of new means of mass media). In times of mass production, such as when the League was active, timber trade accelerated and distribution increased.[38]

A closer inspection of timber, and a comparison with other raw materials (which seem more essential in terms of food demands and industrial needs) suggest that timber received special attention. In an Economic Committee report from the mid-1930s addressing various aspects of international economic collaboration, a central commodity like wheat received no more than a single page of attention.[39] Despite its importance as a basic staple food, and although the League had experienced earlier in the 1920s[40] outbreaks of famine in Communist Russia, and Ukraine in

36 Walter Grottian, Die Umsatzmengen im Weltholzhandel 1925–1938, 144 (1942).

37 Perhaps except Norway. But Sweden and Finland were key players.

38 Partial data from leading European industrial economies show that in both Britain and Germany in particular, there was a growing demand for imported timber. In Britain, timber imports per year rose from fewer than one million cubic meters in 1835 to more than fourteen million in 1927 (*see* Thorsten Streyffert, *Die Holzwirtschaft Europas*, 52 Forstwissenschaftliches Centralblatt 825, 825–36, 869–78 (1930). In Germany, the annual industrial consumption of timber dramatically expanded from almost five million cubic meters between 1860 and 1862, to no less than thirty-five million cubic meters between 1925 and 1929 (*see, e.g.*, Kurt MANTEL, Holzmarktlehre: Ein Lehr und Handbuch der Holzmarktökonomie und Holzwirtschaftspolitik 73 [1973]). These European examples also correspond with changes in the American economy: in the 1840s, the American timber consumption stood at no more than 10 million cubic meters; whereas the statistics show consumption skyrocketing to 275 million cubic meters in the mid-1920s. Even the Spanish economy, which was not considered to be a central economy, showed numbers that point to a clear increase in timber trade at the peak of industrialization (*see* Iñaki Iriarte-Goñia & María Isabel Ayudab, *Wood and Industrialization: Evidence and Hypotheses from the Case of Spain, 1860–1935*, 65 Ecological Eco. 177, 179 [2008]).

39 *See* the note of the Secretariat for the Economic Committee on international economic collaboration (Regional Agreements, Various Manifestations, Producers' Agreements), June 5, 1936, LoN Archives, 10A/381/381/xv, at 15 (hereinafter Regional Agreements).

40 *See* the Report on Economic Conditions in Russia: with Special Reference to the Famine of 1921–1922 and the State of Agriculture (1922), LoN Archives, C.705.M.451.1922. II, at 1.

particular, the League and other parties involved seemed to afford this basic cereal attention and concern almost as it did with timber.

Wheat was not alone in that regard. "Since August 31st, 1935, there has been no international sugar agreement,"[41] the Committee mentioned laconically in this report. There was also an International Tea Committee, which was formed in 1933 and "aim[ed] at regulating exports."[42] Compared to timber (half a page), however, the international tea trade discussion amounted to no more than one-third of a page; coal had a page-long survey;[43] and the International Agreement for Restricting the Production of Copper – accepted by producers and representing 75 percent of world production – stretched over fewer than two pages.[44]

One simple letter sent to the League might also highlight the importance of timber in the interwar period: "We consider that, inasmuch as timber is a raw material of *fundamental importance*, closely lined with agriculture, it is deserving of the special attention of the international organizations, and should receive *first* consideration with a view to an improvement in its position in the sphere of international trade."[45]

The special importance that international bodies attributed to timber went hand in hand with the legal mechanisms that were considered to address the tension between international law and domestic-national law. It seems that the international organizations that were involved in the timber issue were aware of the possible obstacles on the ground when it came to national policies. Therefore, they considered several means by which international governance would be able to overcome local legal barriers. The Comité, for instance, as it aimed to organize a timber cartel,[46] declared that it was fully aware of this legal tension and, in order to reach an international agreement, it "devoted special attention to the establishment of national organisations in all its member countries. The national organisations must be in a position to conclude . . . any agreements that may be thought necessary, and to give all the required guarantees."[47]

41 Regional Agreements, *supra* note 39, at 16.
42 *Id.*
43 *Id.* at 17.
44 *Id.* at 18–19.
45 Letter to the League of Nations (Economic Committee) from the General Secretary of the Permanent International Committee on Timber Production and the Timber Industry and Trade, Feb. 9, 1933, LoN Archives, 10A/381/381 E.802, at 1 (emphasis added).
46 Which was one of its main aims at the beginning of its existence, but which it failed to reach.
47 Letter to the League of Nations (Economic Committee) from the General Secretary of the Permanent International Committee on Timber Production and the Timber Industry and Trade, Feb. 9, 1933, LoN Archives, 10A/381/381 E.802, at 4.

4.2.3 *The Timber Wars of the 1930s*

This section will describe how the timber trade of the 1930s was shaped by two major occurrences: the Great Depression and what major players had described as a Soviet dumping policy that followed it. Both of these had a double impact. First, they had a direct impact on timber on an international scale. Second, as a result, they also had an environmental effect, as people started to blame these economic patterns as the reason for the increasing problem of deforestation.

Like other interwar issues, timber was influenced by certain economic and environmental changes that took place during that time. For instance, significant changes in the global economy were reflected in whaling,[48] and the same is true of the timber trade. At that time, the League was called on by certain players to promote preliminary ideas of international economic governance that could better respond to the global challenges posed by the industrial crises of the 1930s.

As in other areas of international trade, the Great Depression affected timber production and its demand in the markets. This put great pressure on timber industries, which suffered from dropping prices and shrinking trade as the crisis intensified. Economic data at the turn of the 1930s show that trade of sawn timber had decreased by almost 50 percent between the late 1920s and 1932, from approximately forty million cubic meters to just twenty million. Though it recovered to about thirty million cubic meters in 1937, this was still much less than the years before.[49]

Given the impact of the Depression on global demand, one might have expected timber production to fall dramatically after 1929. However, the timber reality of the 1930s was quite different and more complex than that. The crisis did affect the global production and trade of timber, but mostly to the extent that there were fears of overproduction as a result of several key players' economic-political decisions – first and foremost, the Soviet Union.

The Soviets, however, chose to handle the Depression in their own way. For the Soviet Union, aside from wheat, timber was *the* commodity that it could export to finance its own industrialization. After the first dramatic Five-Year-Plan, which overlapped with the Depression, the Soviets sought to achieve their goal of massive industrialization by

[48] For instance, an increase in the popularity of margarine as a cheap alternative to butter made the world's whale oil market an important energy stock. *See* William Cronon's introduction to DORSEY, *supra* note 2, at vii, x.

[49] GROTTIAN, *supra* note 36, at 144–45.

exporting huge quantities of timber abroad in order to cover at least some of the loss due to dropping prices.[50] Given the decreasing prices of raw materials, the Soviet timber industry increased its production. This national policy, which followed the growing American crisis, rapidly became a global problem.

The Soviets' industrial campaign had two central impacts. First, the Five-Year-Plan was responsible for the elimination of huge stretches of forest across the Soviet Union.[51] And second, the USSR's dumping policy seriously worried several timber-producing economies abroad, and the Soviet timber industry's stake in the international market was essential.[52]

Following the double negative impact of both the Depression and the Soviet policy, shrinking trade drove timber-producing countries to action. Fearing an industrial collapse, some national industries descended into bitter competition with one another; this pushed timber industries and forests to a dangerous point. Increased production and the Soviet race to the bottom had no real winners because all industries had fallen on such hard times.[53]

Referring to the interwar period as the period of timber wars is not arbitrary. Timber was significant to the national industries of several countries, and the Soviet reaction to crashing prices did not go unnoticed. In an effort to fight dropping prices and to regain their loss of profits, some countries tried to tackle the double crisis of the Depression and the dumping policy head on. The Canadians, for instance, campaigned massively against Soviet timber, and so did the Finnish, and the Swedish, and several more that were furious with the USSR's harvest policy. The Soviet Union was publicly accused of dumping timber, and these voices pushed for an embargo against Soviet timber exportation.[54] These countries also turned to the Comité to help them

[50] Next to other intensive coercive measures that changed the Soviet agriculture and economy. *See* MARK R. BEISSINGER, SCIENTIFIC MANAGEMENT, SOCIALIST DISCIPLINE, AND SOVIET POWER (1988).

[51] *See* AN ENVIRONMENTAL HISTORY OF RUSSIA 71–135 (Paul Josephson et al. eds., 2013).

[52] *See* the data noted by GROTTIAN, *supra* note 36, at 144–45.

[53] The collapse of the Finnish timber industry, due to falling prices and dropping demand, alarmed other nations that were deeply concerned that they would share the same fate.

[54] The main focus was on Britain. The British, lacking an independent timber industry of their own, relied heavily on imported timber to support major branches of the industry, such as their advanced shipping industry. Although this coalition tried to exert pressure on Britain to join the ban, the British government ultimately refused to do so and continued to import shipments from abroad.

push back against the Soviets and to coordinate their timber policies, trade, and – above all – the market price of timber.

In the face of decreasing global demand and consequent dropping prices, different national timber industries struggled to remain afloat. These interwar difficulties pushed timber-producing countries to turn to international law for help. Most tried to create foreign, transregional, and transnational trade mechanisms, such as cartels and consortiums (first and foremost the Comité) to tackle the timber crisis and overproduction. However, the large majority of these mechanisms, which were developed outside the League, were far from successful.[55]

The concerns of timber industries intersected with the League's own political ambitions, as it had institutional aims of its own to gain support and recognition worldwide. Together, they overlapped in the search for an international solution. Unlike other kinds of transnational collaborations that preceded the League or existed during its time, the League had a greater number of applicable tools to offer. The League entered the timber crisis against this backdrop, just as timber-producing countries were introducing international export agreements in an effort to stabilize the market.

The characteristic of timber, and its influence on the landscape, introduced environmental considerations into the timber discussion. These economic characteristics and historic circumstances overlapped with the League's own agenda to promote modes of international governance. The timber issue was both an opportunity and a challenge to fulfill that. The timber wars allowed for economic interests and industrial incentives to be considered alongside environmental and conservationist agendas. This supported the economic-driven demand to limit and control forest harvest. In the battle to stabilize prices and ensure the survival of the timber industry, the danger of deforestation gained prominence in the timber discussion.

4.3 The Timber Challenge and Concerns of Deforestation: The League Harmonizes Economic, Industrial, and Environmental Perspectives

As the previous sections have shown, timber was a common problem for the Soviet Union, Europe, and North America in the first half of the twentieth century. When the League entered this complicated battlefield

[55] *See* Kuorelahti, *supra* note 6.

of conflicting national and industrial interests, it was acting as an international institution whose chief concern was the economic greater good of the world. The recovery from the results of World War I in terms of civilian and national infrastructures took its toll for several long years. Together with the Soviet dumping policy, it all had a tangible effect on the international trade of goods, and timber in particular. As a result, supporting the global timber industry became a top international priority, since the recovery of different nations' economies also appeared to be dependent on the stability of their timber industries.

This section will show how the timber wars, the resultant trade issues, and the calls for an international timber regime intertwined with environmental concerns and added to the general economic-industrial framework. Seeing how the crisis of 1929 had affected the global demand for timber, some diplomats were also concerned in the 1930s about the environmental outcomes of accelerating timber production on wooded landscapes.

Because timber production was tied to increasing environmental phenomena such as deforestation and erosion, the League eventually began to address the relationship between economic interests regarding the control of timber production, and a growing environmental awareness of the impact of timber production on nature.

The issue of timber production across the world was a meeting point of several different perspectives: economic, industrial, political-institutional,[56] and environmental. In the case of deforestation, I will show that the contrast was particularly stark in terms of timing. No more than one year separated the League's discussions on how to protect forests using international law, and the termination of the League's reign over internationalism. Though the League fought intently to safeguard trees in the late 1930s, World War II brought a swift end to its evolutionary legal process of crafting solutions out of diplomacy.

Section 4.3 comprises two sections. Section 4.3.1 will focus on the continuing efforts of the League (mostly through the Economic Committee) and other international bodies to support the introduction of a binding international timber regulation throughout the 1930s. I will analyze the main events throughout the 1930s, including two international timber conferences that were organized in Berlin (1933) and Vienna (1934) respectively. In Section 4.3.2, I will then address the

[56] The League discussed the timber question as other institutions such as the Comité and the IIA were considering the same tensions.

environmental concerns about the effect of timber production on forests around the world. Here, I will argue that environmental calls were added to the League's existing economic-industrial framework, in which it wished to protect timber industries around the world as well.

4.3.1 *Regulation of the Timber Trade to Support the Industry*

As previously mentioned, the League was already discussing raw materials when the timber trade met with the challenge of the Great Depression and Soviet timber production.[57] Prior to its focus on timber, the League monitored international production and trade of a variety of materials for industrial use and commerce.[58] However, given the obstacles timber-producing countries faced and the League's (and some of its bodies') interests, the League added the timber challenge to its long list of responsibilities in the turbulent 1930s.

Although timber trade had been a topic for some of the League's bodies since 1928–29, the main steps started in 1932. Moreover, the League was using largely the same methods that characterized its legal and diplomatic-bureaucratic procedures in other inquiries, and not just in this case. As the following section will show, these mechanisms included information gathering and sharing, the distribution of formal technical inquiries, and placing technical experts (such as economists) at the forefront of international law and international governance, sometimes ahead of political representatives. At this time, the Economic Committee was primarily involved in tackling issues that reflected different economic perspectives and environmental concerns.

As with other parallel environmental challenges, timber was a professional issue for professional experts. Following the IIA's request for assistance with forestry data a few years earlier in 1926, the Economic Committee in January 1932 sent an invitation to experts from all member states to attend a special professional conference. The conference was to focus on the poor state of the international timber trade. Later that year, in April, delegations of officials, and interest and advocacy groups from fourteen states[59] met in Geneva for a three-day conference. The delegations reconvened in Vienna two months later for another, larger international

[57] K. William Kapp, The League of Nations and Raw Materials: 1919–1939 (1941).

[58] *See* the discussion in Section 4.2.1 above.

[59] Mostly European, but Canada had also joined the initiative.

conference,[60] in which they agreed to establish the Comité International du Bois.

Although the League's Economic Committee did not establish the Comité, the moves and deliberations between these private actors and semi-state organizations were followed by the League's secretariat.[61] As the 1932 conference, for instance, was concluded, two main aims were identified for the future. To achieve these aims, it was recommended that the steady and efficient trade of timber worldwide should be maintained. The first aim was to establish a joint collaboration between states to tackle the dropping prices of timber. The second aim was to promote internationalization and institutionalized supervision of timber production from that point on.

The delegations also specifically agreed – in a rather precedential manner – to establish a central international bureau to monitor and coordinate production, supply, exportation, and imports on an international scale. The Secretariat informed the Economic Committee that these "steady effort[s]," beginning in 1932 "ha[d] been made to stabilise the international timber market."[62]

The conference recommendations called for an internal department or office in Geneva to handle the issue of timber. However, the international bureau of timber that was actually established in practice was an external, and fairly independent, body, working for economic and commercial interests of its members. The Comité was active as a professional international institute from 1932 in Vienna.[63] Like other interwar concerns with which the League was entangled, the timber issue had its own headquarters, a forum, and a routine complete with professional experts, national representatives, reports, and publications. Other departments within the League relied on the Comité's bureaucratic and legal output,

[60] Economic Committee, Timber: International Conferences of Timber-Exporting Countries (Berlin, Dec. 1933; Vienna, Oct. 1934) – Note by the Secretariat, Jan. 18, 1935, LoN Archives, 10A/381/381/E.871, at 1 (hereafter Economic Committee, Timber: Note by the Secretariat).

[61] Series of the League of Nations Publications, Economic Committee: The Timber Problem – Its International Aspects (Series of League of Nations Publications, 1932.II. B.6) (1932), LoN Archives, at 5–12.

[62] Economic Committee, Timber: Note by the Secretariat, *supra* note 60, at 1.

[63] The conceptual question of the possible ties and influence of the League on the Comité might stand in the center of other studies. One can argue that without the security of general internationalism, international frameworks, and legal-institutional mechanisms, an institution like the Comité – an international organization to focus on timber supply and trade concerns – would probably not have been created.

such as papers, proposals for circulation, and drafts as part of an interwar institutional routine.

The will to exert control over areas of law previously considered the domain of sovereign states seems as a rather bold idea. In retrospect, it is impressive that five countries – Roumania, Yugoslavia, Poland, Austria, and Czechoslovakia (the countries that founded the Comité) – who were not leading timber-producing powers, were daring enough to propose the idea of a legally binding quota for timber. Moreover, this move echoed other mechanisms the League discussed in parallel economic-environmental problems: the whaling dilemma, for instance.[64] These legal mechanisms fit the League's advocacy of international management of common natural resources, especially in terms of supervising raw materials.

The joint timber effort got more and more compelling. Although Scandinavian countries were reluctant at first, tough market conditions eventually brought them in. As the Economic Committee explained: "Yet the evolution which has occurred in the international timber market has increasingly lessened the weight of the latter [the Scandinavian countries'] objection."[65]

Sharing the Economic Committee's agenda, the League tried to encourage an international legal-economic arrangement that would overcome the difficulties of the timber trade. In summer 1933, the League also advocated for timber in the World Economic Conference in London (probably because of the lobbying of the Comité). The June–July conference was an international gathering of representatives from more than sixty-five states and lasted almost a month and a half. The conference aimed to reach an agreement on the measures required to overcome the global depression. Different delegations discussed the ways in which international trade could be revived and which steps should be taken to restore international markets and the global economy.[66] In preparation for the conference, the League declared that "the [international economic] settlement should relieve the world."[67] Moreover, during the conference, a subcommittee of technical, economic, and industrial experts further developed the principle of a fixed quota. This

[64] The idea of global quota was fiercely discussed throughout the 1930s, especially concerning the Antarctic waters.

[65] Economic Committee, Timber: Note by the Secretariat, *supra* note 60, at 1.

[66] *See* Rodney J. Morrison, *The London Monetary and Economic Conference of 1933: A Public Goods Analysis*, 52 AM. J. ECON. & SOC. 312 (1993).

[67] Draft Annotated Agenda, C.48.M.18 (Conference M.E.1.) II, LoN Archives, at 7–9.

subcommittee also recommended that the Comité serve as a central international office for timber trade and collaborate with the League's Committee of Statistical Experts and the International Institution of Agriculture. Furthermore, the Comité was to draft relevant recommendations for national-domestic timber production.

Following these preliminary discussions on the supervision of timber, several timber-producing countries agreed to strengthen collaboration at the first International Conference of Timber Exporters, which was convened in Berlin on December 11, 1933. Following the exchange of professional views between experts and representatives, the Berlin Conference introduced a special timber deal based on statistical data.[68] According to the 1933 deal, exports in 1934 were not to exceed those of the previous year. The Economic Committee explained that these arrangements were made based on mutual estimations between the parties, and on an estimate of the world timber requirements that importing countries provided for the year of 1934.[69] In this way, the Comité would be better able to secure stable timber prices globally, control timber trends – and prices, too – and regain the confidence of the international community, whose trust had been lost during the Depression and the Soviet policy. As the Berlin Conference concluded, it declared that it had succeeded "in adjusting supply to demand and that prices could therefore be expected to remain steady during the following season."

In view of the "favourable results" of the Berlin Conference, as the Economic Committee defined them, the participants of the Conference expressed a "unanimous desire" in the summer of 1934 to resume the negotiations and to deepen the modification of international trade.[70] In October, more countries joined the next international meeting, the Vienna Timber Conference. Two important parties joined this timber regime of the Comité. The Director of the Timber Section and the Senior Vice-Chairman of the Export Office arrived from Moscow to represent Soviet interests, which often conflicted with the interests of other timber-producing countries. Moreover, several Baltic states joined the collaboration, including Estonia, Latvia, and Lithuania, which sent a tripartite delegation to Austria consisting of State Forests and the private timber industry.[71] International interest in this timber regime encouraged the

[68] Economic Committee, Timber: Note by the Secretariat, *supra* note 60, at 2.
[69] *Id.*
[70] *Id.*
[71] *Id.* at 3.

Canadian government, for instance, to take part too, and it sent the Commissioner for Timber to the conference.[72]

The efforts seemed to be successful, having gained global attention. The League pointed out that Vienna Conference had gathered representatives from almost "all the countries of the world"[73] who were involved in timber exports. Moreover, the League noted that even states that were absent either followed or were influenced by the international timber regime, and understood that the rules had changed as a result of the ambitious campaign. "In the United States as in Canada, efforts are now being made to set up a central organisation of timber exporters; this would facilitate future participation in international activities."[74] Generally speaking, the Vienna Conference continued the general line of the Berlin Conference of gaining international control over timber production, as the delegates were of the "unanimous opinion" that the 1933 deal should be updated: exports would need to be 10 percent below the quota of sawn timber, and quantities would need to be reduced in 1935 accordingly.[75]

Some of the subsequent steps in this monitoring policy did not actually take place under the formal auspices of the League, such as the timber exporters' organizations agreement of November 1935, signed in Copenhagen.[76] However, the League's international and procedural routines reflected a certain pattern that we can trace, as it might influenced other neighboring frameworks that were working toward ad hoc cooperation. Some of the ways in which the League practiced its legal arrangements are reflected in the Copenhagen trade agreement of 1935. The central articles of the agreement were to be renewed and reapproved annually by the signing parties, just as the League used to revise formal arrangements after a certain period when it addressed economic-environmental issues.[77]

[72] *Id.*

[73] *Id.* With the exception of Norway, Yugoslavia, and the United States. As for the Americans, the memorandum mentioned that they nevertheless "showed their interest by proposing to send a Government representative as observer." (*Id.* at 3).

[74] *Id.*

[75] *Id.* at 4.

[76] The European Timber Exporters' Convention (ETEC) – and its predecessors, the gentlemen's agreements of 1933 and 1934 – provided for export quotas and voluntary production restrictions of Europe's softwood and lumber industry. *See* S. V. CIRIACY-WANTRUP, RESOURCE CONSERVATION: ECONOMICS AND POLITICS 325 (1952).

[77] Such as in the case of the international whaling regulations of the 1930s (both the 1931 Convention and that of 1937). *See* the discussion in Chapter 2.

The supervision of timber – and the binding quota in particular – is an example of how and to what extent the interwar world turned away from ad hoc initiatives and procedures, which had characterized earlier international campaigns, including environmental ones. The League explicitly pointed out this principle of continuity after the conferences in Berlin and Vienna had concluded. The League distanced the new proposed regime from earlier attempts to regulate timber production through international law:

> Mention should be made of a final – perhaps the most important – result of the Conference: it was unanimously resolved that meetings of the same kind should be held at least once a year . . . . This resolution should *prevent a repetition of the slumps* which occurred so often . . . . and should help to reinforce confidence. Under this advisory agreement, the various competent organisations will be able to take *speedy and energetic action* when the situation requires . . . a common line of policy . . . . It will therefore be possible . . . to discuss the international problems connected with timber on the *widest scale* and with the assistance of all the competent organisations.[78]

Was is the League's daily work as an institution that triggered and reignited the discussion on timber and did not let it become obscured or marginalized by other pressing problems? Perhaps. One way of the other, this procedural legal mechanism of the Copenhagen agreement, which is an interwar example, would last until World War II.[79]

In summer 1936, the Economic Committee concluded the implications of the Depression and the Soviet dumping policy: "The forestry industry has suffered for some years from over-production, while, at the same time, consumption has been restricted."[80] Despite the international ongoing efforts, the dumping still posed a very real threat. According to that report, prices in 1935 dropped by 25 percent on average compared with 1934 but improved thereafter, mainly as a result of the Copenhagen agreement. The League concluded at that stage that although prices were "extremely low," thanks to international cooperation (simply put, trade control), these prices had "risen steadily since the conclusion of the

[78] Economic Committee, Timber: Note by the Secretariat, *supra* note 60, at 5 (emphasis added).

[79] On the history of the European Timber Exporters' Convention *see* Jorma Ahvenainen, *The Competitive Position of the Finnish Sawmill Industry in the 1920s and 1930s*, 33 SCANDINAVIAN ECON. HIST. REV. 173 (1985).

[80] Report by the Economic Committee on International Economic Collaboration: Regional Agreements, Various Manifestations, Producers' Agreements, June 5, 1936, LoN Archives, 10A/381/381/xv, at 18 (hereafter Report by the Economic Committee, June 5).

[Copenhagen] Agreement, and [were] now approaching a fairly satisfactory level . . . ."[81]

The League continued to deal with timber regulation in the years that followed. As I will elaborate in the next section, the Nineteenth Ordinary Session of the League Assembly, held in September 1938, focused on the issues of timber production and deforestation and brought together economic-industrial interests and environmental goals. Whereas other environmental discussions at the League reveal tensions caused by *competing* economic and environmental perspectives, in the case of timber, calls for an international regime (even if an external one, led by the Comité) and fears of deforestation went hand in hand – an interwar example of economic-environmental harmony. The Depression's impact on timber production and forestation was raised in the minutes of the Economic Committee during the September Session of the Assembly.

This discussion might be linked to parallel discussions on international economic policy at the time and the role the League could and should play in it. "There is no need . . . to stress the importance of the discussions we shall have on the general economic situation. It is quite possible that the general framework of our society would not survive another crisis equal in severity to what we call 'The Great Depression.'"[82] In order to fight dumping and decreasing prices, harvest or exploitation of natural resources had to be placed under a global trade regime:

> Therefore, whatever concerted action we may be able to take . . . . whether with regard to setting up buffer stocks to reduce the extreme variability of raw materials prices, or whether with regard to the avoidance of mutually harmful policies, in so far as we are successful, there will be no measuring our reward in human happiness and content.[83]

Eventually, the timber question resulted in the entanglement of mass production, forest overexploitation, and deforestation with international law and governance. Instead of the free movement of goods and classic ideas of liberal capitalism, the League supported a much more systematic and regulated environment of trade *through* the issue of timber. "The

[81] *Id.* at 18.

[82] Records of the 19th Ordinary Session of the Assembly, Meetings of the Committees, Minutes of the 2d Committee (Economic, Financial, and Transit Questions), Special Supplement No. 185, League of Nations Official Journal (1938), Annex 1, A.64.1938.II.B, LoN Archives, at 24 (hereafter Records of the 19th Ordinary Session). This quote is taken out of a speck of the former Australian Prime Minister Stanley M. Bruce (read by his substitute, F. L. McDougall).

[83] *Id.*

scientific investigations carried out in the Economic Intelligence Service . . . have paved the way for this enquiry into the practical measures which . . . prevent or mitigate trade depressions." The League concluded that this kind of (deep) institutional involvement "will prove a most striking example of the value of international consultation and collaboration."[84]

The turbulence of timber production and the bitter national-economic rivalries of the 1930s seemed to push aside other general and more acceptable economic conventions. To the League, the crisis of raw materials, particularly timber, justified turning to other means of dealing with international (economic) relations. "The appropriate policies for mitigating depressions may vary from country to country," the League admitted in late 1938. But it was clear that "unless we have an effective international centre for the joint consideration of such methods and their repercussions, we can hardly hope to find means of bringing the phenomena of the trade cycle under control."[85]

Moreover, in the case of international concern over raw materials other than timber, the League was actually advocating for bilateral negotiations and it encouraged states to reach any relevant agreement amongst themselves. In fact, one of the League's publications mentioned that the Economic Committee "insists"[86] that sight should not be lost of the object of restoring a greater degree of freedom and economic liberalism in the international exchange of goods that were not timber. In the case of other raw materials, these modes of operating international law and governance were, at that time, "perhaps the most promising method that can be used to realise the objects set out in the resolutions of recent Assemblies." Control, supervision, and coordination seemed to be specific *only* to the issue of timber: "In particular, is it important that all Governments should refrain at the present time from any measures which are likely to depress still further the prices . . . on world markets . . . ."[87]

Furthermore, the ways in which the League pushed to introduce a regulated regime for timber trade is intriguing when one takes into

[84] *Id.*

[85] *Id.* at 25.

[86] Draft Report of the Economic Committee, May 20, 1939, LoN Archives, 10A/37915/1952 (E.1081), at 1.

[87] Records of the 19th Ordinary Session of the Assembly, Meetings of the Committees, Minutes of the 2d Committee (Economic, Financial, and Transit Questions), Special Supplement No. 185, Annex 1: Economic and Financial Questions: Report of the Second Committee to the Assembly, A.64.1938.II.B., League of Nations Official Journal (1938), at 64.

account the worsening geopolitical context. Times were tough, especially in the late 1930s with tensions increasing among the Berlin-Rome-Tokyo Axis as their respective powers grew, which dramatically endangered collective security and peacekeeping – the original assignments for which the League was established.[88]

Zooming out, both primary economic aims and environmental concerns widened the stage of institutional internationalism and enabled other, noninvolved states to participate in the creation of international law. The League itself emphasized the need to expand its political framework. The role and contribution of these economic-environmental dimensions were central to such action:

> [W]e shall all recognize that, while the absence of certain great nations from our counsels is a serious handicap to our work, it need not prevent us from making great progress in the economic field. Here we have the co-operation of the United States . . . and of certain other nations who are not members of the League. We shall be fortified by the realisation that effective progress towards greater . . . stability and human betterment cannot be without beneficial repercussions in the political field.[89]

Giving this backdrop, the Nineteenth Session of the Assembly (also) on the matter of deforestation allowed for broader considerations that included not only economic and industrial aspects, but also obvious environmental ones. In these times of severe international problems, the League decided to address the challenge of timber and deforestation as an issue.

4.3.2 Environmental Concerns Added to the General Economic-Industrial Framework

As briefly discussed earlier, the League encouraged the development of an ambitious timber regime in the 1930s to ensure the survival of the timber industry. This campaign was mostly promoted by other international organizations that were active during the interwar period. The League was focused on the Depression's economic impact on timber as a priority raw material; however, the protection of forests from rapid,

[88] On the other hand, one could argue that the oncoming war should have increased the League's motivation to deal with raw materials that were crucial to war and economic resilience during times of expected hardship.

[89] Records of the 19th Ordinary Session of the Assembly: Minutes of the 2d Committee (Economic, Financial, and Transit Questions), Special Supplement No. 185, Sept. 22, 1938 League of Nations Official Journal (1938), Annex 1, A.64.1938.II.B., at 26.

intensive, or inefficient industrial timber production entailed other considerations. The League realized that it was not only dropping prices that were of concern, but also the natural landscape, which had been suffering from rapid development and industrial activity. These environmental concerns added a new dimension to the economic-industrial framework and the voices that aimed to stabilize the timber industries.

Certain bodies and representatives within the League encouraged it to focus on the environmental effects of timber production on wooded landscapes. This environmental and conservationist awareness evolved gradually until it reached a peak in the late 1930s. However, the League was not of one mind on how to tackle this aspect of the timber issue. Some bodies, primarily the Economic Committee, enthusiastically supported international cooperation in timber trade in order to secure profitable prices and to protect the industry. Other voices, and mostly certain delegations, had suddenly realized that the cost of a full-scale industrial and economic initiative – not to mention the alleged rapid Soviet forest harvest – could have devastating impacts on nature.

The first time we can identify the link between timber production and deforestation in the League's discussions is during the preparations and preliminary discussions of the Economic Committee between 1937 and 1938. In a summary of one of the Economic Committee's discussions in December 1937 on the difficulties of timber trade, the Committee identified the need to protect forests from overexploitation. The summary went on to describe how, at its third meeting, the Committee examined a document about the development of natural resources with regard to forest preservation in different mandated lands. Pietro Stoppani, the Director of the Economic Relations Section of the Economic Committee at that time, pointed out that "certain activities were reserved for nationals, while the development of forestry was subject to certain restrictions connected with their preservation irrespective of the nationality of the persons developing them."[90] Following that, the French representative to the discussion, Paul Elbel[91] (with whom we shall soon become more closely acquainted), noted that in the case of the exploitation of forests as a natural resource, certain guarantees should be provided "against any intensive and abusive exploitation by foreigners

90 Summary of the Discussions of the Economic Committee at its 47th Session held at Geneva (Dec. 6–9, 1937), Mar. 7, 1937, LoN Archives, 10A/31956/1952, at 4 (hereafter Summary of the Discussions of the Economic Committee at its 47th Session).

91 P. Elbel, Deputy, Honorary Director of Agreements, French Ministry of Commerce, and a member of the Economic Committee during the 1930s.

of the resources of a colonial territory to the detriment of the present or future interests of the natives."[92]

As they discussed the need for the international regulation of timber trade, Elbel – and later the Economic Committee – became aware of the environmental costs of industrial timber activity. I will show, however, that these economic and environmental considerations did not conflict with each other as they had in other issues the League handled, such as in the case of whaling or oil pollution of the sea. On the contrary, these concerns complemented the Comité's endeavors (and the League's support) to assist the timber industry during hard times, when dropping prices, dumping, and overproduction were rife. These belated environmental or conservationist concerns of disappearance of forests[93] became enmeshed with industrial and commercial restrictions, which international organizations (including the League) wish to use in order to control the timber trade.

In July 1938, the Economic Committee decided to refer the issue of nature protection to the Assembly, the League's broadest international forum. In a draft of the Report of the Forty-Eighth Session of the Economic Committee, the Director mentioned that "Monsieur Elbel . . . [has] drawn the Committee's attention to the *danger of deforestation* in several parts of the world . . . ."[94] Moreover, unlike the timber report from the Nineteenth Ordinary Session of the Assembly (which would be held in September later that year), this report did not express nearly as much concern for other raw materials, such as oil, silver, cotton, or sugar, as it did for timber and forests. "Finally, the attention of the Committee was

[92] Summary of the Discussions of the Economic Committee at its 47th Session, *supra* note 90, at 5.

[93] One might argue that the French warnings of advancing deforestation did not match the reality on the ground. However, the question of whether or not there was a (real) deforestation problem in certain regions in the 1930s is not the main focus of this study. At any rate, reflections on this concern attended the League's ongoing discussion on deforestation as an international problem, and as a challenge for international law. James Webb, for instance, has studied the gap between the *impression* of deforestation as a result of industrial campaign and the *reality* on the ground. In his study on the clearing of the highlands of Sri Lanka, Webb argued that this is the largest case of tropical deforestation in the nineteenth-century British Empire. Owing to the difficulty of the mountainous terrain, the trees were simply burned on site. However, no tropical woods entered the international market. JAMES L. A. WEBB, TROPICAL PIONEERS: HUMAN AGENCY AND ECOLOGICAL CHANGE IN THE HIGHLANDS OF SRI LANKA, 1800–1900 (2002).

[94] (Draft) Report on the 48th Session of the Economic Committees held at Geneva, July 4–9, 1938, Oct. 19, 1938, LoN Archives, 10A/34675/1952 (E.1046), at 25 (emphasis added).

drawn to the dangers of deforestation and soil erosion in various parts of the world and the Committee decided to request the Economic and Financial Organisation[95] to study this question in collaboration with the International Institute of Agriculture."[96]

The preliminary discussions of the Economic Committee laid the foundation for the general discussion on the problem of deforestation that was to be held at the Assembly. The report declared: "[I]t was decided that the Economic Committee should draw the Assembly's attention to the advisability of investigation of the problem, and of conducting the investigation in collaboration with the International Institute of Agriculture."[97]

The Economic Committee did indeed draw the Assembly's attention to the question of deforestation and how it was entangled with the international timber regime. A couple of months after the Economic Committee's

[95] *See* note 10.

[96] Records of the 19th Ordinary Session of the Assembly, Meetings of the Committees, Minutes of the 2d Committee (Economic, Financial, and Transit Questions), Special Supplement No. 185, Annex 1: Economic and Financial Questions: Report of the Second Committee to the Assembly, A.64.1938.II.B., League of Nations Official Journal (1938), at 65.

[97] (Draft) Report on the 48th Session of the Economic Committees held at Geneva, July 4–9, 1938, Oct. 19, 1938, LoN Archives, 10A/34675/1952 (E.1046), at 25.

One can notice certain differences between the Economic Committee (which in this case represented Elbel's environmental concerns) and the Assembly, as they were reflected in the work of the editor who prepared the draft report. This analysis offers some insights into the layers of legal texts and possible meanings of their geology. A comparison of the texts prepared for the formal published conclusion of the Economic Committee's recommendations to the Assembly (and the League as a whole) could reveal the hidden agenda of certain officials who tried to downplay some of the environmental concerns.

The first draft of the report on the 48th Session of the Committee, handed in to the Committee's Chairman (F. van Langenhove), summarized Elbel's environmental warning reluctantly. The original minutes used the word "however" before presenting Elbel's argument against the outcome of increasing timber production around the world. Chairman van Langenhove, however, seems to have been more supportive of Elbel than the original drafter. He removed the wary tone of the first draft by dropping the word "however," which somehow strengthened Elbel's call to immediately recruit the League.

But on the other hand, the Chairman was also more cautious than the original drafter (and Elbel himself, probably) in other parts of the discussion. While the original report declared that the Economic Committee "*would* draw the Assembly's attention" to the concern of deforestation and encourage it to conduct a special investigation, the Chairman preferred to articulate the conclusion with more (legal) room for interpretation and possible action (if any) in the future; he replaced the word "would" with "should."

Publication, Report (Economic Committee) to the Council on the Work of its 48th Session (Held in Geneva from July 4–9, 1938), July 11, 1938, LoN Archives, C.233. M.132.1938.II.B., at 5.

preparations, the Nineteenth Ordinary Session of the Assembly was held in September 1938. It followed up on the Committee's recommendations and dealt also with the problem of deforestation. The discussion in the Assembly shows that the League used as a forum in which certain voices publicly started to acknowledge that the timber question merged the international community's industrial-economic aims with environmental concerns over rapidly advancing deforestation and erosion worldwide. In this way, the environmental concerns that the League discussed *supported* the original mission to regulate international timber trade and protect the industry.

Almost six years after the League had first begun to discuss the timber issue – at the meeting of experts in January 1932 in Geneva – the League now began to consider the environmental impact of industrial timber activity, and not merely as a side effect of timber production. Elbel, the French diplomat, asked for an inquiry into the state of global deforestation, given the increasing production of timber.

As the Assembly discussed the issue of worsening deforestation, it took the opportunity to align the international situation of trees with environmental history. According to that discussion, this "period of intense [economic] civilisation" was not the first time humanity had faced this kind of challenge:

> In antiquity also, great civilisations had been destroyers of forests. . . . [In] the case of China, where vast regions were a prey to soil erosion as the result of the disappearance of trees, and that of the Tigris and Euphrates had caused those rivers to silt up, and would perhaps mark the close of civilisation already thousands of years old.[98]

The Assembly also discussed the ways in which both Europe and Northern Africa had suffered from "similar devastations" in the matter of diminishing forests and wooded landscapes. At that time, there was awareness of the conflicting human interests this entailed:

> That was a problem that could not fail to interest the League both from the human point of view and from the commercial standpoint, which was the special province of the [Economic] Committee. Forests were not merely valuable agents in regulating climates and protecting rivers; they also constituted an immense reservoir for raw materials which was being depleted with alarming rapidity.[99]

[98] Records of the 19th Ordinary Session of the Assembly: Minutes of the 2d Committee (Economic, Financial, and Transit Questions), Special Supplement No. 185, Sept. 22, 1938 League of Nations Official Journal (1938), Annex 1, A.64.1938.II.B., at 27.

[99] *Id.*

As in the (parallel) case of whales and whaling, the interwar discussion was focused on the tensions and interests of a powerful industry that was in need of a constant supply of a shrinking natural resource. This particular case substituted whales for forests, but the core problem was the same. Instead of large marine mammals, this time trees were being depleted across the West and elsewhere. "The cellulose industries . . . were amongst those to which the future seemed to offer ever greater possibilities. Cellulose could not be replaced as a raw material, and trees would be difficult to replace as a vehicle for the production of cellulose."[100] Moreover, an increase in industrialized processes and mass production raised the value and demand for trees as a natural resource: "The developments of modern civilisation and of the numerous uses to which cellulose was put – newsprint in particular – constituted a terrible danger to forests throughout the world."[101]

According to the discussion in the Assembly, the global situation of the survival of forests was urgent – and not just in Europe. The reported data revealed a terrible reality: the Assembly's Session records claimed that two-thirds of forests in the United States had already "disappeared."[102] Similarly, though vast reserves still existed in neighboring Canada, the Canadian government was alarmed at the steady rate of decline of forests. According to that warning, Scandinavian countries were also suffering from a rapid and dangerous industrial hunger that had led to severe deforestation: no less than "fifty per cent of the former wooded areas had ceased to exist." Additional records of the Assembly concluded that the situation "was no less alarming" in Central Europe.

The French delegation recommended that the League take up the fight against deforestation. France further argued that the issue should be brought to the Economic Committee's notice, since its mechanisms and legal-diplomatic routine were better suited to handle the issue than anything the League as a whole was able to offer. In September 1938, the Assembly also noted that forestation and deforestation were indeed relevant for international regulations and solutions, such as the fixed timber-quota mechanism for annual production in 1934 and 1935 (to which each timber-producing country would commit to produce or export no more than its annual reported yield of that year). Therefore,

[100] *Id.*
[101] *Id.*
[102] *Id.*

additional cooperation between international institutions was needed. "Obviously ... the investigation should be undertaken in co-operation with the International Institute of Agriculture," the Report concluded.

By calling for further investigation, the League not only induced other relevant and professional international institutions to join a mutual campaign to save forests around the world, but also promised – for the sake of humanity – that it would "be rendering a service to every one of the countries represented ... and indeed *to* mankind ... ."[103]

The French government was anxious to see an international investigation of the consequences of these measures of supporting industrial production of timber on the condition of forests around the world. The Nineteenth Ordinary Session of the Assembly also emphasized that one of the most troubling resulting problems of this economic progress in the field of timber was the phenomenon of deforestation. According to the French delegation, the League had been notified of these evolving problems "prior to that point ... ." Moreover, the delegation pointed to the "question of deforestation" as one of the "certain great problems to which Governments could not remain indifferent."[104]

The League was certainly not indifferent to deforestation. Some parties urged it to work on a solution to deforestation as part of the timber question. As an institution seeking to strengthen its own authority and legitimacy worldwide, the League was interested in placing the issue of deforestation on its agenda, and was even motivated to solve it. The Assembly, in that sense, served as a forum for promoting this question in a most explicit and direct manner: "Deforestation was one of the perils threatening mankind, and it was all the more to be feared because it always corresponded to a period of intense civilisation."[105] War was definitely on the horizon, and the fragile future was tangible even during the League's discussions on deforestation. Whereas raw materials (and timber too, of course) were considered necessary goods to support the state economy during difficult times, concern for nature in times of war seemed to be a secondary consideration.

In its report to the Assembly from September 1938, as the Economic Committee considered possible recommended actions concerning

103 Records of the 19th Ordinary Session of the Assembly: Minutes of the 2d Committee (Economic, Financial, and Transit Questions), Special Supplement No. 185, Sept. 22, 1938 League of Nations Official Journal (1938), Annex 1, A.64.1938.II.B., at 27 (emphasis added).

104 *Id.* at 26.

105 *Id.* at 26–27.

deforestation,[106] it explicitly referred to the unstable geopolitical context. The Swedish rapporteur, M. B. Ohlin, explained that the Committee should focus on questions relating to international economic collaboration and the present world economic situation of the late 1930s. However, the Committee claimed that the reports it possessed on the issue of raw materials control showed that

> in the present state of political tension and economic instability, it is not possible to take any joint action in these matters along the lines contemplated in the resolution of the last Assembly . . . . [C]oncerted international action could not be fruitfully undertaken with regard either to exchange control or to raw materials at the present time.[107]

In spite of widespread global tension, the French delegation and the Assembly encouraged the League not to dismiss the issue of deforestation just because war was looming. Deforestation was once again placed on the agenda for the following general Session of the Assembly, set for early spring 1939. In preparation for the next discussion, the Economic Committee worked on the dangers of both deforestation and soil erosion.[108]

Moreover, in the 105th meeting of the League's Council that followed in May 1939, the Economic Committee was encouraged to sketch out a plan for a joint international effort to control timber production *with* the aim of stopping deforestation. However, in light of the geopolitical tension of the late 1930s, the Committee declined. The Committee explained that the political context and lack of stability made it impossible to create any joint effort in the matter of deforestation and to restrain timber production and trade, which had slowly been recovering from the economic crises of the early 1930s.

Unlike 1938, when the League was relatively deeply involved in trying to solve the problem of deforestation, 1939 marked a shift in that willingness to accept the challenge. Perhaps it was the sound of swords being honed, or perhaps the League preferred to better invest its energy and power before they were compromised by the threat of Nazi Germany. And perhaps there were other reasons for that. The final stages of the deforestation issue were not very optimistic. The League did

[106] Records of the 19th Ordinary Session of the Assembly: Minutes of the 2d Committee (Economic, Financial, and Transit Questions), League of Nations Official Journal, Special Supplement No. 184, Annex 1, A.64.1938.II.B., at 62.

[107] *Id.* 62.

[108] Agenda for the 49th Session of the Economic Committee (Mar. 27, 1939), Mar. 8, 1939, LoN Archives, 10A/35687/1952 (E.1066), at 7–8.

generally support an international solution to fight increasing deforestation. Moreover, the discussion was starting to move toward sketching international legal measures to address deforestation, such as strengthening the binding timber quotas.[109] However, war broke out and disrupted these relatively early plans to handle the crisis of shrinking forests.

Following the Assembly's Nineteenth Ordinary Session in 1939, the Economic Committee continued, on the one hand, to discuss the problem. However, and on the other hand, it seems as it tried to bury the new initiative. Similarly, the Assembly did not seem to be as motivated as before, even attempting to remove itself from the anti-deforestation initiative. Under the fifth subtitle of its summary, "Soil Erosion, Deforestation and Reafforestation," the Committee concluded the ways in which it would carry out the recommendations of the last Assembly.[110] This time however, the involvement of other organizations did not serve as a basis for mutual cooperation – as it did in many of the League's other interwar endeavors – but rather as a justification for leaving the table. The draft of the final report to the League's Council concluded:

> In the course of the investigation undertaken by the Secretariat, it was revealed that various organisations throughout the world are engaged in far-reaching enquiries into the problem . . . . The Imperial Bureau of Soil Science in England is showing particular activity in this field, and keeps the appropriate authorities in various countries regularly informed of action taken.[111]

The Economic Committee also mentioned Elbel, the driving force behind the League's developing awareness of the link between timber production and its environmental outcomes. Perhaps it did so to justify its withdrawal from the fight against deforestation. The Committee asked Elbel

[109] Based on the 1933–34 national yield. Unfortunately, these preliminary solutions for possible global timber regulation did not develop as the special conferences in Berlin (1933) and Vienna (1934) had hoped. Although the double quota decision was articulated in each of the timber conferences' resolutions, it was not obligatory. (*See* Report by the Economic Committee: International Conference of Timber-Exporting Countries, Jan. 18, 1935, LoN Archives, 10A/381/381/E.871, at 4).

[110] Summary of the Discussions Held and Decisions Taken at the Economic Committee's 49th Session (Mar. 27–29, 1939), Apr. 24, 1939, LoN Archives, 10A/3784/1952 (E.1080), at 3.

[111] Drafts of the Economic Committee's Report to the Council on the Work of its 49th Session (Held at Geneva from Mar. 27–30, 1939), Apr. 3, 1939, LoN Archives, C.116. M.70.1939.II.B, at 7.

himself "to indicate the direction to be pursued by the Secretariat's investigation."

As the Economic Committee prepared to adjourn the ongoing discussion on deforestation, it composed three consecutive drafts of a report and intended to publish the final version. The differences between the drafts are clear. The first (internal) preliminary draft discussed the status quo of forests using stronger language than the drafts that followed. This draft focused mainly on the worrying problems associated with deforestation, and on suggested solutions: "Elbel points out that one of the most effective remedies for deterioration of the soil is the cessation of deforestation, followed by reafforestation."[112] The first draft also mentioned the importance of the support of professional experts in this regard: "Expert authorities all agree that erosion is greater wherever the soil's covering of vegetation, especially trees, shrinks or disappears. This phenomenon seems to be common wherever erosion occurs, even if any other protective measure than that of reafforestation be employed."

Moreover, in the first version, Elbel further pointed out that in view of the "rapid exhaustion" of those forests that provide the material for paper pulp, "it is in the economic interest of the States not merely to discourage deforestation, but to increase their forest resources and to select with care those kinds of timber to plant."[113]

Whereas in the first draft, states and experts specifically were calling for the need to stop deforestation and erosion, the second draft[114] was more general, stating only that "several members" had drawn attention to these issues. Moreover, rather than using the term "danger,"[115] the Committee instead described the great "damage" that was caused by large-scale deforestation when it was not followed by reafforestation.

The Institute of Agriculture, as the League suggested, seemed to provide a perfect solution at that problematic unstable time. The League recommended that the IIA deal with the issue of deforestation instead of the League. Perhaps the League's desire to relinquish its responsibility for deforestation is also evident in the final draft of the Committee's report. This version stated that "the great damage caused by

[112] *Id.*

[113] *Id.* at 7–8.

[114] Drafts of the Economic Committee's Report to the Council on the Work of its 49th Session (Held at Geneva from Mar. 27–30, 1939), Apr. 3, 1939, LoN Archives, C.116. M.70.1939.II.B (all three drafts are included in the same dossier).

[115] This time, the Committee did not use the term "danger," as the Assembly had during its Nineteenth Ordinary Session.

soil erosion" was not entirely or necessarily ascribed to the phenomenon of deforestation alone. Perhaps, as the Committee suggested on page three, there were also "other causes" of the problem.

This time, the parallel involvement of multiple other international organizations led the League to withdraw from the discussion. The League preferred to allow other bodies to take the lead.

Given what we know of parallel environmental challenges, it seems likely that had this been another time, and had the League not been on the brink of collapse in the middle of 1939, things might have been different. Dramatic periods like the late 1930s highlight the ambivalence of institutional internationalism at the time. When it came to other dilemmas that the League was entangled in, it seemed determined to maintain its superiority over the other parties (and institutions) involved; however, trying times had affected its resilience. Whereas the League's rise reflected a shift from transnationalism to intense internationalism – governed from its headquarters in Geneva – its fall marked a retreat to "traditional" transnationalism in favor of other institutions, which were encouraged to take the lead *instead* of the League. "Several national institutions, public or private, are keeping information on this subject up to date and are continually revising it." The League withdrew from the problem of deforestation, pointing out:

> During recent years, the particular question of the prevention of deforestation and the encouragement of reafforestation has been discussed at several international congresses .... [I]n these circumstances, the [Economic] Committee is inclined to think that any enquiries or studies on this subject that it undertook might, for the moment at any rate, *duplicate* others which are already completed or are still in progress.[116]

Who knows? With an alternative hypothetical history of the League of Nations – one that did not have to become "the interwar period" and whose existence would have extended beyond September 1, 1939 – perhaps the history of deforestation (and the crisis of timber prices) in the world of international law could have ended differently. If Germany had not started World War II that summer, would Elbel – like his contemporary colleague Professor José Léon Suarez, who fiercely advocated for the restriction of the whaling industry to prevent the extinction of whale species – have allowed the Economic Committee and the League to dodge

[116] Economic Committee's Report to the Council on the Work of its 49th Session (Held at Geneva from Mar. 27–30, 1939), Apr. 3, 1939, LoN Archives, 10A/37843/37843, C.116. M.70.1939.II.B, at 3 (emphasis added).

his persistent demands to combat deforestation with tools of international law? This kind of question cannot, of course, be answered.

However, what we have is the history as it was and as it unfolded, on record. The summary of March 1939 stated, "An exchange of views took place to ascertain in what directions the Committee could usefully take action in this field," showing that the Economic Committee was not as willing to pursue the mission against deforestation. However, though the League tended to respond to other missions ahead of deforestation, it did not abandon forests entirely. International law was still being used, to an extent, to address environmental concerns. The future looked bleak, but the League still thought it would prevail and made plans for summer/autumn 1939:

> It feels, however, that the question might usefully be taken up again as a part of the work of the European Conference on Rural Life planned for the autumn. Some of the countries participating in that Conference are experiencing ... the harmful effects of erosion, due mainly to deforestation. Their attention might with advantage be drawn to the experiments made in other countries to check this adverse development.[117]

History, however, had other plans. Regretfully, neither the Conference on Rural Life – to which the Economic Committee happily handed over the task of protecting the forests – nor the general global interest in stopping deforestation, became a reality that year. Hitler's armies stormed Europe, driving the world into chaos.

4.4 Conclusions: A (Comparative) Glimpse of the post-1945 Period, Forest Conservation, and International Law

As I have shown, forests gained substantial attention during the interwar period. The League's involvement in the discussion on international timber trade and the ways in which it discussed international deforestation provide ground for new discoveries. Even if they have eventually failed, these attempts – and especially the will – to put timber trade under supervision, and the need to fight deforestation, seemed to found common ground. These two aspects can assist us in two ways.

First, they can contribute to the mapping of those ideas that shaped the League's environmental regime as a whole. And second, they can assist us in better understanding the historical evolution of international environmental law and environmentalism in general. As mentioned previously, scholars have studied many different chapters of forestation and deforestation, both

[117] *Id.*

prior to the interwar period and after. Nevertheless, the history of deforestation during the interwar period – like the study of other interwar environmental issues – has remained mostly untouched.

Nature and the environment in the interwar period were, to a certain extent, a secondary aspect of a broader – and more urgent – economic campaign. The focus on economic-industrial problems in a time of global financial crisis revealed interconnected environmental concerns, which then became part of the League's developing agenda.

Nevertheless, it must be stressed that this study does not aim to "color" the discussions, reports, and diplomatic activity as more environmental than they really were. In my analysis, I distinguish between the commercial-industrial and the environmental aspects of interwar forestry policy. According to the recorded discussions, it was the economic agenda that took precedence. Environmental and conservationist perspectives played only a supporting role. In some cases that I have examined, these voices were mostly concerned with the future implications of the overexploitation of forests as a source of timber; others feared overproduction and dumping. The interwar discourse was rather different than our own. Indeed, the unexpected harmony between supporting the timber trade and protecting the future of forests was not always discussed as an environmental concern. The League, as well as the independent bodies involved, primarily talked in terms of sustainability and economic support in its efforts to ensure the efficient trade of timber – particularly when it was dealing with the Great Depression and the claimed Soviet dumping policy.

Moreover, the relations between intensive (but inefficient) timber production and deforestation were seldom discussed as a necessary consideration to balance economic growth and the protection of nature. Compared with other interwar environmental problems, such as the whaling dilemma or oil pollution of the sea, the tension between competing interests in timber was not as overt. The League became aware of the outcomes of uncontrolled forest harvest for industrial reasons, not because of a clash between interests. Unlike other economic-environmental challenges of that period, where industry (such as whaling companies and shipping lobbies that advocated for industrial interests on the matter of international whaling law or antipollution of sea by oil convention) and the pro-environment missionaries often came into conflict, in the matter of timber, these parties were on the same side.[118]

[118] Such as P. Elbel, the French representative to the discussion of the Economic Committee, and one of the leading characters in the timber story.

While exploring the role of the League – and that of other bodies that were involved in the timber issue – one might be tempted to question the League's "practical" involvement. In other words, did the League have some kind of impact on the ground and on forests in particular? Did it influence international law of that time?

This retrospective of the interwar period does not point to changes and reactions at the national-domestic level. Moreover, its aim is not to focus entirely on the legal (and practical, if any) outcomes of the increasingly scientific, economic, technical, and professional discourse on the combined issues of timber, deforestation, and erosion. The bottom line is that no new binding legal solutions were finalized during the interwar period to tackle the timber and deforestation crisis. In contrast, in the parallel dilemmas of whaling and oil pollution of the sea, relatively developed legal mechanisms were employed. In the case of timber, the League never reached the same stage in legal terms, such as through treaties and conventions. All in all, apart from the preliminary idea for a timber quota based on the annual yield of 1933–34, the League did not introduce any "practical" solutions or legally articulated instruments to solve the problem. Possible critique of my analysis might claim that the agreements and the more formal export cartel had been made between private or semi-state commercial actors to regulate production and trade, and that they were not legally binding in the sense to which traditional international lawyers refer. However, history, (legal) discourse, primary sources, and historical context as well are up for our cautious interpretation – or several competing interpretations.

Influence, however, does not necessarily mean success. Our current study of the role of the League should also focus on the failures of legal arrangements, and on ways to better understand and interpret them. An evaluation of the League's actions in terms of international law reveals another claim. A comparative analysis of later, and even current, developments sheds a different light on the interwar period. After the fall of the League[119] and the rise of later more developed international

[119] On the one hand, one might claim that WWII was a high time of international activity in the field of forest products. In 1939, an international forestry organization was founded (which officially was a sub-institution of the IIA). But on the other hand, it was in fact an instrument of Nazi efforts to gain control over European forest resources and timber industry. This Berlin-based organization developed a most intense research activity in forestry and wood utilization, including the establishment of sophisticated techniques to measure and eventually control timber flows internationally. During the war, little "authentic" international activity took place in the field. The Comité found kind of exile in the United States in 1941. Its Secretary-General, Egon Glesinger, tried to

organizations, the problem of deforestation seemed to stay locked mainly within the realm of international education and publicity, and did not lead to concrete binding legal measures[120] – at least none that the interwar international bodies were trying to introduce, even if only in a preliminary way.

Perhaps the League's failure to fight deforestation with tools of international law had an effect on international environmental law, at least to an extent. Today, the certain absence of international law from the fight over trees and forests continues to be a feature of global environmentalism. An analysis of the development of a possible international forest law, or timber regulations, for instance, following the dissolution of the League reveals that later campaigns failed to achieve these kinds of solutions. At the 1992 United Nations Conference on Environment and Development, for instance, some parties assumed that the creation of an international forest treaty would secure wooded landscapes and lead to the global aim of sustainable forest management. Powerful opposition, however, meant this initiative was largely in vain and the suggested treaty eventually failed. Since then, a variety of nonbinding legal instruments has been introduced *instead* of international regulation, and a list of bodies worldwide are still working to reduce deforestation – so far, rather unsuccessfully as far as practical results are concerned.[121] Moreover, the international activity against deforestation of central institutions such as the United Nations Educational, Scientific, and Cultural Organization (UNESCO) largely focuses on encouraging international awareness of the problem or educational advocacy, and does not really promote legal regulations.[122]

A general comparative perspective shows that legal and practical difficulties that emerged as a result of international endeavors to

convince the American government to engage in the field on the international level. Both, the Comité and the Berlin-based organization were taken over by the newly founded Food and Agriculture Organization in 1946.

[120] Compare the (relatively) far-reaching preliminary solution of international timber regulation based on binding quotas, which the League discussed as a way to fight spreading deforestation (*see* the discussion in Sections 4.3.1 and 4.3.2 above).

[121] *See, e.g.*, C. P. Mackenzie, *Future Prospects for International Forest Law*, 14 INT'L FORESTRY REV. 249 (2012).

[122] *See*, for instance, one of UNESCO's current international environmental campaigns against global deforestation. The campaign is titled "Educating to Slow Deforestation," and on its public agenda, it mentions themes such as (formal and informal) education and knowledge transmission: http://en.unesco.org/greencitizens/stories/educating-slow-deforestation.

introduce a global forest treaty also exist in the early twenty-first century. In one of the recent responses to the global problem, the relative absence of firm international law (such as a interwar quota mechanism) can be noticed. Policymakers have developed a family of policies – collectively known as Reducing Emissions from Deforestation and Degradation (REDD+) – to provide a financial incentive to governments, agribusinesses, and communities to maintain and possibly increase, rather than reduce forest cover. Under REDD+, incentives for forest protection are offered to countries, communities, and individual landowners in exchange for slowing deforestation, and carrying out activities that promote reforestation and sustainable forest management. However, current alarming results also provide a certain estimation as for the success of REDD+ on the ground, especially in developing countries (in which most of the tropical forests are located), as alternative land uses (such as palm oil) can offer more immediate and guaranteed cash returns.[123] Moreover, given current pro-forest advocacy calls to find means other than international legal mechanisms to better protect forests around the globe – such as the creation and support of regional initiatives on the ground, and the strengthening of existing domestic-national institutions working on forest preservation – the League's failure almost eighty years ago deserves to be revisited.

[123] *See* Danilo Mollicone et al., Elements for the Expected Mechanisms on 'Reduced Emissions from Deforestation and Degradation, REDD' under UNFCCC, 2 Envtl. Res. Letters 1 (2007).

5

Evaluating the Environmental Regime of the League of Nations: Comparative Discussion

The following comparative discussion will offer an evaluation of the League's environmental regime. As the discussion unfolds, it will compare different parts of this regime and track differences, common ground, and repeating patterns throughout the 1920s and 1930s. In order to provide a more profound analysis of the League's environmental regime, I will highlight similarities and common ideas in the way that the League handled the issues of oil pollution of the sea and ocean, rural hygiene and sanitation, endangered whales and whaling regulations, and views of timber production that were woven with fears of deforestation.

I will discuss how these different challenges merged a variety of economic and environmental considerations and aims. This evaluation relies on parallel elements that characterize the League's initiatives in terms of international law.

It should first be noted that most of the interwar environmental problems that I have addressed – if not all of them – came about as a result of fundamental technological, economic, or industrial changes. As each chapter has shown, this period overlapped major changes in modern industry and manufacturing, economy, and popular culture too. Each chapter shows that in terms of periodization, the League was established at a time when technical improvements had already changed – or were literally changing – the surrounding environment: the sea, the shore, rural peripheries, and sea ports, as well as wooded landscapes around the globe. The problem of oil pollution of the sea, for example, was a direct consequence of the discharge of oil from ships, which was in turn attributable to increasing marine transportation in the late nineteenth and early twentieth centuries – an increase that did not cease after the war had ended. Commercial fleets and leisure culture brought about the need for relatively intensive marine transportation, which caused oil discharge along shores in different countries as an environmental side effect.[1] Similarly, new, faster whaling fleets equipped with explosive harpoons and enhanced means of hunting, introduced in the last third of the nineteenth century by Norwegian ship crews, put several species of whale at risk.[2] In fact, each of the environmental problems the League tried to solve was a result of technological advances, or similar phenomena. In that sense, most of the League's environmental regime was a reaction either to technological developments, or to economic changes.

However, in addition to the obvious overlaps I have found between the rise of the League, technological and industrial changes, and emerging resulting environmental challenges, the discussion that follows presents further similarities that I have identified in my study of the League's environmental regime.

5.1 Environmental Challenges and Problems As an Accelerator for Collective International Action

In this section, I will provide a general comparative overview of how different environmental problems served as a motive for collective international action during the interwar period. My analysis will offer an explanation for why these environmental challenges, which seemed to be secondary concerns – or even marginal at first sight, generated intensive campaigns that involved the League, a variety of states, and different bodies that were not part of an official bureaucracy (such as NGOs, scientists, and the media) or completely independent.

This general evaluation of the League and its collective environmental actions is not a given. Scholars who study the interwar period in general, and those who focus on specific humanitarian challenges of that time in particular, usually claim that despite the variety of pressing problems the world of the 1920s and 1930s was facing, real collective action was not possible during that time.

This assumption is also reflected in discussions on environmental dilemmas as a whole. With regard to the whaling case, for instance, historians have argued that "in a world of big problems, it was nearly

[1] *See* my introductory discussion in Section 1.1.1 of Chapter 1, in which I elaborate on concerns of oil pollution (mostly in Britain and the United States) in the period under examination.

[2] *See* Section 2.2 of Chapter 2, in which I focus on the impact of modern new technologies in the fields of marine transportation and whaling, which changed this industry in the last third of the nineteenth century and early twentieth century.

impossible to generate action to regulate whaling, especially when whaling took place so far from civilization . . . ."[3]

Whether we believe that the League was successful in generating collective action, the interwar period does show that environmental concerns prompted many in the international community to turn to the League as joint collaborator to solve these issues using international law. As I have shown, the League was not incompetent in this regard; after all, international law today faces many of the same difficulties in terms of enforcement and coercion that the League had do lead with in the interwar period. The League worked intensively to introduce a variety of legal mechanisms that aimed to move states and governments towards feasible solutions (whether they were ultimately successful or not).

In all of the cases that I have discussed – from the pollution of the sea by oil to the rural hygiene campaign, to the whaling dilemma and the problem of timber production and warnings of spreading deforestation – the League was not only involved, but instrumental, in leading the interwar world to collective environmental actions and the forming of an environmental regime. This is not to suggest, however, that the League was the only player in town. As I have demonstrated, the League served as driver of these different endeavors, surrounded and encouraged by NGOs, scientific associations, commercial and industrial consortiums, civil society groups, and others. However, all in all, the League was the central forum to which all bodies ultimately turned, and the one that organized and articulated these initiatives in legal terms.

Moreover, apart from the institutional relevancy of the League as an international forum, there was something about these different subjects that the League saw as vital to the formation of the interwar environmental regime. The characteristics of these issues made them a focus of international legal arrangements, which worked to promote collective global actions. Apart from the trees growing in the ground, all of these interwar challenges had something in common: their international character. Migratory animals and other transnational subjects frequently moved across borders, which encouraged collective action and made them obvious subjects for international law. The behavior of wild birds, spreading diseases, and the whales' disregard for territorial jurisdictions placed concerns about them on an international scale.

[3] Kurkpatrick Dorsey, Whales and Nations: Environmental Diplomacy on the High Seas 9 (2013).

Despite their clear differences, at the heart of (most of)[4] these environmental campaigns stood either migrating species as international creatures, or spreading epidemics as common threats. Migratory species of birds, such as Audubon's Shearwater or Waxwings, and blue whales as well, challenged the notion (and capability) of national or domestic sovereignty. Epidemics advancing in rural peripheries due to poor sanitation or environmental risks were a mission that states, and even empires, could not face alone. Similarly, the campaign against pollution of the seas was both a "common" part of international law but was also used by states to dodge or escape national domestic obstacles. A central institution that was able to negotiate and develop international law in these matters was certainly a valuable asset. The League was not only capable of solving international problems, but also served as a way for NGOs, concerned scientists, and in this case also for the British government to overcome political pressure and interest groups at home. As environmental awareness was rising in Britain, and as political pressure increased accordingly in London, the government decided to turn – perhaps strategically – to an international framework in order to avoid confrontation with its powerful shipping industry in Britain. In this case, however, compared to the whaling dilemma, it was a sovereign state, and not organizations, that asked international law for rescue.

Any measure taken by an individual state, no matter how progressive it might be, was not enough to solve threats to the survival of endangered species or suffering animals, since migrating seabirds and whales constantly crossed national borders and sovereign territories. The very existence of these species in the world of internationalism and the inability of domestic law to adequately protect them, made birds and whales obvious subjects for international law. This backdrop invited the League to step in, as the only relevant power that was able to discuss and grasp the supranational identities of these species and to sketch relevant legal solutions to assist them.

Indeed, endangered wild animals also gained international attention prior to the establishment of the League. Colonial frameworks, mostly British, French, and German, tried to protect "their" lions, elephants, zebras, tigers, and other exotic species and developed legal mechanisms that reflected cross-border patterns.[5] However, the range and scale of the institutional procedures the League shaped during the 1920s and 1930s, not to mention

[4] Except the timber trade and fears of deforestation.

[5] *See* RECHELLE ADAM, ELEPHANT TREATIES: THE COLONIAL LEGACY OF THE BIODIVERSITY CRISIS (2014).

the much broader international scope the interwar legal arrangements covered (since the League strove to be as universal as possible), were different than former (and also parallel) legal attempts to regulate nature.

Whales, birds, oil pollution, and spreading dangerous epidemics do not respect national borders.[6] Because they were not confined within states' borders, most of these environmental concerns escalated as collective tasks of international law. Due to the economic and industrial interests of powers such as Norway and Japan in the whaling dilemma, or Britain in the case of oil pollution of the sea, it became obvious that any feasible legal solution aimed at preserving these dwindling lucrative resources would have to be carried out by international regulation. The uncertainties about the effectiveness of states' power to safeguard nature led different players to shift their discussions to the international arena.

The sea, in particular, became a turbulent site of common problems and international law at the same time. Oil fueled not only global mobilization and the acceleration of traffic, trade, and industry, but the globalization of environmental awareness too.[7] In that sense, the sea served as a common environmental space for migratory and sea birds, for oil pollution drifting towards the shore, and for whales and whalers – all of which constantly and inherently crossed borders again and again. This challenged the very notion of national sovereignty and threatened different interests and local communities.[8] These diving, flying, and floating elements – sea creatures and natural resources – reflected an early environmental awareness of some of the interwar players.[9] As the case of the League shows, these different environmental concerns were not only shared by a variety of political and social circles during the interwar period, but also climbed all the way up the ladder of the framework of (institutional) international law.

[6] William Cronon, *Foreword* to DORSEY, *supra* note 3, at vii, viii.

[7] Anna-Katharina Wöbse, *Oil on Troubled Water? Environmental Diplomacy in the League of Nations*, 32 DIPLOMATIC HIST. 519, 528 (2008).

[8] The international characteristic of the oil problem and its effects upon nature and society brought together several interest groups who were concerned about the deteriorating situation. As I have shown, the coalition of this campaign was much more diverse than in other environmental challenges: the petitions of NGOs and birds lovers were discussed alongside claims of sea resorts (complaining about the effect oil pollution had on their business), public health officials, and other interests groups that were harmed by the techno-environmental problem.

[9] *See, e.g.*, Richard Grove's discussion on certain similar (earlier than the interwar period) environmental awareness. RICHARD GROVE, GREEN IMPERIALISM: COLONIAL EXPANSION, TROPICAL ISLAND EDENS AND THE ORIGINS OF ENVIRONMENTALISM, 1600–1860 (1995).

Stopping oil pollution of the sea,[10] improving rural hygiene and sanitation,[11] fighting spreading infectious diseases,[12] and regulating whaling in the oceans[13] were all part of legal discussions that had evolved from domestic attempts to handle these issues. However, the emergence of the League made it *the* center of international negotiations and collaboration. Transnational frameworks and other initiatives for cooperation no longer seemed suitable for these missions.

In the case of oil pollution, for instance, neither of the interwar international conventions that aimed to solve the disturbing problem (one was introduced without the League's involvement in Washington in June 1926, and the second was introduced by the League in 1935) was ever ratified. However, the fact that Washington saw a collaboration between the delegations of twelve industrialized maritime states, whereas the League's convention involved no less than twenty-eight countries – including a variety of maritime states and states that did not have a direct interest in shipping (such as China or Austria)[14] – points to the League's growing influence as a driver of international law.

All in all, although these different examples point to an eclectic variety of environmental problems – from the conservation of wild animals to coping with spreading diseases due to poor rural sanitation – they also show how environmental challenges mobilized the League to consider comprehensive initiatives in order to solve these problems.

5.2 Legal and Procedural Ways in Which the League Handled the Environmental Questions As Evolving Complex Dilemmas

The following cross-cutting argument focuses on the legal and procedural ways in which the League operated its environmental regime, as part of its general institutional routine.

[10] *See* my discussion in Sections 1.1.1 (on the domestic steps) and 1.1.2 (on the transnational steps) in Chapter 1.

[11] *See* my discussion in the first part of Chapter 3, in which I describe the sanitary initiatives in the period before the establishment of the League.

[12] *See* my discussion in the first part of Chapter 3, in which I describe the sanitary initiatives in the period before the establishment of the League.

[13] *See* my discussion in the second section of Chapter 2, in which I give a historical background on whaling arrangements in the period before the establishment of the League.

[14] Report of the Organisation for Communication and Transit: Pollution of the Sea by Oil (Replies of Governments Relating to the Draft Convention and Draft Final Act), Aug. 18, 1936, League of Nations Archives [hereinafter LoN Archives], A.18.1936.VIII, at 3.

As each chapter has shown, the League was neither the first body to discuss these environmental challenges, nor did it offer the first opportunity to address them. When one considers earlier conservation and nature-protection initiatives during the shift from the nineteenth to the twentieth century, one sees that such ideas and preliminary suggestions had already been articulated before 1919. However, as earlier parts of this study have demonstrated, the interwar environmental regime was different – certainly more advanced – than earlier attempts to cope with the variety of problems that troubled states and communities.

As I have already shown, preventing oil pollution of the sea and protecting the marine environment were both discussed at least two transnational conferences – including in Paris (in 1923) and in Washington (in 1926).[15] Rural hygiene issues, however, were addressed by a series of international conferences throughout the second half of the nineteenth century.[16] Similarly, conservationists who were concerned about whales had been advocating for this cause since before World War I, and the problem was discussed as a transnational issue years before the League was born.[17] As noted, during the years that preceded World War I, certain officials in Great Britain, for example, raised explicit warnings of the severe danger perceived to the whale population, and of the reluctance of whalers to halt their exploitation, even in the face of a catastrophe.[18]

Whaling was considered a problem that existed within the international arena and could not be solved either by national action or domestic

[15] *See* Section 1.1.2 in Chapter 1, in which I introduce the transnational phase that preceded the League in terms of trying to solve the problem of oil pollution of the sea and the lethal effect on seabirds. As I elaborate there, both the 1923 Paris nongovernmental international conference of the Congress on the Protection of Flora, Fauna, and Natural Sites and Monuments, and more vigorously the 1926 Washington Preliminary Conference on Oil Pollution of Navigable Waters, dealt with similar concerns.

[16] *See* my discussion in Chapter 3 on the series of International Sanitary Conferences, which started to convene in 1851 in order to cope with concerns that the League would also become concerned about in the 1930s.

[17] *See* the general summary of the historical background of whaling in the second section of Chapter 2.

[18] *See*, for instance, the Sir Sidney Harmer's warning (as I quote it in Section 2.2 of Chapter 2) of a coming "destruction of whales" in certain parts of the globe. According to Harmer's observation from 1913 (while serving as keeper of zoology for the British Museum), this nearby future would take place due to the "deadly nature of modern whaler's weapons." (Untitled excerpt, source unknown, Nov. 7, 1913, presumably transcribed by Remington Kellogg, Smithsonian Institution, Washington, DC, International Whaling Conference and International Whaling Commission, 1930–1968, [Record Unit 7165], Box 8, Folder I).

regulation alone. Imperial or transnational endeavors, in that sense, were not sufficient. A vivid example of this is the International Fisheries Commission, a regional economic framework formed between the United States and Canada in 1918 to solve the problem of the overexploitation of marine fauna. Although both countries agreed that whaling was a problem common to both of them, the international characteristics of the whale made any solution or regulation that was not international in scope, irrelevant. The joint commission concluded that whales' natural migration patterns, and the ax ante legal inability of any state to achieve authority beyond its territorial waters, left any action that did not draw on international means doomed to failure. The commission called for a convention of maritime nations once the war had ended, in which a future convention would secure the future of the industry by preventing extinction.[19]

There was quite a difference between the official calls for an international legal solution before and during the war, and governments' thinking on this issue often varied substantially – at least in some central ministries. While the Canadians and Americans proclaimed their intention to convene a special whaling conference right after the war, other parts of the whaling community thought differently. The official British statement suggested that bilateral treaties covering specific problems were acceptable, but that scientific data on whales at that time were insufficient to support the creation of an international convention to rein in whaling. Actually, it seems that the British – like the Norwegians and other whaling nations – viewed the idea of such a conference with reluctance.[20] Any move towards putting responsibility (or supervision) for whaling in the open seas in the hands of an unfamiliar international body raised great concern – even at this early stage – from Anglo-Norse whaling industries.[21]

As I have shown in the case of oil pollution, the League addressed largely the same problems and tensions that earlier legal attempts had (just as in the case of whaling).[22] The Paris nongovernmental conference for nature protection, and the 1926 Washington Preliminary Conference on Oil Pollution of Navigable Waters in particular, tried to fight oil pollution with similar legal mechanisms. However, the League managed

19 *See* my discussion on the joint committee in Section 2.2 of Chapter 2.

20 *See* the examples of states' reluctance in my analysis in Section 2.3.2 of Chapter 2.

21 Dorsey, *supra* note 3, at 33.

22 *See* Section 1.1.2 in Chapter 1, in which I elaborate on the transnational phase of the antipollution campaign, and discuss the preliminary phase of the 1923 Paris Conference and the 1926 Washington Convention.

to revive the unratified 1926 Washington antipollution convention, given its technical and procedural toolbox. As the interwar environmental regime's procedural methods unfolded, the role of the League's committees, as well as its scheduled sessions, circulated documents, and draft conventions became central. In many ways, as I have described for instance in Chapter 1, the broad feedback to the special questionnaire that the committee of experts distributed enabled the Assembly to eventually introduce a tougher convention, one that included the mandatory installation of (relatively expensive) separators, about which the shipping industry was so concerned.

Certain parts of this institutional routine produced different modes of international law that the League practiced during its environmental regime. These several modes are also exemplified by the rural hygiene campaign. As the historical background briefly sketched earlier, the League revived the international sanitary discussion, but did not invent it. The international sanitation campaign was on the move throughout the second half of the nineteenth century, and it moved from one city to another (mostly in the West).[23]

As with the idea of separators as a tool to prevent oil pollution (and the awful poisoning and subsequent death of birds), at least some of the central notions for improving sanitation by removing environmental threats already existed – especially with regard to certain epidemics that had the international community on high alert in the post-Spanish influenza period of the 1920s and 1930s. The League, however, offered its rich and expert scientific collaboration on these matters and contributed to the magnitude and the scope of *its* two special international conferences. Moreover, it seems that despite the continuing endeavors of pre-League sanitation campaigns and the recurrence of sanitary conferences from 1851 onwards, the scope of detailed professional, scientific, and expert preparatory work that was carried out before each of the two conferences[24] is incomparable.

As in other tasks the League had taken upon itself, this procedural routine kept the sanitation campaign alive and kicking. As the Health Organisation concluded the first rural hygiene conference of 1931, delegates and officials approached the League once again, asking it to use its institutional framework to prevent this initiative from becoming ad hoc

[23] *See* the introduction to the historical background of the sanitation campaign in Section 3.1 of Chapter 3.

[24] *See* my discussion in Section 3.2.2 and 3.2.3 in Chapter 3.

in nature. They implored the League to instead fix it as an ongoing routine. Dr. Chodźko, acting on behalf of the Polish government, did not wait long. A short time after the first conference of 1931 had concluded, he initiated another professional committee.[25] Its mission was to translate or transform the conference results, decisions, and (mostly) recommendations into a list of questions for future studies and inquiries, to be conducted by the League.[26]

However, as with other evolving environmental issues, World War I brought a stop to the early vibrant transnational discussion on sanitation. The League's role, however, involved more than "merely" discussion, and it did more than simply assume institutional responsibility for environmental sanitary concerns once the war had ended. The League's fixed routine and the direct focus of the Health Organisation on the issue of rural hygiene enabled a concentrated and constant effort. As I have exemplified in Chapter 3, the preparatory work carried out by special committees of experts before and after the two main conferences, kept the ongoing international campaign – led directly by the League – on the international agenda. The recommendations and solutions offered by the League constituted feasible protocols that states and countries could use to handle common environmental risks, such as pollution of water sources, fly breeding, and lacking sanitation. The League's institutionalized procedures organized and compared relevant policies of different states, and made these more easily accessible than its predecessors and former frameworks, which had handled similar problems.[27]

The League's constant procedure transformed some of these ideas, solutions, and discussions from ad hoc transnational initiatives into a regular institutional routine. As with other tasks it promoted,[28] the professional and technical frameworks that the League (and the Economic Committee in particular) used to handle these challenges

[25] *See* the beginning of Section 3.2.3 of Chapter 3.

[26] *See* the discussion in Section 3.2.3 in Chapter 3, in which I describe the follow-up to the first Rural Hygiene Conference that was held in Geneva in 1931.

[27] *See* Sections 3.2.3 (in which I describe the steps taken as a follow-up to the 1931 Conference on Rural Hygiene in preparation for the second intergovernmental conference of 1937), and 3.2.4 (in which I elaborate on the 1937 Intergovernmental Conference of Far Eastern Countries on Rural Hygiene in Bandoeng) in Chapter 3.

[28] Such as the professional committees that discussed possible legal solutions to the problems of drug trafficking (*see* Liat Kozma, *The League of Nations and the Debate over Cannabis Prohibition*, 9 Hist. Compass 61 [2011]) or trafficking of women (*see* Magaly Rodríguez García, *The League of Nations and the Moral Recruitment of Women*, 57 Int'l. Rev. Soc. Hist. 97 [2012]).

were intensely dynamic and, to an extent, more efficient. The League's fixed schedule of meetings, committees, preparatory work by experts and professionals, recurring sessions, and official publications strengthened and supported a variety of international missions. The intensive work of the committee of experts in late 1934 to combat pollution of the sea, for instance, in which they deliberated on possible technical-environmental solutions, enabled the League to introduce an improved version of the 1926 Washington Convention. Another notable committee of experts was the one led by Professor José Léon Suárez, which encouraged not just the League but the entire international community of that period to take part in the evolving discussion on the future of whales and whaling. Despite the League's busy schedule, its bureaucratic and technical nature ensured that environmental issues were tackled head on, and not allowed to fade away.

The legal instruments that were in use during that period not only show that the League understood and interpreted the issues of birds, oil pollution, rural hygiene, whales, timber, and deforestation as problems of international law; these instruments, which moved between hard and soft law, also speak to the many procedural and functional mechanisms that interwar international law used to tackle environmental challenges. A number of important elements kept the environmental regime alive: committees, special sessions and discussions, scientific reports, conferences, recommendations for protocols to deal with spreading diseases and other issues of rural hygiene, official standards, and of course binding legal agreements and conventions along with other means of the diplomatic toolkit. The League's choice to invest so much of its power, budget, and institutional energy in different expressions of law relating to complex environmental issues should not be overlooked or taken for granted in a historical interpretation.

Nevertheless, in terms of procedures and institutional structure, compared to its predecessors, the League's framework brought something new and unfamiliar to the complex world of international relations that existed prior to the League. This assessment is useful in efforts to unpack the evolution of international law. As mentioned, certain basic notions were already part of a transnational and diplomatic discussion before the rise of the League: such as the belief that oil pollution in the sea posed a threat to different countries, that sanitary failures and spreading diseases put other societies in danger, or that the riches of the sea were an international common. However, during the interwar period and under the auspices of the League, the same discourses and goals did not necessarily apply – and certainly not the same routine. These case studies[29] show how and to what extent the League marked a period of turning away from ad hoc initiatives and procedures that characterized earlier international campaigns, many of which tried to cope with some of these same concerns. Often throughout the routine of the League's special committees of experts, which discussed these issues frequently, it was the daily, almost bureaucratic, work of the League and its fixed schedule that triggered and reignited these environmental discussions. On the matters of oil pollution of the sea and whaling regulation, various committees of experts – along with preparatory committees working to coordinate an international effort to improve rural hygiene – joined the institutional routine work of the Economic Committee as it revised different policies with which international bodies could supervise and monitor timber production, and bring it under control. Along with the important subject matter of these environmental issues, it was primarily the routine as an institutional praxis that ensured these issues were not eclipsed by other pressing problems that occupied interwar diplomacy.

These environmental issues had a place and a forum within the League, with the attention of officials, national representatives, professional experts, scientists, continuous reports, and publications. As I have highlighted in each chapter, internal bodies, departments, and professional forums within the League all worked hard to develop these issues. Of particular importance to this work was the central role played by the committee of experts in distributing the special questionnaire in January 1935, and the preparations of the antipollution convention carried out by the League's Communications and Transit Organisation, not to mention the preparatory committees who organized the international conferences on rural hygiene. Similarly, it seems that without the Committee of Experts for the Progressive Codification of International Law, the League would have had serious difficulty in introducing any of the international whaling conventions it had prepared in the 1930s. Following the ongoing discussion on possible means of regulating a variety of raw materials – including timber – the Economic Committee was the first to discuss the spreading problem of deforestation. The French representative to the Committee, Paul Elbel, also pushed for further action at the Assembly, which later ordered the Committee to further investigate the question in the late 1930s.[30]

[29] Except for that of timber production and deforestation in particular.

[30] *See* the different subsections in Section 3.3 of Chapter 4.

> In each of these cases, other bodies and departments within (and in some cases also outside) the League were waiting on these committees' bureaucratic and legal products, such as preparatory papers, proposals for circulation, and drafts before international distribution or publication. This routine was not a unique scenario in matters concerning nature and the environment, but rather a regular part of the League's institutional routine.[31]

The procedural routine of the League's daily work, which marked a shift from the ways in which international law was previously performed, influenced and shaped the substance of some of the issues at stake. For instance, as I have shown, starting as early as 1851, international conferences were held every few years as part of several transnational attempts[32] to promote collective action to combat the discharge of oil into the sea, and to develop common concern on the matter of rural hygiene. Indeed, some of the issues that were revised during this continuing cooperation were similar to the ones covered by both the first rural hygiene conference of 1931 (held in Geneva) and the second rural hygiene conference of 1937 (held in Bandgoeng). However, what distinguished the League from other international efforts to tackle these same problems was the fact that previously, there was no central institution with its own permanent personnel, regularly working to implement and follow up on former decisions. Likewise, earlier parallel transnational attempts to regulate whaling, for instance, or to modify timber production, also used some of the same mechanisms as the League, such as conferences, special conventions, and scheduled meetings; however, the League offered an overall experience of ongoing international law and international governance.

Once the Codification Committee, the Economic Committee, and other departments within the League began to hold repeat sessions, or to revise different documents, recommendations, and proposals for other bodies of the League – whether the Council, the Assembly, or Secretary General himself – issues such as oil pollution, rural hygiene and sanitation, whaling, and timber got their own continuing routine. As I have demonstrated, many of the interwar campaigns introduced legal tools

[31] *See*, for instance, Susan Pedersen's account on the general institutional framework of the League: Susan Pedersen, *Back to the League of Nations*, 112 AM. HIST. REV. 1091, 1108 (2007).

[32] *See* my description of the 1923 Paris Congress on the Protection of Flora, Fauna, and Natural Sites and Monuments, and the 1926 Washington Preliminary Conference on Oil Pollution of Navigable Water in Section 1.1.2 of Chapter 1.

and achieved positive results thanks to the League's institutional framework. This framework supported the continuing and evolving effort surrounding environmental issues. No matter whether these issues ultimately succeeded or failed, various departments and officials within the League remained committed to supervising and monitoring the legal arrangements that other parts of the League (and sometimes those of external bodies – such as in the case of timber production) had prepared. Unlike earlier or parallel transnational initiatives that tried to achieve similar goals, such as the 1926 Washington antipollution convention, or the management of marine fauna (between the United States and Canada), the League supervised and kept track of its own activities, maintaining them as developing campaigns.

The League carried with it not just a strong faith in its ability to solve different problems across the globe,[33] but also in its new means of participating – and literally shaping and creating – international law right at its core in Geneva. The modes of operation and mechanisms in play, such as open-for-discussion questionnaires and draft conventions, were unfamiliar to most of the players that took part in the League's new international, legal, and diplomatic game. As the timber and deforestation question shows, the League also offered new procedural opportunities, through which professional diplomacy developed a different type of routine: one with a fix procedure, and committed and professional diplomatic staff and experts who leaned on an ambitious institution. As in the whaling dilemma, in which the forum involved the Copenhagen Council,[34] the League worked with several other international organizations and interested parties who had expressed concern on the issue of raw materials in general, and timber in particular. I have traced the interplay between the League and the Comité International du Bois (or the International Timber Committee). Moreover, the timber plot also included the involvement of the International Institute of Agriculture (IIA), whose role I discussed in Chapter 4. Besides states, as obvious "natural" parties in the process of international policymaking, the League's diplomatic and legal activity also integrated other types of bodies into its schedule. The League consulted with various governments,

[33] For an overview of the different missions for which the League took enthusiastic responsibility, *see* The League of Nations' Work on Social Issues: Visions, Endeavors and Experiments 75 (Davide Rodogno, Magaly Rodríguez García & Liat Kozma eds., 2016).

[34] *See* my discussion on the entry of the Council as a (powerful) advisory body in Section 2.3.3 of Chapter 2.

experts, technical professionals, and relevant bodies who were involved in shipping, whaling, and the international timber trade. Moreover, in the timber case for instance, the involvement of these (independent) bodies allowed[35] for a broader scope of discussion and consultation, becoming international per se.[36]

It seems that none of the states, regardless of their ties to the matter at hand, wished to miss out on the opportunity to distribute the draft of what might become a relevant basis for further discussion – not to mention for legal articulation, as the Economic Committee had managed to do in the matter of oil pollution of the sea, and the Codification Committee had done in the case of whaling regulation.

As I have demonstrated in the comparative analysis, I conclude this section with the argument that it was not only the environmental cause itself in each case study that was central to the intensifying environmental regime, but also the technical and procedural ways in which the League and its bodies discussed and handled these issues as part of its institutional framework and routine.

5.3 The League Practiced Different Modes of International Law through Its Environmental Regime

The League's environmental regime covered different modes of international law: traditional hard law, as well as soft law. As I argue in this section, this regime did not only include conventions and official agreements. Chapter 3 in particular has shown that the environmental regime enabled the League to practice different modes of international law that were not intended to be articulated into conventional legal products; the environmental regime also promoted information sharing and its distribution.

Most of the campaigns I have explored ultimately aimed to introduce a concrete legal result. The endeavors of the parties involved in the

[35] Or gave the League a possible excuse to drop the timber and deforestation questions. *See* my concluding remark in Section 4.3.2 of Chapter 4, in which I describe the justifications the Economic Committee introduced in its final reports from April 1939 on the problem of deforestation.

[36] *See*, for instance, Section 4.3.1 of Chapter 4, in which I demonstrate the role of "external" (and independent) bodies in the timber problem as it was handled by the League. The League, as I have mentioned, was not the only international organization to study the timber issue in that period. The Comité also conducted its own surveys as early as 1934; it published monthly and annual timber trade statistics and information. These formal publications served as a common ground for negotiations and means of coordination between parties involved in timber trade (producing countries, industry, and others).

campaign against sea pollution, and of NGOs in particular, called for strict and binding legal measures achieved by means of an international convention, such as the one that was globally introduced by the League in 1935.[37] In its efforts to control and regulate international whaling, the Codification Committee prepared different legal agreements throughout the 1930s, such as the 1931 Geneva Convention,[38] or the 1937 Convention and the 1938 Protocol.[39]

The case of the rural hygiene campaign in particular stands out as an example in which the League practiced and developed other means of soft international law. The League's role in rural hygiene and sanitation was rather different than in the other test cases I have covered. Here, the League did not practice "hard" international law: there no conventions, no agreements, and no continuing discussions on what constituted the "right" legal terms in a particular circulated draft. In contrast, one can easily trace such elements in the case of the international agreement against the pollution of the sea by oil, whaling conventions, and also in the preliminary discussion on the limited timber quota.[40]

In retrospect, the sanitation campaign revealed the full capacity of the League in terms of international law and international governance. The League's environmental regime included different modes of the practice of international law: the issues of the pollution of the sea by oil and the whaling dilemma introduced, among others, concrete and feasible features of international law such as special conventions; whereas, the fears of deforestation were mainly discussed in the Assembly and "translated" into the formal publications of the institution, but nothing further. The sanitation campaign, with its unique focus on rural hygiene, introduced other procedural directions to which the League turned during the 1920s and 1930s. However, one can still identify defining characteristics of the environmental regime, such as the central role of experts and professional technocrats, as well as the institutional routine of committees that frequently convened to discuss these matters. And yet of the way in which recommendations were decided on differed across the League's parallel discussions on environmental concerns.

Although the various recommendations on rural hygiene matters did not enjoy the legal power and authority of a convention or a treaty, these

[37] *See* my discussion on the final legal result of the campaign in Section 1.3.4 of Chapter 1.
[38] *See* Section 2.3.5 of Chapter 2.
[39] *See* Section 2.3.6 of Chapter 2.
[40] See the discussion on that preliminary proposal in Section 4.3.1 of Chapter 4.

formal texts exerted a strong normative force.[41] At the end of the day, the recommendations were part of the legal spectrum that the League was committed to making a reality. Moreover, they were also legally significant, since states referred to these recommendations as relevant sources or examples of sanitary policy. Modes of reporting, collecting, sharing, and producing information between states, agencies, experts, committees, and the international forum exemplify how the League created soft international law on its own. The fact that the League gathered so many different voices – Western powers, and lands under colonial rule – indicates that it intended to bring about a new kind of international standardization.

This is not only a retrospective conclusion. Even at that time, the League was aware of the inadequacies of "compulsory" law, even when such law was based on international cooperation. In the opening remarks of Chapter Number 3 on Sanitation to the Preparatory Papers (of the second rural hygiene conference) during a discussion on the need for compulsory latrines to be installed in villages and other improvements necessary to defeat sanitary risks, the League's diplomats identified the relevance of a bottom-up legal change in international law:

> Modern hygienic habits are often difficult to inculcate in the East because of customs of long standing. Thus, peasants may be driven *by compulsion* to construct latrines, to make openings in their dwellings, or to protect their wells; but, unless they can be *convinced* that these measures are useful, or at any rate shown evidence that they have been adopted with satisfactory results by their neighbours, the latrines they have constructed will frequently remain unused, the openings will be blocked up, and despite the fact that a hygienic well is available, water will continue to be drawn from the river.[42]

An evaluation of the rural hygiene campaign as a form of soft international law further reveals that the League's decision to use this mode of international law enabled it to overcome other legal, diplomatic, and mostly political and commercial obstacles it had to face in its other campaigns. In other words, *instead* of turning to conventions, agreements, and binding legal arrangements, which seemed impossible in the complex rural reality on the ground of such vast territories, it might be

[41] Iris Borowy, Coming to Terms with World Health: the League of Nations Health Organisation 1921–1946, 338 (2009).

[42] Preparatory Papers for the Intergovernmental Conference of Far Eastern Countries on Rural Hygiene, LoN Archives, 6098/8A/29782/8855, at 49–50 [hereinafter Preparatory Papers] (emphasis added).

possible that the League relied on soft law to accommodate the fact that multiple countries shared the same environmental concerns, and therefore would likely use similar sanitation policy to respond to them.

The difficult entanglements surrounding the convention against the pollution of the sea by oil, or the whaling law crusade, were for the most part avoided in the sanitary campaign. Perhaps this was because the League treated sanitation as a technical issue that required professional solutions and policies that had been tested in different countries, which allowed it to dodge those conflicts that characterized other environmental initiatives. One should remember that the League used soft law in this campaign since it knew that proposing any binding conclusion would mean the involvement of other authorities (not to mention interfering with their jurisdiction), the building of new (and expensive) infrastructures across the countryside and so on, which would doubtless be met with opposition.

Moreover, the League responded to the rural hygiene problem efficiently. At both the first and second special conferences, the League enjoyed the facade of being the only relevant and legitimate forum for international law and international governance. European governments and Asian authorities were first asked to provide information on their rural hygiene policies and issues. Then, these data were shared, compared, and distributed at the conferences.

This was a facade, but one with very real results. The League was furnished with detailed reports and special scientific surveys all throughout the 1930s: both in preparation of the special conferences, and after. In the case of the second rural hygiene conference of 1937, for instance, the British Government furnished the League's Health Committee with a comprehensive report on rural hygiene issues in Colonial India: it was 400 pages long.[43]

Therefore, the case of rural hygiene stands as a real-time example of the interwar environmental regime's focus on these dimensions of international law:

> In order to establish a rational plan of campaign against tuberculosis, and especially of protection for districts hitherto largely immune, it is *essential* to have *full information* as to the situation, not only in each country, but also in each province and to consider separately towns and rural districts,

[43] Intergovernmental Conference of Far-Eastern Countries on Rural Hygiene: Preparatory Papers Relating to British India, Apr. 1937, LoN Archives, C.H. 1235 (b), R 6098/8A/29782/8855.

distinguishing, among the latter, between those which do or do not provide labour for industry and agriculture.[44]

5.4 Who Gets to Play the Game of International Law: New States and NGOs

As Britain suspected in 1927, the League changed international whaling law not only in terms of routine, legal mechanisms, and procedures, but also in terms of who got to play the game of international law. The special British Interdepartmental Conference on the Question of International Control of Whaling of 1927, for instance, concluded that all possible diplomatic means should to be used to stall any drive towards international whaling regulation that would remove control over whaling from Britain and other marine powers.[45] In this section I will introduce how the League indeed "met" Britain's expectations by including a variety of new players and voices in the process of creating and shaping international law.

This section will be divided into two subsections. The first will discuss the different participants: "minor" states (as I choose to call them) or less powerful ones, as well as states who were not directly involved in the environmental issues the League was tackling, but did participate later on. The second subsection will introduce the growing role of NGOs who strove in the 1920s and 1930s to promote their agenda and turned to the League as a forum that could help them to achieve success.

Unlike earlier attempts to regulate marine navigation and transportation in order to fight oil pollution, to fight rural sanitary risks in the countryside, or to regulate whaling, the League, loyal to its belief in internationalism, shattered the closed doors of the traditional diplomatic club. Even the most negative evaluation of the interwar environmental regime would probably agree with the claim that the League changed the rules of the game. States, diplomats, scientists, industrial lobbies and

[44] Preparatory Papers, *supra* note 42, at 86 (emphasis added).

[45] *See* the description of the British Interdepartmental Conference on the Question of International Control of Whaling (held in October 1927) in Section 2.3.4 of Chapter 2. Despite its central role in the creation of what would become the international forum of the League, Britain – with its role in the whaling dilemma – was cautious (certainly at first) of any drive towards international whaling regulation. Minutes of Interdepartmental Conference on the Question of International Control of Whaling, Oct. 12, 1927, National Archives of Canada, RG 32, vol. 1081, File 721-19-5[3] (quoted by Dorsey, *supra* note 3, at 34).

commercial companies, professional unions, conservationist associations – all turned to the League as an institution, and a place, where they negotiate and share their agendas.

5.4.1 *Minor States Practicing International Law*

The League changed the framework of international environmental law by enabling nontraditional players to step in and participate in crafting different arrangements. This was particularly true for "minor states." Rather than relying on traditional powers to make the decisions, the League opened the floor to less familiar nations that it nevertheless believed to be relevant and legitimate players such as Roumania, China, or Brazil, all of which took an active role in the different environmental campaigns and shaped their legal discourse. As the whaling example demonstrates, certain states used or turned to the environmental discussion to gain some sort of hold on internationalism in general, not necessarily because they were concerned for the survival of the whale (or at least, not for that reason alone). Explicit declarations such as those of Brazil, for instance, support my claim that environmental concerns actually helped these (relatively) new voices to get their foot in the door. In its reply to the 1926 Questionnaire, the government of Brazil mentioned, "The democratisation of the world, the equality of States . . . are the constituent elements of a new international order which necessitates the careful definition of reciprocal rights and duties."[46]

Both Brazil and China took on an important and mostly influential role in the whaling dilemma. As I have elaborated in Chapter 2 in my analysis of states' and different organizations' responses to the League's initiative, the Chinese reply also related to broader reflections on a planned international whaling law. Although it did not support a progressive codification concerning the exploitation of marine fauna in general, and whales in particular, China also interpreted whaling regulation as an important concern. However, unlike Brazil, the Chinese government saw possible regulation as a direct threat to its – and other states' – sovereignty. Roumania also influenced international environmental governance, though to a lesser degree. It submitted a scientific report that warned of the dangers of overexploitation (as the country too had suffered as a result of its unsustainable management of

[46] *See* Section 2.3.2 of Chapter 2, in which I analyze both the Brazilian and the Chinese replies to the special questionnaire.

marine exploitation under its jurisdiction), which served as a relevant source for the Codification Committee to refer to.

Moreover, some of the environmental concerns made it possible for different players to dodge or overcome broader political global power relations. As I have claimed in the discussion on the whaling dilemma, although Wilsonian America refused to become a member state of the League, certain environmental issues[47] allowed for official American positions and policies to shape international law.[48] A similar observation can be made with regard to Japanese involvement in the environmental regime. Although Imperial Japan had withdrawn from the League in 1933, it nevertheless participated in the rural hygiene joint effort, and collaborated both with the League and the international community on these (environmental) concerns. This was not, it should be emphasized, merely a move to fulfill a formal duty: Japan organized its preparatory papers prior to the second rural hygiene conference (of 1937) and sent its formal delegation to Java, perhaps because it believed in international law as a way to overcome (environmental) challenges that put vast regions at risk.

The League's international focus turned some of these environmental issues into common concerns for all peoples – they did not remain conflicts between only those states that had a direct interest in these issues. It seems that in this way, the institutional aspects of the League led to new conceptions of the environment. Opening up the issues of oil pollution and whaling to international discussion, as the League had begun to do, brought new voices and perspectives that did not necessarily favor or protect certain nations' – notably the Dutch, British, Norwegians, and

[47] This was also the case in certain interwar social and humanitarian issues, in which American experts and officials were moderately involved. *See*, among others, Paul Knepper's discussion on Americans and American perspectives in interwar period Geneva: Paul Knepper, *The Investigation into the Traffic in Women by the League of Nations: Sociological Jurisprudence as an International Social Project*, 34 L. & HIST. REV. 45 (2015).

[48] One can also see similar American involvement under the same separatist Wilsonian administration on the matter of oil pollution of the sea. The United States, for instance, sent an official representative to the special committee of experts that had been formed to study the question: Commander Chester H. G. Keppler, Naval Attaché to the American Embassy in Berlin. The United States, it should be mentioned, obtained a seat on the professional committee, though no more than seven experts were appointed to the mission and as many different member states were not invited to send a delegate to represent them. *See* my description on the formatting of the committee in Section 1.3.1 of Chapter 1.

Japanese[49] – obvious desire to keep their shipping and whaling industries intact and free of international interference. On the matter of whaling, I have shown that dozens of states became involved in the discussion, some of which – like Switzerland – were landlocked and did not have a whaling fleet at all.[50] Similarly, in the matter of oil pollution and dying birds, the government of the Netherlands claimed in its reply to the Transit and Communications Organisation's questionnaire of January 1935, that there were no deleterious effects of oil pollution. However, other states – such as Spain, Canada, and Egypt – notified the League of their numerous observations on the implications of pollution for birds.[51] With the League's intensifying involvement, and its efforts to make environmental challenges more democratic and accessible to (almost) every interested party, traditional shipping and whaling nations appeared to be slowly losing their grip on an industry that they had dominated for a long time.

In that sense, early concerns that international law would negatively affect dominant nations and their industries came true. A short while before the introduction of the League, the British concluded that a call for international involvement on a large scale would simply invite other states to join and develop their own whaling industries. Moreover, right after the League took the lead on the whaling issue, the British government argued that any agreement that did not include all the great maritime powers would be "rendered futile" by those powers.[52]

However, the relatively broad international involvement in environmental concerns was not typical in all of the issues the League dealt with. States did not reply to all the initiatives, legal documents, and special questionnaires promoted by the League. While studies focusing on parallel international challenges, such as the trafficking of women and children[53] or the transnational illicit trade or distribution of drugs

[49] Though Japan claimed throughout the 1930s (probably intentionally and in order to dodge any international limitation by regulation) that its whaling industry was still "young" and underdeveloped in comparison to that of Western nations (especially Norway and Great Britain).

[50] *See* my discussion on the variety of states that replied to the 1926 Questionnaire in Section 2.3.2 of Chapter 2.

[51] *See* Section 1.3.3 in Chapter 1, in which I analyze states' and organizations' replies to the special questionnaire the League distributed in January 1935.

[52] *See* my concluding remarks in Chapter 2.

[53] *See*, among others, Knepper, *supra* note 47, or Keith David Watenpaugh, *The League of Nations' Rescue of Armenian Genocide Survivors and the Making of Modern Humanitarianism: 1920–1927*, 115 Am. Hist. Rev. 1315 (2010).

(mostly opium),[54] do show a growing interest among states and experts in discussions and cooperation, the number of states and other bodies involved was much smaller and more concentrated.[55]

The invitation to reply to the League's initiatives to regulate or track oil pollution, rural hygiene, whaling, and timber production enabled states to express their interpretation of international law. This way, states could elevate common international interests over the commercial interests of either states themselves (such as Japan or Norway in the whaling dilemma) or industries (shipping and whaling). The new format of the League, for perhaps the first time in modern history, gave states a voice in international matters, putting them on an equal footing with stronger and richer powers. The new format also encouraged the launch of many of the campaigns. The states that supported introducing international whaling law backed up Professor Suárez and "his" Codification Committee. International evidence reached the League's Secretariat from across the globe, reinforcing the hope of a possible new convention that would save the whale from disaster. Given the involvement of member and nonmember states alike in the issue, and the great concern they expressed, the Codification Committee gave the League a source of legitimacy – and perhaps also of authority – to further develop its initiative.

The League's routine, together with its new sense of internationalism and international law, promised these new players equality and partnership with leading nations who had controlled traditional diplomacy in the times preceding the League. This, the antipollution campaign shows, was not "only" on the books but is reflected in the law in action too. Whereas during the deliberations of the special committee of experts the attitude of (mostly Western industrialized) states' representatives towards the solution of obligatory separators was fairly reluctant, the more general, pluralistic, and perhaps even democratic bodies of the League, such as the Assembly, presented a more progressive, open, and welcoming attitude of a variety of states who were not necessarily involved in the shipping industry, by which obligatory installation of separators became one of the central articles of the final version of the antipollution convention of 1935.[56]

[54] Kozma, *supra* note 28.

[55] In the case of fighting the trafficking of women, Knepper has shown, for instance, that the United States (or American professional experts) were mainly in the campaign led by the League. *See* Knepper, *supra* note 47, at 47.

[56] *See* my discussion in Sections 1.3.2 and 1.3.3 in Chapter 1, in which I describe the (mostly) pro-industrial affiliation of the committee of experts, which was followed by a more

The test case of the antipollution campaign serves as an example of an almost "combined" environmental move from below. The original initiative started its journey with the grassroots agendas of NGOs, where it managed to find its way to the highest levels of institutional international law, overcoming national barriers and challenging conventional international frameworks of state-to-state mechanisms and rationalities.[57] And then, as traditional and marine powers attempted to bury this threatening action in "their" committee of experts, early international law – secured by the mechanisms and agenda of interwar internationalism – managed to break the chains of hegemonic power and to promise, at least at this stage, democratic progress and the introduction of a progressive new antipollution convention.

This argument, it should be noted, demonstrates and revalidates several claims that have been suggested in recent literature on the League. Both a close reading of the ways in which states that were not hegemonic actors during the interwar period used the capacity of the League to take part in setting international relations through environmental case studies and parallel studies that looked into other realms the League handled are helpful in sustaining this contention. Susan Pedersen's recent work on the Permanent Mandate Commission (PMC),[58] for instance, appears especially relevant to such claim that the League was dominated by imperial dynamics and Great Powers dominance, but at the same time – as a new and in-transition institution – used by new and peripheral states to further their interests and affirm their presence in international affairs.

Pedersen focuses there on the PMC and the legal routine of the supervising the mandate system from Geneva, but some of her claims are relevant to the interplays (that I have identified in the environmental case studies) between the geopolitical atmosphere of the interwar period and the unfamiliar options the new structure of the League had to offer to states which were not powers.[59]

balanced policy of the Assembly, when the League distributed the antipollution questionnaire and a draft convention in early 1935.

57 *See* Section 1.3.1 in Chapter 1, in which I describe how the Save-the-Seabirds campaign reached the League after the domestic civil-society activity (led by the RSPB and RSPCA) in Britain, and how the League put the antipollution issue on its agenda.

58 Susan Pedersen, The Guardians: The League of Nations and the Crisis of Empires (2015).

59 The PMC was, on the one hand, a complex innovative mechanism of international law and governance, set mostly to enable the (imperial) powers to practice their control and influence overseas in the Middle East, Africa, and Pacific. However, on the other hand,

Likewise, and as another example to the ways in which my general arguments on the League's environmental regime echo resemble conclusions made by other scholars, I shall mention Patricia Clavin's research on the role of the League's Economic and Financial Organisation (EFO), that gives similar ideas in that respect.[60] Clavin's approach as a practitioner of the "new diplomatic history" emphasizes the multiplicity of actors and forms of power that were operating above, beyond, and across traditional powers and nations states throughout the 1920s and 1930s. There was, as Clavin writes, no "single [L]eague at Geneva."[61] Rather, there were multiple actors, new states, old powers, and a variety of agendas, all working together and often also competing with each other at the same time in the complex structure of the institution and its international milieu.

The League was, in that sense, and as the environmental regime demonstrates as well, a "multiverse"; a body that constantly spawned "new universes" and which was therefore subject to constant reinvention. As certain economic aims of the EFO, side by side with the wide involvement in environmental challenges indicate together, the League was a defining feature of their national identity for states which were not Western empires or European powers. With the internationalism enshrined in its bureaucratic routine, the League enables their voices to be heard on terms of nominal quality[62] with great powers that had heretofore determined and shaped international law, relations, and politics.

Yet, it should be noted that these observations with regard to those of Pedersen, Clavin, and other new scholars of the League do not mean that the League deviated from the common, perennial, Western-Eurocentric narrative of modern history. The League was never a truly global body in a sense that post-colonial interpretations would use in the late twentieth and early twenty-first centuries. The League comprised or reflected parts of the globe, and never the whole. In that sense, and although the environmental regime I have uncovered brought to the surface non-

Pedersen's legal-history analysis shows this was not in no way homogeneous and that the Wilsonian moment was rather real, as a non-European world and new emerging voices started to gain their attention, thanks to the opportunities and tools the League had to offer.

60 Patricia Clavin, Securing the World Economy: The Reinvention of the League of Nations, 1920–1946 (2013).

61 *Id.* at 7.

62 *Id.*

Western voices, such as those of Asian countries under colonial and imperialist rule (as the rural hygiene campaign has demonstrated), for instance, or those of Brazil, Japan, and China (as in the whaling dilemma), the absence of African voices[63] prevails also during this chapter of the interwar period and history of international law. Africa, in that sense, is an important example, as it was an object of the League but not as an actor in its own right.

Moreover, the environmental regime also changed other political patterns of that period regarding minor states, countries, lands, and peoples that were not considered equal players in terms of international relations. As I have shown, the concern about infectious diseases that spread from vast rural areas in the global periphery, East Asia in particular, and put Western population centers at risk made the picture of colonial and imperialist power relations much more complex. The ways in which the League framed parts of the discussions on sanitary dangers in these peripheries as a threat to collective security enabled and invited other parties, some of which were still subjected to Western powers in East Asia, to participate in and share methods on how to handle the issue of rural hygiene.

The League, with its developing environmental expertise, should be considered a force in the changing world of the new century. True, full-scale decolonization had not yet been achieved; but the fact that states including Burma, China, Egypt, and Brazil were participating – in an (almost) equal fashion – in the everyday diplomatic routine of discussing and shaping international law shows that an important step had been taken towards a new historical era – at least in terms of formal international law, diplomacy, and international relations.

Recent revisionist descriptions of the story of environmentalism tend to look into the historical long process and explore the early modern roots of international environmental thought –[64] and relevant legal arrangements that followed it – only in the late imperial time.[65] The

[63] Though Ethiopia and Liberia were member states of the League (next to the Union of South Africa).

[64] *See*, among others, ADAM, *supra* note 5; Mario Prost & Yoriko Otomo, *British Influences on International Environmental Law: The Case of Wildlife Conservation*, *in* BRITISH INFLUENCES ON INTERNATIONAL LAW: 1915–2015, 192 (Robert McCorquodale & Jean-Pierre Gauci eds., 2015); GROVE, *supra* note 9.

[65] *See*, among others, the discussion of Hairudin bin Harun, *Colonialism and Medicine in Malaysia*, *in* ENCYCLOPEDIA OF THE HISTORY OF SCIENCE, TECHNOLOGY AND MEDICINE IN NON-WESTERN CULTURES 211 (Helaine Selin ed., 1997).

chapter of the League, however, enables us to trace the ways in which imperial environmentalism started to lose its outposts.[66]

The League's second rural hygiene conference of 1937, for instance, gave room to a variety of voices to present their different reflections on sanitation problems and environmental concerns, which touched on issues of policy-making, at an international forum. It was the League that very deliberately opened the floor of international law and international governance to new and unfamiliar players and perspectives,[67] just as it had in most of the missions in its environmental regime. As I describe in Chapter 3,[68] the procedures of the second rural hygiene conference revealed that different representatives in charge of lands under Western colonial or imperial rule (such as Burma, India, or Indonesia) worked alongside official representatives of the League, scientifically and professionally comparing, discussing, and sharing possible means to overcome environmental risks, such as rats and pollution of water sources. The diverse environmental regime the League developed was an opportunity to challenge the idea of one universal, hegemonic, Western model for international law during discussions on sanitation, fly control in rural areas, and refuse treatment in East Asian countryside areas.

As different parts of my study explore, particularly the complex rural hygiene campaign, the League's environmental regime serves as a unique lens through which to examine the different legal, historical, and political layers that made up imperialism. While delegations and experts discussed public health and sanitation in the changing world of the interwar period, certain conventional or common notions of the imperial world

66 When Rachel Adam, for instance, studied the earliest treaties for territorial species and for saving world (and mostly, African) biodiversity, she revealed that much later conventions – such as those that created by the International Union for Conservation of Nature (IUCN) – actually "predated IUCN itself by almost fifty years" (ADAM, *supra* note 5, at 4), meaning the early 1920s. Going back to last third of the nineteenth century and the early 1900s, such scholars focused on Imperial India and Africa at the peak of Western colonialism, revealing the untold story of environmental history through the lenses of imperialist and colonialist expertise, knowledge, and networks. The environmental story of the League contributes another angle to this scholarship.

67 Some of the participants, including on behalf of the League, who also complained about the diversity of viewpoints and experiences in different countries and even regions in East Asia made it difficult to reach agreed conclusions on the matters discussed. *See* the Report of the Health and Medical Services to the plenary meeting of the Conference (by Dr. J. L. Hydrick), Aug. 10, 1937, LoN Archives, R 6107/8A/37714/8855.

68 *See* Section 3.2.4 of Chapter 3, in which I explore the second rural hygiene conference of 1937, which focused on East Asia.

can be revised, such as the need to promote professional education of local Asian medical staff. Imperial powers expanded their control over regions beyond European borders to combat the environmental and sanitary threats posed by East Asian countries. Western powers were concerned that such threats would place their metropolises at risk.

Colonialism in East Asia also created tension between the West and its colonial spaces. After all, cholera, for instance, spread in modern Europe from its origin in India, carried by busy trade routes and waterways between Asia and the West. These "imported Eastern" dangers were understood by policymakers and experts to be side effects of the Industrial Revolution – including, most certainly, inadequate sanitation. However, the League's own sanitation campaign, especially the one that focused on the "Far East," expressed other reflections of (and attitudes toward) this tension. Although imperial and colonial power relations did not just suddenly disappear, the structure the League was offering marked a different practical and procedural approach to the Eastern dangers about which the West was so concerned. Unlike other transnational frameworks, mostly colonial ones, which already focused on sanitation at a regional (and not "only" domestic) level, the League offered institutional opportunities to discuss and handle colonial and imperial concerns and "local" concerns in an almost equal fashion, suggesting different examples of information sharing, consultation, and comparing a variety of policies. The turn to a scientific and professional discourse enabled colonial power relations to be surmounted, at least to a certain (and maybe temporary) extent. Therefore, when the League discussed different sanitation concerns, such as water purification and fly control, this interwar discussion actually introduced a picture that is rather different from certain conventional depictions of colonial relations.[69]

[69] *See*, for instance, my discussion on the example of training local medical staff in rural East Asian communities in Section 3.2.4 of Chapter 3. Rural hygiene issues showed how and to what extent concerns relating to local communities were part of the discussions on health, sanitation, and environmental problems. These issues also describe how the League – as an institution – encouraged and motivated efforts that aimed to improve the living conditions of agrarian societies. In that sense, it was a more elusive context than the pattern of the "white man's burden." The discussion should be viewed, as in the case of this campaign, as more complex and layered than polarized "bad" or "good" colonialism and other systematic and familiar patterns of postcolonial studies. We can find, on the one hand, "familiar" descriptions of the difference between the Western world and other parts of the globe, where rural hygiene and sanitation serve as a lens through which this gap is reflected. On the other hand, however, concerns relating to local populations were also involved in a genuine process of crafting international law.

Similarly, on the matter of whaling, it seems the League was the only power that was able to generate a collective action between nations – both major powers and minor states – from Asia (such as Japan), Oceania, Europe, and the Americas that would be able to regulate the hunt for whales far off in the ocean. Unlike the problem of wildlife in northern America, Africa,[70] or Europe,[71] the League enabled solutions – or at least discussions on possible ones – that aimed to overcome the constraints of local, regional, and imperial arrangements.[72] Until the establishment of the League, most of the early environmental legal or diplomatic developments were stymied by such barriers, and could not expand into a broad and global spectrum.[73]

5.4.2 NGOs and Non-state Actors' Involvement in the Environmental Regime

Other than minor or emerging countries that got their chance to participate in the game of international law, the new modes of operation also enabled other bodies to step in and to directly influence international law in real time. The "spectacular gathering"[74] of the world's statesmen, jurists, experts, and scientists from different fields also inspired the international engagement of NGOs. As I have elaborated in the variety of case studies I have presented, many of these participants identified the new forum as an opportunity for non-state actors of different kinds – from commercial organizations and industrial consortiums to scientific boards of museums and research centers – to take part in the making of global governance. Through the environmental discussions on stopping oil pollution of the

[70] For a discussion on the colonial influence on biodiversity conventions in the late nineteenth and the twentieth centuries *see* ADAM, *supra* note 5.

[71] Raf de Bont, *Extinct in the Wild: Finding a Place for the European Bison – 1919–1932, in* SPATIALIZING THE HISTORY OF ECOLOGY: SITES, JOURNEYS, MAPPINGS 165 (Raf de Bont & Jens Lachmund eds., 2017).

[72] For a discussion on certain imperial perspectives that influenced transnational environmental-legal regimes, *see*, among others, *see* Prost & Otomo, *supra* note 64.

[73] Some of the environmental historians, however, argue that one can identify early transnational or international characteristics in environmental initiatives taken by colonial powers *beyond* the metropoles such as those of London or Paris. These conservationist and legal norms record a Eurocentric view of nature that meant excluding colonized populations in order to preserve nature and natural heritage. *See* David Anderson and Richard Grove, *The Scramble for Eden: Past, Present and Future in Africa Conservation, in* CONSERVATION IN AFRICA: PEOPLE, POLICIES, PRACTICE 1 (David Anderson & Richard Grove eds., 1987); Prost & Otomo, *supra* note 64.

[74] Wöbse, *supra* note 7, at 521.

sea, overcoming spreading diseases, or saving the whales and their future, many of these NGOs and non-state actors "re-imagined themselves as actors in global governance,"[75] thanks to the League and its diverse toolbox. Although these parties did not constitute a formal part of the League, the interwar period was, at least with regard to their activity as a new developing type of agency, a golden age for NGOs.

The campaign for the Convention on Pollution of the Sea by Oil was led by devoted persons of external organizations such as the Royal Society for the Prevention of Cruelty to Animals (hereinafter RSPCA) and the Royal Society for the Protection of Birds (hereinafter RSPB).[76] These civil society organizations and scientific professional associations were advocating for environmental and nature-protection initiatives, and they challenged states who were reluctant to join the antipollution initiative. Hence, their role in the antipollution campaign was essential. After all, the NGOs and non-state actors *interpreted* post–World War I international law as an open game, especially for *themselves*. The unfamiliar framework of the new forum, which was literally under construction, was particularly convenient in the case of environmental issues that disregarded national sovereignty and borders. Even when these kinds of bodies did not take a leading role in environmental challenges, their voices were nevertheless heard: examples include the case of the Austrian Association of Workers in Agriculture and Forestry,[77] which complained to the League that its members were suffering from poor sanitary and environmental conditions in the workplace, or the case of the International Mercantile Marine Officers Association, which wrote to the League after the distribution of the questionnaire concerning the exploitation of the products of the sea, and whaling in particular.[78]

Moreover, NGOs strove for conservationist and preservationist causes even when the exact facts and details were yet not completely clear (such as in the early 1920s and the beginning of the pollution and whaling

[75] Steve Charnovitz, *The Emergence of Democratic Participation in Global Governance (Paris, 1919)*, 10 IND. J. GLOBAL LEGAL STUD. 45, 77 (2003).

[76] *See*, for instance, the discussion in Section 1.2.1 (in Chapter 1), in which I elaborate on the involvement of these British organizations in the campaign against pollution and for the protection of birds. First, they fought against oil pollution as a domestic problem; and then (as I show in Section 1.3.3) their calls and petitions became part of the League's discussion (mostly through its committee of experts).

[77] The Austrian Association of Workers in Agriculture and Forestry (die Wohnverhältnisse der landwirtschaftlichen Arbeiter Österreichs, Bericht des österreichischen Land- und Forstarbeiterverbandes), Feb. 26, 1931, LoN Archives, R 5927/8A/275438/26690.

[78] *See* my discussion also on the association's reply, next to the variety of replies from all around the world, in Section 2.3.2 of Chapter 2.

sagas). Devoted NGOs quickly identified a connection between increasing marine transportation and the disturbing number of seabird carcasses covering European shores, but the common knowledge at that time still did not fully realize the hazardous chemical effects of oil on aquatic life-forms. It would take some time, and several intensive campaigns led by ambitious NGOs,[79] to raise awareness among the public and media about the lethal effects of oil on birds. But it ultimately became clear, even without proved scientific data (during the early stages of the antipollution campaign), that it took no more than just a small amount of oil to cause lethal consequences to both to birds and their eggs.[80]

These NGOs – such as the RSPB and the RSPCA (in the oil pollution case), and the American Society of Mammalogists (in the case of whaling) – encouraged different states and representatives towards collective actions of international law. These NGOs were quick enough to identify political vacuums in certain issues, and managed to set the tone *before* other players came along: especially in the cases of the antipollution convention and the whaling regulation. These campaigns illustrate the role of non-state actors in the interwar period as a whole. Once the League was established, it served as a greenhouse for diplomatic and international law initiatives that challenged states' interests and motivations. Until more "conventional" agencies, primarily state officials and governmental representatives, stepped in to take *their* part in the discussion (whether on oil pollution, or on the whaling dilemma), NGOs – sometimes together with scientists[81] – made the most of their relative freedom to shape these initiates.[82]

[79] As I have elaborated in Chapter 1, these were primarily British-led campaigns, but Dutch, French, German, and American NGOs also eventually became involved.

[80] *See* my preliminary discussion on the developing awareness about the reasons for the marine phenomenon in Section 1.2.1 of Chapter 1.

[81] In recent years, environmental scholars have pointed out the evolving popular involvement of individuals (who are not professional scientists) in what is called citizen science, a variety of environmental efforts, initiatives, and campaigns. The increase in community science or volunteer monitoring of environmental issues is becoming a significant part of the study of the Anthropocene.

Some parts of the interwar environmental regime, especially in the case of regulating the marine environment, also showed a civil network of bird lovers, for instance, gathered around the RSPB and RSPCA's activity. *See, e.g.*, ALAN IRWIN, CITIZEN SCIENCE: A STUDY OF PEOPLE, EXPERTISE, AND SUSTAINABLE DEVELOPMENT (1995); Trisha Gura, *Citizen Science: Amateur Experts* 496 NATURE 259 (2013); Hauke Riesch & Clive Potter, *Citizen Science as Seen by Scientists: Methodological, Epistemological, and Ethical Dimensions*, 23 PUB. UNDERSTANDING OF SCI. 107 (2014).

[82] In the antipollution case, for instance, it was the RSPB and the RSPCA, and not official representatives, who suggested specific tort law mechanisms in order to drive the shipping industry to install separators on board ships.

Indeed, compared to devoted nature-protection associations striving to save migratory birds from polluted waters, or to scientific societies appealing to the League on the possible extinction of the whale, rural hygiene issues did not involve "independent" organizations and NGOs, or at least not to the same degree that these other issues did. Most of the bodies that accepted the League's invitation to become involved in improving water management, diseases control, preventing fly breeding and so on were state agencies or official institutions. And yet, as it revised the recommendations of the first rural hygiene conference of 1931, the Health Section of the League urged researchers and experts to engage with other institutions and bodies: peasants' associations, media and press, agrarian cooperatives, and more.[83] Once again, the League not only stepped beyond earlier initiatives on rural hygiene and public health (including transnational ones), but actually offered and positioned itself as a relevant institutional partner to various groups beyond their national governments, sometimes effectively bypassing their domestic authority.

As I have shown, the League's environmental regime saw an institutional shift: interwar diplomacy was much less strict than traditional bilateral frameworks of pre-WWI diplomacy, which was based on states and international organizations alone. The interwar regime, in contrast, was based on a triangle structure of member states, the League, and a variety of NGOs taking part in international governance. These NGOs pushed the League to introduce international environmental regulations and initiatives.

All in all, the role of new and minor states, along with NGOs, should be acknowledged in discussions on the League's institutional shift. All of these parties turned to the League to help them shape international law and international governance, and used the unpaved road of environmental law to promote their agendas.

5.5 The Central Role of Scientific Expertise

Next to unfamiliar actors such as minor states and NGOs, the League's environmental regime leaned on another type of non-state agent. This main argument focuses on the central role of scientific expertise in almost

[83] *See* Section 3.2.3 of Chapter 3, in which I discuss the steps that followed the first rural hygiene conference of 1931, and the preparations for the second rural hygiene conference of 1937; or the specific example to which I refer on this matter: Letter from Vacel to Ludwik Rajchman, Report on the Progress of the Rural Hygiene in Czechoslovakia, (undated), LoN Archives, R5932/8A/30078/30078.

each of the environmental case studies of the interwar period. Scientists and scientific-based discourse were a genuine part of the League's different discussions as it tried to regulate the relations between humans and nature.

The League's institutional framework was not just open and accessible to representatives of science – it literally invited them to take an active part in its everyday activities. Together with its routine procedures of regular and special committees, circulated reports, and methods of information producing and sharing, the League encouraged the discourse of professionals and experts throughout its daily schedule. The "spirit of the League"[84] was nourished and supported by this kind of civilian-scientific diplomacy, and the environmental campaigns relied on scientific argumentations and calls for (collective) action.

Scientific experts and NGOs, and not states or governmental agencies, were the ones who initiated and led the campaigns against oil pollution and poisoned birds. Experts were the first to connect industrial and technological developments and their considerable impact on nature. At first, and in the aftermath of World War I, ornithologists had assumed that sunken submarines and naval wrecks lost during battle were to blame for oil pollution, and they mistakenly believed that the oil would quickly disappear from the shores. However, in its Annual Report bulletin four years after the war had ended, the RSPB reported that instead of fading away slowly with the ocean waves, oil not only remained present in the oceans, but had actually become even worse – "developed with alarming rapidity until now the cry is heard from all round our shores."[85]

As I have shown in the case of rural hygiene, for instance, most of the preparatory work and the sessions of the international conferences leaned on professional experts: biologists, physicians, engineers, medical doctors, and public health experts.[86] Furthermore, the whaling dilemma gave center stage to scientific observations, warnings, and recommendations.[87] In many ways,

[84] *See* Pedersen, *supra* note 31, at 1113.

[85] Annual Report of the Royal Society for the Protection of Birds (Presented at the Annual General Meeting, Mar. 7, 1923) 8 (London; 1922). *See* my introductory discussion on concerns about oil pollution in Britain and the United States in Section 1.2.1 of Chapter 1.

[86] The Interchange Program of 1928, one of the first steps in the rural hygiene campaign of the League, was based on a professional scientific report that paved the League's way into the field of rural hygiene. *See* my discussion in Section 3.2.1 of Chapter 3.

[87] *See*, for instance, the discussion in Section 2.3.4 of Chapter 2, in which I elaborate on the role of the biologist Remington Kellogg, who joined the discussion on whaling regulations and promoted the conservationist lobby within the League; or the role of the American Society of Mammalogists.

this campaign was triggered *by* scientists and scientific observations, and also actively *brought* biologists and marine experts to the forefront of international law. In the issue of timber and deforestation, some of the parties involved used scientific data in order to strengthen their arguments.[88]

In all of these environmental battles, the League and other parties emphasized the importance of scientific knowledge to strengthen their respective positions. In many ways, the need for international law to be seen as a source of legitimacy, especially during its formative period, reflects the increased use of scientific databases by the League and its personnel, as well as by states and other bodies that were negotiating with the League.[89] This characteristic was not unique to the environmental regime alone: scientific experts made different professional contributions during much of the League's deliberations and considerations. Between the wars, expertise grew in importance not only in the administration and politics of nation-states, but in the international handling of a variety of international matters as well. For example, scholars have recently focused on the scientific features of the League's campaign against the trafficking of women, in which organs of the League collaborated with experts of different disciplines.[90]

This fundamental role of scientists and professional experts worked in both directions. First, as I have shown, the League built its environmental campaigns on scientific rationalization and justification. When the League's Organisation of Communications and Transit, for instance, distributed the special questionnaire on the matter of pollution of the sea by oil in January 1935, the states were asked to reply by supporting their answers with scientific facts and data. The eight-question document specifically asked replying states to supply scientific evidence regarding the extent of oil pollution at sea. The final question[91] asked replying states to supply any evidence, based on scientific or other observations made in their country that might have a bearing on this question.[92] Likewise, the

[88] *See*, for instance, the emphasis the French delegate placed on scientific expertise as an essential part of the international discussion on the timber question, as I elaborate in Section 4.3.2 of Chapter 4.

[89] *See*, *e.g.*, the role of expert economists in interwar international law, as described by CLAVIN, *supra* note 60.

[90] *See*, *e.g.*, Knepper, *supra* note 47.

[91] In which states were asked to provide their observations on the effect of oil discharge and oily mixtures from ships on marine and coastal environments (including information on the distance of oil discharge from the shore).

[92] *See* Section 1.3.3 of Chapter 1, in which I elaborate on the scientific discourse used in the inquiry on behalf of the League (and in the questionnaire in particular).

role of professional experts from public health services, as well as the fields of biology or civil engineering, was central to the preparations and running of the special rural hygiene conferences the League organized in the 1930s. In reports on the problem of deforestation, in which matter the French plea was able to push the League to investigate the issue further in the late 1930s, it was agreed that collaboration with the International Institute of Agriculture would provide much-needed objective data that would assist the League in facilitating future possible steps.[93]

Second, science and professional output were also the basis of communication between other bodies and the League. When different associations and societies approached the League on the matter of dying migratory birds due to oil pollution of the sea,[94] or when the American Society of Mammalogists warned the international community of the impending extinction of the whale, they articulated their negotiations and correspondence with the League by using scientific discourse.[95] It seems that in order to place an issue on the agenda of interwar international law, one had to use the language of science.

Scientists influenced early international agendas as a whole, and environmental aims and concerns in particular. On the one hand, they operated within the orbit of national institutes such as the American Society of Mammalogists and the Natural History Museum of San Diego, urging their national governments and the League to take up a central role in whaling diplomacy efforts, and to save "these wonderfully adapted creatures, the greatest mammals that have ever inhabited the globe";[96] and on the other hand, also within the orbit of international (independent) organizations – such as the International Conseil of Copenhagen, the industrial consortium of whaling states – furnishing the League with different data on the whaling industry.[97] Scientific expertise was therefore instrumental in connecting the international, environmental, and industrial spheres.

93 *See* my discussion on the collaboration between the International Institute of Agriculture and the League in Sections 4.3.1 and 4.3.2 of Chapter 4.

94 *See* my analysis of different petitions sent to the League by nature-protection societies in Section 1.3.3 of Chapter 1.

95 *See*, for instance, my discussion on the role of the society in Section 2.3.5 of Chapter 2.

96 Clinton Abbott, Director, Natural History Museum of San Diego, to Secretary Stimson, Mar. 2, 1932, United States National Archives, RG 59, File 562.8Fi.

97 *See*, for instance, my discussion on the involvement of the pro-whaling consortium in Section 2.3.3 of Chapter 2, in which I present how the Codification Committee summarized the replies of the 1926 Questionnaire on the matter of the exploitation of the products of the sea.

It was the League that enabled scientific warnings to gain a foothold in and (to an extent) set the course of international law. Given the fast technological and industrial developments in terms of oil pollution, transportation (carrying infectious diseases much more easily than in the past), whaling, and timber production, it seemed impossible that "a few men on a remote speck of land could affect the whale population of a vast ocean."[98] However, the League's environmental regime shows how and to what extent scientific experts, and their alarming concerns, formed part of and stimulated the interwar period discussions on these dilemmas, and sometimes (as in the case of whaling, for instance), literally changed the course of international law.

True, scientists had warned of the devastating outcomes of discharge of oil in the sea, the link between polluted water resources and spreading diseases in rural areas, and the possible extinction of whales even before the birth of the League. The Canadian scientist William Wakeham, for example, concluded several years before the League's establishment that whaling on the North American east coast of Canada had maybe one more season before the whales were all chased away or driven to extinction due to the big bang in modern whaling.[99] Moreover, in 1911, scientists and diplomats discussing the status of the North Pacific fur seal agreed that other sea creatures would be fruitful, and relevant, subjects,[100] for diplomacy. However, as I have argued earlier with regard to NGOs, the League provided a practical focus for the scientists' and activists' activism. Before the League was born, this scientific discourse was mostly articulated as warnings. The League enabled scientists' alarming predictions to become a regular consideration in possible legal solutions.

With this comparative perspective, two conclusions can be drawn. First, even though earlier scientific calls had warned of environmental threats to fauna and flora in the sea and on land, these worried calls at the same time acknowledged the *lack* of practical or feasible solutions to beat these concerns. The British government, for instance, understood that the unique problems on the high seas could only be solved by monitoring and controlling whaling on a much broader scale. Based on scientific warnings, the Colonial Office mentioned that this issue was ultimately

[98] J. N. Tønnessen & A. O. Johnsen, The History of Modern Whaling, 167, 183–84 (1982).

[99] William Wakeham to Fisheries Secretary, July 26, 1913, National Archives of Canada, Records of the Ministry of Fisheries, vol. 1081, File 721-19-5[1].

[100] Dorsey, *supra* note 3, at 31.

one that would have to be solved internationally. However, at the turn of the century, and during the first two decades, the farthest-reaching solution that the British could conceive of was an abstract transnational agreement with their dominions, Norway, and several whaling states from South America.[101]

Second, scientific expertise also allowed both official and unofficial American views to influence the directions in which the League was heading.[102] We can find other examples of American influence managing to find its way into the League's diplomatic routine,[103] *chiefly* by using scientific discourse and studies in areas that seemed to be secondary missions that the League handled in addition to the tremendous social and economic challenges of the postwar period. Furthermore, although the United States stubbornly refused to become a member state, scientific and professional American involvement can be seen in almost every environmental discussion: in the antipollution campaign,[104] when American experts participated in the preparations for the rural hygiene

[101] *See* my concluding remarks in Chapter 2, where I discuss these British observations.

[102] In Paul Knepper's analysis of the League's worldwide investigation of different patterns of trafficking of women and children, he argued that the League strove to build an international legal regime based on a foundation of professional "sociological jurisprudence," as he called it. Throughout this socio-legal campaign, the role of American social scientists was significant, if not what actually prompted the League to focus on this campaign. Knepper's study also analyzed the role of the American Social Hygiene Association (ASHA), the American Sociological Society, and trained social scientists. *See* Knepper, *supra* note 47.

[103] Erez Manila, on the other hand, focused on different patterns in which interwar diplomacy and international relations were shaped, or at least very much influenced, by American attitudes and statesmanship that came from the White House and the State Department in Washington (and not just from NGOs, civil society associations, and committed individuals). President Wilson's promise of self-determination proved to be the genie that was let out of the bottle: the Poles and Serbs, Armenians in the Turkish new state, Jews and Arabs in Mandatory Palestine, all were thrilled by the American declaration. Although the United States insisted that it did not want to become a member state, its decisions and policies nevertheless impacted on the routine of the League. *See* EREZ MANELA, THE WILSONIAN MOMENT: SELF-DETERMINATION AND THE INTERNATIONAL ORIGINS OF ANTICOLONIAL NATIONALISM (2007).

[104] *See*, for instance, the pioneering involvement of the American biologist, Dr. George Wilton Field (as I elaborate in Section 1.3.1 of Chapter 1, in which I describe how the campaign for the protection of seabirds reached the League). In 1931, Field introduced his petition to the League, which urged them to fight against oil pollution in the ocean. Moreover, one can also focus on the role of scientific American organizations (such as the American Humane Association or the Audubon Society of Illinois) that wrote to the League on this matter in the mid-1930s (*see* also my analysis of some of these petitions in Section 1.3.3 of that chapter).

conferences,[105] and throughout the whaling dilemma with the significant role of Kellogg and the American Society of Mammalogists. Scientific expertise revealed the indirect ways in which American policies gained a central position in the League's environmental regime. These were not only "private" crusader individuals, reaching out to Geneva in order to take part in the making of international environmental law, and to protect birds, mammals, oceans, and nature. Different American scientific associations and NGOs literally diverted some of the directions and actions of the League on these matters.

The League, with its in-transition framework, enabled and even encouraged this kind of practical and participatory international law. However, other historians have so far tended to overlook this involvement, or refer to it only laconically.[106]

The American involvement represented a certain desire for rationality that was reflected in interwar diplomacy as part of a broader sociopolitical agenda. Science was also part of the language of international law or jargon. The League's interest in ensuring the international supply of raw materials such as cotton, sugar, coal, and timber, and of supporting their industries during a time of crisis, were based on statistical information received from bureaus, ministries of economic affairs, and official experts from different countries.[107] Provided with this data on the current production of these materials, and expectations of future production, the League encouraged to establish international institutional mechanisms of cooperation and supervision to improve management of the international economy.

The League's – and other bodies' – focus on information, data, and statistics sharing as a mode of international governance also dominated the timber issue.[108] The League used this mode as a basis for international

[105] As I discuss, for instance, in Section 3.2.2 of Chapter 3 (in which I analyze the preparations for the first rural hygiene conference (1931), the United States sent an official delegation of professional experts and scientists to the conference.

[106] Dorsey, for instance, mentions the American involvement very briefly, while other historians (on which I elaborate in Section 2.2 of Chapter 2) skip it altogether: "Because this was a league effort, it also drew attention from nations with no direct stake and from some that were not league members, like the United States." (DORSEY, *supra* note 3, at 40).

[107] *See* the preliminary discussion in Section 4.2.1 in Chapter 4, which introduces the special interest of the League in raw materials in general.

[108] *See*, for instance, my discussion on the ways in which the League (and other independent organizations involved) was looking for assistance with forestry and timber data, as I explain in Section 4.3.1 (covering the interest in timber trade, which intended to support the timber industry) in Chapter 4. Moreover, I return to some of these methods

discourse that was clearly industrial and economic. In this sense, one can study the timber case as an issue that exemplifies the increasing importance of economic data and statistics, and the role of information-sharing culture, in the international commercial trade in general,[109] especially in the post–World War I world.

This mode of science-based international discourse characterized different realms that troubled the international community during that time: from pressing humanitarian social problems, such as fighting narcotics and their distribution beyond national borders,[110] to environmental challenges. The League, together with other transnational organizations and bodies (such as the Comité), contributed to the international scientific observations and studies on wood and timber, which at that point were not as developed as they had been under the (pro-scientific) auspices of the League.

The notion of a knowledge society in the context of the League is a fairly new concept in the research.[111] Nevertheless, as far as it was used in international relations studies, it usually applied to sociological and humanitarian discussions rather than environmental perspectives. By the end of the nineteenth century, the belief in scientific data had become widespread across Western Europe and beyond. The European elite believed that the continent had to build a technological, scientific, and professional foundation for peace, prosperity, and stability. Thus, in that respect, the League continued to develop preceding notions and socio-political phenomena. In this sense, the League joined other newly created international organizations[112] that were working to improve different universal realms.

The League, however, was different from the institutions that preceded it as well as those working during its active period. Unlike these other turn-of-the-twentieth-century transnational organizations, it did not

in Section 4.2.2, which deals with the institutional energy the League applied to international timber production and trade.

[109] Adam Tooze, Statistics and the German State, 1900–1945: The Making of Modern Economic Knowledge (2001).

[110] Philippe Bourmand, *Turf Wars at the League of Nations: International Anti-Cannabis Policies and Oversight in Syria and Lebanon, 1919–1939*, *in* The League of Nations' Work on Social Issues, *supra* note 33, at 75.

[111] *See*, among others, The Knowledge Society: The Growing Impact of Scientific Knowledge on Social Relations (Gernot Böhme & Nico Stehr eds., 1986).

[112] Wolfram Kaiser & Johan Schot, Writing the Rules for Europe: Experts, Cartels, and International Organizations 16 (2014).

focus on one specific or coherent aspect (such as setting standards for an industrializing world), but aimed to serve the international community in *all* matters that reflected and shaped international relations.

That desire, based on scientific conclusions, was emphasized more vigorously in the environmental realm, and therefore strengthened the role of scientists. The fear of the extinction of wild birds and whales, or of losing control over environmental risks in the rural periphery, had intensified not only the involvement, but also the importance, of scientific discourse in environmental matters.

5.6 Devoted Individual Pioneers

This argument relates to the role taken by figures such as Professor José Léon Suárez, the Argentinian scholar[113] who served as the Chair of the Committee of Experts for the Progressive Codification of International Law, and led an intensive campaign to regulate whaling through international law.

Professor Suárez was an example of a group of professional experts and representatives whom I described as pioneers and dedicated visionaries that shaped central parts of the League's environmental regime. Working alongside him was Dr. Remington Kellogg, an American doctor of zoology and paleontology and a member of the American Society of Mammalogists. Like his Argentinean colleague Suárez, Kellogg also became a true and passionate advocate for whale conservation, promoting progressive whaling regulation under the auspices of the League.[114] Other examples of such individuals who shaped interwar international environmental law were experts such as Dr. George W. Field, who encouraged the League to save migratory birds from oil pollution of the sea. Like his American peer Kellogg, Dr. Field was also a trained biologist, who presented a petition in 1931 urging the League and the international community to fight against oil pollution in the oceans. Like Suárez, Field approached the League (and the Economic Committee in particular), sharing and furnishing it with his "private" scientific findings on the pollution problem.[115] This group of pioneers also includes diplomats

[113] *See*, among other examples, my discussion on his role in the whaling dilemma in Section 2.3.1 (on the preparations led by Suárez to launch the special questionnaire) in Chapter 2.

[114] *See* my discussion on the role of Kellogg in Section 2.3.4 of Chapter 2.

[115] *See* my discussion on Field's involvement in the antipollution campaign in Section 1.1.1 of Chapter 1.

such as the French statesman, Paul Elbel, who single-handedly alerted the League to the problem of deforestation in the second half of the 1930s.[116]

Field, Suárez, Kellogg, Elbel, and other conservationists or preservationists were unsatisfied with some aspects of the interwar environmental regime: and they expressed that in certain notes, diplomatic memoranda, and official petitions. As I have shown, their legal environmental efforts can be viewed as "private" crusades in the turbulent and complex world of interwar international law. Although the League viewed these pioneers as representatives of their homelands, and mentioned their national affiliation whenever it discussed their role in various environmental issues – protecting migratory birds, keeping the seas and oceans clean of oil, regulating whaling and protecting the whale from extinction, and defending forests and landscapes from spreading deforestation around the globe – these different pioneers frequently acted as interwar lone rangers, detached from their nations' policies and formal views, instead choosing to advocate for the sake of nature and its creatures.

In fact, the challenges these individuals worked so hard to solve would probably not have received such institutional and international attention without the efforts of these individuals. As I have explained in each chapter, it was Suárez – and not the Codification Committee – who led the League towards the idea of international whaling regulation, when most maritime powers (such as Britain, Norway, Japan, and Denmark) were reluctant to support the international management of whaling. And it was Elbel who managed to persuade the Assembly in 1938 to order a special investigation into the spreading problem of deforestation and erosion, and who encouraged the Economic Committee to further consider possible legal solutions with which the international community could overcome this challenge and the environmental costs that increasing timber production had created.

This is not to argue that the League would not have promoted these environmental aims at all without the involvement of these pioneers. However, the fact that several environmental problems became such central issues in the interwar period should be at least partially attributed to these individuals. While this certainly had something to do with their personal involvement and agendas, it was also because of the institutional, technical, and procedural opportunities that the League – with its committees of experts and special bodies – was able to offer these individuals. The

[116] On Elbel's involvement and warnings, which stood alone against the League and spreading deforestation, *see* my discussion in Section 4.3.2 of Chapter 4.

committee of Experts, acting on behalf of the League's Communication and Transit Organisation, was a forum in which persons such as Dr. Field could promote their own agendas, regardless of their homelands' official agendas. Similarly, the Committee of Experts for the Progressive Codification of International Law, for which the League appointed Professor Suárez as the Chairman, enabled Professor Suárez to guide central parts of the interwar international legal agenda towards solving the whaling dilemma. Moreover, the general open forum of the Assembly gave Elbel a platform through which he could address the problem of deforestation in front of the entire international community. As the environmental missions were carried out at a time when the League (and international law in general) was in transition, the impact of these individuals and their role appears to have grown. In that sense, the League attracted, facilitated, and encouraged these individuals' efforts and their belief in the ability of the League to find solutions to these environmental challenges.

5.7 The League Did Not Suddenly Become an Environmental Shrine

Last but not least, my final concluding argument tries to place the evaluation of the League's environmental regime in a more balanced context.

All of the abovementioned does not mean, however, that the League had suddenly become a global institute of environmentalism. Indeed, although several bodies that were involved in the different campaigns prioritized concern for nature or animals, the League and other bodies did necessarily make nature the priority of every case, whether the discussion focused on dying migratory birds, polluted rivers and water sources, hunted whales, or shrinking forests. As I have demonstrated, the different dilemmas the League was working to solve integrated both conservationist and preservationist perspectives almost simultaneously.[117] But the League and other

[117] Scholars tend to divide early environmentalism into two central approaches: conservation (which preceded preservation on the historical timeline), and preservation. The idea of conservation is based on the belief that public land and natural resources should be managed by methods of conservation, meaning that the environment and its resources should be used by humans and managed in a responsible manner. According to this notion, the value of the environment depends on the goods and services that it can provide to humans. This viewpoint requires that the environment be used in a way that is sustainable, and it ensures that the natural resources will be used in a manner that will meet present-day needs for the resource without jeopardizing the supply of the natural resource for future generations.

bodies were sometimes more concerned about economic, industrial, and political interests when they acted on these matters. The preservationist agenda was sometimes only as a secondary consideration, if any at all.

When the League and other bodies became involved in the whaling dilemma, they mostly treated whales as a lucrative source of raw materials. The special Codification Committee's report from February 9, 1926 outlined its conclusions and stated that "it is possible, by means of adequate regulation, to secure the economical exploitation of the products of the sea."[118] There, the Committee touched on a core environmental and commercial-materialist dilemma: economic exploitation versus nature protection. The whaling case exemplifies the conflict between environmental considerations and the economic interests of whaling nations and the mighty whaling industry.

In many ways, the interwar discussions on oil pollution of the sea, dangerous epidemics due to lacking sanitation in rural areas, possible extinction of the whale, and rapid deforestation worldwide reflected the basic dilemma of environmentalism in the early twentieth century. The League was simply facing a tension between conservation and preservation in many of these matters. Looking at the internal discussion of the Codification Committee as it reviewed the dozens of replies to the 1926 Questionnaire, one can sense the tension the League had identified between different possible aims of its initiative:

Above all, we must realize that our efforts cannot be directed solely to preventing the destruction of certain species of animals – quite apart

On the other side of the dilemma is the notion of preservation. The method of preservation is much stricter than the conservationist approach. Under preservation of the environment, the land and its natural resources should not be consumed by humankind and should instead be maintained in their pristine form. Nature and land have an intrinsic value – each is valuable in itself, simply by existing.

These two views (conservation and preservation) have been at the center of many historical environmental debates. *See*, for instance, the debate over the Hetch Hetchy water project of the Hetch Hetchy Valley. In the early 1880s, the valley was being considered as a potential site for a reservoir. At the same time, the city of San Francisco was facing a water shortage. With the damming of the river and the creation of a reservoir in the valley, it would be possible to supply ample drinking water to the people of the city and its metropolis. However, this caused historical damage to nature in the valley. *See*, for instance, John W. Simpson, Dam!: Water, Power, Politics, and Preservation in Hetch Hetchy and Yosemite National Park Hardcover (2005).

118 Communication to the Council, the Member of the League of Nations and other Governments, Feb. 9, 1926, LoN Archives, 19/49113/47284, at 6. *See* my discussion in Section 2.3.1 of Chapter 2.

from their relative importance – which man's rapacity threatens with extermination, such as the cetaceans and pinnipeds (whales and seals). *Our aim should be a wider one* – to preserve intact the whole productive force of the riches of the sea, animal, vegetable and mineral, and by a rational system of exploitation to make the sea permanently provide the human race with the quantity and quality of food and economic products of which it is capable.[119]

The Codification Committee relied on both conservationist and preservationist approaches. On the one hand, it put the blame on humans; the Codification Committee specifically declared there was no purpose in dedicating effort to preventing the destruction of only certain species, and called to defend all[120] marine fauna. But on the other hand, it did not go the extra mile to choose preservation. Indeed, it also announced that the League's aim should be much wider in scope: to protect all of the creatures and inhabitants of the sea. However, this agenda of favoring preservation meant that "the whole productive force of the riches of the sea" would be kept intact. This meant that nature was not necessarily being protected because it was thought to have intrinsic value, but because it was viewed as a reservoir of marine treasures that belonged to humankind and its prosperity.

Similarly, in the case of deforestation, the League first discussed timber as part of its interest in raw materials.[121] As the Great Depression deepened into a global crisis, the League supported the involvement of other independent bodies that worked to save timber industries from collapse, especially in the face of the claims arguing against Soviet dumping. It was only then that the timber question evolved into a problem of deforestation, revealing an alignment of the commercial interests of Western nations – controlling the timber market and

[119] Report of the Committee of Experts of the Exploitation of the Products of the Sea, Jan. 24, 1927, LoN Archives, 19/55517/47284, at 108 (emphasis added). *See* my analysis in Section 2.3.2 of Chapter 2.

[120] Compare with the suggestion mentioned in the later Conclusion Report of the Economic Committee – Exploitation of the Products of the Sea: Note by the Secretariat – the History of the Question, Oct. 14, 1927, LoN Archives, 19/62527/62527 (I), at 2, and more specifically the reference the Economic Committee made (on p. 2) to "several Governments," which were of opinion that, "in any case," protection measures should be adopted for "certain species." (*See* my discussion in Sections 2.3.2 and 2.3.4 of Chapter 2).

[121] *See*, for instance, my discussion in Section 4.2.2 (in which I elaborate on the institutional energy the League applied to timber production and trade) and 4.3.1 (in which I describe the League's will to see regulation of timber trade in order to support the industry) in Chapter 4.

restraining production in order to prop up prices – with environmental considerations – which promoted the idea of limitations on forest harvest and timber production to prevent deforestation.[122]

Following this careful argument, it seems the League understood that environmental protection was an important part of fortifying international security and building a new defense system in a rapidly changing new world. In the case of rural hygiene, the League viewed the environment in a completely different way than it did in the other cases it handled. Here, the environment – such as polluted water sources – was considered to be danger threat from which the global community had to protect itself.[123] In Geneva and Bandoeng, when the League and the Health Organisation were discussing different ways to protect rivers, lakes, and springs, they did so not because they believed these water sources had intrinsic value, but for other reasons: they wished to prevent polluted water sources from becoming a sanitary-environmental danger that might pose a threat to the (surrounding) human community.

In these discussions, the League used a discourse of security. The growing fear about the surrounding environment – first across the periphery, and then from the rural front into the urban centers of these regions – did not stop in Eastern Europe or in East Asia: the League was concerned the rural villages would find ways to transfer their pathogens to the West.

As opposed to previous periods in modern times, as the historical background briefly explained earlier, it was the League that depicted the rural periphery as a dangerous environmental and sanitary space. Instead of the common perspective that sanitary threats originated in densely populated cities, it was the environment of the agrarian, remote, and backward periphery in Europe and beyond that was highlighted as the source of this global concern. Both conferences, and the campaign as a whole, hoped to improve rural sanitation and hygiene: first in Europe, and then – as the broader geographical perspective of the second rural hygiene conference of 1937 had shown – around the world. The sanitary security discourse the League and the other agencies used during the campaign might actually have bridged the League's more conventional activities and its unexpected environmental initiatives. After all, when it comes to peacekeeping in general and global security in particular, the

122 *See* Section 4.3.2 in Chapter 4.

123 *See*, for instance, my discussion in Section 3.2.2 (which covers the preparations for the first rural hygiene conference of 1931) of Chapter 3.

League was supposed to confront other threats, and not polluted water, rats, or breeding Asian flies.

To conclude this comparative discussion, the interwar environmental regime was on many occasions depicted as a story of the tension between clear economic, commercial, and industrial incentives on the one hand, and environmental concerns on the other hand – just as it is sometimes described today. As in the interwar period, conflicting interests of this kind are still evident in our current discussions on the need for joint international campaigns to save nature. In most of the case studies that were analyzed, we see the same fundamental tension between development (powerful industries) and environmentalism (devoted NGOs and scientific associations) that exists today. In the antipollution campaign and in the whaling dilemma, there were those who refused to acknowledge the warnings of NGOs and scientists, because these industries were trying to dodge suggested initiatives. One can trace, for instance, the powerful influence of industrial, commercial, and governmental corporations on discussions for an international agreement to install separators on board ships. The shipping industry claimed that the financial burden of obligatory separators would lead to its collapse.[124] Shipping and whaling[125] industries clashed with the League and other bodies that tried to limit these industries' exploitation of natural resources. In many instances, these industries claimed that the legal restrictions were not feasible in terms of keeping the industry stable and businesses running.

As part of the general discussion on the exploitation of natural raw materials, the issues of sea pollution, sanitary entanglements, whaling diplomacy, and timber production and deforestation were all brought to the attention of international law through a variety of national sovereignty dilemmas. This expanded scientific research and databases, and increased the involvement of different NGOs, but it also heightened institutional-political tensions between the League, these NGOs, and scientific associations, and other states and bodies with their own industrial and economic motivations.

As in other discussions, many states were reluctant to consider *any* intervention in their national interests or domestic policies. In many of

[124] *See*, for instance, the remarks made by the Chairman of the committee of experts, C. H. Grimshaw, as I elaborate in Section 1.3.2 of Chapter 1.

[125] In the case of timber, the will to regulate and control timber production and trade went hand with hand with the warnings of the French delegation about spreading deforestation due to timber trade.

these environmental concerns, as well as other humanitarian campaigns that faded away as a result of political pressure within the League,[126] different nations feared that international institutions, indifferent to their interests, would interfere in their national interests and affect their policies as a result. These patterns were reflected in other environmental test cases handled by the League.

[126] For example: refugees, women's political rights, drug trafficking, and minorities – problems that concerned both the newborn states in the aftermath of the Great War, and the more stable nations of Europe. *See*, among others, THE LEAGUE OF NATIONS' WORK ON SOCIAL ISSUES: VISIONS, ENDEAVOURS AND EXPERIMENTS (*supra* note 33).

Conclusion

The League of Nations failed in many of its actions, initiatives, and its performance of international law. The renaissance that has been flourishing in the old chambers of the Art Deco Palais des Nations and its archives cannot create an alternative history that did not occur. Scholars should study the League – something too few of them did in the second half of the twentieth century – but like us, they should not attempt to sketch a different history than the one that occurred.

As I have elaborated in each previous chapter, most of the League's environmental regime ended up as an apparent failure: none of the conventions (in the case of polluted oceans and beaches, or the case of the endangered whales),[1] or the soft law mechanisms and other techniques of international law and governance (like those used in the matter of rural hygiene and fighting deforestation), ultimately succeeded in protecting the surrounding nature.

Some might continue to dismiss the League's role or significance in the evolution of international environmental law, even if we manage to convince them that such an environmental chapter in the interwar chronicles existed. Since none of the League's endeavors achieved any real measurable success, the League's contribution to the development (and to the history) of environmentalism might continue to be viewed in a minimal, almost skeptical, way.

Perhaps, indeed, all the League managed to do in the 1920s and 1930s was to fail, again and again. Assuming, for the purpose of this discussion, that such an assessment of the League is correct – even though recent studies on the League have certainly challenged our assumptions about its effectiveness – I believe there is still value in studying these failures.

[1] This was particularly true in the whaling dilemma. Despite the series of detailed legal arrangements of the 1930s, the whale nevertheless faced the danger of extinction in the 1930s and 1940s. Most of the scholars who have explored the history of whaling completed their studies with an almost definitive conclusion that the League had failed in its efforts to protect the whale by means of international law.

We do not discourage studies on other controversial steps in the history of early environmentalism, or in the history of international environmental law, because of the outcomes of their research objectives. In some instances, the contrary is true. Scholars such as Mario Prost and Yoriko Otomo, concluding their study of the (failing) 1900 London Convention, are not afraid to agree that the "1900 London Convention ... was arguably never intended to abolish the large-scale extermination of wild animals in Africa but rather to provide a legal framework within which the symbolic hunt could continue." They go on to say that, despite this, "the significance of the 1900 London Convention on the international conservation project should not be underestimated. The Convention ... established key concepts and ideas of preservation that came to dominate international conservation efforts in the twentieth century."[2]

No matter how much it failed, the League certainly had an important role in the *evolution* of modern international environmental law, which continues to impact legal arrangements today. I am not at all sure if any of policymakers, scientists, environmental activists, jurists, and scholars of the interwar period realized that the Convention against the Pollution of the Sea by Oil[3] (unsuccessful though it was) would set the tone and legal mechanisms for marine protection for the rest of the century. Similarly, in the case of whaling, it is likely that no one foresaw that a legal "lapdog of the major whaling nations – would one day be transformed into an anti-whaling institution, though in fact that is what happened in 1982."[4]

Moreover, with regard to the layered structure of international environmental law (and its history), the interwar period should not be overlooked in terms of comparative legal history. Was there something new under the sun[5] in the 1920s and 1930s? This research shows there certainly was. Although legal history tends to skip this period altogether, it was not merely made up of a patchwork of incidental issues – some more successful than others. As I have argued, several aspects of the

[2] Mario Prost & Yoriko Otomo, *British Influences on International Environmental Law: The Case of Wildlife Conservation*, *in* BRITISH INFLUENCES ON INTERNATIONAL LAW: 1915–2015, 192, 200 (Robert McCorquodale & Jean-Pierre Gauci eds., 2016).

[3] Which was originally started with environmentalist-conservationist applications for international treaties for the sake of avian protection.

[4] MARC CIOC, THE GAME OF CONSERVATION: INTERNATIONAL TREATIES TO PROTECT THE WORLD'S MIGRATORY ANIMALS 10 (2009).

[5] J. R. MCNEILL, SOMETHING NEW UNDER THE SUN: AN ENVIRONMENTAL HISTORY OF THE TWENTIETH-CENTURY WORLD (2013).

League's environmental regime intertwined in the different cases it handled, and we can track parallel sets of ideas and legal mechanisms in some of its environmental campaigns. If we turn to a legal history perspective, and comparative legal history methodology in particular, these similarities can provide us with some relevant insights into the toolbox that the League had in mind for its environmental initiatives. An examination of the agenda for the 1900 London Conference on African Wildlife, for instance, reveals similar provisions to those found in the League's whaling campaign.

This should not come as a surprise. Although the environmental problems of the interwar period were very different, they did share some common characteristics – such as a clear intersection between nature, historical tradition, and economic interests – and players. For instance, the idea to establish special reserves or sheltered areas in which the killing of wild animals was prohibited appeared in the 1900 London Convention, as well as in some of the drafts for whaling conventions that were circulated between the League and other political centers and capitals in the 1930s. Both conventions also tackled the issue of how best to manage these reserved areas, and who would be trusted with the responsibility for this international agreement. Moreover, the question on the need for additional measures to reinforce the efficacy of hunting (in the case of the 1900 London Conference) and whaling (in the case of 1931 Geneva Convention for Regulation of Whaling) was not limited only to the early phase of 1900, the first decades of the twentieth century, and interwar period.[6]

Before going into detail on the "practical" legal questions regarding where and to what extent the League changed different aspects of international environmental law per se, I would briefly like to discuss the general overview of the League's contribution to the course of legal environmentalism, and the shift that it effected in this regard.

As I have shown, in order to facilitate their way into the world of international law, many interwar players turned to an urgent scientific-based discourse. In its deliberations with other bodies on the issues of whaling, deforestation, or oil pollution of the sea, the League was actually

[6] This parallel–comparative question includes, among other things, the establishment of closed hunting/whaling seasons to facilitate the rearing of young; the protection of immature animals and mammals; the use of international hunting or whaling licenses to raise revenue and control access to game or to whaling; and the prohibition of certain hunting techniques that were deemed primitive and wasteful (nets and pitfalls), or means that were considered unethical, such as poison and the use of explosives.

aware of the urgent need to find solutions, before it was too late. NGOs repeatedly urged the League to use its force and authority to protect whales, poisoned, dying birds, contaminated water sources in rural areas, and disappearing forests.

Interwar environmentalism was, in many ways, a global discussion with a clear sense of urgency. However, a look at several relevant works reveals that this sense of urgency has not always been characteristic of international environmental law.[7] Largely due to the actions of NGOs and subnational agents that identified the League as a relevant target and partner for their advocacy, the League made it a priority to find solutions to the modern environmental hazards and dilemmas that each test case encompassed. As I have shown, these different solutions had to be crafted using the toolbox of international law: whether they were concrete agreements, standards, methods of information sharing, procedural diplomatic routines of fixed committees and planned conferences, and more. In response to this urgent and alarming discourse on environmental challenges and risks, the League introduced a variety of possible international legal solutions.

In many ways, this broad environmental perspective of the interwar period resonates with key features of international environmentalism at the turn of the (twentieth) century. As I discussed earlier, the dilemma between conservation and preservation, for instance, which was reflected in other initiatives of early international environmental law, was also evident in the League's policies. However, the League also presented other elements. Unlike environmental discussions that took place outside the League,[8] where the Anglo-American influence was keenly felt, the environmental discussions and missions negotiated in Geneva were more global in character, if one can use this term. Norway, Germany, China, Australia, New Zealand, Japan, Romania, Venezuela, Argentina, and other countries – whether independent or under colonial rule – were involved in this phase of international environmental law.

[7] *See, e.g.*, Jan Schneider, World Public Order of the Environment: Towards an International Ecological Law and Organization (1979); Lynton Caldwell, In Defense of Earth (1972); Edith Brown Weiss, In Fairness to Future Generations (1989).

[8] British and American officials, scientists, and representatives of nongovernmental organizations (who were promoting preservation, conservation, and environmental causes) were deeply involved in the bird treaties of 1916 and 1936. Moreover, Anglo-American perspectives also gained a leading role in the matter of the Africa Wild Animal agenda, whereas North-Atlantic statesmen and colonial administrators promoted their nations' own agendas.

The general overview of the interwar environmental regime supports the claim that the League symbolized and facilitated the shift from transnational modes to internationalism. By saying this, however, I do not mean to claim that the League was solely responsible for this shift. Moreover, it should go without saying that the League was not the only institution to deal with environmental concerns, conservationist agendas, or preservationist initiatives either in the first half of twentieth century or during the interwar period. Certainly, other frameworks and collaborations used law to address environmental causes and they developed it in complex ways, often crossing sovereign national borders. The 1900 London Conference on African Wildlife, for instance, and the Second International Conference for the Protection of the Fauna and Flora of Africa[9] that followed it, operated under the auspices of British Empire[10] at the beginning of the new century, and later in the 1930s. Apart from the League, there were other institutions that had their own international environmental agendas, and they promoted similar ideas both before the rise of the League and also during its lifetime. The world has seen, for example, the creation of the International Union of Biological Science, which was established in 1925 by P. G. van Tienhoven, the founder of the Netherlands Commission for International Nature Protection. Almost one decade later, in the mid-1930s, this Union had evolved into the International Office for the Protection of Nature.[11]

Moreover, my analysis here does not claim that the League was, relatively speaking, the most progressive institution in terms of environmentalist scale or criteria. There were also other environmental initiatives that were promoted shortly before and during the interwar period as well. Some of these other environmental measures sometimes offered more comprehensive environmental perspectives on certain issues than the League was able to contribute. Some would claim, for instance, that the 1900 London Conference and the Second International Conference for the Protection of the Fauna and Flora of Africa (from 1938) revealed a much stronger commitment to protecting the world's fauna. Similarly, the Second International Conference of 1938, for which the League was not responsible, reflected an "emerging sense of the wild animal's welfare ... [that attributed] characteristic[s] such as innocence and

[9] Of May 1938.

[10] With the colonial self-esteem of the British, as suggested by Prost & Ottomo. (*See supra* note 2, especially between pages 197–205.)

[11] Which is known today as the International Union for the Conservation of Nature (IUCN). *See* Cioc, *supra* note 4, at 40–41.

beauty to those beings,"[12] as some of the scholars suggested.[13] Some of these were, perhaps, more advanced environmentalist approaches than the ones expressed in the discussions on the whaling dilemma or poisoned birds in the 1920s and 1930s, under the (direct) auspices of the League.

However, having said that, it is important to remember that during the interwar period, both regional and superregional problems were at stake. Since local domestic steps were inadequate to address these issues, collective action between the nations of Europe, the Americas, Asia, and Oceania was necessary. This was something that could not have been promoted by any international institution but the League. Unlike earlier or parallel campaigns that also turned to super-state legal mechanisms, such as the case of protecting wildlife in Africa and Northern America, the League came up with solutions that aimed to overcome constraints of national-domestic and regional-international legal dimensions.

This shift to internationalism was not only reflected in the substantive issues that were at stake. The interwar environmental regime was primarily based on a procedural and legal routine that supported the environmental challenges that confronted the League. Handling environmental concerns (including the ones handled by the League) with transnational legal measures was not an interwar invention. As I have described in each chapter, in most of the test cases, transnational frameworks preceded the League.

However, the League brought something completely different to the table. Earlier attempts to cope with the fear of overexploitation or extinction of world fauna (such as whales, seals, and migrating birds), or with rural hygiene, took place before the establishment of the League. As I have described, some of these issues not only became subjects for domestic and national conservationist regulations, but were transferred into several legal transnational arrangements. Yet, most of these attempts were based on specific, isolated ad hoc, initiatives.

These environmental law missions show how and to which extent the League shifted these discussions (which were generally of interest to some of the parties involved) and kept them going, thanks to its regular institutional routine. With the daily agenda of the different departments in Geneva, scheduled discussions, meetings, sessions, and conferences,

[12] Prost & Otomo, *supra* note 2, at 9.

[13] *See, e.g.*, Yoriko Otomo & Cressida Limon, *Dogs, Pigs and Children: Changing Laws in Colonial Britain*, 40 Australian Feminist L. J. 163 (2014).

most of these environmental issues continued to be addressed. It was the regular, systematic – almost bureaucratic – institutional work of the League that triggered and reignited these discussions, squeezing them into different modes of operation. In this way, these issues developed their own dynamic as part of international law. Indeed, earlier and parallel transnational attempts to regulate whaling used some of the same mechanisms as the League (such as conferences, conventions, and scheduled meetings), but the League offered – and practiced – an overall experience of ongoing international law and international governance.

Moreover, as I have demonstrated, many of the League's environmental initiatives were put on hold because of World War II. However, some of these initiatives continued regardless of the deteriorating stability of the 1930s, even though they had been directly affected by the Nazi invasion of Poland. The League's continuing bureaucratic institutional work did not let the whaling dilemma, the efforts for the special convention against the pollution of the sea by oil, the campaign to improve rural hygiene policies, and to an extent the fight against deforestation, to become overshadowed by other pressing problems that troubled the interwar world. These environmental challenges had a place and a relevant forum at the League, with the attention of officials, national representatives, professional experts, scientists, formal reports, and publications. Internal bodies and departments of the League relied on this institution for its bureaucratic and legal products (such as papers, proposals for circulation, and drafts for submission) – not only in the case of the environment and natural resources, but as part of an institutional routine.

In each of the environmental challenges, I have woven the interwar story between the past and future. This shows that the stories are not isolated in the time capsule of the 1920s and 1930s, but are part of a larger, continuing plot of environmental legal history. Moreover, in the evolving process of codifying an international environmental regime, the League did not only contribute the "substantive" issues of whaling or antipollution mechanisms per se. It had also supplied international environmental law with mechanisms of procedure that allowed for the *maintenance* of environmental challenges. An example of this is the Conferences of the Parties (COP) method, which literally flourished during the interwar period and was promoted by the League.[14] This method of performance, which

[14] Early, and – as I argue – rather formative experiences of that kind can be seen in the variety of international gatherings that the League was working towards. As a matter of fact, the League began convening regular conferences on environmental questions (such as for the whaling problem, first in 1931 and then in 1937; as well as on the increasing

usually takes place annually or biennially, has become the most common practice of multilateral environmental agreements in operation today.

In the institutional realm, the Economic Committee stands as one of the prominent centers of the League's environmental regime. In almost every case that involved environmental considerations, whether they had to do with conservation, preservation, or proto-sustainability, it was the Economic Committee that managed and supervised the translation of the discussion (in the relevant cases) into precise legal terms. Some might wonder why the League handled such a large volume of environmental missions when there were so many other problems that were considered far more dangerous to global security and peacekeeping than the future of whales, trees, and migrating birds. Perhaps this study can shed some light on this question.

The Economic Committee, with its intensive involvement in a variety of environmental concerns, took the League one step further. The Committee considered all of these issues to be an important part of postwar stability and security. In that sense, timber was part of economic security and stability because of its importance for global economic recovery. Similarly, rural hygiene and proper sanitation in global peripheries were crucial to assuring international security.

These environmental concerns were not at all part of the League's official, legal, charter. It was the institutional routine and the daily work – and a broad legal interpretation – of the League (and the Economic Committee in particular) that made the environmental challenges an integral part of its activity.

It also seems that the transition from an ad hoc routine to international law and international governance was assisted by two other general characteristics of interwar diplomacy. First, it was a time of science and scientific discourse. In each environmental story, the central role of scientific expertise and scientists from a variety of disciplines cannot be overlooked.

The League and the other bodies involved (both those who supported environmental causes as well as those who were opposed) often turned to scientific terms, discourse, and data when they discussed nature in terms of international law. There was something in the League's institutional

danger of pollution of the sea by oil, and the special rural hygiene conferences in Geneva, 1931, and Bandoeng, 1937). During these conferences, the League, either through special committees or certain institutes within its framework (such as the Health Organisation), reviewed reports on the current status and on the progress that had been made towards the implementation of these international legal arrangements.

framework that was not only accessible to representatives of science, but literally invited them to take part. Together with its procedural routine, the League not only enabled, but actually supported and encouraged, the discourse of professionals and experts throughout its daily schedule. Each environmental dilemma – the whaling dilemma, the campaign that fought against the pollution of the sea by oil, the sanitation missions to improve rural hygiene in Eastern Europe and East Asia, and deforestation – all relied on scientific argumentations and calls for action. Moreover, some of the test cases in this study – whaling and the rural hygiene campaigns in particular – were initiated *by* scientists and scientific observations, but also actively *brought* biologists, medical doctors, and other experts together.

Second, when the League first started to handle environmental issues, the developing environmental regime changed the framework of who got to play the game of international law – something that worried certain powers, who were concerned for their economic and industrial interests. The different test cases that I have analyzed show how the League was loyal to its belief in international law, international governance, and cooperation, and how it was not as loyal to old-school, traditional, diplomacy. The interwar environmental regime shattered the closed doors of the diplomatic club that dominated international relations until 1914. New states, old powers, diplomats, scientists and scientific associations, subnational agents, industrial consortiums, independent economic-commercial organizations, devoted NGOs, and the media – all worked with or turned to the League as a forum where they could bargain, promote their agendas for protecting nature, or defend their interests and assets.

Instead of the familiar powers that typically governed world politics, other states identified the environmental dilemmas and discussions as a chance to influence internationalism. In other words, it is uncertain, perhaps, whether all the participants were concerned specifically for the survival of whales, migrating birds, and forests, or whether they were concerned *only* to the extent of keeping the sea and shores clean of drifting black oil, or fighting pollution of water sources in rural areas. Whereas previously, these states and other bodies had rarely been offered the chance to make themselves heard on the international stage, suddenly, they had access to unfamiliar tools and possibilities. This allowed them to become involved in shaping international law and the world order in ways that had not been possible before – at least not to that extent or with these modes of operation. When the League distributed a questionnaire, or gathered a professional committee, the game of international law became much more pluralistic, democratic, and open for (almost) anybody who wished to be heard.

Indeed, powers such as Britain and France participated in many of the discussions, including those that incorporated reflections – and policies – from their colonial territories. However, states that did not play a leading role (if any at all) prior to the Paris Peace Conference soon realized the value that the League's new modes offered them. Brazil, Roumania, Norway, China, Argentina, New Zealand, Czechoslovakia, the Soviet Union, and other countries influenced the interwar environmental regime in a variety of ways: either by actively participating in the ongoing crafting of international law, or by carrying out the League's actions. The way the League managed the environmental regime brought new voices and fresh perspectives – ones that did not necessarily favor or protect the obvious British, French, and other hegemonic nations' interests. As the Brazilian government was quick to point out in its reply to the League during the discussion on the matter of developing an international whaling law, "[T]he democratization of the world, the equality of States . . . are the constituent elements of a new international order which necessitates the careful definition of reciprocal rights and duties."[15] In that sense, the League also contributed to the expansion of the scope of international environmental law. When earlier stages in the evolution of transnational environmental law were confined to the circle of "civilized" European imperial powers – France, Germany, Belgium, Spain, Italy, Portugal and, most eminently, Britain[16] – the interwar phase changed the rules of the game, at least to a certain extent.

Alongside states that were interested in becoming part of international law and international governance, the League especially welcomed – perhaps more than ever before – NGOs and subnational bodies. This pattern of opening the floor of international law to non-state actors was not unique to environmental causes (either conservationist or preservationist), and one can characterize the interwar period as the golden hour of NGOs and organized civilian diplomacy. As I have demonstrated, these environmental challenges not only enabled NGOs to be part of the discussion, but also allowed them to push the League to use its capacity to set in motion an environmental regime.

This is not to argue, however, that these new voices – of either "supporting actor" states or devoted NGOs – completely changed the

15 Opinion of Professor Clovis Bevilaqua, Legal Advisor to the Ministry of Foreign Affairs, Received on Feb. 28, 1927, League of Nations Archives, 19/57699/47284, at 2–3.

16 For instance, these states were the ones which took part at the 1900 London Conference on the Preservation of Wild Animals.

course of interwar international law. International environmental law was still governed by traditional powers, and they did not disappear once the League stepped into the picture. And yet, as a result of the intensifying involvement of the League in these campaigns, these traditional powers did seem to be losing their exclusive grip on internationalism as a whole, and early environmental frameworks in particular. In Britain's view (in the matter of the whaling dilemma), the League's involvement jeopardized the future of international law. It believed that the call for open involvement in the crafting of international (environmental) arrangements would simply invite other states to join the game.[17]

Moreover, throughout its environmental regime, the League was a beacon for international law and cooperation – an institution that humanity could trust and believe in. After all, the League was meant to lead the world into a phase of peace, stability, progress, and international cooperation. By offering its innovative toolbox to these new participants, the League allowed them to "[re-imagine] themselves as actors in global governance."[18] It was not just the League's desire to become a relevant and accessible institution that secured it such status in international governance; by turning to the League for solutions to environmental problems, states and non-state bodies also ensured the League's prominence in this regard.

Moreover, the League offered functional, feasible, and practical tools with which these new players could access and shape international law directly. It seems that genuine hope was not enough, and if the League had not had as much to offer as it did, it is likely that internationalism would have been generated rather differently from how I have depicted it. The technical modes of operation, such as open-for-discussion questionnaires and legal documents, were not familiar to most of the players who took part in the new international, legal, and diplomatic game of the League. But, the League also practiced other, semilegal mechanisms that made the sense of international law less elusive and more approachable – inviting, even.

In many ways, the "spectacular gathering"[19] of the world's statesmen, jurists, experts, and scientists from different fields would not have been possible without the soft law practices the League offered to its audience.

[17] Minutes of the Interdepartmental Conference on the Question on International Control of Whaling, Oct. 12, 1927, National Archives of Canada, RG 23, vol. 1081, File 721–19–5[3].

[18] Steve Charnovitz, *The Emergence of Democratic Participation in Global Governance (Paris, 1919)*, 10 IND. J. GLOBAL LEGAL STUD. 45, 77 (2003).

[19] Anna-Katharina Wöbse, *Oil on Troubled Water? Environmental Diplomacy in the League of Nations*, 32 DIPLOMATIC HIST. 519, 521 (2008).

The collecting, sharing, and distributing of information, for instance, regardless of the core issues of environment, nature protection, and exploitation of natural resources, was one of the central characteristics of the interwar period in general, and the environmental regime in particular. These mechanisms of supervision and monitoring characterized much of the work and negotiations of the League's environmental regime.

Since I started this concluding part with a general assessment of the League's (environmental) policy that failed, this is perhaps an appropriate place to explain what the League was *not* doing in terms of environmentalism. Among the issues that did not feature in any international discussions in the 1920s and 1930s are climate change (with the exception of singular single note made by the French delegation on the matter of deforestation in the late 1930s), depletion of the ozone layer, or recycling as a systematic policy of treating human garbage. Some of which, if not all, were not yet known to scientists and experts during that period, but that is perhaps a question for another research in legal history and environmental studies.

However, one might also question why the League did not address – whether intentionally or inadvertently – several other issues that were *known* to interwar political, environmental, and economic circles. Issues such as air pollution, for instance, had been part of the public discussion in the urban regions of several countries as early as the second third of the nineteenth century, and also at the turn of the century. What is more, in Britain, for instance, policymakers successfully argued that there was a link between the prevention of air pollution,[20] public health (and mortality), and relevant legislation. Why, then, did the League's environmental regime not address these many issues that were part of different public discussions, such as mining and its environmental effect on scenic areas and the natural landscape, coastal protection (beyond the oil pollution issues), and more?[21] These other environmental issues were clearly recognized as problems that humankind (through industrial-economic development in particular) was responsible for – not only in the case of carbon emissions. The same argument can be made for

[20] Mostly in industrialized urban centers.

[21] International conservation law, with its special focus on the governance of animal life, played a leading – and quite intensive – role in international diplomacy long before the Paris Peace Conference established the League. Different colonial nations, superpowers, and states invested great effort in trying to promote transnational concern for conservation measures, especially in Africa.

endangered migrating species other than whales and seabirds (which the League advocated for so intensively). The European bison, for instance, another species that became endangered due to human expansion, was the subject of an ongoing international media campaign during the interwar period.[22] However, unlike the whale or certain bird species, the migrating bison never found its way to Geneva and never had the chance to become a subject of international environmental law.

The example of the European bison serves as a relevant example of what the League avoided doing during the interwar period in terms of concrete environmental concerns. Like the whale, the bison too was hunted for meat (and sport). Moreover, the bison was also an international creature that frequently crossed several European borders and jurisdictions during its seasonal journeys (also like the whale). I have focused on the territorial-sovereignty barrier that justified the protection of migratory birds and international whales using international law (as well making spreading rural diseases a subject of international sanitation policies), but the woeful example of the bison challenges my earlier explanation. It seems that the League (or its bodies, departments, and officials) simply did not consider all endangered species to be equal or worthy of protection. Based on its legal-environmental characteristics, the bison too became a subject of certain transnational legal arrangements – but not ones managed by the League. Like other less fortunate species of that period, the European bison sadly remained dependent on domestic, inter-imperial, and regional legislations for survival. This intriguing (counter) case[23] perhaps deserves further comparative study, especially given the fact that just like whales and birds, the bison also had

[22] Raf de Bont, *Extinct in the Wild: Finding a Place for the European Bison – 1919–1932, in* SPATIALIZING THE HISTORY OF ECOLOGY: SITES, JOURNEYS, MAPPINGS 165 (Raf de Bont & Jens Lachmund eds., 2017).

[23] One might claim there are a few alternative explanations for the League's "indifference" on other environmental issues. When such concerns were handled by other bodies, such as in the case of the protection of wild animals (which was discussed as part of a transnational framework of the multilateral 1900 London Convention for the Preservation of Wild Animals, Birds, and Fish in Africa), perhaps the League felt that there were other forums that could solve these issues using transnational arrangements. Another explanation as to why these issues were not addressed in the interwar regime is that they did not have a powerful agency (either a state, NGO, or devoted scientist) to advocate for them, such as in the case of deforestation, whaling, or migrating birds. For a study on the London Convention of 1900 *see*, among others, JOHN M. MACKENZIE, THE EMPIRE OF NATURE: HUNTING, CONSERVATION, AND BRITISH IMPERIALISM (1997).

independent conservationist and preservationist civilian associations that drew international attention for their campaign.

Having briefly described the environmental problems that the League did not tackle, I shall also mention which states did not participate in its environmental regime. The absence of Germany (as a state) from almost all of the League's discussions on the central issues at stake seems rather surprising. Environmental historians have studied the relatively developed German conservationist approaches and tendencies in the late nineteenth and early twentieth centuries, and yet there was not a single case in which Germany (or German voices) took on a leading role in the international relations of the environmental regime. Indeed, Germany had a strained relationship with the League, especially after Hitler and the Nazis came to power.[24] But given the fairly developed environmental political streams within German society and politics at that time, not to mention Germany's experience in transnational environmental networks and frameworks,[25] the fact that German officials and NGOs did not play a significant role in the League's environmental regime (which was not restricted to member states alone, as the American case shows), is surprising.

But besides this seeming exception, one can identify a general characteristic that was in common to most of the League's environmental regime: the notion of migration and constant movement. This notion challenged and triggered interwar international environmental law. In the case of the gray whale, for instance, migration meant that it could travel almost 10,000 miles between its feeding ground in the Bering and Chukchi seas and its breeding grounds in Baja California – a track that is the longest known migration route of any mammal on Earth. Likewise, the League faced issues to do with migration and traveling in the form of spreading rural diseases, poisoned seabirds, ships and oil slicks drifting out in the ocean, and strove to find legal solutions for these problems.[26]

[24] In October 1933, Nazi Germany announced its withdrawal from both the Disarmament Conference and the League.

[25] On early German environmentalism *see, e.g.*, Frank Uekötter, The Greenest Nation? A New History of German Environmentalism (2014), or Bernhard Gissibl, The Nature of German Imperialism: Conservation and the Politics of Wildlife in Colonial East Africa (2016).

[26] However, it should also be noted that the definitions and frameworks of internationalism sometimes rather restricted the League's competence when it came to migration. Diplomacy, for instance, used a narrower definition of *migration* than scientists and biologists. In that sense, interwar international law was restricted only to those species that regularly crossed and challenged national borders by their seasonal movements.

Moreover, the League was also enthusiastic about developing forms of soft international law (such as the collecting, producing, and sharing of information, scientific exploration, and involvement of experts and professionals) when it came to combating spreading diseases in rural peripheries as environmental threats.

Moreover, it seems that in most cases where the League was willing to step in to solve environmental problems, it mostly only did so if these issues were not locked within sovereign states, their territories, or subjected to any domestic applicable law. Indeed, in some cases, such as the whaling campaign and the discharge of oil, the League grappled with the notion of state sovereignty. Yet in general, while biologists and early environmentalists were deeply worried for the survival of species that remained within the confines of a single state, in these issues the League – and international law – generally kept out of the way.

This ambivalent line continues as one attempts to draw conclusions about the interplays between the League, its environmental regime, and the multilayered imperialist and colonialist world. As some of the environmental case studies I have presented show, the League did enter into the complex relations between imperial powers and other countries (including those that were subject to the political influence of imperial powers in regions beyond Europe). The rural hygiene campaign pictured how the interwar story – and its environmental concerns – challenged imperial networks and power relations. During its work on the different sanitary problems that put local, national, and global public health at risk, the League invested a great deal of scientific, comparative, and professional effort into revising possible policies with which these dangers could be confronted. After the first international Rural Hygiene Conference (Geneva, 1931), the League convened a second, larger conference: the Intergovernmental Conference on Rural Hygiene in Far Eastern Countries (Bandoeng, Java 1937) assimilated colonial and imperial tensions into the campaign. As I have demonstrated, some of these depict the imperial world (or worlds) not as a simplistic, bipolar, or dichotomous system, but rather as a multilayered, complex, and heterogeneous universe.[27]

[27] At this point, it is worth mentioning another relevant historical fact. Whether or not this was nothing more than a coincidence, Bandoeng (which also spelled "Bandung") also held another conference that related directly to colonialism. Bandung Conference of April 1955 was the first large-scale Afro-Asian conference convened in order to coordinate a common policy in a postcolonial world. Twenty-nine states, most of which were newly independent, aimed to promote Afro-Asian political, economic, and cultural

It is unrealistic to think that we can fully comprehend an issue simply by looking at its pros and cons, and the same is true of the environmental agenda. The League (which was not a single, unified entity, as I have noted before), as a new and unfamiliar institution focused on recognition, legitimacy, and support worldwide, also had its own considerations, interests, and agenda to worry about. As I have argued in the case of the whaling, when several popular newspapers and magazines approached the Secretariat to mobilize the League for certain measures to protect the whale, officials within the League identified this as an opportunity to bolster the League's international public relations and image.

Along with devoted scientists, mammalogists, jurists, businessmen, representatives of different industries, diplomats, NGOs, officials, and professional experts, the League's environmental regime had enough room to include journalists and newspapers, too. Thanks to petitions from the *Herald Tribune* and the *Times*, high-ranking League officials saw the fierce battle of whaling (also) as an opportunity to promote the growing legitimacy, authority, and public relations of the League as a newborn institution – and to support the survival of the whale of course.

I opened these concluding remarks with a general "acknowledgment" of the failures of the League's environmental regime. However, I would like to adjust that conclusion slightly. After all, even if we agree that the League failed, how successful is our own current international environmental law? And can we point at great or successful milestones in the ways in which global environmentalism faces the challenges of the ecological crisis? In spite of the rapidly growing number of legal instruments, data collections, new technologies, awareness, and mechanisms, only a few international arrangements have been labeled as successful in managing to halt environmental degradation to any great degree: first and foremost, the Vienna Convention for the Protection of the Ozone Layer.[28] The rest, or at least a large number – including climate change

cooperation and to oppose declining colonialism or neocolonialism in any nation. Historians of postcolonial studies tend to identify this conference, and Bandung, as a central event in the rise of the Third World movement and in the evolution of decolonialism. On the interplays between Bandung Conference and colonialism *see* JAMIE MACKIE, BANDUNG 1955: NON-ALIGNMENT AND AFRO-ASIAN SOLIDARITY (2005), MAKING A WORLD AFTER EMPIRE: THE BANDUNG MOMENT AND ITS POLITICAL AFTERLIVES (Christopher J. Lee ed., 2010), BANDUNG 1955: LITTLE HISTORIES (Antonia Finnane & Derek McDougall eds., 2010).

[28] *See*, DANIEL BODANSKY, THE ART AND CRAFT OF INTERNATIONAL ENVIRONMENTAL LAW (2010); PHILIPPE SANDS, JACQUELINE PEEL, ADRIANA FABRA & RUTH MACKENZIE, PRINCIPLES OF INTERNATIONAL ENVIRONMENTAL LAW (2012);

regulations, unfortunately – are still either controversial and suffer from a powerful anti-coalition, or they are difficult to enforce in our twenty-first century world, despite its alleged improved possibilities compared to those of the League. Moreover, considering that environmental degradation continues to worsen, and that regional and global problems remain unsolved, it seems that a more cautious legal-historical assessment of the discipline is relevant. It is necessary to understand the possible reasons why international environmental law failed to introduce an accepted solution, and why it has not been (successfully) enforced on the ground with regard to today's pressing environmental challenges.

By trying to sum up where the League succeeded and where it fell short, one should take note of the involvement, of several "penitent butchers"[29] in at least some of the campaigns I have analyzed in this study. On the other side of diplomats, scientists, officials, and NGOs that were advocating for wild animals, birds, clean shores, and forests, there were also the lobbies of hunters and the industries that threatened these creatures and environmental interests in Geneva. Their presence during decisions and articulations of the legal arrangements might provide another explanation for why several nations were willing to sign and participate in these measures of global environmental regulations. However, the involvement of game protective and propagation associations, whaling industries, and shipping companies in the negotiating process of each realm can also elucidate some of the treaties' inherent weaknesses.

Some scholars have argued that in this involvement, the "hunting" agencies were largely working to establish "uniform game regulation across national borders."[30] All that these interest groups were doing was trying to provide a level playing field for hunters, and to reduce the illegal international transport of products, which jeopardized and damaged their commercial interests. Further research might review this assumption vis-à-vis the interwar environmental regime. At the closure of this research, I believe it is also the appropriate place to note that much of what I have traced is a (or another) "history of privileged men," as Prost and Otomo have pointed out.[31] After all, I have looked at persons, departments, and organizations that have been recorded as primary

Patricia Birnie, Alan Boyle & Catherine Redgewell, International Law and Environment (2009).

[29] As Cioc calls them. *See* Cioc, *supra* note 4, at 11.

[30] *Id.*

[31] Prost & Otomo, *supra* note 2, at 194.

actors in the international domain: diplomats, representatives, scientists, NGOs, and officials, side by side with interest groups such as the industry (in the cases of the Convention on the Pollution of the Sea by Oil, as well as in the whaling dilemma and the timber problem), administrators, and politicians who have shaped the terms of what Arjun Appadurai called "tournaments of value."[32] One can argue that without further research that would uncover the role of others – for instance, indigenous peoples, who were subjects of or influenced by the decisions made by the League (as well as by those it did not make) – we cannot claim that we have a full understanding, or a full picture, of this chapter in the evolution of international environmental law.

[32] Arjun Appadurai, *Introduction: Commodities and the Politics of Value, in* THE SOCIAL LIFE OF THINGS: COMMODITIES IN CULTURAL PERSPECTIVE 21 (Arjun Appadurai ed., 1988).

BIBLIOGRAPHY

Main Archives

Foreign Office records (FO) and Foreign and Commonwealth Office (FCO), The National Archives, Kew, London.

League of Nations Archives, Geneva, Switzerland.

Secondary Sources

Adam, Rachelle, Elephant Treaties: the Colonial Legacy of the Biodiversity Crisis (2014).

Alston, Philip, *Does Past Matter? On the Origins of Human Rights*, 126 Harvard Law Review 2043 (2013).

Amrith, Sunil S., Decolonizing International Health: India and Southeast Asia – 1930–65 (2006).

Amrith, Sunil S. & Clavin, Patricia, *Feeding the World: Connecting Europe and Asia, 1930–1945*, 218 (Suppl. 8) Past and Present 29 (2013).

Anghie, Antony, Imperialism, Sovereignty and the Making of International Law (2004).

'The Heart of My Home': Colonialism, Environmental Damage, and the Nauru Case, 34 Harvard International Law Journal 445 (1993).

Anker, Peder, Imperial Ecology: Environmental Order in the British Empire, 1865–1945 (2002).

Anyanova, Ekaterina, *Oil Pollution and International Marine Environmental Law*, *in* Sustainable Development – Authoritative and Leading Edge Content for Environmental Management 29 (Sime Curkovic ed., 2012).

Arnold, David, Colonizing the Body: State Medicine and Epidemic Disease in Nineteenth-Century India (1993).

Arnold, David & Guha, Ramachandra, Nature, Culture, Imperialism: Essays on the Environmental History of South Asia (1995).

BALINSKA, MARTA A., FOR THE GOOD OF HUMANITY: LUDWIK RAJCHMAN, MEDICAL STATESMAN (Rebecca Howell Trans., 1998).

Barona, Josep L., *The European Conference on Rural Hygiene (Geneva, 1931) and the Spanish Administration, in* HEALTH AND MEDICINE IN RURAL EUROPE: 1850–1945, 127 (Josep L. Barona & Steven Cherry eds., 2005).

BARNES, DAVID S., THE MAKING OF A SOCIAL DISEASE: TUBERCULOSIS IN NINETEENTH-CENTURY FRANCE (1995).

BARROS, JAMES, BETRAYAL FROM WITHIN: JOSEPH AVENOL, SECRETARY-GENERAL OF THE LEAGUE OF NATIONS, 1933–1940 (1969).

BARRY, JOHN M., THE GREAT INFLUENZA: THE EPIC STORY OF THE DEADLIEST PLAGUE IN HISTORY (2004).

BEINART, WILLIAM AND HUGHES, LOTTE, ENVIRONMENT AND EMPIRE (2007).

BENDINER, ELMER, A TIME FOR ANGELS: THE TRAGICOMIC HISTORY OF THE LEAGUE OF NATIONS (1975).

Biermann, Frank & Pattberg, Philipp, *Global Environmental Governance: Taking Stock, Moving Forward*, 33 ANNUAL REVIEW OF ENVIRONMENTAL RESOURCES 277 (2008).

BIRNIE, PATRICIA W., INTERNATIONAL REGULATION OF WHALING: FROM CONSERVATION OF WHALING TO CONSERVATION OF WHALES AND REGULATION OF WHALE-WATCHING (1985).

BLANDON, PETER, SOVIET FOREST INDUSTRIES (1983).

Bonneuil, Christophe, *Development as Experiment: Science and State Building in Late Colonial and Postcolonial Africa, 1930–1970*, 15 (2ND SER) OSIRIS, 258 (2000).

Bont, Raf de, *Extinct in the Wild: Finding a Place for the European Bison – 1919–1932, in* SPATIALIZING THE HISTORY OF ECOLOGY: SITES, JOURNEYS, MAPPINGS 165 (Raf de Bont & Jens Lachmund eds., 2017).

Borowy, IRIS, COMING TO TERMS WITH WORLD HEALTH: THE LEAGUE OF NATIONS HEALTH ORGANISATION 1921–1946 (2009).

BROUWER, G. A., THE ORGANISATION OF NATURE PROTECTION IN VARIOUS COUNTRIES (1938).

CALDWELL, LYNTON K., IN DEFENSE OF EARTH (1972).

INTERNATIONAL ENVIRONMENTAL POLICY: FROM THE TWENTIETH TO THE TWENTY-FIRST CENTURY (1996).

Cherry, Steven, *Medicine and Rural Health Care, in* HEALTH AND MEDICINE IN RURAL EUROPE: 1850–1945, 19 (Steven Cherry & Josep Barona, eds., 2005).

CIOC, MARC, THE GAME OF CONSERVATION: INTERNATIONAL TREATIES TO PROTECT THE WORLD'S MIGRATORY ANIMALS (2009).

Clavin, PATRICIA, SECURING THE WORLD ECONOMY: THE REINVENTION OF THE LEAGUE OF NATIONS, 1920–1946 (2013).

The Austrian Hunger Crisis and the Genesis of International Organization after the First World War, 90 INTERNATIONAL AFFAIRS 265 (2014).

COATES, PETER, NATURE: WESTERN ATTITUDES SINCE ANCIENT TIMES (1998).

Cronon, William, *A Place for Stories: Nature, History, and Narrative*, 78 JOURNAL OF AMERICAN HISTORY 1347 (1992).

The Trouble with Wilderness, in UNCOMMON GROUND: RETHINKING THE HUMAN PLACE IN NATURE (1996).

Crosby, Alfred W., *The Past and Present of Environmental History*, 100 AMERICAN HISTORICAL REVIEW 1177 (October 1995).

DESOMBRE, ELIZABETH, THE GLOBAL ENVIRONMENT AND WORLD POLITICS (2007).

DOMINICK III, RAYMOND, THE ENVIRONMENTAL MOVEMENT IN GERMANY: PROPHETS AND PIONEERS, 1871–1971 (1992).

DORSEY, KURKPATRICK, THE DAWN OF CONSERVATION DIPLOMACY: U.S.-CANADIAN WILDLIFE PROTECTION TREATIES IN THE PROGRESSIVE ERA (1998).

WHALES AND NATIONS: ENVIRONMENTAL DIPLOMACY ON THE HIGH SEAS (2013).

Drayton, R. H., NATURE'S GOVERNMENT: SCIENCE, IMPERIAL BRITAIN AND THE 'IMPROVEMENT' OF THE WORLD (2000).

ELLIS, ERLE C., ANTHROPOCENE: A VERY SHORT INTRODUCTION (2018).

FAIRHEAD, JAMES & Leach, Melissa, MISREADING THE AFRICAN LANDSCAPE: SOCIETY AND ECOLOGY IN A FOREST–SAVANNA MOSAIC (1996).

Fakhri, Michael, *The 1937 International Sugar Agreement: Neo-Colonial Cuba and Economic Aspects of the League of Nations*, 24 LEIDEN JOURNAL OF INTERNATIONAL LAW 899 (2011).

FINK, CAROLE, DEFENDING THE RIGHTS OF OTHERS: THE GREAT POWERS, THE JEWS, AND INTERNATIONAL MINORITY PROTECTION: 1878–1938 (2004).

Ford, Caroline, *Nature, Culture, and Conservation in France and Her Colonies, 1840–1940*, 183 PAST AND PRESENT 173 (2004).

Frank, David J., *Science, Nature and the Globalization of the Environment: 1870–1990*, 76 SOCIAL FORCES 409 (1997).

Frank, David J. et al., *The Rationalization and Organization of Nature in World Culture, in* CONSTRUCTING WORLD CULTURE 82 (John Boli & George M. Thomas eds., 1999).

Gambell, Ray, *The International Management of Marine Mammals, in* CONSERVATION AND MANAGEMENT OF MARINE MAMMALS 179 (John R. Twiss Jr. & Randall R. Reeves eds., 1999).

García, Magaly Rodríguez, *The League of Nations and the Moral Recruitment of Women*, 57 INTERNATIONAL REVIEW OF SOCIAL HISTORY 97 (2012).

Gissibl, Bernhard, The Nature of German Imperialism: Conservation and the Politics of Wildlife in Colonial East Africa (2016).

Glacken, Clarence, Traces on the Rhodian Shore: Nature and the Culture in Western Thought from Ancient Times to the End of the Eighteenth Century (1976).

Gold, Edgar, Handbook on Marine Pollution (1998).

Gottlieb, Robert, Forcing the Spring: The Transformation of the American Environmental Movement (2005).

Grove, Richard, Ecology, Climate and Empire: Colonialism and Global Environmental History 1400–1940 (1993).

Green Imperialism: Colonial Expansion, Tropical Island Edens and the Origins of Environmentalism, 1600–1860 (1996).

Guha, Ramachandra, Environmentalism: A Global History (1999).

Radical American Environmentalism and Wilderness Preservation: A Third-World Critique, 11 Environmental Ethics 71 (1989).

Halman, Gerald B., *Saving Failed States*, 89 Foreign Policy 3 (1992–93).

Harrison, Mark, Public Health in British India: Anglo-Indian Preventive Medicine: 1859–1913 (1994).

Harvey, Peter A., *Environmental Sanitation Crisis: More than Just a Health Issue*, 2 Environmental Health Insights 77 (2008).

Hayden, Sherman S., The International Protection of Wild Life: An Examination of Treaties and Other Agreements for the Preservation of Birds and Mammals (1942).

Hays, Samuel, Conservation and the Gospel of Efficiency: The Progressive Conservation Movement: 1890–1920 (1959).

Hironaka, Ann, Greening the Globe: World Society and Environmental Change (2014).

Honigsbaum, Mark, Living with Enza: The Forgotten Story of Britain and the Great Flu Pandemic of 1918 (2009).

How Green Were the Nazis? Nature, Environment and Nation in the Third Reich (Franz-Josef Brüggemeier, Mark Cioc & Thomas Zeller eds., 2005).

Howard-Jones, Norman, *The Scientific Background of the International Sanitary Conferences: 1851–1938*, 1 History of International Public Health (1975).

Huber, Valeska, *The Unification of the Globe by Disease? The International Sanitary Conferences on Cholera, 1851–1894*, 49 The Historical Journal 453 (2006).

Hughes, J. Donald, *Ancient Deforestation Revisited*, 44 Journal of the History of Biology 43 (2011).

Global Dimensions in Environmental History, 70 The Pacific Historical Review 91 (2001).

Jefferies, Cameron, Mammal Conservation and the Law of the Sea (2016).

Kaiser, Wolfram & Schot, Johan, Writing the Rules for Europe: Experts, Cartels, and International Organizations (2014).

Knepper, Paul, *The Investigation into the Traffic in Women by the League of Nations: Sociological Jurisprudence as an International Social Project*, 34 Law and History Review 45 (2015).

Koskenniemi, Martti, The Gentle Civilizer of Nations: The Rise and Fall of International Law, 1870–1960 (2002).

Kozma, Liat, *The League of Nations and the Debate over Cannabis Prohibition*, 9 History Compass 61 (2011).

Landscapes of Exposure: Knowledge and Illness in Modern Environments (Gregg Mitman, et al. eds., 2004).

MacKenzie, C. P., *Future Prospects for International Forest Law*, 14 The International Forestry Review 249 (2012).

MacKenzie, John M., The Empire of Nature: Hunting, Conservation, and British Imperialism (1997).

Maher, Neil, Nature's New Deal: The Civilian Conservation Corps and the Roots of the American Environmental Movement (2008).

Mauch, Christof, The Growth of Trees: A Historical Perspective on Sustainability (Katie Ritson trans., 2014).

Mazower, Mark, Dark Continent: Europe's Twentieth Century (1998).

Enchanted Palace: The End of Empire and the Ideological Origins of the United Nations (2009).

Governing the World: the History of Idea, 1815 to the Present (2013).

Minorities and the League of Nations in Interwar Europe, 126 Daedalus 47 (1997).

McEvoy, Arthur F., The Fisherman's Problem: Ecology and Law in the California Fisheries, 1850–1980 (1986).

McNeill, John R., Something New Under the Sun: An Environmental History of the 20th-Century World (2000).

Melosi, Martin V., Garbage in the Cities: Refuse, Reform, and the Environment (Rev. ed., 2005).

Merchant, Carolyn, *Shades of Darkness: Race and Environmental History*, 8 Environmental History 380 (2003).

Meyer, John W. Frank, David J. Hironaka, Ann, Schofer, Evan & Tuma, Nancy B., *The Structuring of a World Environmental Regime, 1870–1990*, 51 International Organization 623 (1997).

Miller, Char, Gifford Pinchot and the Making of Modern Environment (2001).

SEEKING THE GREATEST GOOD: THE CONSERVATION LEGACY OF GIFFORD PINCHOT (2013).

Mitchell, Ronald, *International Oil Pollution of the Oceans, in* INSTITUTIONS FOR THE EARTH: SOURCES OF EFFECTIVE INTERNATIONAL ENVIRONMENTAL PROTECTION 241 (Peter M. Hass, Robert O. Keohane & Marc A. Levy eds., 1993).

MITCHELL, TIMOTHY, RULE OF EXPERTS: EGYPT, TECHNO-POLITICS, MODERNITY (2002).

MITMAN, GREGG, THE STATE OF NATURE: ECOLOGY, COMMUNITY, AND AMERICAN SOCIAL THOUGHT, 1900–1950 (1992).

MOWAT, FARLEY, SEA OF SLAUGHTER (1989).

Nagtzaam, Gerry J., *The International Whaling Commission and the Elusive Great White Whale of Preservationism*, 33 WILLIAM & MARY ENVIRONMENTAL LAW AND POLICY REVIEW 375 (2009).

NASH, LINDA, INESCAPABLE ECOLOGIES: A HISTORY OF ENVIRONMENT, DISEASE, AND KNOWLEDGE (2006).

Natarajan, Usha, *Creating and Recreating Iraq: Legacies of the Mandate System in Contemporary Understanding of Third World Sovereignty*, 24 LEIDEN JOURNAL OF INTERNATIONAL LAW 799 (2011).

Natural Enemy, NATURAL ALLY: TOWARD AN ENVIRONMENTAL HISTORY OF WAR (Richard P. Tucker & Edmund Russell eds., 2004).

NORTHEDGE, F. S., THE LEAGUE OF NATIONS: ITS LIFE AND TIMES, 1920–1946 (1986).

Oberthür, Sebastian, *The International Convention for the Regulation of Whaling: From Over-Exploitation to Total Preservation, in* YEARBOOK OF INTERNATIONAL CO-OPERATION ON ENVIRONMENT AND DEVELOPMENT *1998/99*, 29 (Helge Ole Bergesen, Georg Parmann & Øystein B. Thomnessen eds., 1998).

Owen, Daniel, *The Marine Implementation of the EC Birds and Habitats Directives: The Cases of Shipping and Oil Exploration Compared, in* CHALLENGING COASTS BOOK SUBTITLE: TRANSDISCIPLINARY EXCURSIONS INTO INTEGRATED COASTAL ZONE DEVELOPMENT 159 (Leontine E. Visser ed., 2004).

PEDERSEN, SUSAN, *Back to the League of Nations*, 112 THE AMERICAN HISTORICAL REVIEW 1091 (2007).

THE GUARDIANS: THE LEAGUE OF NATIONS AND THE CRISIS OF EMPIRE (2015).

PEPPER, DAVID, THE ROOTS OF MODERN ENVIRONMENTALISM (1984).

Percival, Robert V., *Global Law and the Environment*, 86 WASHINGTON LAW REVIEW 579 (2011).

PONTING, CLIVE, A NEW GREEN HISTORY OF THE WORLD: THE ENVIRONMENT AND THE COLLAPSE OF GREAT CIVILISATIONS (2007).

PRATT, JOSEPH A., BLACK WATERS: RESPONSES TO AMERICA'S FIRST OIL POLLUTION CRISIS (2008).

PRITCHARD, SONIA Z., OIL POLLUTION CONTROL (1987).

Prost, Mario and Otomo, Yoriko, *British Influences on International Environmental Law: The Case of Wildlife Conservation, in* BRITISH INFLUENCES ON INTERNATIONAL LAW: 1915–2015, 192 (Robert McCorquodale & Jean-Pierre Gauci eds., 2016).

RADKAU, JOACHIM, NATURE AND POWER: A GLOBAL HISTORY OF THE ENVIRONMENT (2008).

THE AGE OF ECOLOGY (Patrick Camiller trans., 2014).

Raitz VON FRENTZ, CHRISTIAN, A LESSON FORGOTTEN: MINORITY PROTECTION UNDER THE LEAGUE OF NATIONS – THE CASE OF THE GERMAN MINORITY IN POLAND: 1920–1934 (1999).

Rajan, Ravi, *Imperial Environmentalism or Environmental Imperialism? European Forestry, Colonial Foresters and the Agendas of Forest Management in British India 1800–1900, in* NATURE AND THE ORIENT 324 (Richard H. Grove, Vinita Damodaran & Satpal Sangwan eds., 1998).

Rothschild, Emma, *Forum: The Idea of Sustainability Introduction*, 8 MODERN INTELLECTUAL HISTORY 147 (2011).

Rubin, Alfred P., *Pollution by Analogy: The Trail Smelter Arbitration*, 50 OREGON LAW REVIEW 259 (1971).

RUSSELL, EDMUND, WAR AND NATURE: FIGHTING HUMANS AND INSECTS WITH CHEMICALS FROM WORLD WAR I TO SILENT SPRING (2000).

SCHNEIDER, JAN, WORLD PUBLIC ORDER OF THE ENVIRONMENT: TOWARDS AN INTERNATIONAL ECOLOGICAL LAW AND ORGANIZATION (1979).

Schorr, David, *Forest Law in the Palestine Mandate: Colonial Conservation in a Unique Context, in* MANAGING THE UNKNOWN: ESSAYS ON ENVIRONMENTAL IGNORANCE 71 (Frank Uekötter & Uwe Lübken eds., 2014).

SCOTT, GEORGE, THE RISE AND FALL OF THE LEAGUE OF NATIONS (1973).

SCOTT, JAMES C., SEEING LIKE A STATE: HOW CERTAIN SCHEMES TO IMPROVE THE HUMAN CONDITION HAVE FAILED (1998).

SHAH, SONIA, CRUDE: THE STORY OF OIL (2006).

DE STEIGUER, J. E., THE ORIGINS OF MODERN ENVIRONMENTAL THOUGHT (2006).

Steinberg, Theodore, *Down to Earth: Nature, Agency, and Power in History*, 107 AMERICAN HISTORICAL REVIEW 798 (2002).

STOETT, PETER J., THE INTERNATIONAL POLITICS OF WHALING (1997).

Sutter, Paul S., *Reflections: What Can U.S. Environmental Historians Learn from Non-U.S. Environmental Historiography*, 8 ENVIRONMENTAL HISTORY 109 (2003).

Sweeney, Joseph C., *Oil Pollution of the Oceans*, 37 FORDHAM LAW REVIEW 155 (1968).

THE CAMBRIDGE COMPANION TO INTERNATIONAL LAW (James Crawford & Martti Koskenniemi eds., 2012).

THE LEAGUE OF NATIONS' WORK ON SOCIAL ISSUES: VISIONS, ENDEAVOURS AND EXPERIMENTS (Magaly Rodríguez García, Davide Rodogno & Liat Kozma eds., 2016).

THE ORIGINS, STRUCTURE AND WORKING OF THE LEAGUE OF NATIONS (CHARLES HOWARD ed., 2003).

THE SPANISH INFLUENZA PANDEMIC OF 1918–19 (Howard Phillips & David Killingray eds., 2003).

THE SPANISH INFLUENZA PANDEMIC OF 1918–19: NEW PERSPECTIVES (Howard Phillips & David Killingray eds., 2003).

TUCKER, RICHARD P., INSATIABLE APPETITE: THE UNITED STATES AND THE ECOLOGICAL DEGRADATION OF THE TROPICAL WORLD (2000).

UEKÖTTER, FRANK, THE GREENEST NATION? A NEW HISTORY OF GERMAN ENVIRONMENTALISM (2014).

Victor, David G., *Whale Sausage: Why the Whaling Regime Does Not Need to Be Fixed, in* TOWARD A SUSTAINABLE WHALING REGIME 292 (Robert L. Friedheim ed., 2000).

WALTERS, F. P., THE LEAGUE OF NATIONS (1950; reprint ed., 1969).

Watenpaugh, Keith D., *The League of Nations' Rescue of Armenian Genocide Survivors and the Making of Modern Humanitarianism: 1920–1927*, 115 AMERICAN HISTORICAL REVIEW 1315 (2010).

WEISS, EDITH BROWN, IN FAIRNESS TO FUTURE GENERATIONS (1989).

Wheatley, Natasha, *Mandatory Interpretation: Legal Hermeneutics and the New International Order in Arab and Jewish Petitions to the League of Nations*, 227 PAST & PRESENT 205 (2015).

White, Lynn, *The Historical Roots of Our Ecological Crisis*, 155 SCIENCE 1203 (1967).

White, Richard, *From Wilderness to Hybrid Landscapes: the Cultural Turn in Environmental History*, 66 HISTORIAN 557 (2004).

The Nationalization of Nature, 86 JOURNAL OF AMERICAN HISTORY 976 (1999).

Wilde, Ralph, *From Danzig to East-Timor and Beyond: The Role of International Territorial Administration*, 95 AMERICAN JOURNAL OF INTERNATIONAL LAW 583 (2001).

Williams, Raymond, *Ideas of Nature, in* PROBLEMS OF MATERIALISM AND CULTURE: SELECTED ESSAYS 67 (1980).

WILSON, WALTER J., GEORGE WILTON FIELD, 1863–1938: A PIONEER CONSERVATIONIST (1968).

WINTERS, ROBERT K., FOREST AND MAN (1974).

Wirth, John D., *The Trail Smelter Dispute: Canadians and Americans Confront Transboundary Pollution, 1927–41*, 1 ENVIRONMENTAL HISTORY 34 (1996).

WORSTER, DONALD, NATURE'S ECONOMY: A HISTORY OF ECOLOGICAL IDEAS (1994).

Worster, Donald et al., *A Roundtable: Environmental History*, 74 JOURNAL OF AMERICAN HISTORY 1087 (1990).

Wöbse, Anna-Katharina, *Oil on Troubled Water? Environmental Diplomacy in the League of Nations*, 32 DIPLOMATIC HISTORY 519 (2008).

YERGIN, DANIEL, THE PRIZE: THE EPIC QUEST FOR OIL, MONEY, AND POWER (1991).

Zhu, Ling, *Do We Need a Global Organization for the Protection of the Marine Environment, in* INTERNATIONAL MARITIME ORGANIZATIONS AND THEIR CONTRIBUTION TOWARDS A SUSTAINABLE MARINE DEVELOPMENT 157 (Peter Ehlers & Rainer Lagoni eds., 2006).

INDEX

Introductory Note

References such as '178–79' indicate (not necessarily continuous) discussion of a topic across a range of pages. Wherever possible in the case of topics with many references, these have either been divided into sub-topics or only the most significant discussions of the topic are listed. Because the entire work is about the 'League of Nations', the use of this term (and certain others which occur constantly throughout the book) as an entry point has been minimised. Information will be found under the corresponding detailed topics.

CAMBRIDGE STUDIES IN INTERNATIONAL AND COMPARATIVE LAW

Books in the Series

160 *Rewriting Histories of the Use of Force: The Narrative of 'Indifference'*
Agatha Verdebout

159 *The League of Nations and the Protection of the Environment*
Omer Aloni

158 *International Investment Law and Legal Theory: Expropriation and the Fragmentation of Sources*
Jörg Kammerhofer

157 *Legal Barbarians: Identity, Modern Comparative Law and the Global South* Daniel Bonilla Maldonado

156 *International Human Rights Law Beyond State Territorial Control*
Antal Berkes

155 *The Crime of Aggression under the Rome Statute of the International Criminal Court*
Carrie McDougall

154 *Minorities and the Making of Postcolonial States in International Law*
Mohammad Shahabuddin

153 *Preclassical Conflict of Laws*
Nikitas E. Hatzimihail

152 *International Law and History: Modern Interfaces* Ignacio de la Rasilla

151 *Marketing Global Justice: The Political Economy of International Criminal Law*
Christine Schwöbel-Patel

150 *International Status in the Shadow of Empire*
Cait Storr

149 *Treaties in Motion: The Evolution of Treaties from Formation to Termination*
Edited by Malgosia Fitzmaurice and Panos Merkouris

148 *Humanitarian Disarmament: An Historical Enquiry*
Treasa Dunworth

147 *Complementarity, Catalysts, Compliance: The International Criminal Court in Uganda, Kenya, and the Democratic Republic of Congo*
Christian M. De Vos

146 *Cyber Operations and International Law*
François Delerue

145 *Comparative Reasoning in International Courts and Tribunals*
Daniel Peat

144 *Maritime Delimitation as a Judicial Process*
Massimo Lando

143 *Prosecuting Sexual and Gender-Based Crimes at the International Criminal Court: Practice, Progress and Potential*
Rosemary Grey

142 *Capitalism As Civilisation: A History of International Law*
Ntina Tzouvala

141 *Sovereignty in China: A Genealogy of a Concept Since 1840*
Adele Carrai

140 *Narratives of Hunger in International Law: Feeding the World in Times of Climate Change*
Anne Saab

139 *Victim Reparation under the Ius Post Bellum: An Historical and Normative Perspective*
Shavana Musa

138 *The Analogy between States and International Organizations* Fernando Lusa Bordin

137 *The Process of International Legal Reproduction: Inequality, Historiography, Resistance*
Rose Parfitt

136 *State Responsibility for Breaches of Investment Contracts*
Jean Ho

135 *Coalitions of the Willing and International Law: The Interplay between Formality and Informality*
Alejandro Rodiles

134 *Self-Determination in Disputed Colonial Territories*
Jamie Trinidad

133 *International Law as a Belief System*
Jean d'Aspremont

132 *Legal Consequences of Peremptory Norms in International Law*
Daniel Costelloe

131 *Third-Party Countermeasures in International Law*
Martin Dawidowicz

130 *Justification and Excuse in International Law: Concept and Theory of General Defences*
Federica Paddeu

129 *Exclusion from Public Space: A Comparative Constitutional Analysis*
Daniel Moeckli

128 *Provisional Measures before International Courts and Tribunals*
Cameron A. Miles

127 *Humanity at Sea: Maritime Migration and the Foundations of International Law*
Itamar Mann

126 *Beyond Human Rights: The Legal Status of the Individual in International Law*
Anne Peters

125 *The Doctrine of Odious Debt in International Law: A Restatement*
Jeff King

124 *Static and Evolutive Treaty Interpretation: A Functional Reconstruction*
Christian Djeffal

123 *Civil Liability in Europe for Terrorism-Related Risk*
Lucas Bergkamp, Michael Faure, Monika Hinteregger and Niels Philipsen

122 *Proportionality and Deference in Investor-State Arbitration: Balancing Investment Protection and Regulatory Autonomy*
Caroline Henckels

121 *International Law and Governance of Natural Resources in Conflict and Post-Conflict Situations*
Daniëlla Dam-de Jong

120 *Proof of Causation in Tort Law*
Sandy Steel

119 *The Formation and Identification of Rules of Customary International Law in International Investment Law*
Patrick Dumberry

118 *Religious Hatred and International Law: The Prohibition of Incitement to Violence or Discrimination*
Jeroen Temperman

117 *Taking Economic, Social and Cultural Rights Seriously in International Criminal Law*
Evelyne Schmid

116 *Climate Change Litigation: Regulatory Pathways to Cleaner Energy* Jacqueline Peel and
Hari M. Osofsky

115 *Mestizo International Law: A Global Intellectual History 1842–1933*
Arnulf Becker Lorca

114 *Sugar and the Making of International Trade Law*
Michael Fakhri

113 *Strategically Created Treaty Conflicts and the Politics of International Law*
Surabhi Ranganathan

112 *Investment Treaty Arbitration As Public International Law: Procedural Aspects and Implications* Eric De Brabandere

111 *The New Entrants Problem in International Fisheries Law*
Andrew Serdy

110 *Substantive Protection under Investment Treaties: A Legal and Economic Analysis*
Jonathan Bonnitcha

109 *Popular Governance of Post-Conflict Reconstruction: The Role of International Law*
Matthew Saul

108 *Evolution of International Environmental Regimes: The Case of Climate Change*
Simone Schiele

107 *Judges, Law and War: The Judicial Development of International Humanitarian Law*
Shane Darcy

106 *Religious Offence and Human Rights: The Implications of Defamation of Religions*
Lorenz Langer

105 *Forum Shopping in International Adjudication: The Role of Preliminary Objections* Luiz Eduardo Salles

104 *Domestic Politics and International Human Rights Tribunals: The Problem of Compliance*
Courtney Hillebrecht

103 *International Law and the Arctic*
Michael Byers

102 *Cooperation in the Law of Transboundary Water Resources*
Christina Leb

101 *Underwater Cultural Heritage and International Law*
Sarah Dromgoole

100 *State Responsibility: The General Part*
James Crawford

99 *The Origins of International Investment Law: Empire, Environment and the Safeguarding of Capital*
Kate Miles

98 *The Crime of Aggression under the Rome Statute of the International Criminal Court*
Carrie McDougall

97 *'Crimes against Peace' and International Law*
Kirsten Sellars

96 *Non-Legality in International Law: Unruly Law*
Fleur Johns

95 *Armed Conflict and Displacement: The Protection of Refugees and Displaced Persons under International Humanitarian Law*
Mélanie Jacques

94 *Foreign Investment and the Environment in International Law*
Jorge E. Viñuales

93 *The Human Rights Treaty Obligations of Peacekeepers*
Kjetil Mujezinović Larsen

92 *Cyber Warfare and the Laws of War*
Heather Harrison Dinniss

91 *The Right to Reparation in International Law for Victims of Armed Conflict*
Christine Evans

90 *Global Public Interest in International Investment Law*
Andreas Kulick

89 *State Immunity in International Law*
Xiaodong Yang

88 *Reparations and Victim Support in the International Criminal Court*
Conor McCarthy

87 *Reducing Genocide to Law: Definition, Meaning, and the Ultimate Crime*
Payam Akhavan

86 *Decolonising International Law: Development, Economic Growth and the Politics of Universality*
Sundhya Pahuja

85 *Complicity and the Law of State Responsibility*
Helmut Philipp Aust

84 *State Control over Private Military and Security Companies in Armed Conflict*
Hannah Tonkin

83 *'Fair and Equitable Treatment' in International Investment Law*
Roland Kläger

82 *The UN and Human Rights: Who Guards the Guardians?*
Guglielmo Verdirame

81 *Sovereign Defaults before International Courts and Tribunals*
Michael Waibel

80 *Making the Law of the Sea: A Study in the Development of International Law*
James Harrison

79 *Science and the Precautionary Principle in International Courts and Tribunals: Expert Evidence, Burden of Proof and Finality*
Caroline E. Foster

78 *Transition from Illegal Regimes under International Law*
Yaël Ronen

77 *Access to Asylum: International Refugee Law and the Globalisation of Migration Control* Thomas Gammeltoft-Hansen

76 *Trading Fish, Saving Fish: The Interaction between Regimes in International Law*
Margaret A. Young

75 *The Individual in the International Legal System: Continuity and Change in International Law*
Kate Parlett

74 *'Armed Attack' and Article 51 of the UN Charter: Evolutions in Customary Law and Practice*
Tom Ruys

73 *Theatre of the Rule of Law: Transnational Legal Intervention in Theory and Practice*
Stephen Humphreys

72 *Science and Risk Regulation in International Law*
Jacqueline Peel

71 *The Participation of States in International Organisations: The Role of Human Rights and Democracy*
Alison Duxbury

70 *Legal Personality in International Law*
Roland Portmann

69 *Vicarious Liability in Tort: A Comparative Perspective*
Paula Giliker

68 *The Public International Law Theory of Hans Kelsen: Believing in Universal Law*
Jochen von Bernstorff

67 *Legitimacy and Legality in International Law: An Interactional Account*
Jutta Brunnée and Stephen J. Toope

66 *The Concept of Non-International Armed Conflict in International Humanitarian Law*
Anthony Cullen

65 *The Principle of Legality in International and Comparative Criminal Law*
Kenneth S. Gallant

64 *The Challenge of Child Labour in International Law*
Franziska Humbert

63 *Shipping Interdiction and the Law of the Sea*
Douglas Guilfoyle

62 *International Courts and Environmental Protection*
Tim Stephens

61 *Legal Principles in WTO Disputes*
Andrew D. Mitchell

60 *War Crimes in Internal Armed Conflicts*
Eve La Haye

59 *Humanitarian Occupation*
Gregory H. Fox

58 *The International Law of Environmental Impact Assessment: Process, Substance and Integration*
Neil Craik

57 *The Law and Practice of International Territorial Administration: Versailles to Iraq and Beyond*
Carsten Stahn

56 *United Nations Sanctions and the Rule of Law*
Jeremy Matam Farrall

55 *National Law in WTO Law: Effectiveness and Good Governance in the World Trading System*
Sharif Bhuiyan

54 *Cultural Products and the World Trade Organization*
Tania Voon

53 *The Threat of Force in International Law*
Nikolas Stürchler

52 *Indigenous Rights and United Nations Standards: Self-Determination, Culture and Land*
Alexandra Xanthaki

51 *International Refugee Law and Socio-Economic Rights: Refuge from Deprivation*
Michelle Foster

50 *The Protection of Cultural Property in Armed Conflict*
Roger O'Keefe

49 *Interpretation and Revision of International Boundary Decisions*
Kaiyan Homi Kaikobad

48 *Multinationals and Corporate Social Responsibility: Limitations and Opportunities in International Law*
Jennifer A. Zerk

47 *Judiciaries within Europe: A Comparative Review*
John Bell

46 *Law in Times of Crisis: Emergency Powers in Theory and Practice*
Oren Gross and Fionnuala Ní Aoláin

45 *Vessel-Source Marine Pollution: The Law and Politics of International Regulation*
Alan Khee-Jin Tan

44 *Enforcing Obligations* Erga Omnes *in International Law*
Christian J. Tams

43 *Non-Governmental Organisations in International Law*
Anna-Karin Lindblom

42 *Democracy, Minorities and International Law*
Steven Wheatley

41 *Prosecuting International Crimes: Selectivity and the International Criminal Law Regime*
Robert Cryer

40 *Compensation for Personal Injury in English, German and Italian Law: A Comparative Outline*
Basil Markesinis, Michael Coester, Guido Alpa and Augustus Ullstein

39 *Dispute Settlement in the UN Convention on the Law of the Sea*
Natalie Klein

38 *The International Protection of Internally Displaced Persons*
Catherine Phuong

37 *Imperialism, Sovereignty and the Making of International Law*
Antony Anghie

36 *Principles of the Institutional Law of International Organizations*
C. F. Amerasinghe

35 *Necessity, Proportionality and the Use of Force by States*
Judith Gardam

34 *International Legal Argument in the Permanent Court of International Justice: The Rise of the International Judiciary*
Ole Spiermann

33 -

32 *Great Powers and Outlaw States: Unequal Sovereigns in the International Legal Order*
Gerry Simpson

31 *Local Remedies in International Law*
(second edition) Chittharanjan Felix Amerasinghe

30 *Reading Humanitarian Intervention: Human Rights and the Use of Force in International Law*
Anne Orford

29 *Conflict of Norms in Public International Law: How WTO Law Relates to Other Rules of International Law*
Joost Pauwelyn

27 *Transboundary Damage in International Law*
Hanqin Xue

25 *European Criminal Procedures*
Edited by Mireille Delmas-Marty and J. R. Spencer

24 *Accountability of Armed Opposition Groups in International Law*
Liesbeth Zegveld

23 *Sharing Transboundary Resources: International Law and Optimal Resource Use*
Eyal Benvenisti

22 *International Human Rights and Humanitarian Law*
René Provost

21 *Remedies against International Organisations*
Karel Wellens

20 *Diversity and Self-Determination in International Law*
Karen Knop

19 *The Law of Internal Armed Conflict*
Lindsay Moir

18 *International Commercial Arbitration and African States: Practice, Participation and Institutional Development*
Amazu A. Asouzu

17 *The Enforceability of Promises in European Contract Law*
James Gordley

16 *International Law in Antiquity*
David J. Bederman

15 *Money Laundering: A New International Law Enforcement Model*
Guy Stessens

14 *Good Faith in European Contract Law*
Reinhard Zimmermann and Simon Whittaker

13 *On Civil Procedure*
J. A. Jolowicz

12 *Trusts: A Comparative Study*
Maurizio Lupoi and Simon Dix

11 *The Right to Property in Commonwealth Constitutions*
Tom Allen

10 *International Organizations before National Courts*
August Reinisch

9 *The Changing International Law of High Seas Fisheries*
Francisco Orrego Vicuña

8 *Trade and the Environment: A Comparative Study of EC and US Law*
Damien Geradin

7 *Unjust Enrichment: A Study of Private Law and Public Values*
Hanoch Dagan

6 *Religious Liberty and International Law in Europe*
Malcolm D. Evans

5 *Ethics and Authority in International Law*
Alfred P. Rubin

4 *Sovereignty over Natural Resources: Balancing Rights and Duties*
Nico Schrijver

3 *The Polar Regions and the Development of International Law*
Donald R. Rothwell

2 *Fragmentation and the International Relations of Micro-States: Self-Determination and Statehood*
Jorri C. Duursma

1 *Principles of the Institutional Law of International Organizations*
C. F. Amerasinghe

For EU product safety concerns, contact us at Calle de José Abascal, 56–1°,
28003 Madrid, Spain or eugpsr@cambridge.org.

www.ingramcontent.com/pod-product-compliance
Lightning Source LLC
LaVergne TN
LVHW010341220926
848484LV00004BB/1023

* 9 7 8 1 1 0 8 8 3 8 1 9 1 *